W9-CAS-046

STATE OF THE ART REVIEWS (STARs)

SUBJECT	FREQUENCY	PRICE (U.S.)	PRICE (Foreign)	PRICE (Single)
☐ ADOLESCENT MEDICINE	Triannual	$63.00	$ 73.00	$33.00
☐ CARDIAC SURGERY	Triannual	$96.00	$106.00	$42.00
☐ OCCUPATIONAL MEDICINE	Quarterly	$78.00	$ 88.00	$36.00
☐ PATHOLOGY	Biannual	$60.00	$ 70.00	$40.00
☐ PHYSICAL MED & REHAB (PM&R)	Triannual	$68.00	$ 80.00	$32.00
☐ SPINE	Triannual	$86.00	$ 96.00	$35.00

☐ 1993 subscription   ☐ 1992 subscription   ☐ Single Issue
   Check subject title above.   Title _____

Name _____   I enclose payment: ☐ Check ☐ Visa ☐ MasterCard
Company/Hospital _____   Credit Card # _____
Street Address _____   Expiration Date _____
City/State/Zip _____   Signature _____

Send order to:
HANLEY & BELFUS, INC.
210 South 13th Street / Philadelphia, PA 19107 / 215-546-7293 / 800-962-1892

STATE OF THE ART REVIEWS (STARs)

SUBJECT	FREQUENCY	PRICE (U.S.)	PRICE (Foreign)	PRICE (Single)
☐ ADOLESCENT MEDICINE	Triannual	$63.00	$ 73.00	$33.00
☐ CARDIAC SURGERY	Triannual	$96.00	$106.00	$42.00
☐ OCCUPATIONAL MEDICINE	Quarterly	$78.00	$ 88.00	$36.00
☐ PATHOLOGY	Biannual	$60.00	$ 70.00	$40.00
☐ PHYSICAL MED & REHAB (PM&R)	Triannual	$68.00	$ 80.00	$32.00
☐ SPINE	Triannual	$86.00	$ 96.00	$35.00

☐ 1993 subscription   ☐ 1992 subscription   ☐ Single Issue
   Check subject title above.   Title _____

Name _____   I enclose payment: ☐ Check ☐ Visa ☐ MasterCard
Company/Hospital _____   Credit Card # _____
Street Address _____   Expiration Date _____
City/State/Zip _____   Signature _____

Send order to:
HANLEY & BELFUS, INC.
210 South 13th Street / Philadelphia, PA 19107 / 215-546-7293 / 800-962-1892

Physical Medicine and Rehabilitation

Long-Term Consequences of Stroke

Guest Editor:

Robert W. Teasell, BSc, MD, FRCPC
Chief of Physical Medicine and Rehabilitation
University Hospital, and
Assistant Professor of Medicine
University of Western Ontario
London, Ontario

Volume 7/Number 1   February 1993
HANLEY & BELFUS, INC.   Philadelphia

STATE OF THE ART REVIEWS

Publisher: **HANLEY & BELFUS, INC.**
210 South 13th Street
Philadelphia, PA 19107
(215) 546-7293
(215) 730-9330 (Fax)

PHYSICAL MEDICINE AND REHABILITATION: State of the Art Reviews (ISSN 0888-7357)
Volume 7, Number 1   (ISBN 1-56053-127-4)

PHYSICAL MEDICINE AND REHABILITATION: State of the Art Reviews is published triannually (three times per year) by Hanley & Belfus, Inc., 210 South 13th Street, Philadelphia, Pennsylvania 19107.

POSTMASTER: Send address changes to PHYSICAL MEDICINE AND REHABILITATION: State of the Art Reviews, Hanley & Belfus, Inc., 210 South 13th Street, Philadelphia, PA 19107.

The 1993 subscription price is $68.00 per year U.S., $80.00 outside U.S. (add $30.00 for air mail). Single copies $32.00 U.S., $36.00 outside U.S. (add $10.00 for single copy air mail).

Physical Medicine and Rehabilitation: State of the Art Reviews
Vol. 7, No. 1, February 1993

LONG-TERM CONSEQUENCES OF STROKE
Robert W. Teasell, MD, FRCPC, Editor

CONTENTS

Despite considerable advances in diagnostic technology, our ability to diagnose and detect occurrences of stroke has not changed greatly over the past two decades. The incidence and prevalence rates of stroke, mortality rates, risk factors, and patterns of recovery as reported in recent studies are reviewed in this chapter. Stroke remains a condition of the aged with known risk factors and identifiable preventive strategies.

The disability and handicap following stroke have multifactorial etiologies. The extent of disability varies with the extent of recovery, site of lesion, and premorbid status. Other contributing factors include age of the patient and extent of family supports. Short-term goals in the recovery from stroke are usually limited to gaining independence in activities of daily living. Long-term goals involve vocational and avocational interests. One goal throughout management should be prevention of secondary complications, such as contracture, deep vein thrombosis, or aspiration, which might contribute to further disability.

Prevention strategies and risk factors for the various types of stroke are evaluated. The safety and clinical application of tissue plasminogen activator are being reviewed in acute cerebral infarction and subarachnoid hemorrhage. Anticoagulation with heparin and warfarin has been selectively applied in suspected cardioembolic stroke. Carotid endarterectomy is more effective than medical care in symptomatic severe carotid stenosis, but it is not recommended for symptomatic mild carotid stenosis. The use of agents such as ticlopidine, aspirin, and newer agents is discussed. Early detection through magnetic resonance angiography promises to help improve management of vascular disorders.

J. Malcolm O. Arnold

Patients surviving a stroke should have a careful cardiovascular evaluation by clinical history, physical examination, and appropriate other investigations. Pre-existing cardiovascular factors which influence risk of developing a primary or recurrent stroke are discussed, and appropriate interventions directed at these factors can be planned to reduce the high mortality that persists. Cardiac abnormalities may be found in up to 50% of patients who suffer stroke. Increased attention needs to be paid to cardiovascular risk factors which may influence long-term outcome.

Samuel Wiebe-Velazquez and Warren T. Blume

The incidence of post-stroke seizures ranges from 7.7 to 42.8% in the various studies, with vascular disease being the most common documentable etiology of seizures. The pathophysiology of these seizures is discussed as they occur in the various types of stroke. The timing of seizure occurrence in relation to the stroke event can be important. Controlling seizures related to vascular disease is usually relatively easy with antiepileptic medications, as it is with most unifocal nonprogressive lesions. Seizures may become refractory in some circumstances.

Robert W. Teasell, Hillel M. Finestone, and Linda Greene-Finestone

Dysphagia is a common consequence of stroke and is associated with various complications, including aspiration pneumonia and malnutrition/dehydration. For patients at high risk of aspiration, special diets and specific compensatory feeding techniques or non-oral tube feedings may be necessary. Malnutrition can be identified through nutritional assessment, which includes collection of appropriate dietary, biochemical, and anthropometric measures as well as evaluation of swallowing status. Subsequent diet therapy may include modification of food consistencies or enteral feeding.

Michael John Borrie

Urinary incontinence is common after stroke, occurring in 51 to 60% of patients. In virtually all patients, incontinence can be resolved, improved, or better contained. An accurate history, physical examination, and residual urine volume testing will determine the pre- and post-stroke factors contributing to incontinence. Improving incontinence will improve patient morale and may well facilitate rehabilitation and reduce the time to hospital discharge.

Karen L. Harburn and Patrick J. Potter

Physiologically, spasticity and contractures are multidimensional and provide formidable challenges in choosing the most appropriate treatment. Measuring spasticity and monitoring the development of contractures are necessary in evaluating treatments. Spasticity is measured in the clinic by quantitatively assessing muscle tone. Pharmacologic treatment and current medical and rehabilitative treatment approaches are described.

Pain following stroke, especially where spastic hemiplegia results, is very common in the upper extremity. Most cases of pain are due to a peripheral mechanism and are generally associated with spastic paralysis and/or joint contractures. Shoulder pain is particularly common and occurs in up to 84% of hemipelgic patients. Shoulder-hand syndrome is a frequent source of upper limb pain in hemiplegics and represents a form of reflex sympathetic dystrophy. Central pain occurs in less than 2% of patients but is always intractable to treatment.

Because lower extremity tasks are more gross in terms of what is necessary for independent movement, less neurologic recovery is required to perform these tasks adequately. As a result, the affected lower limb may be supplemented with the use of aids and orthotics with greater success than what is achieved with upper limb orthotics. Residual recovery of a small percentage of functioning CNS tracts innervating the lower extremity will allow adequate ambulation. More complex functions, such as running, require more extensive neurologic recovery.

The use of orthotics in the hemiplegic patient as the result of a cerebrovascular accident is discussed. Traditional, including conventional (metal), as well as newer thermoplastic, combination types of orthotics and functional electrical stimulation are described. A description of orthotic materials, clinical and laboratory analyses of gait, and gait training are included.

Negative emotional reactions are common following a stroke. Depression is prevalent and may be underdiagnosed and consequently undertreated. The reaction of each patient to a stroke is shaped by his or her premorbid personality, the individual's manner of coping with stress, support of family and friends, and cognitive/perceptual deficits created by the stroke itself. The neurophysiological basis of these psychological difficulties, biological treatment approaches, as well as the psychological causes and treatments of these problems are reviewed.

Stroke may relate to dementia in different ways: it may cause, contribute, or coexist with the cognitive impairment. Stroke may be the main cause of vascular dementia and often unmasks or modifies other underlying impairment, such as Alzheimer's disease. Patients with a history of cerebrovascular disease seem to be at considerable risk of dementia. Evaluation of cognitive abilities, emotional, and social skills is part of the clinical evaluation of stroke patients outlined here.

Colleen Churchill

A stroke is a significant and traumatic event that affects the well-being of the individual as well as that of the immediate family. The subsequent impairment and disabilities are invariably accompanied by significant psychosocial consequences, including social isolation, decreased community involvement, new economic strain, disruption of family functioning, major depression, anxiety, and anger. Family and social issues which affect stroke patients over the long term are emphasized.

Trilok N. Monga

Marked decline in many aspects of sexuality has been reported in stroke victims. Common problems include a decline in libido, coital frequency, vaginal lubrication and orgasm in women, and poor or lack of erection and ejaculation in males. The problems are multifactorial in cause, with the major factors influencing sexuality comprising poor coping skills, psychosocial adjustment to the impairment and disability from the stroke, fear of having another stroke, and the severity of sensory, perceptual, and cognitive deficits.

CONTRIBUTORS

J.M.O. Arnold, MD, FRCPC
Associate Professor, Departments of Medicine (Cardiology) and of Pharmacology and Toxicology, University of Western Ontario, and Staff Cardiologist, Victoria Hospital, London, Ontario

Warren T. Blume, MD, FRCPC
Professor, EEG Laboratory, Department of Clinical Neurological Sciences, University of Western Ontario, London, Ontario

Michael John Borrie, MBChB, FRCPC
Associate Professor, Division of Geriatric Medicine, Department of Medicine, University of Western Ontario, and Head, Division of Geriatric Medicine, Parkwood Hospital, London, Ontario

Colleen Churchill, BSW, MSW
Social Worker, Stroke Rehabilitation Unit, Department of Social Work, University Hospital, London, Ontario

Gail A. Delaney, MD, FRCPC
Assistant Professor, Department of Physical Medicine and Rehabilitation, University of Western Ontario, and Chief, Department of Physical Medicine and Rehabilitation, Parkwood Hospital, London, Ontario

Douglas K. Dittmer, MD, FRCPC
Assistant Professor, Department of Physical Medicine and Rehabilitation, University of Western Ontario, and Chief, Department of Physical Medicine and Rehabilitation, Victoria Hospital, London, Ontario

Timo Erkinjuntti, MD, PhD
Associate Professor in Neurology, Department of Neurology, University of Helsinki, Helsinki, Finland

Hillel M. Finestone, MDCM, FRCPC
Assistant Professor, Department of Physical Medicine and Rehabilitation, University of Western Ontario; Staff Physician, Department of Physical Medicine and Rehabilitation, University Hospital; and Electromyographer, St. Mary's Hospital; St. Joseph's Health Centre, London, Ontario

Andrew P. Gasecki, MD
Clinical Fellow, Department of Clinical Neurological Sciences, University of Western Ontario and University Hospital, London, Ontario

Martin Gillen, MD, FRCPC
Assistant Professor of Medicine, Division of Physical Medicine and Rehabilitation, University of Ottawa, and the Rehabilitation Centre, Ottawa, Ontario

Linda Greene-Finestone, MSc, RPDt
Dietitian–Nutritionist, Clinical Nutrition Services, University Hospital, London, Ontario

Vladimir C. Hachinski, MD, FRCPC, MSc(DME), DSc(Med)
Richard and Beryl Ivey Professor and Chairman, Department of Clinical Neurological Sciences, University of Western Ontario; Chief, Department of Clinical Neurological Sciences, University Hospital; and Director, Stroke and Aging Group, The John P. Roberts Research Institute, London, Ontario

Karen L. Harburn, PhD
Associate Professor, Departments of Occupational and Physical Therapy, Elborn College, University of Western Ontario, London, Ontario

Ian C. Jones, BM, MA
Research Assistant, Department of Physical Medicine and Rehabilitation, Victoria Hospital, London, Ontario

Dawn E. MacArthur-Turner, BSc, CO(C)
Certified Orthotist; President of the Ontario Association of Prosthetists and Orthotists; Examiner for the Canadian Board of Certification of Prosthetists and Orthotists; and President, Custom Orthotics of London, Inc., London, Ontario

Nancy E. Mayo, PhD
Adjunct Professor, Department of Epidemiology and Biostatistics, School of Physical-Occupational Therapy, McGill University, Montreal, and Epidemiologist and Co-Chief, Research Department, Jewish Rehabilitation Hospital, Chomeday-Laval, Quebec

Trilok N. Monga, MD, FRCPC, MRCP(I)
Professor of Medicine, Department of Clinical Physical Medicine and Rehabilitation, Baylor College of Medicine, and Chief, Rehabilitation Medicine Service, Houston Veterans Affairs Medical Center, Houston, Texas

Patrick J. Potter, MD, FRCPC
Assistant Professor, Department of Physical Medicine and Rehabilitation, University of Western Ontario, and Staff Physician, Department of Physical Medicine and Rehabilitation, Victoria Hospital, London, Ontario

Leora Swartzman, PhD
Assistant Professor of Psychology, Department of Psychology, University of Western Ontario, London, Ontario

Robert W. Teasell, BSc, MD, FRCPC
Assistant Professor of Medicine, Department of Physical Medicine and Rehabilitation, University of Western Ontario, and Chief of Physical Medicine and Rehabilitation, University Hospital, London, Ontario

Samuel Wiebe-Velazquez, MD, FRCPC
Clinical Fellow, EEG Laboratory, Department of Clinical Neurological Sciences, University of Western Ontario and University Hospital, London, Ontario

PUBLISHED ISSUES

PUBLISHED ISSUES

1991

Vol 5, No 1   **Rehabilitation of Chronic Pain**
Edited by Nicolas E. Walsh, MD, San Antonio, Texas

Vol 5, No 2   **The Child with Physical Disability**
Edited by Gabriella Molnar, MD, Oakland, California

Vol 5, No 3   **Musculoskeletal Pain**
Edited by Constance D. Schwab, MD, Chicago, Illinois

1992

Vol 6, No 1   **Post-Concussive Disorders**
Edited by Lawrence J. Horn, MD, Houston, Texas
and Nathan D. Zasler, MD, Richmond, Virginia

Vol 6, No 2   **Industrial Rehabilitation**
Edited by Chrisanne Gordon, MD, and Paul E. Kaplan, MD,
Columbus, Ohio

Vol 6, No 3   **Neuropsychological Assessment**
Edited by Stephanie Hanson, PhD, Charlotte, North Carolina
and David Tucker, PhD, Austin, Texas

FUTURE ISSUES

1993   **Long-term Consequences of Stroke**
Edited by Robert W. Teasell, MD, London, Ontario, Canada

Management Issues in Rehabilitation Medicine
Edited by F. Patrick Maloney, MD, and Richard P. Gray, MD,
Little Rock, Arkansas

**Neurologic and Orthopaedic Disorders Following Traumatic
Brain Injury**
Edited by Lance R. Stone, DO, Downey, California

Assessment and Management of HIV-Related Disability
Edited by Michael W. O'Dell, MD, Cincinnati, Ohio

Subscriptions and single issues available from the publisher—Hanley & Belfus, Inc.,
Medical Publishers, 210 South 13th Street, Philadelphia, PA 19107 (215) 546-7293;
1-800-962-1892. Fax (215) 790-9330.

'PREFACE

In managing and following patients who have suffered a stroke, I have been impressed by the wide variety of problems they encounter long after their rehabilitation is complete. Management of the stroke patient still remains largely focused on acute in-hospital care, with its emphasis on medical diagnosis, prevention and treatment including intensive rehabilitation. As a result, the immediate consequences of stroke during this acute phase are well recognized. However, what is too often *not* appreciated is the ongoing difficulties suffered by stroke patients and their families long after they have left the hospital and therapy is completed. Over time, the immediate consequences of stroke are frequently complicated by a variety of medical, musculoskeletal, and psychosocial disorders.

It is hoped that this text will allow an appreciation of the wide variety of problems and complications that can follow a stroke, many occurring long after the stroke patient has been discharged from the hospital. The book is aimed at rehabilitation specialists, neurologists, and family doctors who may be confronted by the long-term problems which affect stroke victims. This text has been written by specialists who have practiced within the Canadian health care system, although the issues discussed are universal in their applications.

ROBERT W. TEASELL, BSc, MD, FRCPC
GUEST EDITOR

ACKNOWLEDGMENT

I would like to thank Mrs. Debbi Harley, who assisted in the organization and preparation of the text.

NANCY E. MAYO, PhD

1. EPIDEMIOLOGY AND RECOVERY

From the
Research Department
Jewish Rehabilitation Hospital
and the
Department of Epidemiology
  and Biostatistics
McGill University
Montreal, Quebec
Canada

Reprint requests to:
Nancy E. Mayo, PhD
Research Department
Jewish Rehabilitation Hospital
3205 Place Alton Goldbloom
Chomeday-Laval, Quebec
  H7V 1R2
Canada

Epidemiology is the study of the distribution and determinants of disease in populations.[122] When the epidemiologic method is applied to the study of stroke, an interesting portrait emerges. Stroke is the most disabling chronic condition[192] and, in Canada, is estimated to newly affect nearly 50,000 persons each year. In the U.S., that number is 500,000.

THE NATURE OF STROKE

The World Health Organization defines stroke as "rapidly developing clinical signs of focal (or times global) disturbance of cerebral function lasting more than 24 hours or leading to death with no apparent cause other than that of vascular origin."[5] Stroke can be either ischemic or hemorrhagic in origin with 5% to 20% of all strokes being classified as hemorrhagic.[34]

Stroke is diagnosed by a combination of history, clinical signs, neuroradiologic evidence, and the ruling out of nonvascular causes. The prevalence of various signs and symptoms associated with stroke[34,162,200] is presented in Table 1 and confirms that the most outstanding feature of stroke is a sudden paralysis or paresis of the extremities on one side.

Even though stroke commonly presents with a dramatic hemiplegia, there are other causes of hemiplegia, and persons presenting with other constellations of signs and symptoms can also have had a stroke. The accurate diagnosis of stroke is crucial not only to instigate appropriate treatment but also for accurate surveillance of the community.

Errors in the diagnosis of stroke can be systematic and nonsystematic, clinical and administrative, and cover both false-positives and

TABLE 1. Prevalence of Presenting Signs and Symptoms of Acute Stroke*

	%
Hemiplegia or hemiparesis of extremities	57–92
Dysphasia or aphasia	46–57
Memory impairment or disorientation	47
Loss of sensation or altered sensation	26–46
Dysphagia or tongue deviation[†]	30–40
Facial weakness or paralysis or ptosis	41
Altered consciousness	17–47
Nausea or vomiting	23
Headache	10–23
Vertigo	15
Convulsions	12
Nuchal rigidity	10
Abnormal vision	8
Limitation of leg extension	2

* Prevalence data from references 34, 161 and 202.
† Data from references 25 and 195.

false-negatives. Systematic error would occur when some types of strokes are always miscoded. For example, if the appropriate diagnostic procedures such as CT scan are not available or if the diagnosis is not made by a neurologist, hemorrhagic strokes could be miscoded as ischemic strokes, but the reverse would be unlikely. Nonsystematic error occurs when an error in diagnosis is made or when there is an administrative error in recording the correct diagnosis. These errors are difficult to eliminate completely, but the quality-control procedures set up in hospital archives are likely to pick up gross coding errors such as transposing numbers. The National Survey of Stroke[155] attributed 11% of errors to administrative error.

Table 2 presents the results of four studies examining the diagnostic accuracy of administrative codes for stroke. At the University of Rochester Medical Center,

TABLE 2. Validity of Administrative Codes to Indicate Acute Stroke

Type of Stroke (ICD9 Code)	Proportion with High Probability of Acute Stroke (%)			
	Barker et al.[27] 1979 (n= 1604)	Phillips[147] 1990 (n= 301)	Mayo[134†] 1990 (n= 96)	Liu et al.[127] 1990 (n= 217)
Subarachnoid hemorrhage (430)	71	33	100	100
Intracerebral hemorrhage(431)	100	100	100	83
Intracranial hemorrhage (432)	—	0	0–33	0
Occlusion and stenosis of precerebral arteries (433)	4	12	44–50	27
Occlusion of cerebral arteries (434)	—	64	90–95	94
Acute but ill-defined CVD (436)	74	66	62–83	93
Other and ill-defined CVD (437)	—	8	60–75	80
Late effects of CVD (438)	—	0	—	33
Transient cerebral ischemia (435)	16	14	—	22
Hemiplegia (342)*	—	—	—	44
Vertigo (780.4)*	—	—	—	71

* For codes 342 and 780.4 (hemiplegia and vertigo), the high proportion of strokes is due to these being considered "probable" according to the algorithm based on the presence of one clinical finding in these cases; only 20% were definite strokes. CVD = cerebrovascular disease.
† Two neurologists reporting.

New York,[27] charts with an administrative code for stroke were reviewed by Stroke Center staff and the accuracy judged. In Saskatchewan,[127] the hospital separation code was compared to the type of stroke determined by an algorithm developed by the National Survey of Stroke[200] that used the presenting signs and symptoms and diagnostic evidence. In Nova Scotia,[147] medical charts of persons with a discharge code of stroke were reviewed by a neurologist and two medical students and the diagnostic accuracy estimated using a combination of clinical judgment and diagnostic evidence. In Montreal,[134] two neurologists independently reviewed medical charts and gave their expert opinion as to the probability and type of stroke. Table 2 illustrates that the diagnostic accuracy was remarkably consistent given that the settings, methods of validation, and time periods differed considerably.

Three studies carried out 10, 15, and 20 years ago[27,140,155] found that approximately 70% of the records with an administrative code indicating cerebrovascular disease or an admitting diagnosis of stroke were true strokes. These three studies agree with the three recent Canadian studies[127,134,147] indicating that our ability to diagnose and detect occurrences of stroke has not changed greatly in the past two decades, despite considerable advances in diagnostic technology.[140]

OCCURRENCE

Sources of Data for Estimating Occurrence

Incidence is the number of new cases of stroke in a population over a defined period of time, and *prevalence* is the total number of cases in the population and includes both new cases and existing cases.

The challenge in estimating the incidence of stroke is to obtain an accurate count, and several strategies have been used. In general, these strategies are of four main types: cohorts, registries, surveys of one or more medical sources, and hospital discharge databases. The most accurate method would be to establish a cohort of individuals free of stroke and follow these persons over time until the onset of stroke or until death. These studies take a very long time and even if large yield only a small number of strokes.[126,137,152] The Framingham study followed a cohort of more than 5,700 people for over 30 years and identified less than 500 events.[208] The Honolulu Heart Program followed 8,006 men for 12 years and identified 288 strokes.[1] A household survey of persons would also yield an accurate estimate of incidence if the stroke diagnosis could be confirmed and the date of the stroke obtained. Usually household surveys are carried out to estimate prevalence and are done infrequently owing to their high cost.

Most often, incidence is estimated by identifying cases of stroke through medical sources. A number of stroke registries[8,17,34,36,83,102,110,124,143,153,161,170,181,183] have been set up to systematically monitor admissions to hospitals, physicians' offices, and records of deaths and autopsies for possible cases of stroke. An important feature of a registry is that the cases are ascertained prospectively and the stroke diagnoses are verified for accuracy. Stroke registries are usually set up only for a short period of time as they are expensive to maintain and, thus, do not permit an evaluation of rates over time.

Other strategies incorporate surveys of one or more sources of stroke cases, either prospectively or retrospectively, with a validation of either all or a sample of the stroke cases.[43,48,50,66,90,201,203] The more sources that are monitored, the more accurate is the estimate of incidence. Finally, the occurrence of stroke has been estimated through large computerized databases of hospital discharges for stroke.[132,202] This strategy has the advantage of being able to cover a large segment of the population over a long period of time at relatively low expense, but it has the disadvantage of being based only on hospitalized cases without the ability to distinguish first-ever strokes. Validation of the discharge code is possible but only on a sample of discharges that permits only an estimate of the accuracy.

A new feature of the computer age is the ability to link multiple databases to obtain a "person-oriented database" that contains, for an individual, information on hospitalizations, ambulatory physician visits, drug prescriptions, and mortality. Eventually, this "person-oriented database" will permit accurate surveillance of stroke and other conditions at a minimum cost and expenditure of time.

Incidence of Stroke

Table 3 presents an international comparison of the rates of first-ever stroke and all stroke during the 1970s and 1980s. The source of the data for estimating occurrence is also given, as the intensity of the case finding will affect the rate.[9] All rates have been directly standardized to the 1986 Canadian population.

For all strokes, the rates varied approximately threefold. The lowest rate (96.2/100,000) was reported from a WHO stroke registry in Nigeria,[143] but the completeness of case ascertainment is questionable; the highest rate (329.1/100,000) was reported from Australia using a prospective survey of all possible sources of stroke cases.[50] For first-ever strokes, the rates varied by a factor of two, with the lowest rate based on hospitalized cases among South African blacks[156] (116.8/100,000) and the highest rate from a registry in Brazil.[124] In general, the countries with the highest rates of stroke are the Nordic countries and Japan.

Stroke is a condition of the aged. Among persons under the age of 50, stroke is a happily rare event. For persons between the ages of 50 and 64 years, stroke occurs at a rate of approximately 3/1,000 persons; between the ages of 65 and 74 years, the incidence of stroke is approximately 12/1,000 and doubles to approximately 25/100,000 for persons 80 years and over.[3,36,39,43,132,137,153,154,163]

Prevalence

Prevalence of stroke can be estimated through a household survey or calculated based on the relationship *prevalence = incidence × duration.* Thus, knowing the incidence of stroke and the average length of survival, it is possible to calculate an estimate of the prevalence of stroke in the community without having to carry out an expensive and time-consuming household survey. Baum and Robins,[30] analyzing data from the National Survey of Stroke, used a life-table approach to estimate that, in the United States in 1976, the prevalence of stroke was approximately 1.7 million or 0.8% of the population. Other estimates of prevalence in the United Sates over the same time period ranged from 0.5% to 1.2%.[30] This calculated estimate agrees very well with the prevalence obtained through the National Interview Survey (0.8%)[30] and through the Copiah County, Mississippi, study (1.06%).[160]

Since the 1970s the mortality due to stroke has declined,[10,33,37,58,105,116,119,174] and thus, we would expect the prevalence to increase. If the American estimate of prevalence of 0.8% is projected to Canada, an estimated 208,000 Canadians are currently living with the sequelae of stroke.

Changing Rates of Stroke

From 1945 to 1980, the incidence of stroke declined.[74,75,79,119] This decline was attributed to modifications in the major risk factors for stroke, particularly improvements in the control of hypertension.[56,68,75] Recently, however, a rise in the hospitalization rate for stroke has been reported.[43,80,121,132,184] One report from Rochester, Minnesota, found that the incidence of stroke was 17% higher for the period 1980 to 1984 compared with the period 1975 to 1979.[43] The National Hospital Discharge Survey[80] from the United States reported a similar rise in the hospitalization rate for cerebrovascular disease over the period 1979 to 1983. Neither of these studies could rule out the possibility that the increases were artifactual due to changes in the admission rates for cerebral angiography and endarterectomy or to changes in the use of CT, a procedure that presumably improved the detection of mild strokes. A study from Sweden[184] found a significant rise in the incidence of stroke among women for the period 1983–86 compared with the period 1975–78; however, no specific mechanism contributing to this increase was identified. The rise was probably not due to changes in diagnostic practice favoring detection of milder strokes because the case-fatality rates were stable over this period of time. In Quebec,[132] the overall rate of hospitalization for cerebrovascular disease increased from 1981 to 1989 with dramatic increases observed in the rates of hemorrhagic cerebrovascular disease (26% to 172% depending on age and sex). These increases did not appear to be attributed solely to changes in diagnostic technology and point to the possibility of a true increase in the occurrence of stroke.

An issue separate to that of occurrence is the amount of hospital resources attributed to stroke care. From 1970 to 1980, the amount of bed-days attributed to stroke in Finland rose from 257,000 to 345,000 or 115 to 144 days/patient.[44] In Scotland, 4.3% of the National Health Budget was attributed to in-hospital and community stroke care, while 2% of all discharges and 7% of all hospital bed-days were for stroke care.[108] In Quebec, stroke accounted for 2% of all acute-care hospital discharges and 5% of total acute-care bed-days.[131] From 1981 to 1990 the number of acute-care bed-days attributed to stroke in Quebec rose from 290,000 to 360,000 or 34 days in acute-care per person.[131,132] In all of Canada, over 3.5 million hospital bed-days were attributed in 1988-89 to stroke care.[178]

Even though, the population of Canada is one-tenth that of the United States, the average length-of-stay for stroke in Canada is two to three times longer than in the United States. Thus, in proportion to the population, the total number of bed-days attributed to stroke in the United States (9.6 million) is less than in Canada.[190]

Mortality

Stroke is the third leading cause of death in Canada and the United States, following cardiovascular disease and malignant neoplasms.[177,188] For stroke, the burden of mortality is greatest in the first 30 days and declines up to 1 year after stroke.[2,30,106] After 1 year, the mortality rate from stroke is no different from the mortality rate of the general population (age-adjusted).[2,30,59] Thirty-day case fatality rates have been reported to range from 10% to 30%[17,36,73,81,90,101,105,124,153,157,170,201]; 1 year after stroke, 30% to 50% will have succumbed,[17,36,90,170] and 2 to 3 years after stroke, the death toll will reach 50% to 60%.[83,161,183] During the first few days after stroke, death is attributed predominantly to cerebral causes, such as transtentorial herniation, but also to pneumonia, cardiac complications, and pulmonary embolism.[2,19,22,40,81,106] After 6 months very few of the deaths were attributed to the stroke;

TABLE 3. International Comparison of Incidence Rates of Stroke

Reference	Source of Data	Place	Time Period	Length of Time (yrs)	Age Range (yrs)	Number of Strokes*	Population at Risk	Rate/year (per 100,000)
First-ever strokes								
156	Hospital records	South Africa (blacks)	1984-85	1	> 20	116	114,931	116.8
201	Medical sources	Perth, Australia	1986	0.8	30–85+	154	927,114†	121.4
154	Hospital records	USA	1975–76	1	15–85+	594,000	211,047,000	124.2
110	Registry	Malmo, Sweden	1989	1	0–85+	524	232,448	124.2
90	Medical sources	Alabama (whites)	1980	1	20–75+	48	25,483	126.1
43	Medical sources	Minnesota	1980-84	5	0–85+	401	300,893	140.4
36	Registry	Auckland, NZ	1981-82	1	15–85+	680	829,464	148.0
119	Registry	Finland	1972–80	4	15–75+	255	136,850	150.9
20	Registry	Oxfordshire, UK	1981–86	4	0–85+	675	105,476	154.8
101	Registry	Netherlands	1978–79	0.5	0–75+	438	157,356	155.1
126	Cohort	Denmark	1976–88	12	35–84	640	15,499	156.2
153	Registry	Umbria, Italy	1986–89	3	0–85+	375	49,218	160.0
3	Hospital records	Manitoba	1970–71	1.5	20–80+	1,367	660,391	162.6
91	Survey	China	1986	1	0–85+	6,367	5,790,864	165.3
17	Registry	Sweden	1986–88	3	25–85+	288	30,005	166.5
137	Cohort	Shibata, Japan	1977–87	10	40–70+	80	2,299	197.8
90	Medical sources	Alabama (blacks)	1980	1	20–75+	91	31,169	220.4
152	Cohort	Finland	1966–72	6	15–85+	310	24,747	233.5
124	Registry	Bahia, Brazil	1979–80	1	15–65+	1,119	783,642	236.8

All strokes

143	Registry	Nigeria	1973–75	2	0–80+	318	881,000	96.2
203	Medical sources	Poland	1985	1	20–90+	1,763	889,139	120.8
83	Registry	Dijon, France	1985	1	15–85+	418	140,000	127.3
90	Medical sources	Alabama (whites)	1980	1	20–75+	53	25,483	141.7
8	Registry	New Jersey	1982–83	1	0–85+	831	497,767	146.7
154	Hospital records	USA	1975–76	1	15–85+	828,000	211,047,000	147.1
48	Medical sources	Bejing, China	1984–86	3	25–74	2,593	700,000	148.9
132	Hospital discharges	Quebec	1981–89	9	15–85+	79,482	5,161,735	151.0
163	Hospital records	Brisbane, Australia	1984	1	25–75+	1,274	1,000,000	174.1
101	Registry	Netherlands	1978–79	0.5	0–75+	526	151,356	186.5
36	Registry	Auckland, NZ	1981–82	1	15–85+	703	613,953	193.2
183	Registry	Sibata, Japan	1976–78	3	20–80+	415	75,168	195.8
17	Registry	Sweden	1986–88	3	25–85+	384	30,005	221.0
66	Medical sources	Israel	1984	1	45–80+	1,149	600,000	226.9
152	Cohort	Finland	1966–72	6	15–85+	343	23,666	258.1
90	Medical sources	Alabama (blacks)	1980	1	20–75+	107	31,169	263.8
181	Registry	Akita, Japan	1983–85	1.5	20–79	1,808	889,812	267.6
170	Registry	Kuopio, Finland	1978–80	1.7	15–75+	373	95,420	269.5
124	Registry	Bahia, Brazil	1979–80	1	15–65+	1,320	783,642	282.6
50	Medical sources	Melbourne, Australia	1978–79	1.5	25–85+	508	160,000	329.1

* Stroke includes cerebral infarction, cerebral hemorrhage, and subarachnoid hermorrhage but excludes transient ischemic attacks. Rates for men and women combined are directly standardized to the 1986 Canadian population.
† Estimated from rates.

however, recurrent stroke, cardiac disease, and noncardiovascular conditions probably secondary to long periods of bed-rest and immobility, increasingly, contributed to mortality in the first year.[2,22,40,106,161]

FACTORS AFFECTING THE OCCURRENCE OF STROKE

Factors that modify the occurrence of an event are called *risk factors*. While *risk* refers to an individual's probability of developing a stroke, *risk factors* are evaluated among groups of persons by comparing the rate of events in a population with the risk factor to the rate in a population without the risk factor. The two rates are either subtracted to obtain the risk difference, or more commonly, a ratio is made of the two risks yielding the relative risk.

Causality

When considering risk factors for stroke, it is essential to distinguish between factors that are associated with the development of stroke and factors that are causally related to stroke so that effective strategies for reducing the occurrence of stroke in the population can be introduced. For example, an evaluation of causality may assist health care planners to judge the relative effectiveness of instituting an antismoking campaign in a community or a hypertension screening program. Table 4 gives a list of criteria for judging whether an association between a factor and stroke could be that of causality.[41]

TABLE 4. Criteria for Causality*

Strength of the association	Relative risks > 2.0 are less likely to be explained by unmeasured confounding variables.
Experiment	Direct or indirect manipulation of the risk factor changes the rate of stroke.
Dose-response gradient	Risk increases with increasing levels of the risk factor.
Temporality	The development of the risk factor precedes the occurrence of the event; this criterion is more relevant to the diseases with an insidious onset but could be applicable if one considers that certain manifestations of an impending cerebrovascular accident could have led to changes in behavior (e.g., aspirin may have been taken for a headache which may have been an early warning sign of stroke) or the consequences of the stroke may also themselves be risk factors (e.g., atrial fibrillation may follow a stroke and not precede it).[146]
Consistency	An association has been observed by different persons in different places, at different times, and under different circumstances.
Biological plausibility	There is a reasonable biologic mechanism whereby the risk factor could cause the disease (of course, this is dependent on the knowledge of the day).
Coherence of the evidence	There is no conflict with what is generally known about the disease such as temporal trends or histopathologic findings from laboratory studies or animal studies.
Specificity	The association is specific to stroke or to certain subtypes of stroke or to certain subgroups of the population.
Analogy	When there is an analagous situation with other similar risk factors, the balance of the evidence would not need to be so strong (e.g., if one illicit drug showed an association with stroke, then similar drugs would be suspect).

*Data from Bradford-Hill.[41]

The etiology of stroke is multifactorial, and therefore, there are a number of factors that, in the population, satisfy the criteria for causality. However, for any one individual, it is not always possible to identify which factor or combination of factors resulted in the stroke. One of the strongest criteria for causality is that of *experimentation*.[41] That is, if the risk factor is removed or modified, does the probability of stroke change? Thus, one of the main criteria for causality depends on the degree to which a risk factor is modifiable. The concept of modifiable and nonmodifiable risk factors is useful for the study of stroke except that the degree to which certain factors are modifiable is not a dichotomy. Table 5 gives a taxonomy for the consideration of risk factors for stroke using the rubrics of modifiable and nonmodifiable, although an informed reader will be able to see that not all factors can be so easily classified. For example, for nonsmokers or exsmokers, smoking probably appears to be a modifiable risk factor; however, for persons living with an addiction to nicotine, the degree to which this is modifiable may be limited. Similarly, the extent to which atrial fibrillation or valvular heart disease are modifiable through medical management could also be questioned. Although use of oral contraceptives and postmenopausal estrogens are given in the modifiable group, their modification may be associated with other unacceptable events that justify their inclusion in this grouping. The variable, blood lipids, has been included in the modifiable group among the variables modifiable through lifestyle changes, although change in blood lipids is not always under individual control but regulated through a variety of metabolic and genetic factors.

Relative Risk and Attributable Risk

Table 6 summarizes the extent to which certain factors have been shown to modify an individual's risk of stroke. The concept of relative risk is pivotal for understanding the etiology of the disease, but it is not the crucial ingredient to disease prevention. The frequency with which a particular factor is present in the population dictates the proportion of cases attributed to this factor. The attributable risk in the population is derived according to the formula:

$$\frac{p_e(RR-1)}{1 + p_e(RR-1)}$$

where RR is the relative risk and p_e is the prevalence of the factor in the population.[122] Table 7 presents the population attributable risk for key risk factors. Estimates of relative risk were drawn from Table 6 and estimates of

TABLE 5. Taxonomy for Classifying Risk Factors for Stroke*

Nonmodifiable	Modifiable

Sociodemographic
  Age, sex, race
	Lifestyle factors
	  Smoking, alcohol consumption, obesity, diet,
	  exercise, illicit drug use, blood lipids

Manifestations of vascular disease
  Previous stroke, transient ischemic attack,
  myocardial infarction, atherosclerosis, left
  ventricular hypertrophy, angiopathy, family
  history of stroke, peripheral vascular disease
	Potentially medically manageable
	  Hypertension, diabetes, platelet aggregation,
	  atrial fibrillation, valvular heart disease,
	  migraine, infections, febrile illness, oral
	  contraceptives, postmenopausal estrogens

* Risk factors given here are those identified by the WHO Task Force on Stroke and Other Cerebrovascular Disorders[212] and by the Council of Cerebrovascular Disease of the American Heart Association Subcommittee on Risk Factors and Stroke[63]; the list is not inclusive.

TABLE 6.   Magnitude of the Risk of Stroke Associated with Selected Factors

	Magnitude of Relative Risk	References
Nonmodifiable		
Sociodemographic variables		
Age	Risk approximately doubles every decade	56,69,159,165,209
Sex	2.0 for males vs. females	56,165
Race	1.5 to 2.5 for blacks vs. whites	70,115
	Association stronger at younger ages	42,70
Manifestations of vascular disease		
Previous stroke	3.8–14.1	65,175,185
Transient ischemic attack	3.5–5	56,95,100
Myocardial infarction	1.7–17	65,95,100,175,185
Family history of stroke	1.5–8.0	95,125,175
	No association	56
Peripheral vascular disease	2.2–4.0	95,175
Left ventricular hypertrophy	2.0	56,179
Modifiable		
Lifestyle variables		
Smoking	Cerebral infarction: 1.9	103,166 (reviews)
	Cerebral hemorrhage: 0.7	51,60,65
	Subarachnoid hemorrhage: 2.9	
	All strokes: 1.5	
	Dose-response effect	78,86
Alcohol consumption	Cerebral infarction: 1.5–3.2	46,77,86
	Cerebral hemorrhage: 2–3	
	Subarachnoid hemorrhage: >3.5	176
	No association or protective	65,176
	J-shaped dose-response curve	176
Obesity	1.6–2.6	100,167
	No association	29,54,65,69,95,175
Diet	No association for vitamin C or salt	24,65
	Cerebral infarction and salt: 1.8	125
	Cerebral hemorrhage and salt: 2.0	
Exercise	No association	69,95,65
	Protective	100
Illicit drug use	6.5 or 49.4 for use within 6 hrs	112
Potentially Medically Manageable		
Hypertension	Cerebral infarction: 2.0–15.0	56,125,159
	Cerebral hemorrhage: 1.3–24.0	125,165
	All strokes: 1.5–7.1	69,85,95,100,128,164,
		175,65,179,185,186
	Dose-response effect	65,128
Blood lipids	Cerebral infarction: 1.8–2.6	109,159
	Cerebral hemorrhage: 0.3–0.8	109,159
	No association	95
Diabetes	1.7–10.5	56,65,69,95,100,175,185
Atrial fibrillation	2.2–12.7	95,100,175
	No association	56,207
Valvular heart disease	Not estimable directly; persons with stroke and valvular prolapse are 7–14 times more likely to have no other risk factor than persons with stroke and no valvular prolapse	28,113,120
Oral contraceptives	Cerebral infarction: 3–12.7	52
	Cerebral hemorrhage: no association	

(Table continued on facing page.)

TABLE 6. Magnitude of the Risk of Stroke Associated with Selected Factors *(Continued)*

	Magnitude of Relative Risk	References
Other		
Pregnancy	13.0	204,205
	1.5	
Epilepsy	4.0	175
Snoring	3.0	175
Migraine	1.7	99
Stress	Cerebral infarction: 1.9–3.0	95
	Cerebral hemorrhage: no association	
	Subarachnoid hemorrhage: no association	
	All strokes: 1.5	

prevalence came from a recent survey of cardiovascular risk factors in Quebec,[136] except for illicit drug use (for which American data were used[189]) and migraine.[99] The greatest proportion of strokes is attributed to hypertension, followed by alcohol consumption which, although not a very strong risk factor, is quite prevalent in modern society (>20%). Diabetes is a strong risk factor but not common, and therefore, a greater proportion of strokes is attributed to the weaker but more prevalent factor, elevated blood lipids. Even though the prevalence of smoking is high (31% of the Quebec population), its attributable risk is low (13%) because it is not as strong a risk factor as some of the others. Of concern is the 10% of strokes in the young that are attributed to abuse of illicit "hard" drugs.

Age and Risk Factors

Is there any evidence that the risk factors for stroke in the young differ from risk factors for stroke in older persons? Stroke in the young is rare; less than 5% of all strokes will occur in persons under 45 years of age.[3,50,110,126,132,153,163,181,191] Cardiac sources of emboli are important contributors to stroke in young persons, whereas in older persons atherosclerosis is the most common underlying pathology.[34,63,67] Approximately 30% to 50% of ischemic strokes in the young can be attributed to emboli,[4,31,64,89,94,96] whereas in older persons only 5% to 14% of

TABLE 7. Risk of Stroke Attributed to Selected Factors

Factor	Relative Risk	Prevalence (%)	Attributable Risk* (%)
Hypertension[†]	1.5–7.1	13	6–44
Alcohol[†]	1.5–3.5	21	9–33
Diabetes[†]	1.7–10.5	5	3–33
Blood lipids[†]	1.8–2.6	19	13–23
Smoking[†]	1.5	31	13
Migraine[‡]	1.7	5	3
Illicit drug use[§]	6.5	5	10 (ages 15–44)
			0.5 (all ages)

* Calculated according to formula: $AR = p_e(RR - 1)/1 + p_e(RR - 1)$, where AR = attributable risk, p_e = prevalence, and RR = relative risk.
† Prevalence from Santé Québec[136]; hypertension defined as diastolic pressure $\geq$ 90 mmHg; alcohol, > 7 glasses/wk; diabetes diagnosed by a physician; blood lipids, > 6.2 mmol/L; regular smoking.
‡ Prevalence data from reference 99.
§ Illicit drug use in persons 15–44 years; prevalence based on US data[189]; AR for all ages based on 5% of strokes occurring in persons < 45 years of age (0.10 × 0.05).

strokes are cardio-embolic.[63] Atherosclerosis is identifiable as a contributor in approximately 25% of the strokes among young persons and is influenced by the same factors as in older persons (diabetes, hypertension, smoking).[4,31,94,96,104,130]

Unrecognized trauma can be an important contributor to stroke in the young,[94,104] and use of oral contraceptives and hematologic disorders arising during the peripartum period are important contributors to stroke in women of childbearing age.[4,31,52,53,96,205]

Is there any evidence that the risk factors for stroke in the very old differ from risk factors for stroke in middle-aged persons? In general, no. The major risk factors for stroke identified through a study of 535 persons whose mean age was 82 years[14] included the known risk factors of systolic or diastolic hypertension, smoking, diabetes, left ventricular hypertrophy, prior stroke or transient ischemic attack, extracranial arterial disease, and coronary heart disease. In addition many of the strategies to reduce the risk of stroke in middle-aged persons are potentially effective in reducing the risk of stroke in much older persons, and given that most strokes occur in older persons, even if less effective, preventive strategies could still reduce considerably the number of new strokes in the population.[149]

While the risk factors for stroke in the elderly do not appear to be greatly different from those in younger persons,[13,15,16,92,168] age may modify the effect of certain risk factors.[149] For example, for persons over the age of 75 years, the risk ratio for stroke and smoking is less than the risk ratio in younger persons, indicating that age modifies the magnitude of the effect of smoking. High cholesterol is putative in young persons but protective in older persons, again implicating age as an effect modifier of the relationship between cholesterol and stroke.[149]

Probability of Stroke

Figure 1 illustrates the probability of a man developing a stroke in the next 10 years according to a cumulative risk factor index derived from data obtained from the Framingham study.[209] The index derived by Wolf and colleagues assigns a variable weighing scale to eight risk factors. Up to 10 points is assigned for age, 1 point for each 3-year age bracket starting at age 57. Up to 10 points is assigned for systolic blood pressure, 1 point for each 11 mm Hg starting at 106 mm Hg. Two points each are assigned for hypertensive therapy and for a history of diabetes; 3 points each are assigned for smoking and a history of peripheral vascular disease or congestive heart failure; 4 points are assigned for history of atrial fibrillation; and 6 points are assigned for electrocardiographic evidence of left ventricular hypertrophy.

Figure 1 shows very clearly how the probability of stroke increases as the burden of risk factors accumulates. For men with only 1 point—for example, a man between the age of 57 and 59 years with no other risk factors or a man under 57 years whose only risk factor is a systolic blood pressure between 106 and 116 mm Hg—the probability of stroke over the next 10 years is estimated at 2.6%. For men with 10 points, an index that can be accumulated by the combination of several risk factors or by being in the oldest age bracket or the highest range for systolic blood pressure, the 10-year probability of developing stroke is estimated at 9.7%. The maximum number of points that can be accumulated is 30, and this degree of burden inflicts a 10-year risk of almost 90%.

Factors Influencing the Rate of Stroke in the Population

Rates of stroke in the population are not solely dependent upon the characteristics of the individuals making up the population but can be affected by

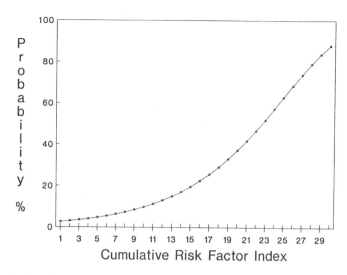

1 point for each 3 years of age starting at age 57 (max 10)
1 point for each 11 mm Hg of systolic blood pressure starting at 106 mm Hg (max 10)
2 points for hypertensive therapy
2 points for a history of diabetes
3 points for smoking
3 points for history of peripheral vascular disease or congestive heart failure
4 points for history of atrial fibrillation
6 points for ECG evidence of left ventricular hypertrophy

FIGURE 1. Probability of Stroke Within 10 Years for Men Aged 55–84 Years According to a Cumulative Risk Factor Index. Cumulative index derived from Framingham study.[209]

the sociopolitical climate of the region. Sociopolitical conditions influence access to medical care, and this influences the management of conditions affecting an individual's risk of stroke (diabetes, hypertension, heart disease). Access to medical care will also influence the probability that an individual will search out medical care for the stroke. As most of the studies on the rates of stroke are based on identifying cases that present themselves for medical attention, the degree to which medical attention is available and affordable will influence the estimation of the rate of stroke. For persons suffering severe strokes, the probability that they will enter the medical system and, therefore, be counted is higher than for persons suffering mild strokes. Case-fatality rates are often used as indicators of stroke severity and are used to determine whether changes in rates may be explained by changes in severity or in diagnostic practices. Estimates of case-fatality rates in areas where access to medical care is fraught with obstacles may be biased if it is based on the mortality experience of persons with relatively severe strokes.

The sociopolitical climate also influences the economic strength of the population, and this influences the health of the community. In Canada, the number of years a person can expect to live in good health is greater in larger communities and among persons with higher incomes.[206] In Quebec, poverty has been shown to be an important contributor to regional mortality rates from cardiovascular disease and from diabetes[144,207] and to be a contributor to overall and disability-free life expectancy.[207] In Montreal, the difference between the wealthiest and poorest neighborhoods in life expectancy and quality-adjusted life expectancy was almost 10 years.[207]

Seasonal Variation

Seasonal variability in stroke rates has been investigated worldwide, and when a pattern has emerged, it is most commonly one of a relative excess in the winter and spring compared to the summer and autumn.[7,32,50,72,76,82,84,93,117,129,135,141,148,150,158,172,181,213] Several groups of hypothetical mechanisms contributing to a seasonal variation in the occurrence of stroke have been suggested. These include meterologic phenomena,[35,45,117,141,182] intrinsic metabolic factors that themselves may be under the influence of extrinsic forces,[93,117,135,162,172] and seasonal variation in the occurrence of other conditions associated with stroke.[129]

Meterologic hypotheses that have been proposed to explain the seasonality of stroke have suggested that decreased temperature causes decreased blood flow to the extremities, increasing blood pressure, which in turn leads to an increase in the likelihood of either a cerebral hemorrhage or cerebral infarction occurring. It has been documented that blood pressure rises in the winter,[93] which may explain the seasonal pattern of stroke.

It has also been hypothesized that an individual's metabolic state is influenced by environmental factors such that meterologic variation causes hemodynamic changes in blood platelets, erythrocyte count, blood viscosity, catecholamines, blood pressure, blood volume, or blood coagulability or blood electrolytic concentrations.[93,172,210] Other hypothesized metabolic changes, which are seasonally influenced, include changing consumption of diuretics and salt loss variation[117] or dehydration.[172]

Although there appears to be some evidence for a seasonal pattern in stroke occurrence, the data are not conclusive because many of the methodologic difficulties inherent to the study of seasonal variation (season not climatically well defined, reduced power to detect a seasonal pattern, and variable statistical treatment) have not been overcome.

In summary, stroke is a condition with known risk factors and identifiable preventive strategies,[62] yet it remains a major contributor to disability and handicap in the population.

RECOVERY FROM STROKE

The Pattern of Recovery

In 1951, Twitchell[187] observed that motor recovery after stroke followed a distinct pattern. After the initial vascular event, motor power was lost in the contralateral extremities. This period of flaccidity was followed by the return of tendon reflexes and the onset of spasticity. The restoration of movement started proximally and moved distally. First, movement was possible only in a synergistic pattern of total flexion for the upper extremity and total extension for the lower extremity; gradually movement came under voluntary control.

Although the degree of restoration differed, the pattern followed was the same except for timing. Among persons making complete recovery, the return of tendon reflexes and the onset of spasticity occurred during the first week. For persons with partial or no recovery, the onset of spasticity was observed 2 to 28 days post-stroke. For persons eventually making full recovery, voluntary movement commenced during the first 2 weeks, but took 3 to 8 weeks to return for persons making only partial recovery.

Of the 19 patients followed by Twitchell throughout the course of recovery, 25% never regained movement in the upper extremity, 25% recovered completely, and the remaining 50% regained movement only at the shoulder and elbow joint.

Decades later, the pattern of recovery following stroke is as described by Twitchell, and the degree of recovery of the upper extremity remains limited.[23,87,88,98,138,145,194,196] Approximately one-third make no recovery, one-third make enough recovery to use the arm in functional activities, and one-third make partial recovery. The restoration of movement in the lower extremity is better, as less than 10% of persons remain with severe motor loss.[138,196]

Recovery of Neurologic Deficits

Although not all strokes present with complete loss of motor function, as described by Twitchell, more than three-fourths will have a moderate to severe disturbance of motor ability in the affected limbs.[101,110,161] Loss of motor function is a reflection of the severity of the neurologic deficit or the degree of impairment. There are many other sequelae of stroke that reflect the nature, location, and size of the neurologic impairment, such as dysphagia, dysphasia, hemianopia, and visual hemi-neglect. These sequelae are not easily assessed, particularly in the acute care setting, and as a consequence our knowledge of their incidence and recovery is limited. What we do know about the recovery comes from studies restricted to the clientele from one center that usually has some unique program comprising complete and comprehensive evaluations and follow-up. As a consequence, the selection criteria for entry into these programs are those same criteria that effect the extent of recovery.

Recently, however, several stroke registries have reported the prevalence of presenting deficits, and one report form Moscow presents data on the recovery of motor disturbance, dysarthria, and aphasia for up to 7 years post-stroke.[161] At 3 weeks post-stroke, 81% had some degree of motor deficit; but by 1 year this proportion had dropped to 50% and continued to decline over the 7-year period, so that by the end of the period of observation only 12% had residual motor deficits. Initially, one-half to two-thirds of persons with stroke will have some disturbance of speech,[101,110,161] but in only 10% will this persist. Barer[25] and Wade and Hewer[196] observed that between 30% and 43% of persons with stroke initially had difficulty swallowing and that more than 98% of those surviving recovered. The data derived from Russia[161] and Great Britain[25,95] may not be entirely applicable to the situation in North America owing to differences in the population studied, the medical after-care for stroke, and the type of diagnostic procedures used to detect various neurologic deficits. For example, the frequency with which swallowing disorders are detected will vary depending on whether the diagnosis is based on radiologic evidence or clinical observation. The degree of diagnostic rigor will not only influence the number of individuals so classified but also will affect the characteristics of the population with swallowing disorders, and so mortality rates from one setting to another would not be comparable.

The proportion of persons with visual hemi-neglect following stroke is variable and depends on the assessment procedure.[71] In general, one-third or less will have this deficit;[57,71,180] however, the degree of recovery has been reported to be as low as 25% and high as 87%.[47,57,180,199]

Incontinence is another prevalent deficit following stroke, occurring initially in more than 58% of stroke victims.[26] Only 7% of those initially incontinent will regain bladder control by 1 week, but 36% will have recovered control by 1 month and 56% by 6 months. However, even by 6 months, 14% of all persons with stroke will still have incomplete bladder control.

There is a paradox in determining the recovery rate from these sequelae: as they are associated with a high degree of mortality, it is only in survivors that the recovery rate is high. In Moscow, the mortality rate for persons with severe motor disturbance was two to three times higher than the mortality rate for persons with mild or moderate motor disturbance. Fullerton et al.[71] reported that persons with visual hemi-neglect had a higher mortality rate than persons without neglect. In the study by Barer,[25] the mortality rate for persons with swallowing disorders was three to six times greater than the mortality rate for persons without difficulty swallowing, so that by 6 months, even though less than 1% of persons still had a swallowing disorder, 57% of those with swallowing disorders had died.

Recovery of Functional Ability and Quality of Life

Usually the first question raised by someone who has survived an acute stroke relates to walking. One-half to three-fourths of those who lose the ability to walk after stroke will regain independence in this very important function. That is, most persons will be able to walk, perhaps with a cane, but without the assistance of another person.[61,97,145,197,198] When disability is looked at globally, in terms of the degree to which a person can carry out basic activities of daily living, at 6 months post-stroke, one-half to two-thirds of survivors will be independent or have only slight dependency and the remaining one-half to one-third will be classified as needing moderate or total assistance.[6,12,21,38,55,59,118,195]

An even more distressing finding is that the quality of life after stroke is poor even in young persons who would be expected to have better recovery than older persons.[139] In the study by Niemi et al.,[139] on quality of life 4 years after stroke, they found that 59% of persons under the age of 65 years had not returned to work, and 83% had not returned to their pre-stroke quality of life. While younger persons have a better chance of returning to work than older persons, overall the proportion of younger or all persons returning to work after stroke is small ($< 20\%$).[107]

Recently Aström, Asplund, and Aström found that persons with stroke reported a very marked reduction in their global life satisfaction 1 year after stroke. Söderback and colleagues[173] also reported that the consequences of stroke for function and personal activity were considerable even after 3 years; two-thirds of persons felt that their lifestyle had been altered considerably by the stroke such that they were unable to return to previous levels of rest and leisure activities, family function, occupation, and quality of life.

Given that quality of life or satisfaction with life is essential to health and well-being, it is remarkable that it has not been studied more often among stroke patients and indicates our preoccupation with the medical and physical aspects of stroke rather than with the social aspects.

The Rate of Recovery

The second question asked following stroke usually refers to the speed at which recovery will take place. The timing of recovery depends upon the degree of impairment, and it also predicts the extent of recovery. Almost all individuals with a lesion that results in a motor deficit only, but spares sensation and language will regain independence in walking and functioning within 3 months.[151] Persons with more extensive deficits will regain function more slowly, within 6 to 8 months, and will have a lower probability of becoming independent. For example, Reding and Potes[151] demonstrated that 90% of persons with a motor deficit only regained the ability to walk independently by 14 weeks. In contrast, persons with motor and sensory deficits or motor, sensory, and language deficits took 22 weeks and 30 weeks, respectively, to reach the same level of independence, and a much lower proportion were successful (35% and 3%, respectively).

Coming back to the early study by Twitchell,[187] persons with full recovery of the upper extremity started the process of recovery within the first 2 weeks. However, persons with only partial or no recovery took 3 to 8 weeks, if ever, to begin recovery. In general, the majority of persons will make the majority of their recovery during the first 3 months.[23,59,114,118,138,171,194,198] That is not to say that recovery after 3 months is not possible. Indeed, many persons continue to progress well past 3 months,[11,12,49,133,138] particularly in their ability to adapt to their new functional level. Rehabilitation professionals must be aware of this latent recovery and continue to offer services.[193] Indeed, the profile of a person living in the community with stroke will change over time, and thus, in order to maintain a person at their maximum level of functioning, this author feels that rehabilitation services that are responsive to changing needs should be accessible long after the acute phase has passed.

Factors Influencing Recovery

Throughout this chapter, the World Health Organization's *International Classification of Impairment, Disability, and Handicap*[211] has provided the conceptual framework for the presentation of the material related to the recovery from stroke. *Impairment* refers to the physical or psychological lesion, *disability* refers to the functional consequence of the impairment such as the inability to walk or carry out basic functional activities, whereas *handicap* is any limitation in a person's ability to perform a role in society (worker, parent, mate, etc.).

Certain disabilities, in particular those that are classified as neurologic deficits, loss of motor function, dysphagia, dysphasia, hemianopia, and visual hemi-neglect reflect the nature, location, and size of the neurologic impairment. Other disabilities such as in walking, dressing, bathing, or managing personal affairs are dependent not only upon the extent of the impairment but also on personal characteristics of the person prior to the stroke. Factors related to the impairment that have been shown to influence the degree of disability after stroke are nature and severity of the stroke,[6,61,142,169] sensory deficits,[87] perceptual deficits,[87,111] and functional ability at the beginning of the period of observation.[97,111,142] The personal characteristics of the individual that have been shown to influence outcome after stroke are age[6,55,87,97,111,169,195] and the occurrence of medical complications or comorbid conditions.[61,123] Such factors as age, perceptual deficit, comprehension difficulties, and depression have been shown to influence the rate of recovery.[133]

The degree of handicap that arises from stroke is even more dependent upon individual characteristics, but more importantly, handicap is dependent upon environmental and sociopolitical factors such as funding for aids and adaptations, transportation, etc. Thus, people with the same degree of impairment can have very different levels of disability, and persons with the same disability can have very different degrees of handicap. It is the role of rehabilitation to reduce the impact of impairment on disability and handicap.

ACKNOWLEDGMENT

The author wishes to thank Mr. Adrian Levy for his assistance in preparing Table 3 and in reviewing the literature on seasonality.

REFERENCES

1. Abbott RD, Yin Y, Reed DM, Yano K: Risk of stroke in male cigarette smokers. N Engl J Med 315:717–720, 1986.
2. Abu-Zeid HAH, Choi NW, Hsu PH, Maini KK: Prognostic factors in the survival of 1,484 stroke cases observed for 30 to 48 months.: I. Diagnostic types and descriptive variables. Arch Neurol 35:121–125, 1978.
3. Abu-Zeid HAH, Choi NW, Nelson NA: Epidemiologic features of cerebrovascular disease in Manitoba: Incidence by age, sex and residence, with etiologic implications. Can Med Assoc J 113:379–384, 1975.
4. Adams HP, Butler MJ, Biller J, Toffol GJ: Nonhemorrhagic cerebral infarction in young adults. Arch Neurol 43:793–796, 1986.
5. Aho K, Harmsen P, Hatano S, et al: Cerebrovascular disease in the community: Results of a WHO collaborative study. Bull WHO 58:113–130, 1980.
6. Allen CMC: Predicting the outcome of acute stroke: A prognostic score. J Neurol Neurosurg Psychiatry 47:475–480, 1984.
7. Alter M, Christoferson L, Resch J, et al: Cerebrovascular disease: Frequency and population selectivity in an upper midwestern community. Stroke 1:454–465, 1970.
8. Alter M, Sobel E, McCoy RL, et al: Stroke in the Lehigh Valley: Incidence based on a community-wide hospital register. Neuroepidemiology 4:1–15, 1985.
9. Alter M, Zhang ZX, Sobel E, et al: Standardized incidence ratios of stroke: A worldwide review. Neuroepidemiology 5:148–158, 1986.
10. Anderson GL, Whisnant JP: A comparison of trends in mortality from stroke in the United States and Rochester, Minnesota. Stroke 13:804–809, 1982.
11. Andrews K, Brocklehurst JC, Richards B, Laycock PJ: The rate of recovery from stroke—and its measurement. Int Rehabil Med 3:155–161, 1981.
12. Andrews K, Brocklehurst JC, Richards B, Laycock PJ: The influence of age on the clinical presentation and outcome of stroke. Int Rehabil Med 6:49–53, 1984.
13. Aronow WS, Schoenfeld MR, Paul P: Risk factors for extracranial internal or common carotid arterial disease in persons aged 60 years and older. Am J Cardiol 63:881–882, 1989.
14. Aronow WS, Starling L, Etienne F, et al: Risk factors for atherothrombotic brain infarction in persons over 62 years of age in a long-term health care facility. J Am Geriatr Soc 35:1–3, 1987.
15. Aronow WS, Gutstein H, Lee NH, Edwards M: Three year follow-up of risk factors correlated with new atherothrombotic brain infarction in 708 elderly patients. Angiology 39:563–566, 1988.
16. Aronow WS: Risk factors for geriatric stroke: Identification and follow-up. Geriatrics 45:37–44, 1990.
17. Asberg KH, Parrow A: Event, incidence and fatality rates of cerebrovascular disease in Enköping-Habo, Sweden, 1986–1988. Scand J Soc Med 19:134–139, 1991.
18. Aström M, Asplund K, Aström T: Psychosocial function and life satisfaction after stroke. Stroke 23:527–531, 1992.
19. Bamford J, Dennis M, Sandercock P, et al: The frequency, causes and timing of death within 30 days of a first stroke: The Oxfordshire Community Stroke Project. J Neurol Neurosurg Psychiatry 53:824–829, 1990.
20. Bamford J, Sandercock P, Dennis M, et al: A prospective study of acute cerebrovascular disease in the community: The Oxfordshire Community Stroke Project 1981–86. I. Methodology, demography and incident cases of first-ever stroke. J Neurol Neurosurg Psychiatry 51:1373–1380, 1988.
21. Bamford J, Sandercock P, Dennis M, et al: A prospective study of acute cerebrovascular disease in the community: The Oxfordshire Community Stroke Project 1981–86. 2. Incidence, case fatality rates and overall outcome at one year of cerebral infarction, primary intracerebral hemorrhage and subarachnoid haemorrhage. J Neurol Neurosurg Psychiatry 53:16–22, 1990.
22. Bamford J, Sandercock P, Dennis M, et al: Classification and natural history of clinically identifiable subtypes of cerebral infarction. Lancet 337:1521–1526, 1991.
23. Bard G, Hirschberg GG: Recovery of voluntary motion in upper extremity following hemiplegia. Arch Phys Med Rehabil 46:567–572, 1965.

24. Barer D, Leibowitz, R, Ebrahim S, et al: Vitamin C status and other nutritional indices in patients with stroke and other acute illnesses: A case control study. J Clin Epidemiol 42:625–631, 1989.

25. Barer DH: The natural history and functional consequences of dysphagia after hemispheric stroke. J Neurol Neurosurg Psychiatry 52:236–241, 1989.

26. Barer DH: Continence after stroke: Useful predictor or goal of therapy? Age Ageing 18:183–191, 1989.

27. Barker WH, Feldt KS, Feibel J: Assessment of hospital admission surveillance of stroke in a metropolitan community. J Chronic Dis 37:609–615, 1984.

28. Barnett HJM, Boughner DR, Taylor DW, et al: Further evidence relating mitral-valve prolapse to cerebral ischemic events. N Engl J Med 302:139–144, 1980.

29. Barrett-Connor E: Obesity, hypertension and stroke. Clin Exp Hyper Theory Pract 12:769–782, 1990.

30. Baum HM, Robins M: Chapter 5: Survival and prevalence. In Weinfeld FD (ed): The National Survey of Stroke. Stroke 12(Suppl):59–68, 1981.

31. Bevan H, Sharma K, Bradley W: Stroke in young adults. Stroke 21:382–386, 1990.

32. Biller J, Jones MP, Bruno A, et al: Seasonal variation in stroke—Does it exist? Neuroepidemiology 7:89–98, 1988.

33. Bisch L, Semenciw R, Wilkins K: Temporal and spatial patterns in stroke mortality and morbidity among the Canadian elderly. Chronic Dis Can 10:63–67, 1989.

34. Bogousslavsky J, Van Melle G, Regli F: The Lausanne Stroke Registry: Analysis of 1,000 consecutive patients with first stroke. Stroke 19:1083–1092, 1988.

35. Bokonjic R, Zec N: Strokes and the weather: A quantitative statistical study. J Neurol Sci 6:483–491, 1968.

36. Bonita R, Beaglehole R, North JDK: Event, incidence and case fatality rates of cerebrovascular disease in Auckland, New Zealand. Am J Epidemiol 120:236–243, 1984.

37. Bonita R, Beaglehole R: Increased treatment of hypertension does not explain the decline in stroke mortality in the United States, 1970–1980. Hypertension 13:69–73, 1989.

38. Bonita R, Beaglehole R: Recovery of motor function after stroke. Stroke 19:1497–1500, 1988.

39. Bonita R: Epidemiology of stroke. Lancet 339:342–344, 1992.

40. Bounds JV, Weibers DO, Whisnant JP, Okazaki H: Mechanisms and timing of deaths from cerebral infarction. Stroke 12:474–477, 1981.

41. Bradford-Hill A: A Short Textbook of Medical Statistics. London, Unibook Hodder and Stoughton, 1977.

42. Broderick JP, Brott T, Tomisk T, et al: The risk of subarachnoid and intracerebral hemorrhages in blacks as compared with whites. N Engl J Med 326:733–736, 1992.

43. Broderick JP, Phillips SJ, Whisnant JP, et al: Incidence rate of stroke in the eighties: The end of the decline in stroke? Stroke 20:577–582, 1989.

44. Brommels M, Tilvis R, Autio L: Cerebrovascular disease: Declining incidence but increasing hospital utilisation. Scand J Soc Med 15:153–157, 1987.

45. Bull GM: Meterological correlates with myocardial and cerebral infarction and respiratory disease. Br J Prev Soc Med 27:108–113, 1973.

46. Camargo CA: Moderate alcohol consumption and stroke: The epidemiologic evidence. Stroke 20:1611–1626, 1989.

47. Campbell DC, Oxbury JM: Recovery from unilateral visuo-spatial neglect? Cortex 12:303–312, 1976.

48. Chen D, Raman GC, Wu G, et al: Stroke in China (Sino-MONICA-Beijing Study) 1984–1986. Neuroepidemiology 11:15–23, 1992.

49. Chen Q, Ling R: A 1–4 year follow-up study of 306 cases of stroke. Stroke 16:323–327, 1985.

50. Christie D: Stroke in Melbourne, Australia: An epidemiological study. Stroke 12:467–469, 1981.

51. Colditz GA, Bonita R, Stampfer MJ, et al: Cigarette smoking and risk of stroke in middle-aged women. N Engl J Med 318:937–941, 1988.

52. Collaborative Group for the Study of Stroke in Young Women: Oral contraception and increased risk of cerebral ischemia or thrombosis. N Engl J Med 288:871–878, 1973.

53. Collaborative Group for the Study of Stroke in Young Women: Oral contraceptives and stroke in young women, associated risk factors. JAMA 231:718–722, 1975.

54. Curb JD, Marcus EB: Body fat, coronary heart disease, and stroke in Japanese men. Am J Clin Nutr 53:1612–1615, 1991.

55. Davaret P, Castel JP, Dartigues JF, Orgogozo JM: Death and functional outcome after spontaneous intracerebral hemorrhage: A prospective study of 166 cases using multivariate analysis. Stroke 22:1–6, 1991.

56. Davis PH, Dambrosia JM, Schoenberg BS, et al: Risk factors for ischemic stroke: A prospective study in Rochester, Minnesota. Ann Neurol 22:319–327, 1987.

57. Denes G, Semenza C, Stoppa E, Lis A: Unilateral spatial neglect and recovery from hemiplegia: A follow-up study. Brain 105:543–552, 1982.

58. Dobson AJ, Gibberd RW, Wheeler DJ, Leeder SR: Age-specific trends in mortality from ischemic heart disease and cerebrovascular disease in Australia. Am J Epidemiol 113:404–412, 1981.

59. Dombovy ML, Basford JR, Whisnant JP, Bergstralh EJ: Disability and use of rehabilitation services following stroke in Rochester, Minnesota, 1975–1979. Stroke 18:830–836, 1987.

60. Donnan GA, McNeil JJ, Adena MA, et al: Smoking as a risk factor for cerebral ischemia. Lancet 643–647, 1989.

61. Dove HG, Schneider KC, Wallace JD: Evaluating and predicting outcome of acute cerebral vascular accident. Stroke 15:858–864, 1984.

62. Dunbabin DW, Sandercock PAG: Preventing stroke by the modification of risk factors. Stroke 21:IV36–IV39, 1990.

63. Dyken ML, Wolf PA, Barnett HJM, et al: Risk factors in stroke: A statement for physicians by the Subcommittee on Risk Factors and Stroke of the Stroke Council. Stroke 15:1105–1111, 1984.

64. Eldar R, Zagreba F, Tamir A, Epstein L: Risk factors and causes of stroke in young women in Israel. Int Disabil Stud 12:81–85, 1990.

65. Ellekjaer EF, Wyller TB, Sverre JM, Holmen J: Lifestyle factors and risk of cerebral infarction. Stroke 23:829–834, 1992.

66. Epstein L, Rishpon S, Bental E, et al: Incidence, mortality, and case-fatality rate of stroke in Northern Israel. Stroke 20:725–729, 1989.

67. Ferro JM, Crespo M: Young adult stroke: Neuropsychological dysfunction and recovery. Stroke 19:982–986, 1988.

68. Folsom AR, Luepker RV, Gillum RF, et al: Improvement in hypertension detection and control from 1973–1974 to 1980–1981: The Minnesota Heart Survey Experience. JAMA 250:916–921, 1983.

69. Folsom AR, Prineas RJ, Kaye SA, Munger RG: Incidence of hypertension and stroke in relation to body fat distribution and other risk factors in older women. Stroke 21:701–706, 1990.

70. Friday G, Lai SM, Alter M, et al: Stroke in the Lehigh Valley: Racial/ethnic differences. Neurology 39:1165–1168, 1989.

71. Fullerton KJ, McSherry D, Stout RW: Albert's test: A neglected test of perceptual neglect. Lancet i:430–432, 1986.

72. Fyfe T, Dunnigan MG: Comparison of seasonal incidence and mortality of stroke and myocardial infarction. Health Bull 30:159–161, 1972.

73. Ganowa M, Morgenstern W, Östör-Lamm E, et al: First results from the MONICA stroke register in Heidelberg. Rev Epidémiol Santé Publique 38:441–445, 1990.

74. Garraway WM, Whisnant JP, Drury I: The continuing decline in the incidence of stroke. Mayo Clin Proc 58:520–523, 1983.

75. Garraway WM, Whisnant JP, Furlan AJ, et al: The declining incidence of stroke. N Engl J Med 300:449–452, 1979.

76. Gill JS, Davies P, Gill SK, Beevers DG: Wind-chill and the seasonal variation of cerebrovascular disease. J Clin Epidemiol 41:225–230, 1988.

77. Gill JS, Shipley MJ, Tsementzis SA, et al: Alcohol consumption—A risk factor for hemorrhagic and non-hemorrhagic stroke. Am J Med 90:489–497, 1991.

78. Gill JS, Shipley MJ, Tsementzis SA, et al: Cigarette smoking: A risk factor for hemorrhagic and nonhemorrhagic stroke. Arch Intern Med 149:2053–2057, 1989.

79. Gillum RF, Gomez-Marin O, Kottke TE, et al: Acute stroke in a metropolitan area, 1970 and 1980: The Minnesota Heart Survey. J Chron Dis 38:891–898, 1985.

80. Gillum RF, Gomez-Martin O, Kottke TE, et al: Cerebrovascular disease morbidity in the United States, 1970–1983: Age, sex, region and vascular surgery. Stroke 17:656–661, 1986.

81. Giroud M, Beuriat P, Vion P, et al: Stroke in a French prospective population study. Neuroepidemiology 8:97–104, 1989.

82. Giroud M, Beuriat P, Vion PH, et al: Les accidents vasculaires cérébraux dans la population Dijonnaise. Rev Neurol 145:221–227, 1989.

83. Giroud M, Milan C, Beuriat P, et al: Incidence and survival rates during a 2-year period of intracerebral and subarachnoid haemorrhages, cortical infarcts, lacunes and transient ischemic attacks: The Stroke Registry of Dijon: 1985–1989. Int J Epidemiol 20:892–899, 1991.

84. Gordon PC: The epidemiology of cerebral vascular disease in Canada: An analysis of mortality data. Can Med Assoc J 95:1004–1011, 1966.

85. Gorelick PB, Rodin MB, Langenberg P, et al: Is acute alcohol ingestion a risk factor for ischemic stroke? Results of a controlled study in middle-aged and elderly stroke patients at three urban medical centers. Stroke 18:359–364, 1987.
86. Gorelick PB, Rodin MB, Langenberg P, et al: Weekly alcohol consumption, cigarette smoking, and the risk for ischemic stroke: Results of a case-control study at three urban medical centers in Chicago, Illinois. Neurology 39:339–343, 1989.
87. Gowland C: Recovery of motor function following stroke: Profile and predictors. Physiother Can 34:77–84, 1982.
88. Gresham GE, Phillips TF, Wolf PA, et al: Epidemiologic profile of long-term stroke disability: The Framingham Study. Arch Phys Med Rehabil 60:487–491, 1979.
89. Grindel AB, Cohen RJ, Saul RF, Taylor JR: Cerebral infarction in young adults. Stroke 9:39–42, 1978.
90. Gross CR, Kase CS, Mohr JP, et al: Stroke in South Alabama: Incidence and diagnostic features—A population based study. Stroke 15:249–255, 1984.
91. Guang-Bo X, Bing-Xue Y, Xiao-Zhong W, et al: Epidemiological Survey Stroke in urban and rural areas of China. Chin Med J 104:697–704, 1991.
92. Guzik HJ, Ooi WL, Frishman WH, et al: Hypertension: Cardiovascular implications in a cohort of old old. J Am Geriatr Soc 40:348–353, 1992.
93. Haberman S, Capildeo R, Rose FC: The seasonal variation in mortality from cerebrovascular disease. J Neurol Sci 52:25–36, 1981.
94. Hachinski V, Norris JW: The Young Stroke. In The Acute Stroke (Contemporary Neurology Series, vol 27). Philadelphia, FA Davis Co, 1985, pp 141–163.
95. Harmsen P, Rosengren A, Tsipogianni A, Wilhelmsen L: Risk factors for stroke in middle-aged men in Göteberg, Sweden. Stroke 21:223–229, 1990.
96. Hart RG, Miller VT: Cerebral infarction in young adults: A practical approach. Stroke 14:110–114, 1983.
97. Heinemann AW, Elliot J, Cichowski K, Betts HBN: Multivariate analysis of improvement and outcome following stroke rehabilitation. Arch Neurol 44:1167–1172, 1987.
98. Heller A, Wade DT, Wood VA, et al: Arm function after stroke: Measurement and recovery over the first three months. J Neurol Neurosurg Psychiatry 50:714–719, 1987.
99. Henrich JB: The association between migraine and cerebral vascular events: An analytical review. J Chron Dis 40:329–335, 1987.
100. Herman B, Leyten ACM, van Luijk JH, et al: An evaluation of risk factors in a Dutch community. Stroke 13:334–339, 1982.
101. Herman B, Leyten ACM, van Luijk JH, et al: Epidemiology of stroke in Tilburg, The Netherlands: The Population-based Stroke Incidence Register: 2. Incidence, initial clinical picture and medical care, and three-week case fatality. Stroke 13:629–634, 1982.
102. Herman B, Schulte BPM, van Luijk JH, et al: Epidemiology of stroke in Tilburg, The Netherlands: The Population-based Stroke Incidence Register: 1. Introduction and preliminary results. Stroke 11:162–165, 1980.
103. Higa M, Davanipour Z: Smoking and stroke. Neuroepidemiology 10:211–222, 1991.
104. Hilton-Jones D, Warlow CP: The causes of stroke in the young. J Neurol 232:137–143, 1985.
105. Howard G, Craven TE, Sanders L, Evans GW: Relationship of hospitalized stroke rate and in-hospital mortality to the decline in US Stroke Mortality. Neuroepidemiology 10:251–259, 1991.
106. Howard G, Evans GW, Murros KE, et al: Cause specific mortality following cerebral infarction. J Clin Epidemiol 42:45–51, 1989.
107. Howard G, Till JF, Toole JS, et al: Factors influencing return to work following cerebral infarction. JAMA 253:226–232, 1985.
108. Isard PA, Forbes JF: The cost of stroke to the National Health Service in Scotland. Cerebrovasc Dis 2:47–50, 1992.
109. Iso H, Jacobs DR, Wentworth D, et al: Serum cholesterol levels and six-year mortality from stroke in 350,977 men screened for the Multiple Risk Factor Intervention Trial. N Engl J Med 320:904–910, 1989.
110. Jerntorp G, Berglund G: Stroke registry in Malmö, Sweden. Stroke 23:357–361, 1992.
111. Jongbloed L, Jones W: Prediction of recovery after stroke: An examination of outcome criteria. Can J Rehabil 2:87–92, 1988.
112. Kaku D, et al: Emergence of recreational drug abuse as a major risk factor for stroke in young adults. Ann Intern Med 113:821–827, 1990.
113. Kelley RE, Pina I, Lee SC: Cerebral ischemia and mitral valve prolapse: Case-control study of associated factors. Stroke 19:443–446, 1988.

114. Kelly-Hayes M, Wolf PA, Kase CS, et al: Time course of functional recovery after stroke: The Framingham Study. J Neurol Rehabil 3:65–70, 1989.
115. Kittner SJ, White LR, Losonczy KG, et al: Black-white differences in stroke incidence in a national sample: The contribution of hypertension and diabetes mellitus. JAMA 264:1267–1270, 1990.
116. Klag MJ, Whelton PK, Seidler AJ: Decline in US stroke mortality demographic trends and antihypertensive treatment. Stroke 20:14–21, 1989.
117. Knox EG: Meteorological associations of cerebrovascular disease mortality in England and Wales. J Epidemiol Community Health 35:220–223, 1981.
118. Kotila M, Waltimo O, Niemi ML, et al: The profile of recovery from stroke and factors influencing outcome. Stroke 15:1039–1044, 1984.
119. Kotila M: Declining incidence and mortality of stroke? Stroke 15:255–259, 1984.
120. Kouvaras G, Bacoulas G: Association of mitral valve leaflet prolapse with cerebral ischaemic events in the young and early middle-aged patients. Q J Med 55:387–392, 1985.
121. Kuller LH: Incidence rates of stroke in the eighties: The end of the decline in stroke? Stroke 200:841–843, 1989.
122. Last JM: A Dictionary of Epidemiology, 2nd ed. New York, Oxford University Press, 1988.
123. Lefkovits J, Davis SM, Rossiter SC, et al: Acute stroke outcome: Effects of stroke type and risk factors. Aust NZ J Med 22:30–35, 1992.
124. Lessa I, Bastos CAG: Epidemiology of cerebrovascular accidents in the city of Salvador, Bahia, Brazil. Paho Bull 17:292–299, 1983.
125. Li SC, Wang CC, Fu YG, et al: Risk factors for stroke in rural areas of the People's Republic of China: Results of a Case-Control Study. Neuroepidemiology 9:57–67, 1990.
126. Lindenstrom E, Boysen G, Nyboe J, Appleyard M: Stroke incidence in Copenhagen, 1976–1988. Stroke 23:28–32, 1992.
127. Liu L, Reeder B, Shuaib A: Validity of hospital separation on cases of stroke in Saskatchewan (abstract). Presented at the International Heart Health Conference, Victoria, BC, May 1992.
128. MacMahon S, Peto R, Cutler J, et al: Blood pressure, stroke, and coronary heart disease: Part 1. Prolonged differences in blood pressure: Prospective observational studies corrected for the regression dilution bias. Lancet 335:765–774, 1990.
129. Marshall RJ, Scragg R, Bourke P: An analysis of the seasonal variation of coronary heart disease and respiratory disease mortality in New Zealand. Int J Epidemiol 117:325–331, 1988.
130. Matias-Guiu J, Alvarez J, Insa R, et al: Ischemic stroke in young adults: II. Analysis of risk factor in the etiological subgroups. Acta Neurol Scand 81:314–317, 1990.
131. Mayo N, Hendlisz J, Goldberg M, et al: Destinations of stroke patients discharged from Montreal area hospitals (1984–85). Stroke 20:351–356, 1989.
132. Mayo NE, Goldberg MS, Levy AR, et al: Changing rates of stroke in the province of Quebec, Canada: 1981–1988. Stroke 22:590–595, 1991.
133. Mayo NE, Korner-Bitensky NA, Becker R: Recovery time of independent function post-stroke. Am J Phys Med Rehabil 70:5–12, 1991.
134. Mayo NE, Danys I, Carlton J, Scott S: Accuracy of hospital discharge coding for stroke. Can J Cardiol 1993 (in press).
135. McDowell FH, Louis S, Monahan K: Seasonal variation of non-embolic cerebral infarction. J Chron Dis 23:29–32, 1970.
136. Ministère de la Santé et des Services sociaux: Faits Saillants De L'enquête Québécoise Sur La Santé Cardio-Vasculaire Santé Québec. Québec, Ministère de la Santé et des Services sociaux, 1991.
137. Mui K: Relationship of risk factors to subsequent development of stroke and ischemic heart disease in a rural community. Osaka City Med J 35:145–171, 1989.
138. Newman M: The process of recovery after hemiplegia. Stroke 3:702–710, 1972.
139. Niemi ML, Laaksonen R, Kotila M, Waltimo O: Quality of life 4 years after stroke. Stroke 19:1101–1107, 1988.
140. Norris JW, Hachinski VC: Misdiagnosis of stroke. Lancet 328–331, 1982.
141. Ohno Y: Biometerologic studies on cerebrovascular disease: I. Effects of meteorologic factors on the death from cerebrovascular accident. Jpn Circ J 33:1285–1298, 1969.
142. Osberg JS, DeJong G, Haley SM, et al: Predicting long-term outcome among post-rehabilitation stroke patients. Am J Phys Med Rehabil 67:94–103, 1988.
143. Osuntokun BO, Bademosi O, Akinkugbe OO, et al: Incidence of stroke in an African City: Results from the stroke registry at Ibadan, Nigeria, 1973–1975. Stroke 10:205–207, 1979.
144. Pampalon R: Géographie de la santé au Québec. Québec, Les Publications du Québec, Gouvernement du Québec, 1985.

145. Partridge CJ, Johnston M, Edwards S: Recovery from physical disability after stroke: Normal patterns as a basis for evaluation. Lancet 373–375, 1987.

146. Phillips SJ: Is atrial fibrillation an independent risk factor for stroke? Can J Neurol Sci 17:163–168, 1990.

147. Phillips SJ, Cameron KA, Chung CR: Stroke surveillance revisited. Can J Cardiol 1993 (in press).

148. Piergentili P, Salmaso S, Stazi MA, Menotti A: Seasonal variations and trends in cardiovascular disease mortality in Naples, 1974–1978. G Ital Cardiol 13:393–398, 1983.

149. Psaty BM, Koepsell TD, Manolio TA, et al: Risk ratios and risk differences in estimating the effect of risk factors for cardiovascular disease in the elderly. J Clin Epidemiol 43:961–970, 1990.

150. Ramirez-Lassepas M, Huas E, Lakarua DJ, et al: Seasonal (circannual) periodicity of spontaneous intracerebral hemorrhage in Minnesota. Ann Neurol 8:539–541, 1980.

151. Reding MJ, Potes E: Rehabilitation outcome following initial unilateral hemispheric stroke: Life table analysis approach. Stroke 19:1354–1358, 1988.

152. Reunanen A, Aho K, Aromaa A, Knekt P: Incidence of stroke in a Finnish prospective population study. Stroke 17:675–681, 1986.

153. Ricci S, Celani MG, La Rosa F, et al: SEPIVAC: A community-based study of stroke incidence in Umbria, Italy. J Neurol Neurosurg Psychiatry 54:695–698, 1991.

154. Robins M, Baum HM: Chapter 4: Incidence. In Weinfeld FD (ed): The National Survey of Stroke. Stroke 12(Suppl 1):45–57, 1981.

155. Robins M, Weinfeld FD: Chapter 2: Study Design. In Weinfeld FD (ed): The National Survey of Stroke. Stroke 12(Suppl 1):1–7, 1981.

156. Rosman KD: The epidemiology of stroke in an urban black population. Stroke 17:667–669, 1986.

157. Sacco RL, Wolf PA, Kannel WB, McNamara PM: Survival and recurrence following stroke: The Framingham Study. Stroke 13:290–295, 1982.

158. Sakamoto Momiyama M: Changes in the seasonality of human mortality: A medico-geographical study. Soc Sci Med 12:29–42, 1978.

159. Salonen JT, Puska P, Tuomilehto J, Homan K: Relation of blood pressure, serum lipids, and smoking to the risk of cerebral stroke: A longitudinal study in eastern Finland. Stroke 13:327–333, 1982.

160. Schoenberg BS, Anderson DW, Haerer AF: Racial differentials in the prevalence of stroke in Copiah County, Mississippi. Arch Neurol 43:565–568, 1968.

161. Scmidt EV, Smirnov VE, Ryabova VS: Results of the seven-year prospective study of stroke patients. Stroke 19:942–949, 1988.

162. Scragg R: Seasonality of cardiovascular disease mortality and the possible protective effect of ultra-violet radiation. Int J Epidemiol 10:337–341, 1981.

163. Shah SK, Bain C: Admissions, patterns of utilization and disposition of cases of acute stroke in Brisbane hospitals. Med J Aust 150:256–260, 1989.

164. Shaper AG, Phillips AN, Pocock SJ, et al: Risk factors for stroke in middle aged British men. BMJ 302:1111–1115, 1991.

165. Shimamoto T, Komachi Y, Inada H, et al: Trends for coronary heart disease and stroke and their risk factors in Japan. Circulation 79:503–515, 1989.

166. Shinton R, Beevers G: Meta-analysis of relation between cigarette smoking and stroke BMJ 298:789–794, 1989.

167. Shinton R, Shipley M, Rose G: Overweight and stroke in the Whitehall Study. J Epidemiol Community Health 45:138–142, 1991.

168. Siegel D, Kuller L, Lazarus NB, et al: Predictors of cardiovascular events and mortality in the systolic hypertension in the elderly program pilot project. Am J Epidemiol 126:385–399, 1987.

169. Silliman RA, Wagner EH, Fletcher RH: The social and functional consequences of stroke for elderly patients. Stroke 18:200–203, 1987.

170. Sivenius J, Heinonen OP, Pyörälä K, et al: The incidence of stroke in the Kuopio area of east Finland. Stroke 16:188–192, 1985.

171. Skilbeck CE, Wade DT, Hewer RL, Wood VA: Recovery after stroke. J Neurol Neurosurg Psychiatry 46:5–8, 1983.

172. Sobel E, Zhang ZX, Alter M, et al: Stroke in the Lehigh valley: Seasonal variation in incidence rates. Stroke 18:38–42, 1987.

173. Söderback I, Ekholm J, Caneman G: Impairment/function and disability/activity 3 years after cerebrovascular incident or brain trauma: A rehabilitation and occupational therapy view. Int Disabil Stud 13:67–73, 1991.

174. Soltero I, Liu K, Cooper R, et al: Trends in mortality from cerebrovascular diseases in the United States, 1960 to 1975. Stroke 9:549–558, 1978.

175. Spriggs DA, French JM, Murdy JM, et al: Historical risk factors for stroke: A case control study. Age Ageing 19:280–287, 1990.
176. Stampfer MJ, Colditz GA, Willett WC, et al: A prospective study of moderate alcohol consumption and the risk of coronary disease and stroke in women. N Engl J Med 319:267–273, 1988.
177. Statistics Canada: Canadian Centre for Health Information Health Indicators, 1990.
178. Statistics Canada: Hospital Morbidity, Catalogue 82-206-1989.
179. Stokes J III, Kannel WB, Wolf PA, et al: Blood pressure as a risk factor for cardiovascular disease: The Framingham Study—30 years of follow-up. Hypertension 13:13–18, 1989.
180. Sunderland A, Wade DT, Hewer RL: The natural history of visual neglect after stroke: Indications from two methods of assessment. Int Disabil Stud 9:60–61, 1987.
181. Suzuki K, Kutsuzawa T, Takita K, et al: Clinico-epidemiologic study of stroke in Akita, Japan. Stroke 18:402–406, 1987.
182. Takahashi E: Geographic distribution of cerebrovascular disease and environmental factors in Japan. Soc Sci Med 15:163–172, 1981.
183. Tanaka H, Ueda Y, Date C, et al: Incidence of stroke in Shibata, Japan: 1976–1978. Stroke 12:460–466, 1981.
184. Terént A: Increasing incidence of stroke among Swedish women. Stroke 19:598–603, 1988.
185. Thompson SG, Greenberg G, Meade TW: Risk factors for stroke and myocardial infarction in women in the United Kingdom as assessed in general practice: A case-control study. Br Heart J 61:403–409, 1989.
186. Tuomilehto J, Bonita R, Stewart A, et al: Hypertension, cigarette smoking, and the decline in stroke incidence in eastern Finland. Stroke 22:7–11, 1991.
187. Twitchell TE: The restoration of motor function following hemiplegia in man. Brain 74:443–480, 1951.
188. US Department of Health and Human Services, Public Health Service: Health Statistics on Older Persons, United States, 1986. Hyattsville, MD, US DHHS, June 1987. DHHS Pub no. (PHS)87-1409.
189. US Department of Health and Human Services: National Household Survey on Drug Abuse, 1985. Bethesda, MD, National Institute on Drug Abuse, 1985.
190. US Department of Health and Human Services, Public Health Service: Vital and Health Statistics: Utilization of Short-Stay Hospitals, United States, 1985 Annual Summary. Hyattsville, MD, US DHHS, May 1987. DHHS Pub no. (PHS)87-1752.
191. Ueda K, Omae T, Hirota Y, et al: Decreasing trend in incidence and mortality from stroke in Hisayama residents, Japan. Stroke 12:154–160, 1981.
192. Verbrugge LM, Lepkowski JM, Imanada Y: Comorbidity and its impact on disability. Milbank Q 67:450–484, 1989.
193. Wade DT, Collen FM, Robb GF, Warlow CP: Physiotherapy intervention late after stroke and mobility. BMJ 304:609–613, 1992.
194. Wade DT, Hewer RL, Wood VA, et al: The hemiplegic arm after stroke: Measurement and recovery. J Neurol Neurosurg Psychiatry 46:521–524, 1983.
195. Wade DT, Hewer RL: Functional abilities after stroke: Measurement, natural history and prognosis. J Neurol Neurosurg Psychiatry 50:177–182, 1987.
196. Wade DT, Hewer RL: Motor loss and swallowing difficulty after stroke: Frequency, recovery, and prognosis. Acta Neurol Scand 76:50–54, 1987.
197. Wade DT, Wood VA, Heller A, et al: Walking after stroke: Measurement and recovery over the first 3 months. Scand J Rehabil Med 19:25–30, 1987.
198. Wade DT, Wood VA, Hewer RL: Recovery after stroke—The first 3 months. J Neurol Neurosurg Psychiatry 48:7–13, 1985.
199. Wade DT, Wood VA, Hewer RL: Recovery of cognitive function soon after stroke: A study of visual neglect, attention span and verbal recall. J Neurol Neurosurg Psychiatry 51:10–13, 1988.
200. Walker AE, Robins M, Weinfeld FD: Chapter 3: Clinical findings. In Weinfeld FD (ed): The National Survey of Stroke. Stroke 12(Suppl 1):13–44, 1981.
201. Ward G, Jamrozik K, Stewart-Wynne E: Incidence and outcome of cerebrovascular disease in Perth, Western Australia. Stroke 19:1501–1506, 1988.
202. Weinfeld FD (ed): The National Survey of Stroke. Stroke (Suppl 1):1–92, 1981.
203. Wender M, Lenart-Jankowska D, Pruchnik D, Kowal P: Epidemiology of stroke in the Poznan district of Poland. Stroke 21:390–393, 1990.
204. Wiebers DO, Whisnant JP: The incidence of stroke among pregnant women in Rochester, Minn, 1955 through 1979. JAMA 254:3055–3057, 1985.

205. Wiebers DO: Ischemic cerebrovascular complications of pregnancy. Arch Neurol 42:1106–1113, 1985.
206. Wilkins R, Adams OB: Health expectancy in Canada, late 1970s: Demographic, regional, and social dimensions. Am J Public Health 73:1073–1080, 1983.
207. Wilkins R: Health expectancy in the territory of the Montreal General Hospital, Department of Community Health. Montreal, Department of Community Health, Montreal General Hospital, 1982.
208. Wolf PA, Abbott RD, Kannel WB: Atrial fibrillation: A major contributor to stroke in the elderly: The Framingham Study. Arch Intern Med 147:1561–1564, 1987.
209. Wolf PA, D'Agostino RB, Belanger AJ, Kannel WB: Probability of stroke: A risk profile from the Framingham Study. Stroke 22:312–318, 1991.
210. Woo J, Kay R, Nicholls MG: Environmental temperature and stroke in a subtropical climate. Neuroepidemiology 10:260–265, 1991.
211. World Health Organization: International Classification of Impairments, Disabilities, and Handicaps. Geneva, WHO, 1980.
212. World Health Organization: Recommendations on stroke prevention, diagnosis, and therapy. Stroke 20:1407–1431, 1989.
213. Wylie CM: Cerebrovascular accident deaths in the United States and in England and Wales. J Chron Dis 15:85–90, 1961.

GAIL A. DELANEY, MD, FRCPC
PATRICK J. POTTER, MD, FRCPC

2. DISABILITY POST STROKE

From the Department of Physical
   Medicine and Rehabilitation
Parkwood Hospital (GAD)
   and
Victoria Hospital (PJP)
University of Western Ontario
London, Ontario
Canada

Reprint requests to:
Gail A. Delaney, MD, FRCPC
Chief
Department of Physical Medicine
   and Rehabilitation
Parkwood Hospital
801 Commissioner's Road East
London, Ontario N6C 5J1
Canada

Cerebrovascular accidents are the third leading cause of mortality and rank second as a cause of long-term physical disability among North Americans. Increased mortality is most evident during the initial month after stroke. Mortality rates for the population affected by stroke approach normal after 1 year, although morbidity following stroke remains prevalent.[38,39] The morbidity following stroke imposes economic and social burdens to the survivor, family, and society as a whole.[38] Like the disability imposed by other disease processes and injuries such as multiple trauma and neurodegenerative disorders, disability and handicap[105] following a stroke have multifactorial etiologies.[27,43,44,72,98] The extent of disability varies with the extent of recovery, the site of lesion, and premorbid status. The impairments due to right hemisphere, left hemisphere, and brainstem strokes may all manifest differently; hence, the extent and type of disability seen with these conditions also vary. Other contributing factors to the disability and handicap resulting from stroke include the age of the patient and extent of family supports.

Disability following stroke can be divided into short-term and long-term consequences. The initial goals during the first several weeks after a significant stroke are usually limited to gaining independence in activities of daily living (ADL).

Over the short term, during the months following a major cerebrovascular accident, vocational goals are often a low priority, and avocationally, patients are generally unable to pursue their usual hobbies, social activities, and family life due to initial impairments.[64,79] The extent of independence in ADL achieved during recovery from stroke often dictates a person's ability to return home.[39] Those patients who return home are more likely to maintain gains achieved during rehabilitation.[7] A loss in ADL abilities may occur due to caregivers providing, for the sake of expedience, more assistance than is physically required.[59]

Long-term disability generally involves vocational and avocational interests. Vocational issues may involve a change in job type, which may lead to loss of or a change in the patient's status within the family—i.e., loss of role as the "breadwinner." Avocationally, simple household tasks may no longer be managed by the patient. Although leisure and recreational activities are often pursued following stroke, these are usually not performed as well or to the same extent as they were before the stroke.[79]

One goal throughout the stroke patient's management should be the prevention of complications that might contribute to subsequent disability. The important role of secondary prevention is exemplified by a patient who has hemiparesis and goes on to develop an ankle plantar flexion contracture. The contracture, rather than the weakness, may lead to disability for the patient for whom putting on footwear becomes a problem. Other potentially preventable secondary complications include ipsilateral shoulder pain, deep vein thrombosis, pulmonary embolus, trauma to the neglected limb, pressure sores, aspiration, and dysfunction of bowel and bladder.

ETIOLOGY

Common causes of stroke are thrombotic or embolic infarcts and hemorrhagic lesions, with a significant number unclassified (Table 1).

Thrombotic strokes account for 40 to 55% of all strokes.[37,88,99] Because thrombosis frequently occurs in association with large-vessel atherosclerosis, the insult caused by thrombotic strokes is often extensive with severe unilateral brain involvement.

Embolic strokes are reported to cause 16 to 28% of strokes[37,88,99] and occur when embolic material dislodges from a thrombus in the heart or larger vessels, such as the carotid artery, and lodges in smaller caliber blood vessels, producing large, small, and sometimes multiple areas of infarction. The patient with an embolic stroke may present with a history of transient ischemic attacks or with the sudden onset of neurologic deficits. It is believed that in many instances of emboli, neither transient ischemic attacks nor neurologic deficits occur and the patient is completely aymptomatic.[84]

Lacunar strokes, once thought to be due to small, multiple emboli, are now believed to be associated with small-vessel infarcts associated with hypertension.[46]

TABLE 1.   Strokes by Etiology

Type	Dennis and Warlow[37] (1987)	Thorngren and Westling[99] (1990)	Shah et al.[88] (1991)
Atherothrombotic	55%	42%	57%
Embolic	25%	28%	16%
Hemorrhagic	20%*	25%[†]	16%
Unspecified/unclassified	—	5%	12%

* 15% intracerebral, 5% subarachnoid
[†] All intracerebral

Very specific lacunar syndromes may result. Patients with lacunar infarcts are generally less severely impaired than patients with larger hemispheric infarcts (Table 2).

Hemorrhagic strokes, caused by subarachnoid or intracerebral bleeding, may be catastrophic, with initial mortality rates of up to 50%.[76] If patients survive the initial period, the degree of neurologic recovery often exceeds that seen with infarctions. Intracerebral hemorrhages occur in hypertensive patients at approximately the same sites that lacunar strokes develop: namely, the putamen (50%), thalamus (20%), cerebellum (10%), subcortical regions (10%), and pons (10%).[84]

Hemorrhagic and ischemic strokes may have similar clinical presentations, with the hemorrhagic stroke patient often presenting acutely with obtundation or coma, frequently with associated vomiting and sometimes with nuchal rigidity, decerebrate spasms, and pupillary abnormalities.

Early computed tomography (CT) shows high-density blood in hemorrhagic strokes, whereas following cerebral infarction the CT scan may show no abnormality early on. However, several days later, the CT scan will show a low-density area in cerebral infarction. Intracerebral hemorrhage and subarachnoid hemorrhage may present similarly, but usually the patient with a significant intracerebral bleed demonstrates more localizing signs. Most cases of subarachnoid hemorrhage result from a ruptured aneurysm in the circle of Willis or arteries leading from it, while about 10% of subarachnoid hemorrhages occur consequent to ruptured arteriovenous malformations.[84]

RISK FACTORS AND DISABILITY

The major known risk factors for stroke are age, hypertension, cardiac disease, diabetes mellitus, hyperlipidemia, and a previous stroke or transient ischemic attack.[1,35,42,65,67,93] A more inclusive discussion of the risk factors is presented in Chapter 1 of this issue.

Risk factors for stroke may also be major contributors to the disability seen with stroke. Each of these risk factors carries with it a degree of morbidity. In particular, as the incidence of cerebrovascular accidents rises with increasing age (moderate increases after age 55),[2,28] those affected by stroke often have one or all of these comorbid factors, which results in increased disability. Cardiac diseases, such as myocardial infarction, atrial fibrillation, mitral stenosis, and, in times past, rheumatic heart disease, may interfere with rehabilitation efforts and play a role in the disability seen following stroke. Patients with preexisting congestive heart failure are at risk for exacerbation of the heart failure at the time of stroke.[85] Diabetes, peripheral vascular disease, renal failure, obesity, and chronic obstructive pulmonary disease are commonly seen comorbid diseases which may also act as limiting factors in recovery. Comorbid diseases occur more frequently in the stroke population than in age-matched controls.[55] Concomitant and unrelated diseases, such as cancer, decrease the stroke patient's ability to cope with the residual sequelae. Coexisting medical conditions serve to compound the impairment and resultant disability of the stroke victim.

TABLE 2. Common Lacunar Syndromes

Pure motor hemiplegia	Pyramidal syndrome
Pure hemisensory syndrome	Syndrome of slurred speech
Cerebellar syndrome	Clumsy arm and hand syndrome

RIGHT-HEMISPHERE STROKE

The right hemisphere is dominant for visuospatial orientation, constructional praxis, and judgment in over 90% of the population. Various neuropsychologic batteries have been used to delineate the deficits seen with right hemisphere strokes.[3,26,95,101,104]

Stone et al.[95] reported on deficits using a modified test battery that included (1) pointing to objects located about the ward; (2) pointing to named food items on a plate; (3) reading a menu; (4) reading a newspaper article; (5) line cancellation; (6) star cancellation; (7) coin selection; and (8) figure copying from the left. This battery was based on work reported by Wilson et al.[3,104] Visuospatial neglect was found to be equally common in patients with right-hemisphere and left-hemisphere stroke 3 days after stroke (72% vs. 62%). However, it was more severe in right-hemisphere stroke and resolved more frequently in those with left-hemisphere stroke.[95]

Anosognosia has been described with right-hemisphere lesions. Such patients may perceive they have no deficit and disregard the existence of the affected half of their bodies. As an example, a man may shave only one half of his face and appear totally unaware of the problem, even upon confrontation with a mirror. Frequently, there is an associated left homonymous hemianopsia which may compound the deficit.

Titus et al.[101] used a large battery of perceptual tests on subjects and found that patients with right-hemisphere lesions performed similarly to those with left-hemisphere lesions except on the Haptic Visual Discrimination Test.

Campbell et al.,[26] using the Michigan Neuropsychological Battery and the self-care component of the Howard University Activities of Daily Living Scale, found "left-sided somatosensory and motor functions were the best predictors of self-care skills, showing that in these stroke patients lower cerebral functions mediated by the right hemisphere are more strongly related to the self-care skills examined than higher cerebral functions." This supported findings previously reported by others showing a strong relationship between visual, spatial, perceptual, and motor dysfunction and the ADL performance of right-hemisphere stroke victims.

Right and left confusion, astereognosis, and figure-ground disorientation may occur in patients with right-hemisphere strokes. An example of the latter can be seen when a brown hairbrush on a brown table is not peceived and cannot be detected by the patient due to impaired figure-ground discrimination. Such perceptual impairments have been shown to adversely influence the rate of achieving independent sitting and stair-climbing.[75]

Hier et al.[61] studied 41 patients with right-hemisphere stroke and reported rapid recovery for left neglect, prosopagnosia, anosognosia, and unilateral spatial neglect on drawing with slower recovery for hemianopsia, hemiparesis, motor impersistence, and extinction. In those patients with constructional apraxia and dressing apraxia, rates of recovery were intermediate. Patients with hemorrhages were reported to recover more rapidly from constructional apraxia, neglect, and motor impersistence than patients with infarcts.

A New Zealand study reviewed gait recovery after hemiplegic stroke and found the best predictors of independent ambulation among 113 subjects still not walking 7 days after stroke were low age, low bisection line error (indicative of lack of neglect), and high leg power.[48] Patients with right-hemisphere lesions tended to have a higher bisection line error than those with left-hemisphere lesions.

However, looking at functional outcome of rehabilitation in Australia, Shah et al.[88] noted that the severity of the paralysis was an important determinant of outcome while the side of paralysis did not influence the outcome.

As the extent of perceptual, motor, and sensory deficits and left-sided neglect increases, a summation effect often occurs in regard to the disability seen. Such difficulties together restrict safety in locomotion and many specific daily tasks such as cooking. However, when only isolated lesions are present such as sensory deficit without neglect, homonymous hemianopsia without neglect, or perceptual problems, patients can often learn to accommodate to the discrete deficits. In a person with right-hemispheric lesions, the presence of associated deficits (i.e., neglect and homonymous hemianopsia) often precludes safe operation of any form of motorized vehicle, including a bicycle or electric wheelchair.

Although aphasia is commonly noted to occur with left-hemisphere lesions, it may rarely occur with right-hemisphere lesions. One study showed aphasia occurred after right-hemisphere lesions in 30% of left-handers and 5% of right-handers.[8] However, patients with nondominant hemisphere lesions often have other specific associated communication problems, with difficulty in utilizing intact language skills effectively. The patient may not observe turn-taking rules of conversation, may have difficulty with metaphorical speech (tending to be concrete), may have difficulty telling jokes (frequently missing the punchline), and may have less tendency to appropriately initiate conversation. This tends to result in social dysfunction that may erode family and social supports.

LEFT-HEMISPHERE STROKE

Ninety-three percent of the population is right-handed, with the left hemisphere being dominant for language in 99% of right-handed individuals. In left-handed individuals, 70% have language control in the left hemisphere, 15% in the right hemisphere, and 15% in both hemispheres.[80] Thus, 96.9% of the population has language control mainly in the left hemisphere. The prevalence of and disability caused by aphasia has led to extensive interest in this area and development of an accepted classification system.[4] Most aphasias fit into several categories (Table 3). However, extensive hemispheric involvement in large-vessel infarctions often leads to a mixed picture of aphasia clinically. Also, atypical cases of aphasia have been described with lesions involving the basal ganglia and internal capsule[5,33] which may not be able to be classified according to the widely used Boston Diagnostic Classification.

In a patient with language deficits, events in the environment are often misinterpreted. A paranoid reaction may occur in those with significant comprehension deficits.[14] Expressed feelings of support from family members, in particular the patient's spouse, may be misinterpreted by the patient as verbal aggression, even to the point where the patient feels the spouse is plotting against them.

Neglect tends to be less severe in left than in right-hemisphere stroke.[95] The presence of right-sided neglect increases the extent of disability with respect to safe use of a motorized vehicle, despite the relative absence of the typical visuospatial and other perceptual deficits seen in those with right-hemisphere lesions.

Left-hemisphere stroke patients often demonstrate apraxias which can adversely affect function and result in disability. The term *apraxia* refers to a range of complex disorders involving motor functions in which alert and oriented patients with apparently preserved motor and sensory function are unable to carry

TABLE 3.   Characteristic Features of Aphasias

Type	Fluency	Comprehension	Repetition
Broca's aphasia (motor, expressive)	Nonfluent	Good	Poor
Transcortical motor	Nonfluent	Good	Good
Wernicke's aphasia (sensory, receptive)	Fluent	Poor	Poor
Transcortical sensory	Fluent	Poor	Good
Global	Nonfluent	Poor	Poor
Conduction	Fluent	Good	Poor

out voluntary movements on command. There are general apraxias known as the motor or ideational apraxias and specific apraxias that include constructional apraxias, apraxias of speech, dressing apraxia, and apraxia of gait (Table 4).[103] For instance, in a dressing apraxia, patients demonstrate a frustrating inability to dress independently. They are unable to put on a garment in the manner in which it is expected to be worn, often placing clothing on backwards, on the wrong extremity, or in the wrong sequence.

Many studies have shown no relationship between laterality and functional independence.[20,71,102] However, recent work by Campbell et al.[26] has produced evidence that patients with left-hemisphere lesions perform better than patients with lesions in the right hemisphere in such self-care skills as bed mobility, dressing, grooming, hygiene, and object manipulation.

Depression and its influence on disability is controversial. Depression and comprehension have been reported to influence the recovery time for walking.[75] Decreased language function has been correlated with an increase in incidence of depression.[49] In a 2-year follow-up after stroke, patients who had an inhospital diagnosis of depression (either major or minor depression) were significantly more

TABLE 4.   Types of Apraxias

Type	Site of Lesion	Manifestation
Motor or ideomotor	Often left hemisphere	Can automatically perform a movement but cannot repeat it on demand
Ideational	Often bilateral parietal	Can perform separate movements but cannot coordinate all steps into an integrated sequence
Constructional	Either parietal lobe but right more often than left	Unable to synthesize individual spatial elements into a whole (e.g., cannot draw a picture)
Articulatory or verbal	Commonly associated with Broca's aphasia	Sparse verbal output, poor articulation, abnormal phrase length and melody[15]
Dressing	Either hemisphere, right more often than left	Inability to dress oneself despite adequate motor ability
Gait	Frontal lobes	Difficulty initiating and maintaining a normal walking pattern when sensory and motor functions seem otherwise unimpaired

impaired in both physical activities and language functioning than were nondepressed patients.[81] In the depressed patients, 60% had left-hemisphere lesions compared to 37% in the nondepressed group. In contrast, 28% of the depressed group had right-hemisphere lesions compared to 50% in the nondepressed group. Although the correlation has been observed, no definite cause-and-effect between language impairment per se and depression has been shown. Depression following stroke is discussed in more detail in Chapter 12.

BRAINSTEM STROKE

In contrast to the major cognitive or language disorders seen with hemispheric strokes, brainstem strokes generally spare cognitive and language functions. Intact cognitive abilities are important in later regaining functional abilities lost as a result of the stroke.[45]

The vertebral arteries give rise to small branches which supply the brainstem and cerebellar peduncles. In rare circumstances, the initial physical manifestations of a brainstem stroke may be so marked as to result in a "locked-in syndrome" during which the patient is cognitively aware but is unable to use any facial movement or upper-extremity movement except eye contact and lid movement to allow communication.[56] Approximately two-thirds of brainstem stroke patients survive the acute stroke period.[82] Survivors often continue to suffer moderate impairments.

Brainstem strokes have been categorized into a variety of well-defined syndromes depending on the vascular territory involved. Common examples of these syndromes include Wallenberg's syndrome, in which the medulla is affected and the patient presents with vertigo, dysarthria, ataxia, and horizontal gaze nystagmus. Other clinical presentations include lesions in the lower pons (Millard-Gubler, Fouille's and Raymond's syndromes), in the upper pons (superior cerebellar artery syndrome), and in the superior colliculus (Parinaud's syndrome) (Tables 5 and 6).

As the list of brainstem stroke syndromes grows longer, it has become more useful to describe the brainstem stroke in terms of the actual cranial nerve or motor and sensory involvement rather than by the named syndrome. Specific impairments resulting from brainstem syndromes include ipsilateral cranial nerve involvement and pyramidal and sensory tract involvement, resulting in hemisensory deficits and hemiparesis. With involvement of the cerebellar tracts, significant ipsilateral ataxia and incoordination results.

Dysarthria and dysphagia are common sequelae after brainstem stroke. Dysarthria is characterized by unclear speech of various types including slurred, scanning, spastic, monotonous, lisping, nasal, or explosive speech.[84] Dysphagia following brainstem stroke often requires the use of prolonged feeding by an alternate route, initially with a nasogastric tube and later by a G-tube. The dysphagia seen after brainstem stroke is often very gradual in its recovery, and changes may be seen up to 12 to 24 months. In spite of the prolonged need for G-tube or nonoral feedings, the recovery following brainstem stroke may allow a patient to change back to oral feeding on a gradual basis.

OUTCOME

Recovery

Initial recovery following stroke is felt to occur due to resolution of local edema, resolution of any mass effect, and recovery of ischemic but noninfarcted

TABLE 5.   Classic Brainstem Syndromes of Medulla and Lower Pons

Syndrome	Lesion Location	Clinical Picture
Wallenburg's	Lateral medulla (posterior inferior cerebellar artery and/or vertebral artery)	Vertigo Nausea and vomiting Sensory loss of ipsilateral face or contralateral limbs Ipsilateral ataxia Rotatory or horizontal gaze nystagmus Hoarseness and dysphonia Dysphagia and dysarthria Ipsilateral Horner's syndrome
	Medial medulla	Contralateral limb paralysis (facial sparing) Contralateral decrease in position and vibration sense Ipsilateral tongue paralysis
Jackson's	Medulla	Hoarseness and dysphonia Weakness of trapezius and sterno-cleidomastoid muscles
Millard-Gubler	Lower pons	Alternating or crossed hemiparesis Unilateral UMN facial palsy Contralateral limb paralysis with no contralateral facial paralysis
Fouille's	Lower pons	Crossed (alternating) hemiparesis Ipsilateral lateral gaze palsy
Raymond's	Lower pons	Abducens nerve palsy Contralateral hemiparesis

areas. Clinically, rapid improvement is often seen in the first 2 weeks, with slower improvements over the next several months. Residual healthy brain tissue may compensate for lost function of damaged areas, and it is postulated that

TABLE 6.   Classic Brainstem Syndromes of the Cerebellum, Midbrain, and Superior Colliculus

Type	Lesion Location	Clinical Picture
Parinaud's	Superior colliculus	Paralysis of upward conjugate convergence and frequently of downward gaze
Cerebellum	Cerebellum	Unilateral ataxia Vertigo Headache Occasionally patient may become comatose
Weber's	Midbrain	Contralateral hemiparesis Ipsilateral oculomotor paralysis with dilated pupil, lateral gaze only, ptosis
Benedict's or Claude's	Midbrain	Contralateral hemiparesis Tremor in paretic limbs on voluntary movement Frequently contralateral sensory loss Ipsilateral oculomotor paralysis

neuroplasticity also plays a major role in later recovery.[10] Brain plasticity is purported to include regeneration of neurons and synaptic sprouting.[10,46] By 3 months, the majority of improvement has occurred, and by 6 months almost all of the neurologic recovery likely to occur has been realized.[27]

Hier et al.[61] have reviewed the rates of recovery of arm weakness, leg weakness, extinction on bilateral sensory stimuli, dressing apraxia, motor impersistence, and hemianopsia. Recovery was better for smaller than for larger lesions. Recovery of neglect or dressing apraxia was also better than the recovery seen of leg weakness and arm weakness when the impairment persisted longer than 20 weeks. Function and quality of life, however, are dependent on multifactorial effects and not simply dependent on the degree of neurologic recovery.[34,54,72,96]

Functional Activities

After a stroke, the initial rehabilitation goals are to acquire basic skills in personal care and to achieve independent function.[22] These goals can best be expressed by the mnemonic *BB ADEPT,* in which, *A* signifies ambulation and locomotion; *D,* dressing; *E,* eating and ability to feed oneself; *P,* personal care and hygiene; and *T,* transfers. Associated with this are bowel *(B)* and bladder *(B)* control facilitated by specific bowel and bladderr training techniques. These rehabilitation tasks aim to provide an adequate degree of functional independence in order to return the patient to the usual home environment. Achieving sufficient neurologic and functional recovery to allow partial independence in these areas often determines whether a patient will be able to return home as opposed to institutional care.

When considering disability outcome following stroke, one must consider the degree of prestroke disability. This is particularly true with the elderly, who have the greatest prevalence of both stroke and other causes of disability.[6] The Perth Community Stroke Study[6] demonstrated that at least 50% of surviving stroke patients achieved complete functional independence 4 months after their acute episode. In looking at the 50% who were still disabled 4 months after their initial event, the authors noted that 19% had been disabled prior to the onset of their stroke. This suggested that in only 30% of elderly patients in their study could an actual new disability be attributed to the stroke 4 months after the acute event.

Anderson et al.[7] studied the ability to maintain gains following stroke rehabilitation. They assessed patients 2 to 12 years after stroke, looking at abilities in self-care, mobility, the amount of time spent for daily activities, vocational status, and overall rehabilitative status or abilities. Living at home rather than in a nursing home, which may be a partial measure of the extent of recovery, correlated positively with the ability to maintain and achieve gains. Ability to maintain gains also appeared to be dependent on the family's attitude and their support with respect to patients performing activities for themselves. When changes in ability occurred several years after the initial stroke, it was usually related to other superimposed health problems. Seventy percent of the patients studied experienced complicating health problems following their initial discharge. Eight percent of the total stroke population studied had one or more additional cerebral vascular accidents. Obesity resulted in further disability in 4% and fractures in 8%, and 13% suffered from other injuries as a result of falls. General medical problems were cited as the other major cause of increase in disability in the rest of this group.

Gowland[53] reviewed 23 clinical variables to identify a clinically useful method of predicting the sensorimotor recovery a patient will make during rehabilitation following stroke. Those variables which played a significant role in predicting outcomes, ranked from most to least important, were as follows: stage of recovery of the leg; weeks post-stroke; gross motor performance; age; perception; postural control; stage of recovery of the arm; urinary incontinence; major medical complications; family support; gait; length of stay; locomotion; mental status; sensation; gender; shoulder pain; and side of hemiplegia.

Listianingsih et al.,[74] in reviewing disability and functional outcome seen in children with sickle cell disease affected by stroke, found that all of the children were physically independent. The impairments seen were mainly due to intellectual deficits, with reduced language function, problems of adjustment, and problems of intelligence quotient. In general, results from this study indicated that psychosocial deficits far outweigh the physical disability seen. Long-term rehabilitation of these patients, and by inference other children, should emphasize cognitive training.

A recent study by Davidoff et al.[34] suggests that for those stroke patients who are conscious at onset, who had a significant hemiparesis or hemiplegia, and were able to be discharged home, inpatient rehabilitation appeared to be an effective tool in improving function. Most patients in this group had maintained their achieved goals at 1 year follow-up.

In general, the outcome for those individuals who survive a stroke is good, with approximately 70% managing to maintain a reasonable quality of life.[40,94]

VOCATIONAL AND AVOCATIONAL OUTCOME

For the patient who acquires enough functional ability to overcome the initial barriers of self-care and mobility, social and vocational barriers become a major focus.

It has been reported that for stroke victims of various ages, approximately 10% of survivors of acute stroke return to work without disability, 40% have a mild disability, 40% are moderately disabled, and 10% require institutionalization.[94] Czyrny et al.[32] recently reported that 5% of patients at 116 days after discharge from rehabilitation were employed. An additional 5% were homemakers. Twelve percent were of working age but not working, and 78% were retired (66% due to age and 12% due to disability).

Physical handicap alone does not determine degree of disability. Lawrence and Christie[72] looked at 45 people 3 years post-stroke and reported that physical handicap itself may be less important than people's response to their disability. The distribution in work activity immediately before the stroke was compared with that 3 years later. Prestroke, over 70% of males and females were fully occupied, compared to 20% of males and approximately 25% of females after stroke. *Fully occupied* was defined as fulltime work or, in the case of most of the women (9 out of 14), fulltime housework for more than one person. In addition to work, negative change in leisure activities proved to be an important sequel to stroke.

In return to work after stroke, differences in studies occur likely secondary to the population studied. Black-Schaffer and Osberg[19] studied a select group of patients between the ages of 21 and 65 years who had been employed at the time of their first stroke. In this group of 79 patients, 6 months after discharge from rehabilitation, 49% had returned to work. The mean time to return to work was 3.1 months after discharge. Ninety percent of those returned to their initial job, while 10% changed jobs. Of those who returned to work, only 32% returned to the same number of working hours per week as before. The average reduction in those unable to work a full week was a mean of 17.4 hours. In this population, those likely to return to work were not aphasic, had shorter rehabilitation lengths of stay, and had higher Barthel index scores on discharge.

Less specific but equally disabling and handicapping consequences of stroke include seizures and fatigue. The incidence of seizures post-stroke is estimated to be 10 to 15%.[77] This results in a handicap of not being able to drive or operate machinery, which may result in disability for certain occupations. This may also result in limited travel outside the home due to fear by the patient. Fatigue following stroke compounds the deficits already present.[11] This fatigue described by most patients after stroke exceeds that which would be predicted on the basis of energy consumption,[30,86] suggesting a central mechanism.

PREDICTING OUTCOME

The importance of predicting outcome is apparent in reviewing the need for discharge planning and for determining to what degree resource allocation will be of benefit to the patient after cerebral vascular accident. It is also important for family members and the patient, as much as possible, to understand long-term outcomes as part of their acceptance of the sequelae of stroke. In this regard, numerous studies have looked at predictors of functional outcome after stroke. Such predictors are based on clinical appraisal, family assessment, and specific neuropsychological testing.

Clinical Predictors of Outcome

Negative predictors of outcome are coma at onset, incontinence 2 weeks after stroke, poor cognitive function, severe hemiparesis or hemiplegia, no motor return within 1 month, previous stroke, perceptual spatial deficits, left-sided neglect, significant cardiovascular disease, a large or deep lesion on CT scanning, and multiple neurologic deficits.[38] Similarly, in the same study, postulated negative predictors were hemi-sensory deficit, left hemiparesis, homonymous hemianopsia, advanced age, language disorder/dysphasia, low premorbid intelligence, lack of spouse or close family members, and low socioeconomic class.

Another predictor of outcome is the presence of other premorbid or concurrent illnesses. Ec et al.[41] noted that in a population of 100 elderly stroke patients, concomitant diseases were present in 43% of patients, with a high prevalence of hypertension. Of these 100 elderly stroke victims, 80% improved their level of self-care and 60% improved their level of mobility. Those patients with dense hemiplegia at the outset were likely to remain dependent. Age, gender, delay in rehabilitation, duration of rehabilitation, presence of dysphasia, and side of the deficit did not appear to have a bearing on outcome.

Patients continue to improve functionally after discharge from rehabilitation. Gains have been reported by Czyrny et al.[32] using the FIM (Functional Independence Measure) more than 100 days after discharge. In looking at specific tasks related to the maintaining of independence within the patients' own homes, Thorngren and Westling[99] suggest that of those patients discharged to independent living, 90% were still living in their own home after 12 months. Of these 90% who were still living at home, 99% could walk independently indoors, 92% could climb stairs, and 90% could manage their daily hygiene. Clinically apparent abilities which may also help predict outcome after discharge include the patient's cognitive integrity, frontal lobe function, their ability to transfer, and their communication skills, in addition to those predictors already noted.[102]

Using other physical signs and tests to determine long-term predictors of ambulation in 113 subjects, Friedman[48] suggests that the best multivariate predictors of independent ambulation by patients who were unable to walk by day 7 (i.e., that group of subjects who have experienced a moderately severe cerebral vascular accident) were age, line bisection error (performed on a 200-mm line), and leg power as measured using the Medical Research Council Scale. Ninety-five percent of those patients who are able to walk independently by day 7 were able to continue their independence. Forty percent of the remaining group were able to walk 4 months after stroke. Other predictors of ambulation which were significant included mental state score, homonymous hemianopsia, arm power, and type of stroke (lacunar vs. nonlacunar). Independent mobility was measured as the ability to walk greater than 0.15 meters/second.

On psychological battery measures, the best predictors of self-skills are those of left-sided somatosensory and motor functions.[26] In general, the evidence from neuropsychological studies demonstrates that in self-care categories, patients with cerebrovascular accidents in the left hemisphere are able to perform better than those patients with right-hemisphere lesions, further indicating that right-hemisphere processes have a special role to play in these self-care activities as measured by an adaption of the Klein-Bell ADL scale.[26]

External Influences on Outcome

Following stroke, patients and families undergo an adjustment process similar to the stages of grief. Adjustment and attitude of family members can serve as external influences on the outcome of the stroke victim.[6,23] Bray[23] studied 180 families of severely disabled patients and identified three stages of family adjustment. Initially there are several months of **anxiety and denial,** followed by **acceptance** of problem, with a third stage of **assimilation** back into the family.

Attitude of family members may also play a role. Anderson et al.[6] looked at attitudes of family members with interviews and compared the functional status of the stroke patients. Interestingly, all of the stroke patients in the "nonaccepting family member group" were walking, which points out that the nonacceptance was not related to independent ambulation status (Table 7).

Maladjusted marital relationships, a decline in caregiver health and depression all commonly contribute to problems with care at home.[43,87,89] The patient's ability to adjust and adapt to the disability may be influenced by these factors

Once home in a previously familiar environment, the stroke victim and his or her family is often faced with an alteration in family dynamics and altered roles

TABLE 7.   Rehabilitation Status as Affected by Attitude of Family Members*

Rehabilitation Status	Accepting Attitude	Nonaccepting Attitude
Maintained or improved	86%	75%
Independent in self-care	72%	50%
Ambulatory	83%	100%
Activity level over 50%	61%	50%
Employed	50%	0%

* Data from Anderson et al.[6]

within the family. Household chores previously done by the individual fall on other family members instead. Disability due to physical and cognitive impairments are compounded by limited community resources and supports available to facilitate adaptation. Vocational and avocational pursuits frequently have to be altered.

REFERENCES

1. Abbot RD, Yin Y, Reed DM, Yano K: Risk of stroke in male cigarette smokers. N Engl J Med 315:1717–1720, 1988.
2. Abu-Zeid HAH, Choi NW, Nelson NA: Epidemiologic features of cerebrovascular disease in Manitoba: Incidence by age, sex and residence, with etiologic implications. Can Med Assoc J 113:379–384, 1975.
3. Albert ML: A simple test of neglect. Neurology 23:658–664, 1973.
4. Albert ML, Helm-Estabrooks N: Diagnosis and treatment of aphasia: Part I. JAMA 259:1043–1047, 1988.
5. Alexander MP, Naeser MA, Palumbo CL: Correlations of subcortical CT lesion sites and aphasia profiles. Brain 110:961–991, 1987.
6. Anderson C, Jamrozik K, Stewart-Wynne E: Physical disability after stroke in the Perth Community Stroke Study. Clin Exp Neurol 27:121–124, 1990.
7. Anderson E, Anderson T, Kottke F: Stroke rehabilitation: Maintenance of achieved gains. Arch Phys Med Rehabil 58:345–352, 1977.
8. Annet M: Hand preference and the laterality of cerebral speech. Cortex 11:305–328, 1975.
9. Arthur G: The Arthur Point Scale of Performance Tests: Vol. I. Clinical Manual, 2nd ed, rev. Chicago, Stoetling, 1943.
10. Bach-y-Rita P: Central nervous system lesions: Sprouting and unmasking in rehabilitation. Arch Phys Med Rehabil 62:413–417, 1981.
11. Baker CA: Activity tolerance in the geriatric stroke patient. Rehabil Nurs 16:337–343, 1991.
12. Baum B, Hall KM: Relationship between constructional praxis and dressing in the head-injured adult. Am J Occup Ther 35:438–442, 1981.
13. Baylor University Medical Center, Occupational Therapy Department: Adult Visual-Perceptual Assessment. Dallas, Baylor University Press, 1980.
14. Benson DF: Psychiatric aspects of aphasia. Br J Psychiatry 123:555–566, 1973.
15. Benson DF: Aphasia, Alexia and Agraphia. New York, Churchill Livingstone, 1979.
16. Benton AL, Fogel ML: Three-dimensional constructional praxis: A clinical test. Arch Neurol 7:347–354, 1962.
17. Benton AL, Varney NR, deS Hansher K: Visuospatial judgment: A clinical test. Arch Neurol 35:364–367, 1978.
18. Benton AL: Test of Three-Dimensional Constructional Praxis. Iowa City, IA, University of Iowa Hospital, 1973.
19. Black-Schaffer RM, Osberg JS: Return to work after stroke: Development of a predictive model. Arch Phys Med Rehabil 71:285–290, 1990.
20. Bourestom NC: Predictors of long-term recovery in cerebrovascular disease. Arch Phys Med Rehabil 48:415–419, 1967.
21. Bowman BR, Baker LL, Waters RL: Positional feedback and electrical stimulation: Automated treatment for hemiplegic wrist. Arch Phys Med Rehabil 60:497–502, 1979.
22. Brandstater ME: An overview of stroke rehabilitation. Stroke 21(9 Suppl):1140–1142, 1990.
23. Bray GD: Reactive patterns in families of the severely disabled. Rehabil Counsel Bull 236–239, 1977.
24. Buros OK (ed): Tests in Print 2. Highland Park, NJ, Gryphon, 1974.
25. Buros OK (ed): The Eighth Mental Measurements Yearbook (vols. 1 & 2). Highland Park, NJ, Gryphon, 1978.
26. Campbell A, Brown A, Schildroth C, et al: The relationship between neuropsychological measures and self-care skills in patients with cerebrovascular lesions. J Natl Med Assoc 83:321–324, 1991.
27. Carroll D: The disability in hemiplegia caused by cerebrovascular disease: Serial studies of 98 cases. J Chronic Dis 15:179–188, 1961.
28. Christie D: Stroke in Melbourne, Australia: An epidemiological study. Stroke 12:467–469, 1981.
29. Collen FM, Wade DT, Bradshaw CM: Mobility after stroke: Reliability of measures of impairment and disability. Int Disabil Stud 12:6–9, 1990.

30. Corcoran PJ, Jebsen RH, Brengelmann GL, Simons BC: Effects of plastic and metal leg braces on speed and energy cost of hemiparetic ambulation. Arch Phys Med Rehabil 51:69–77, 1970.
31. Coughlan AK, Humphrey M: Presenile stroke: Long-term outcome for patients and their families. Rheum Rehabil 21:115–122, 1982.
32. Czyrny JJ, Hamilton BB, Gresham GE: Rehabilitation of the stroke patient. Adv Clin Rehabil 3:64–96, 1990.
33. Damasio AR, Damasio H, Rizzo M, et al: Aphasia with non-hemorrhagic lesions in the basal ganglia and internal capsule. Arch Neurol 39:15–20, 1982.
34. Davidoff GN, Keren O, Ring H, Solzi P: Acute stroke patients: Long-term effects of rehabilitation and maintenance of gains. Arch Phys Med Rehabil 72:869–873, 1991.
35. Davis PH, Dambrosia JM, Schoenberg BS, et al: Risk factors for ischemic stroke: A prospective study in Rochester, Minnesota. Ann Neurol 22:319–327, 1987.
36. DeJong G, Branch LG: Predicting the stroke patient's ability to live independently. Stroke 13:648–655, 1982.
37. Dennis MS, Warlow CP: Stroke: Incidence, risk factors and outcome. Br J Hosp Med (Mar):194–198, 1987.
38. Dombovy ML, Sandok BA, Basford JR: Rehabilitation for stroke: A review. Stroke 17:363–367, 1986.
39. Dombovy ML, Basford JR, Whisnent JP, Bergstra EH: Disability and use of rehabilitation services following stroke in Rochester, Minnesota 1975–1979. Stroke 18:830–836, 1987.
40. Dove HG, Schneider KC, Wallace JD: Evaluating and predicting outcome of acute cerebral vascular accident. Stroke 15:858–864, 1984.
41. Ec CH, Kwan PE, Tan ES: Stroke rehabilitation of elderly patients in Singapore. Singapore Med J 32:55–60, 1991.
42. Ellekjaer EF, Wyller TB, Sverre JM, Holmen J: Lifestyle factors and risk of cerebral infarction. Stroke 23:829–834, 1992.
43. Evans RL, Bishop DS, Haselkorn JK: Factors predicting satisfactory home care after stroke. Arch Phys Med Rehabil 72:144–147, 1991.
44. Feibel JH, Springer CJ: Depression and failure to resume social activities after stroke. Arch Phys Med Rehabil 63:276–278, 1982.
45. Feigenson JS, McCarthy ML, Greenberg SD, et al: Factors influencing outcome and length of stay in a stroke rehabilitation unit: Part II. Comparison of 318 screened and 248 unscreened patients. Stroke 8:657, 1977.
46. Fisher CM: Concerning the mechanism of recovery in stroke hemiplegia. Can J Neurol Sci 19:57–63, 1992.
47. Fisher SV, Gullickson G: Energy cost of ambulation in health and disability: A literature review. Arch Phys Med Rehabil 59:124–133, 1978.
48. Friedman PJ: Gait recovery after hemiplegic stroke. Int Disabil Stud 12:119–122, 1990.
49. Gainotti G: Emotional behavior and hemispheric side of the lesion. Cortex 8:41–55, 1972.
50. Garrison SJ, Rolak LA, Dodaro RR, O'Callaghan AJ: Rehabilitation of the stroke patient. In Delisa JA (ed): Rehabilitation Medicine: Principles and Practice. Philadelphia, J.B. Lippincott, 1988, pp 565–584.
51. Geshwind N: Aphasia. N Engl J Med 284:654–656, 1971.
52. Geshwind N: Late changes in the nervous system: An overview. In Stein D, Rosen J, Butters N (eds): Plasticity and Recovery of Function in the Central Nervous System. New York, Academic Press, 1974.
53. Gowland C: Predicting sensorimotor recovery following stroke rehabilitation. Physio Canada 36:313–320, 1984.
54. Granger CV, Hamilton BB, Gresham GE: The stroke rehabilitation outcome study: Part I. General description. Arch Phys Med Rehabil 69:506–509, 1988.
55. Gresham GE, Phillips TF, Wolfe PA, et al: Epidemiological profile of long-term stroke disability: The Framingham Study. Arch Phys Med Rehabil 60:487–491, 1983.
56. Haig AJ, Katz RT, Sahgal V: Mortality and complications of the locked-in syndrome. Arch Phys Med Rehabil 68:24–27, 1987.
57. Hariman LMF, Griffith ER, Hurtig AL, Keehn MT: Functional outcomes of children with sickle-cell disease affected by stroke. Arch Phys Med Rehabil 72:498–502, 1991.
58. Harris JM: Stroke rehabilitation: Has it proven worthwhile? J Fla Med Assoc 77:683–686, 1990.
59. Heinemann AW, Roth EJ, Cichowski K, et al: Multivariate analysis of improvement and outcome following stroke rehabilitation. J Arch Neurol 44:1167, 1987.
60. Hewer RL: Outcome measures in stroke: A British view. Stroke 21:1152–1155, 1990.

61. Hier DB, Mondlock J, Caplan LR: Recovery of behavioral abnormalities after right hemisphere stroke. Neurology 33:345–350, 1983.
62. Hiller F: The vascular syndromes of the basilar and vertebral arteries and their branches. J Nerv Ment Dis 116:988–1016, 1952.
63. Jongbloed L: Prediction of function after stroke: A critical review. Stroke 17:765–776, 1986.
64. Jongbloed L, Morgan D: An investigation of involvement in leisure activities after a stroke. Am J Occup Ther 45:42–47, 1991.
65. Kannel WB: Current status of the epidemiology of brain infarction associated with occlusive arterial disease. Stroke 2:295–318, 1971.
66. Kannell WB, Dawber T, Sordie P, Wolfe PA: Components of blood pressure and risk of athero-thrombotic brain infarction: The Framingham Study. Stroke 7:327–331, 1976.
67. Kannel WB, Wolfe PA: Epidemiology of cerebrovascular disease. In Ross Russell RW (ed): Vascular Disease of the Central Nervous System, 2nd ed. Edinburgh, Churchill Livingstone, 1983, pp 1–24.
68. Kaplan J, Hier D: Visuospatial deficits after right hemisphere stroke. Am J Occup Ther 36:314–321, 1982.
69. Katz S, Ford AB, Chinn AB, Newell VA: Prognosis after strokes: Part II. Long term course of 159 patients. Medicine 45:236–246, 1966.
70. Kelly JF, Winograd CH: A functional approach to stroke management in elderly patients. J Am Geriatr Soc 33:48–60, 1985.
71. Kotila M, Waltimo O, Niemi ML, et al: The profile of recovery from stroke and factors influencing outcome. Stroke 15:1039–1044, 1984.
72. Lawrence L, Christie D: Quality of life after stroke: A three-year follow-up. Age Ageing 8:167–172, 1979.
73. Lehmann JF, DeLateur BJ, Fowler RS, et al: Stroke: Does rehabilitation affect outcome? Arch Phys Med Rehabil 56:375–382, 1975.
74. Listianingsih MF, Hariman MD, Griffith ER, et al: Functional outcomes of children with sickle-cell disease affected by stroke. Arch Phys Med Rehabil 72:498–502, 1991.
75. Mayo NE, Korner-Bitensky NA, Becker R: Recovery time of independent function post-stroke. Am J Phys Med Rehabil 70:5–12, 1991.
76. Mohr JP, Caplan LR, Melski JW, et al: The Harvard cooperative stroke registry. Neurology 28:754–762, 1978.
77. Moskowitz E: Complications in the rehabilitation of hemiplegic patients. Med Clin North Am 53:541–558, 1969.
78. Nakano KK: An overview of stroke: Epidemiology, classification, risk factors, clinical aspects. Postgrad Med 80:82–97, 1986.
79. Niemi ML, Laaksonen R, Kotila M, Waltimo O: Quality of life 4 years after stroke. Stroke 19:1101–1107, 1988.
80. O'Brien MT, Pallet PJ: Total Care of the Stroke Patient. Boston, Little Brown & Co., 1978.
81. Parikh RM, Robinson RG, Lipsey JR, et al: The impact of post-stroke depression on recovery in activities of daily living over a 2-year follow-up. Arch Neurol 47:785–789, 1990.
82. Patrick BK, Ramirez-Lassepas M, Snyder BD: Temporal profile of vertebrobasilar territory infarction: Prognostic implications. Stroke 11:643–648, 1980.
83. Pinsky JL, Jette AM, Branch LG, et al: The relationship of various coronary heart disease manifestations to disability in older persons living in the community. Am J Public Health 80:1363–1367, 1990.
84. Pryse-Phillips W, Murray TJ: Essential Neurology. Garden City, NY, Medical Examination Publishing Company, 1978, pp 4 and 358–385.
85. Roth EJ, Green D: Cardiac complications in stroke rehabilitation. Arch Phys Med Rehabil 71:776, 1990.
86. Saunders JB, Inman VT, Eberhart HD: Major determinants in normal and pathological gait. J Bone Joint Surg 35A:543–558, 1953.
87. Schultz R, Tompkins CA, Rau MT: A longitudinal study of the psychosocial impact of stroke on patients and support persons. Psychol Aging 3:131–141, 1988.
88. Shah S, Vanclay F, Cooper B: Stroke rehabilitation: Australian patient profile and functional outcome. J Clin Epidemiol 44:121–122, 1991.
89. Silliman R, Wagner EH, Fletcher RH: The social and functional consequences of stroke for elderly patients. Stroke 18:200–203, 1987.
90. Silverstein A: Acute infarctions of the brain stem in the distribution of the basilar artery. Conf Neurol 24:37–61, 1964.
91. Sjogren K, Fugel-Meyer A: Sexual problems in hemiplegia. Int Rehabil Med 3:26–31, 1981.

92. Smith DS: Outcome studies in stroke rehabilitation: The South Australian Stroke Study. Stroke 21:1156–1158, 1990.

93. Spriggs DA, French JM, Murdy JM, et al: Historical risk factors for stroke: A case control study. Age Ageing 19:280–287, 1990.

94. Stallones RA, Dyken ML, Fang HCH, et al: Epidemiology for stroke facilities planning. Stroke 3:360–371, 1972.

95. Stone SP, Wilson B, Wroot A, et al: The assessment of visuo-spatial neglect after acute stroke. J Neurol Neurosurg Psychiatry 54:345–350, 1991.

96. Tamiya N, Araki S, Yokoyama K, et al: Factors affecting activity of daily living (ADL) in stroke patients at home. Nippon Koshu Eisei Zasshi 37:315–320, 1990.

97. Tangeman PT, Banaitis DA, Williams AK: Rehabilitation of chronic stroke patients: Changes in functional performance. Arch Phys Med Rehabil 71:876–880, 1990.

98. Teasell R: Musculoskeletal complications of hemiplegia following stroke. Semin Arthritis Rheum 20:385–395, 1991.

99. Thorngren M, Westling B: Rehabilitation and achieved health quality after stroke: A population-based study of 258 hospitalized cases followed for one year. Acta Neurol Scand 82:374–380, 1990.

100. Thorngren M, Westling B, Norrving B: Outcome after stroke in patients discharged to independent living. Stroke 21:236–240, 1990.

101. Titus MND, Gall NG, Yerxa EJ, et al: Correlation of perceptual performance and activities of daily living in stroke patients. Am J Occup Ther 45:410–418, 1991.

102. Wade DT, Wood VA, Hewer RL: Recovery after stroke—the first three months. J Neurol Neurosurg Psychiatry 48:7–13, 1985.

103. Wade DT, Langton Hewer R, Skilbeck CE, David RM: Stroke: A Critical Approach to Diagnosis, Treatment and Management. Chicago, Yearbook Medical Publ, 1985.

104. Wilson B, Cockburn J, Halligan P: Development of a behavioural test of visuo-spatial neglect. Arch Phys Med 68:98–102, 1987.

105. World Health Organization: International Classification of Impairments, Disabilities and Handicaps: A Manual of Classification Relating to the Consequences of Disease. Geneva, World Health Organization, 1980.

ANDREW P. GASECKI, MD
VLADIMIR C. HACHINSKI, MD,
FRCPC, MSc(DME), DSc(Med)

3. STROKE RECURRENCE AND PREVENTION

From the Department of Clinical
   Neurological Sciences
University Hospital
London, Ontario
Canada

Reprint requests to:
Vladimir C. Hachinski, MD,
   FRCPC, MSc, DSc(Med)
Richard and Beryl Ivey Professor
   and Chairman
Department of Clinical
   Neurological Sciences
University Hospital
339 Windermere Road
London, Ontario N6A 5A5
Canada

Stroke remains the third leading cause of death in the United States and the most common reason for major disability, particularly in the elderly.[25,66] Atherosclerosis is the primary cause of coronary heart disease, peripheral vascular disease, as well as atherothrombotic brain infarction, the most frequent type of stroke. Therefore, improved control of the risk factors for ischemic heart disease has also contributed to the dramatic decrease in stroke incidence over the past several decades. Unknown risk factors, however, still contribute to much of the stroke risk.[33,97]

The identification of strokes of cardiac origin still poses some difficulty, although preventive therapy may be very successful. Extracranial carotid artery atherosclerosis is an established source of the artery-to-artery emboli. The efficacy of carotid endarterectomy in symptomatic[29,68] and asymptomatic[91] patients is currently under close scrutiny. Laboratory and clinical research efforts to protect the brain from ischemic injury are underway, and major contributions are expected. At this moment, however, the prevention of stroke remains the most effective treatment modality.

RISK FACTORS AND ATHEROTHROMBOTIC STROKE

Prevention of atherothrombotic strokes attempts to eliminate known risk factors (Table 1). Although many risk factors are potentially correctable (i.e., hypertension, cigarette smoking,

TABLE 1. Stroke Risk Factors

Treatment specifically effective	Treatment of associated factors effective	
Established factors	Established factors	
Hypertension	Age	Increasing hematocrit
Cardiac disease	Gender	Elevated fibrinogen
Transient ischemic attacks	Heredo-familial	Sickle cell disease
Cigarette smoking	Race	Lupus anticoagulant
Alcohol consumption	Diabetes mellitus	Asymptomatic structural
Other drug abuse	Prior stroke	lesions (bruits)
Factors not well established	Factors not well established	
Abnormal lipids	Migraine and migraine equivalents	
Diet		
Oral contraceptives	Treatment not possible	
Sedentary activity	Factors not well established	
Obesity	Geographic location	Socioeconomic factors
Hyperuricemia	Season and climate	Personality type
Infection		
Homocysteinemia	Treatment of factors in combination	

From Dyken ML: Stroke risk factors. In Norris JW, Hachinski VC (eds): Prevention of Stroke. New York, Springer-Verlag, 1991, pp 83–101, with permission.

or diabetes), the management of others is limited (i.e., age, gender, race, or heredo-familial). The overall risk of stroke in the presence of multiple risk factors is greater than the sum of the individual risks.[21,97]

Established Risk Factors with Effective Management. Hypertension is the most important independent risk factor, due to its frequency and strong relationship with both ischemic and hemorrhagic stroke. The overall decline in stroke incidence is partly related to improved treatment of high blood pressure.[47,61] Ischemic heart disease is the major cause of death among stroke survivors[56] (*see* Chapter 4). Although a transient ischemic attack (TIA) is considered a risk factor for stroke, only about 10% of all strokes are preceded by TIAs.[25] Smoking is now a clearly established risk factor for stroke, independent of age and hypertension, according to the 26-year follow-up in the Framingham study[98] and in the meta-analysis of 32 separate studies.[86] Excessive alcohol intake and illicit drug use (opiates, amphetamines, cocaine, and phencyclidine) are associated with both infarction and hemorrhagic stroke.[14,24,38]

Other Established Risk Factors. Other risk factors that identify those patients at particular risk include age, male gender, family history, race, diabetes, previous stroke, increasing hematocrit, increased fibrinogen, sickle cell disease, lupus anticoagulant, anticardiolipin antibodies, and asymptomatic carotid bruits.[25]

Risk Factors Not Well Established. Inconclusive evidence exists for an association between lipid levels, diet, oral contraceptives, sedentary activity, obesity, hyperuricemia, infection, or homocysteinemia and an increased risk for stroke.[25]

Aggregation of Risk Factors. Although some risk factors may appear unimportant independently, when in combination with others (e.g., oral contraceptive use, cigarette smoking, and age over 35), they increase the cumulative risk for stroke.[60] Stroke patients tend to have multiple risk factors in comparison to the relatives of their spouses.[22] Therefore, not surprisingly, at least one-third of strokes in the Framingham study occurred in only 10% of the population.[49]

CARDIOEMBOLIC STROKE PREVENTION

Epidemiology. The second most common cause of stroke is cardiogenic embolism, implicated in approximately 15% of all strokes.[26] This number may even be underestimated, as about 30% of patients with stroke have evidence of heart disease.[84] However, the presence of a potentially cardioembolic source does not establish the stroke type. For example, finding an isolated mitral valve prolapse (without cardiomyopathy or myxomatous valve changes) in a patient with stroke or TIA cannot be automatically related to each other, as mitral valve prolapse is commonly present in the healthy general population.

Diagnosis and Management Problems. Proper identification of cardiac disease to produce stroke is of outmost importance. Unfortunately, echocardiography has a low yield in detection of atrial or small intraventricular thrombi. Holter or prolonged ECG monitoring are still relatively insensitive tools in identification of transient cardiac arrhythmias, such as atrial fibrillation or sick sinus syndrome, with estimated yield at about 2% (range, 0–4%).[84] The diagnosis is particularly important because about 12% of patients with acute stroke of presumed cardiogenic origin have a recurrent stroke within 2 weeks.[16,17,83]

The use of early anticoagulation has to be weighed against the possibility of worsening the hemorrhagic infarction in embolic stroke, which has a special propensity for spontaneous hemorrhagic transformation. The time limit for this transformation has not been established, but most delayed hemorrhage takes place within 2 to 4 days.[70] During the first 6 to 12 hours, the detection by head CT scan may not be possible.[40,57] Therefore, the current practice is to postpone anticoagulation until CT scanning is done at least 48 hours after stroke to exclude the possibility of hemorrhagic transformation.[83] With larger strokes this period should further be extended, as hemorrhagic infarcts are more common in large strokes.

Atrial Fibrillation. Atrial fibrillation is the most common arrhythmia in the elderly population, affecting about 5% of persons over 60 years of age[50] and 13% of 82-year-olds.[4] Therefore, the prevalence increases with age in the elderly. There is at least a fivefold increased risk of stroke in nonvalvular atrial fibrillation,[32] accounting for 45% of all cardioembolic strokes.[16] The overall risk of stroke in patients with chronic atrial fibrillation is about 5% per year.[17]

The currently available data favor the use of chronic anticoagulation with warfarin for stroke prophylaxis in patients with nonvalvular atrial fibrillation.[1,6] The risk reduction in the stroke rate as a result of warfarin therapy in patients with nonvalvular atrial fibrillation varies between 42 and 86% in four major studies conducted (Fig. 1).[2] Low-dose (international normalized ratio of 1.5 to 2.7, prothrombin time ratio of 1.2 to 1.5) is as effective as high-dose anticoagulation with a lower incidence of bleeding complications. Unsuitable patients or those opposing chronic anticoagulation should consider 325 mg/day of aspirin until further data are available.[1] Asymptomatic lone (i.e., without coexisting cardiovascular disease) or paroxysmal atrial fibrillation in patients less than 60 years old should probably be treated with aspirin 325 mg/day rather than warfarin, but the data are inconclusive.[1] Long-term anticoagulation remains the routine treatment for atrial fibrillation associated with rheumatic mitral stenosis or prosthetic valves.[58]

Other High-Risk Groups for Cardiogenic Embolism. Anticoagulation in patients with myocardial infarction and/or ventricular aneurysm (with or without mural thrombus) is not necessary unless the patient is symptomatic with systemic emboli, including cerebral infarction.[41,85] Patients with an acute transmural myocardial infarction with wall motion abnormality on echocardiogram are at special

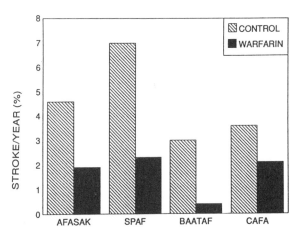

FIGURE 1. Stroke prevention in patients receiving warfarin and controls. AFASAK = Copenhagen Atrial Fibrillation, Aspirin, Anticoagulation Study; SPAF = Stroke Prevention in Atrial Fibrillation study; BAATAF = Boston Area Anticoagulation Trial for Atrial Fibrillation; CAFA = Canadian Atrial Fibrillation Anticoagulation study. (From Albers GW, Atwood JE, Hirsh J, et al: Stroke prevention in nonvalvular atrial fibrillation. Ann Intern Med 115:727–736, 1991; with permission.)

risk for cardiogenic emboli. Cardiomyopathy of any etiology, when associated with congestive heart failure, increases the risk for stroke, with mural thrombi found in 35 to 100% of autopsies on patients who died with cardiomyopathy.[27] Long-term anticoagulation is recommended in such patients. Other high-risk patients for cardioembolic complications with treatment options are presented in Table 2.

CAROTID ATHEROSCLEROSIS AND SURGICAL PREVENTION OF STROKE

Extracranial carotid atherosclerosis is considered one of the most common sources of ischemic stroke or transient ischemic attack.

Asymptomatic Carotid Stenosis. High-grade stenosis in asymptomatic patients is associated with an incidence of approximately 10% for TIA and 5% for strokes per year in a review of the major published studies.[77] Low- or moderate-grade stenosis carries a low risk unless a large ulcer is seen on angiography, in which case the stroke risk may increase up to 12.5% per year.[23,65] The carotid endarterectomy perioperative complication rate (stroke or death) ranges between 0 and 18% in 18 published series.[77] It is, therefore, crucial to identify patients at high risk for stroke whose life expectancy is over 24 months and who will benefit from endarterectomy on the asymptomatic artery.

Lowering the risk of operative mortality, in addition to increased longevity of patients, would potentiate the benefit of surgery. There is currently an ongoing study to evaluate the efficacy of carotid endarterectomy in the high-risk (high-grade) asymptomatic stenosis patients.[91] The value of surgery has not been established; if it is undertaken, it should be in patients with no less than 90% internal carotid stenosis.[92]

Symptomatic Carotid Stenosis. Despite the negative results of the carotid endarterectomy trial for stroke and TIA prevention in 1970,[30] the number of

TABLE 2. Relative Risk for Stroke Associated with Cardioembolic Disorders

	Management*
High risk (>6%/yr)	
Atrial myxoma	Surgery
Infective staphylococci, endocarditis, mechanical prosthetic valve	Anticoagulation (H), antibiotics
Nonischemic cardiomyopathy + thrombus	Anticoagulation (H)
Mechanical prosthetic mitral valve	Anticoagulation (H)
Recent cardioembolic stroke/systemic embolus	Anticoagulation (H)
Mitral stenosis with atrial fibrillation	Anticoagulation (L)
Large anterior MI with thrombus	Anticoagulation (L)
Intermediate or undetermined risk	
Ventricular aneurysm	?, Anticoagulation (L)
Mitral stenosis without atrial fibrillation	Anticoagulation (L)
Nonvalvular atrial fibrillation	Aspirin, anticoagulation (L)
Mitral regurgitation	—
Thyrotoxicosis with atrial fibrillation	Anticoagulation (L)
Mitral valve prolapse + myxomatous changes	Aspirin
Nonbacterial thrombotic endocarditis	Aspirin, anticoagulation (L) ?
Low risk (<1%/yr)	
Mitral valve prolapse young women	—
Lone atrial fibrillation <60 yr old	—
Small inferior myocardial infarction	—
Bioprosthetic aortic valve	Aspirin
Mitral annulus calcification	—

* H = high-dose (prothrombin time 1.5–2.0 times normal); L = low-dose (prothrombin time 1.3–1.5 times normal). (From Sherman DG: Prevention of cardioembolic stroke. In Norris JW, Hachinski VC (eds): Prevention of Stroke. New York, Springer-Verlag, 1991, pp 149–159; with permission.)

operations continued to flourish. The surgical morbidity, however, was unacceptably high (above 10%) in the first 15 years of endarterectomy surgery. With improved surgical skills, the high-risk group was shown to benefit from the surgery. The degree of stenosis at the bifurcation correlates with the frequency of ipsilateral symptoms.[35,79] In the North American Symptomatic Carotid Endarterectomy Trial (NASCET),[68] the patients with 70 to 99% stenosis of the ipsilateral internal carotid stenosis and prior (within 120 days) hemispheric or retinal TIA or minor (nondisabling) stroke benefited from the surgery, with a 17% absolute and a 65% relative risk reduction from ipsilateral stroke. As the degree of stenosis diminished, a declining benefit of surgery was noted in the NASCET (the patients with 70 to 79% stenosis benefited less than those with 80 to 89% or 90 to 99% stenosis). From the European Carotid Surgery Trialists (ECST),[29] we know that patients with a mild degree of carotid stenosis (0–29%) are better off without surgery. No results can be claimed as yet for patients in either study with moderate stenosis (30–69%), and both trials are continuing for this group.

It needs to be emphasized that carotid endarterectomy must be performed by surgeons with validated skill. Should the perioperative stroke and death complications approach 10% (instead of 5.8% in NASCET and 7.5% in ECST), the benefit of the surgery would have vanished in both studies.

ANTITHROMBOTIC THERAPY IN STROKE PREVENTION

Primary Prevention with Aspirin. In primary prevention among British[73] and American physicians,[88] no significant stroke risk reduction was noted, although there was a significant reduction in nonfatal myocardial infarction incidence in patients over 50 years old in the aspirin group.[88] Asymptomatic individuals at risk for coronary or cerebrovascular disease who are over 50 years old are, therefore, advised to take 100 to 325 mg of aspirin daily.[34]

  Acute Stroke.   No data are available on the effect of aspirin therapy initiated immediately after the ischemic stroke and the outcome.[7] Early anticoagulation with heparin in unselected patients is of doubtful efficacy and can be harmful.[83] Its role in treatment of the progressing stroke is controversial, as approximately 20% of patients with acute stroke experience a spontaneous deterioration.[7,63,64] Prevention of infarction of cardioembolic origin with immediate anticoagulation may be beneficial,[18] although the delayed institution of heparin is preferable as cardioembolic strokes have a particular propensity for secondary hemorrhagic complication (*see also* Cardioembolic Stroke Prevention).

  The use of subcutaneous heparin (5000 units twice daily) is empiric but reasonable.[7,83] Thrombolytic therapy (tissue plasminogen activator [alteplase], streptokinase, or urokinase) offers great promise, but further experience is needed to establish its therapeutic index.[13]

  Acute Transient Ischemic Attack.   There are anecdotal reports on the efficacy of heparin after a recent TIA or "crescendo TIA." However, both groups are at a substantial risk for imminent stroke or subsequent TIAs.[8,55,75] These symptoms could be mimicked by cerebral mass lesions, and a significant extracranial carotid stenosis may be found in many cases. Therefore, a thorough investigation should be carried out in an attempt to establish the underlying cause. Antiplatelet treatment, with pending results of ongoing diagnostic evaluation, remains an empiric but reasonable alternative.

  Long-Term Secondary Stroke Prevention.   The risk for stroke in patients with TIA is about 5% per year and 10% per year in patients with previous minor ischemic stroke.[28,83] This risk for stroke is even higher (26% within 2 years) in high-grade (70–99%) carotid stenosis despite aspirin therapy.[68] Again, the detailed investigation, including imaging of the extracranial carotid bifurcation, should be pursued. Long-term anticoagulation following TIA or ischemic stroke is of unknown value[28,48] except for cardioembolic stroke (*see* above). Although the data from 13 major international studies are convincing that aspirin reduces nonfatal stroke by 22%,[39] the optimal dose remains unknown. The efficacious doses reported range between 30[93] and 1300 mg/day.[15] Although the debate continues as to which dose of aspirin is correct for stroke or TIA prevention, the trials that have shown the greatest benefit have used doses of 975 mg and higher. We prescribe the highest tolerable dose starting from 1300 mg/day.

  Ticlopidine in Stroke Prevention.   Ticlopidine is both structurally and biochemically different from all available antiplatelet agents, although the exact mechanism of action remains elusive.[62] Contrary to aspirin, it is not a gastric irritant.[42] The efficacy of ticlopidine was established based upon small[78,94] and large clinical trials.[36,43] In comparison to aspirin, a 12% risk reduction in nonfatal stroke or death from any cause and 21% risk reduction in fatal and nonfatal stroke at 3 years for ticlopidine was obtained in the Ticlopidine Aspirin Stroke Study (TASS).[43] The side effects, including dose-related diarrhea and rash, were more common (2%) with ticlopidine.[36] The most worrisome, although infrequent (1%), adverse effect of ticlopidine is neutropenia that requires complete blood count analyses every 2 weeks for the first 3 months.[36] In the Canadian-American Ticlopidine Study (CATS),[36] the risk reduction for fatal and nonfatal recurrent stroke was 33.5% and 30.2% for stroke, myocardial infarction, or vascular death.

Dipyridamole. Previously widely prescribed to potentiate aspirin effect, dipyridamole failed to demonstrate any benefit in stroke reduction in two large clinical trials.[3,9] Therefore, its use is considered empiric and without any strong scientific support.

STROKE PREVENTION IN CARDIAC SURGERY

Open heart surgery (coronary artery bypass surgery, CABG) has been known to cause strokes since its introduction. With improved techniques and skills of surgeons, the stroke risk has diminished, ranging from 1 to 5%.[12,19,20] Various risk factors for increased stroke risk during CABG surgery were implicated which could be divided into preoperative (e.g., carotid bruits, history of prior stroke, old myocardial infarction, or congestive heart failure), operative (e.g., duration of total bypass or aortic clamp time, drop in blood pressure, or embolic sources), and postoperative (e.g., metabolic derangements, postoperative arrhythmias, ventilatory parameters, reoperation within 48 hours, or duration of intubation).

Preoperative Risk. Most studies failed to document any relationship between asymptomatic carotid bruits and perioperative CABG stroke.[12,19,81] Conflicting results exist as to whether there is an increased risk for perioperative stroke in patients with carotid stenosis determined by noninvasive carotid ultrasound.[5,10] Data are limited and insufficient to draw any conclusions in regards to the risk of peri-CABG stroke in the symptomatic high-grade stenosis.[46] It is suggested that CABG surgery be delayed for 3 months in patients with recent stroke, but an urgent cardiac condition (e.g., unstable angina) may occasionally not allow it.[19,82] Preoperative cerebral perfusion reserve assessment to identify the high-risk group of patients and intraoperative cerebral blood flow monitoring may contribute in lowering the risk of perioperative stroke in the future.[37,44,59,74,80]

Intraoperative Risk. Prolonged pump time during CABG (over 2 hours) was found to be associated with an increased risk for stroke.[71] Profound drops in blood pressure should be avoided, and a mean arterial pressure should be maintained at a minimum of 60 mm Hg in high-risk patients (hypertensive, prior stroke, marked systemic atherosclerotic disease).[19] Potential embolic materials (intraventricular thrombus, air in the heart, aortic plaque, or arrhythmias) should be managed with extreme caution to avoid dissemination.

Postoperative Risk. A three- to fivefold increased risk for stroke in patients with post-CABG transient atrial fibrillation[76] was not substantiated by a prospective study at the Cleveland Clinic.[71] The incidence of postoperative encephalopathy varies from 3 to 12% but may be up to 30% if neuropsychological testing is used.[19] The cause of this condition is multifactorial, probably related to hypoxia, metabolic derangements, medications, fever, sepsis, hemodynamic instability, and intensive care psychosis. Multiple air, fat, platelet/fibrin emboli, and decreased cerebral blood flow on arteriolar level with autoregulation impairment have been postulated.[11,12,19,45,89,90]

PREVENTION OF SUBARACHNOID HEMORRHAGE

Natural History. Approximately 60% of subarachnoid hemorrhages are due to a ruptured aneurysm.[95] The immediate mortality rate is high; as many as 30% of people die before they are admitted to a hospital.[87] A further 65% mortality is present over the first 3 months after aneurysmal hemorrhage.[72] The highest morbidity and mortality occurs, however, in the first 2 weeks after the initial hemorrhage, with a peak incidence of rebleeding in the first 24 hours. Therefore, prompt diagnosis and intervention, prevention of rebleeding (60% of patients die from the second rupture[87]), and prevention of delayed cerebral ischemia (vasospasm) are crucial to increased survival rates.

Diagnosis. Up to 50% of patients describe warning signs weeks before rupture of the aneurysm.[72,96] Focal headache, eye pain, facial pain, and dizziness may be ignored or misdiagnosed by physicians as nonspecific symptoms at a time when the intervention and treatment provide the most satisfying results.[31] Efforts should be directed to identifying those patients with recognizable minor sentinel bleeds, particularly when there was no past history of such nonspecific symptoms. CT may detect subarachnoid hemorrhage as well as the site of aneurysm rupture.[67] Future application of high-resolution magnetic resonance angiography may enable us to screen patients at risk (family members of aneurysm patients) for unruptured aneurysms. Routine screening for patients at risk for unruptured aneurysms associated with organ disease (e.g., polycystic kidneys, Marfan's syndrome, coarctation of the aorta, or fibromuscular dysplasia) is probably not justified, as the prophylactic surgery in asymptomatic patients remains to be determined.[31] The patients with "familial" cases, cases with previous carotid ligation for aneurysm, cases with residual aneurysmal neck noted on postoperative angiogram, and cases with previous remote "'wrapping" or "coating" are at particular risk and may be considered for more aggressive management.[31]

Prevention of Rebleeding. As mentioned earlier, the rate of rebleeding is maximal within the first 24 hours after subarachnoid hemorrhage.[51] Therefore, early surgery has been advocated by many neurosurgeons. The timing, however, was not found to be the most important determinant of the overall outcome in the International Cooperative Study on Timing of Aneurysm Surgery.[52,53] In the prospective randomized study,[69] there was a trend towards better results in early (first 3 days) surgery in patients on nimodipine, although this did not reach statistical significance. Delay in surgery may be warranted in severely debilitated patients or in patients with technically difficult aneurysms when antifibrinolytic therapy may be of value to gain time until the acute effects of hemorrhage (swollen brain) subsides. Unfortunately, antifibrinolytic agents increase the incidence of delayed cerebral ischemia and hydrocephalus.[54]

CONCLUSION

Stroke has varied etiologies; therefore, the treatment is diverse. Over the last several decades, the advances in stroke therapy enabled us to find the most appropriate management for each category of stroke. There is no longer a place for nihilism in stroke therapy. Prevention of stroke by controlling the risk factors is as important as emerging hyperacute treatment of stroke with thrombolytic therapy. The safety and clinical application of the tissue plasminogen activator are being evaluated in acute cerebral infarction and subarachnoid hemorrhage. Anticoagulation with heparin and warfarin has become selectively applied in patients with strong suspicion of cardioembolic source (i.e., in atrial fibrillation or other high-risk group).

An important contribution in the surgical treatment of stroke is the demonstration that carotid endarterectomy in symptomatic severe carotid stenosis (70–99%) is more beneficial than the best medical care. The same surgery is not recommended for patients with a symptomatic mild (<30%) carotid stenosis. Both

British and North American trials are still underway to determine the efficacy of carotid endarterectomy in symptomatic patients with moderate (30–69%) stenosis. These results do not apply to asymptomatic patients; the management of them, associated with carotid stenosis, remains under close scrutiny.

It becomes apparent that currently only randomized, double-blind, placebo-controlled, multicenter clinical trials can determine the efficacy of therapies, including drug trials. Ticlopidine, a new platelet antiaggregating agent, has become established as an important agent in the prevention of stroke in this way. Although the optimal aspirin dose remains to be determined, its role in stroke prevention is established. The emerging role of drugs altering cellular mechanisms (calcium antagonists, N-methyl-D-aspartate receptor antagonists) may become important tools in amelioration of cerebral ischemia by reducing the size of infarction (as shown in animals) in the future.

The technique of magnetic resonance angiography is another breakthrough, providing a noninvasive visualization of extra- and intracranial vessels. An early detection of asymptomatic aneurysms and carotid stenosis will be possible which will revolutionize the management of vascular disorders. Optimism will prevail, leaving nihilistic concepts behind, in the management of patients with stroke.

REFERENCES

1. Albers GW, Sherman DG, Gress DR, et al: Stroke prevention in nonvalvular atrial fibrillation: A review of prospective randomized trials. Ann Neurol 30:511–518, 1991.
2. Albers GW, Atwood JE, Hirsh J, et al: Stroke prevention in nonvalvular atrial fibrillation. Ann Intern Med 115:727–736, 1991.
3. American-Canadian Co-Operative Study Group. Persantine Aspirin Trial in cerebral ischemia: Part II. Endpoint results. Stroke 16:406–415, 1985.
4. Aronow WS, Gutstein H, Fsieh FY: Risk factors for thromboembolic stroke in elderly patients with chronic atrial fibrillation. Am J Cardiol 63:366–367, 1989.
5. Barnes RW, Marszalek PB: Asymptomatic carotid disease in the cardiovascular surgical patient: Is prophylactic endarterectomy necessary? Stroke 12:497–500, 1981.
6. Bazing MA, Morris JJ: Atrial fibrillation: Conventional wisdom reappraised. Heart Dis Stroke 1:78–84, 1992.
7. Biller J: Medical management of acute cerebral ischemia. Neurol Clin 10:63–85, 1992.
8. Biller J, Bruno A, Adams HP Jr, et al: A randomized trial of aspirin or heparin in hospitalized patients with recent transient ischemic attacks. Stroke 20:441–447, 1989.
9. Bousser MG, Eschwege E, Haguenau M, et al: "AICLA" controlled trial of aspirin and dipyridamole in the secondary prevention of athero-thrombotic cerebral ischemia. Stroke 14:5–14, 1983.
10. Brener BJ, Brief DK, Alpert J, et al: A four-year experience with preoperative noninvasive carotid evaluation of two thousand twenty-six patients undergoing cardiac surgery. J Vasc Surg 1:326–338, 1984.
11. Brennan RW, Patterson RH, Kessler J: Cerebral blood flow and metabolism during cardiopulmonary bypass: Evidence of microembolic encephalopathy. Neurology 21:665–672, 1971.
12. Breuer AC, Furlan AJ, Hanson MR, et al: Central nervous system complications of coronary artery bypass graft surgery: Prospective analysis of 421 patients. Stroke 14:682–687, 1983.
13. Brott T: Thrombolytic therapy for stroke. Cereb Brain Flow Metab Rev 3:91–113, 1991.
14. Brust JCM: Stroke and substance abuse. In Barnett HJM, Mohr JP, Stein BM, et al (eds): Stroke Pathophysiology, Diagnosis and Management, vol. 2. New York, Churchill Livingstone, 1986, pp 903–917.
15. Canadian Cooperative Study Group: A randomized trial of aspirin and sulfinpyrazone in threatened stroke. N Engl J Med 299:53–59, 1978.
16. Cerebral Embolism Task Force: Cardiogenic brain embolism: The second report of the cerebral embolism task force. Arch Neurol 46:727–743, 1989.
17. Cerebral Embolism Task Force: Cardiogenic brain embolism. Arch Neurol 43:71–84, 1986.
18. Cerebral Embolism Study Group: Immediate anticoagulation of embolic stroke: A randomized trial. Stroke 14:668–676, 1983.

19. Chimowitz MI, Furlan AJ: Preventing cerebral complications of cardiac surgery. In Norris JW, Hachinski VC (eds): Prevention of Stroke. New York, Springer-Verlag, 1991, pp 219–227.

20. Coffey CE, Massey EW, Roberts KB, et al: Natural history of cerebal complications of coronary artery bypass graft surgery. Neurology 33:1416–1421, 1983.

21. Collaborative Group for the Study of Stroke in Young Women: Oral contraceptives and stroke in young women: Associated risk factors. JAMA 231:718–722, 1975.

22. Diaz JF, Hachinski VC, Pederson L, et al: Aggregation of multiple risk factors for stroke in siblings of patients with brain infarction and transient ischemic attacks. Stroke 17:1240–1242, 1986.

23. Dixon S, Pais SO, Raviola C, et al: Natural history of nonstenotic asymptomatic ulcerative lesions of the carotid artery: A further analysis. Arch Surg 117:1493–1498, 1982.

24. Donahue RF, Abbott RD, Reed DM, et al: Alcohol and hemorrhagic stroke: The Honolulu Heart Program. JAMA 255:2311–2314, 1986.

25. Dyken ML: Stroke risk factors. In Norris JW, Hachinski VC (eds): Prevention of Stroke. New York, Springer-Verlag, 1991, pp 83–103.

26. Easton JD, Sherman DG: Progress in cerebrovascular disease. Stroke 11:433–441, 1980.

27. Easton JD: Present status of anticoagulant prophylaxis. In Norris JW, Hachinski VC (eds): Prevention of Stroke. New York, Springer-Verlag, 1991, pp 139–149.

28. Easton JD, Hart RG, Sherman DG, Kaste M: Diagnosis and management of ischemic stroke: Part I. Threatened stroke and its management. Curr Probl Cardiol 8:1–76, 1983.

29. European Carotid Surgery Trialists' Collaborative Group: MRC European Carotid Surgery Trial: Interim results for symptomatic patients with severe (70–99%) or with mild (0–29%) carotid stenosis. Lancet 337:1235–1243, 1991.

30. Fields WS, Maslenikov V, Meyer JS, et al: Joint study of extracranial arterial occlusion: V. Progress report of prognosis following surgery of nonsurgical treatment for transient cerebral ischemic attacks and cervical carotid artery lesions. JAMA 211:1993–2003, 1970.

31. Findlay JM, Weir BKA: Prevention of aneurysmal subarachnoid hemorrhage. In Norris JW, Hachinski VC (eds): Prevention of Stroke. New York, Springer-Verlag, 1991, pp 247–260.

32. Flegel KM, Shipley MJ, Rose G: Risk of stroke in nonrheumatic atrial fibrillation. Lancet i:526–529, 1987.

33. Friedman MH, Hutchins GM, Bargeron CR, et al: Correlation between intimal thickness and fluid shear in human arteries. Arteriosclerosis 39:425–431, 1981.

34. Fuster V, Cohen M, Halperin J: Aspirin in the prevention of coronary disease. N Engl J Med 321:183–185, 1989.

35. Gasecki AP, Eliasziw M, Fox AJ, et al: Risk factors for extracranial carotid atherosclerosis: Results from NASCET [abstract]. Cerebrovasc Dis 2:196, 1992.

36. Gent M, Blakely JA, Easton JD, et al: The Canadian American Ticlopidine Study (CATS) in thromboembolic stroke. Lancet i:1215–1220, 1989.

37. Gibbs JM, Wise RJS, Leenders KL, et al: Evaluation of cerebal perfusion reserve in patients with carotid artery occlusion. Lancet i:310–314, 1984.

38. Gill JS, Shipley MJ, Hornby RH, et al: A community case-control study of alcohol consumption in stroke. Int J Epidemiol 17:542–547, 1988.

39. Grotta JC: Aspirin in stroke prevention. In Norris JW, Hachinski VC (eds): Prevention of Stroke. New York, Springer-Verlag, 1991, pp 121–126.

40. Hart RG, Putnam C: Hemorrhagic transformation of cardioembolic stroke [letter]. Stroke 20:117, 1989.

41. Hart RG, Sherman DG, Miller VT, et al: Diagnosis and management of ischemic stroke: II. Selected controversies. Curr Probl Cardiol 8:1–80, 1983.

42. Hass WK: Ticlopidine: A new drug to prevent stroke. In Norris JW, Hachinski VC (eds): Prevention of Stroke. New York, Springer-Verlag, 1991, pp 127–138.

43. Hass WK, Easton JD, Adams HP Jr, et al: A randomized trial comparing ticlopidine hydrochloride with aspirin for the prevention of stroke in high-risk patients: Ticlopidine Aspirin Stroke Study Group. N Engl J Med 321:501–507, 1989.

44. Henriksen L, Hjelms E, Rygg IH: Cerebral blood flow measured in patients during open-heart surgery using intraarterially injected xenon-133: The effect of rewarming on cerebral blood flow. J Cereb Blood Flow Metab 1(suppl):432–433, 1981.

45. Henriksen L: Evidence suggestive of diffuse brain damage following cardiac operations. Lancet i:816–820, 1984.

46. Hertzer NR, Loop FD, Beven EG, et al: Surgical staging for simultaneous coronary and carotid disease: A study including prospective randomization. J Vasc Surg 9:455–463, 1989.

47. Hypertension Detection and Follow-up Program Cooperative Group: Five year findings of the hypertension detection and follow-up program: III. Reduction in stroke incidence among persons with high blood pressure. JAMA 247:633–638, 1982.
48. Jonas S: Anticoagulant therapy in cerebrovascular disease: Review and meta-analysis. Stroke 19:1043–1048, 1988.
49. Kannel WB, Wolf PA: Epidemiology of cerebrovascular disease. In Ross Russell RW (ed): Vascular Disease of the Central Nervous System. London, Churchill Livingstone, 1983.
50. Kannel WB, Abbott RD, Savage DD, McNamara PM: Epidemiologic features of chronic atrial fibrillation: The Framingham study. N Engl J Med 306:1018–1022, 1982.
51. Kassell NF, Torner JC: Aneurysmal rebleeding: A preliminary report from the Cooperative Aneurysm Study. Neurosurgery 13:479–481, 1983.
52. Kassell NF, Torner JC, Haley EC Jr, et al: The International Cooperative Study on the Timing of Aneurysm Surgery: Part I: Overall management results. J Neurosurg 73:18–36, 1990.
53. Kassell NF, Torner JC, Jane JA, et al: The International Cooperative Study on the Timing of Aneurysm Surgery: Part II: Surgical results. J Neurosurg 73:37–47, 1990.
54. Kassell NF, Torner JC, Adams HP Jr: Antifibrinolytic therapy in the acute period following aneurysmal subarachnoid hemorrhage: Preliminary observations from the Cooperative Aneurysm study. J Neurosurg 61:225–230, 1984.
55. Keith DS, Phillips SJ, Whisnant JP, et al: Heparin therapy for recent transient focal cerebral ischemia. Mayo Clin Proc 62:1101–1106, 1987.
56. Knutsen R, Knutsen SF, Curb JD, et al: Predictive value of resting electrocardiograms for 12-year incidence of stroke in the Honolulu Heart Program. Stroke 19:555–559, 1988.
57. Laureno R, Shields RW Jr, Narayan T: The diagnosis and management of cerebral embolism and hemorrhagic infarction with sequential computerized cranial tomography. Brain 110:93–105, 1987.
58. Levine HJ, Pauker SG, Salzman EW: Antithrombotic therapy in valvular heart disease. Chest 95(suppl): 98S–106S, 1989.
59. Levine RL, Lagreze HL, Berkoff HA, et al: Noninvasive testing of cerebral perfusion reserve prior to coronary artery bypass graft surgery. Angiology 39:421–428, 1988.
60. Longstreth WT Jr, Swanson PD: Oral contraceptives and stroke. Stroke 15:747–750, 1984.
61. MacMahon S, Cutler JA, Stamler J: Antihypertensive drug treatment: Potential, expected and observed effects on stroke and on coronary heart disease. Hypertension 13:145–150, 1989.
62. Maffrand JP, Defreyn G, Bernot A, et al: Reviewed pharmacology of ticlopidine. Angiologie 5(suppl):5–13, 1988.
63. Miller VT, Hart RG: Heparin anticoagulation in acute brain ischemia. Stroke 19:403–406, 1988.
64. Millikan CH, McDowell FH: Treatment of progressing stroke. Stroke 12:397–409, 1981.
65. Moore WS, Boren C, Malone JM, et al: Natural history of nonstenotic asymptomatic ulcerative lesions of the carotid artery. Arch Surg 113:1352–1359, 1978.
66. Mortality trends—United States, 1986–1988. MMWR 38:117–118, 1989.
67. Nehls DG, Flom RA, Carter LP, et al: Multiple intracranial aneurysms: Determining the site of rupture. J Neurosurg 63:342–348, 1985.
68. North American Symptomatic Carotid Endarterectomy Trial Collaborators: Beneficial effect of carotid endarterectomy in symptomatic patients with high-grade carotid stenosis. N Engl J Med 325:445–453, 1991.
69. Ohman J, Heiskanen O: Timing of operation for ruptured supratentorial aneurysms: A prospective randomized study. J Neurosurg 70:55–60, 1989.
70. Okada Y, Yamaguchi T, Minematsu K, et al: Hemorrhagic transformation in cerebral embolism. Stroke 20:598–603, 1989.
71. O'Neill BJ III, Furlan AJ, Hobbs RD: Risk of stroke in patients with transient postoperative atrial fibrillation/flutter. Stroke 14:133, 1983.
72. Pakarinen S: Incidence, aetiology, and prognosis of primary subarachnoid hemorrhage: A study based on 589 cases diagnosed in a defined urban population during a defined period. Acta Neurol Scand 43(suppl 29):1–128, 1967.
73. Peto R, Gray R, Collins R, et al: Randomised trial of prophylactic daily aspirin in British male doctors. BMJ 296:313–315, 1988.
74. Powers WJ, Press GA, Grubb RL Jr, et al: The effect of hemodynamically significant carotid artery disease on the hemodynamic status of the cerebral circulation. Ann Intern Med 106:27–35, 1987.
75. Putnam SF, Adams HP Jr: Usefulness of heparin in initial management of patients with recent transient ischemic attacks. Arch Neurol 42:960–962, 1985.
76. Reed GL III, Singer DE, Picard EH, et al: Stroke following coronary artery bypass surgery: A case control estimate of the risk from carotid bruits. N Engl J Med 319:1246–1250, 1988.

77. Ricotta JJ: Carotid endarterectomy in patients with asymptomatic carotid stenosis. In Norris JW, Hachinski VC (eds): Prevention of Stroke. New York, Springer-Verlag, 1991, pp 177–194.

78. Rieger JS, Picho JLT: Effect of ticlopidine on the prevention of relapses of cerebrovascular ischemic disease. Med Clin (Barcelona) 82:62–64, 1984.

79. Riles TS, Lieberman A, Kopelmann I, Imparato AM: Symptoms, stenosis and bruit. Arch Surg 116:218–220, 1981.

80. Robertson WM, Welch KMA, Tilley BC, et al: Cerebral blood flow asymmetry in the detection of extracranial cerebrovascular disease. Stroke 19:813–819, 1988.

81. Ropper AH, Wechsler LR, Wilson LS: Carotid bruit and the risk of stroke in elective surgery. N Engl J Med 307:1388–1390, 1982.

82. Rorick M, Furlan AJ: Risk of cardiac surgery in patients with prior stroke. Neurology 40:835–837, 1990.

83. Rothrock JF, Hart RG: Antithrombotic therapy in cerebrovascular disease. Ann Intern Med 115:885–895, 1991.

84. Sherman DG: Prevention of cardioembolic stroke. In Norris JW, Hachinski VC (eds): Prevention of Stroke. New York, Springer-Verlag, 1991, pp 149–159.

85. Sherman DG, Dyken ML, Fisher M, et al: Cerebral embolism. Chest 89(suppl):83S–98S, 1986.

86. Shinton R, Beevers G: Meta-analysis of relation between cigarette smoking and stroke. BMJ 298:789–794, 1989.

87. Solomon RA, Fink ME: Current strategies for the management of aneurysmal subarachnoid hemorrhage. Arch Neurol 44:769–774, 1987.

88. Steering Committee on the Physicians' Health Study Research Group: Final report on the aspirin component of the ongoing physicians' health study. N Engl J Med 321:129–135, 1989.

89. Stockard JJ, Bickford RG, Schauble JF: Pressure dependent cerebral ischemia during cardiopulmonary bypass. Neurology 23:521–529, 1973.

90. Taylor KM: Brain damage during open-heart surgery. Thorax 37:873–876, 1982.

91. The Asymptomatic Carotid Atherosclerosis Study Group: Study design for randomized prospective trial of carotid endarterectomy for asymptomatic atherosclerosis. Stroke 20:844–849, 1989.

92. The CASANOVA Study Group: Carotid surgery versus medical therapy in asymptomatic carotid stenosis. Stroke 22:1229–1235, 1991.

93. The Dutch TIA Trial Study Group: A comparison of two doses of aspirin (30 mg vs. 283 mg a day) in patients after a transient ischemic attack or minor ischemic stroke. N Engl J Med 325:1261–1266, 1991.

94. Tohgi H: The effect of ticlopidine on TIA compared with aspirin: A double-blind twelve-month follow-up study. Agents Actions 15(suppl):279–282, 1984.

95. Torner JC: Epidemiology of subarachnoid hemorrhage. Semin Neurol 4:354–369, 1984.

96. Waga S, Ohtsubo K, Handa H: Warning signs in intracranial aneurysms. Surg Neurol 3:5–20, 1975.

97. Wolf PA, Kannel WB, Verter J: Current status of risk factors for stroke. Neurol Clin 1:317–343, 1983.

98. Wolf PA, D'Agostino RB, Kannel WB, et al: Cigarette smoking as a risk factor for stroke: The Framingham study. JAMA 259:1025–1029, 1988.

J.M.O. ARNOLD, MD, FRCPC

4. CARDIOVASCULAR ASSOCIATIONS OF STROKE

From the Department of Medicine
(Cardiology)
and
Department of Pharmacology and
Toxicology
University of Western Ontario
London, Ontario
Canada

Correspondence to:
J.M.O. Arnold, MD, FRCPC
Division of Cardiology
Victoria Hospital
375 South Street
London, Ontario N6A 4G5
Canada

Because stroke is caused by underlying disease of the cerebral large or small arteries, it is not surprising that it is likely to occur in patients who have evidence of vascular disease elsewhere, such as coronary heart disease or peripheral vascular disease. The Framingham epidemiological study was originally conceived as a study of the consequences of hypertension and arteriosclerosis on the heart and peripheral vascular system, but attention turned to cerebral vascular disease after about 10 years when stroke began to occur in the cohort. At the end of the first examination, 5,184 men and women were free of stroke and underwent biennial examinations over 24 years. During that period, 345 strokes occurred and appeared to be athero-thrombotic in origin in 59%, embolic in 14%, due to subarachnoid hemorrhage in 10%, intra-cerebral hemorrhage in 5%, a transient ischemic attack in 9%, and other causes in 3%.[96] The incidence of atherothrombotic infarction increased significantly with age after 55 to 60 years and, from a cardiovascular perspective, was associated with hypertension, cardiac disease, and impaired cardiac function. Both temporal and geographic variability was noted.[97]

While cerebrovascular and other cardiovascular disease therefore frequently occur together within individual patients, the problem of whether one caused the other is harder to define. Both Koch's postulates and the criteria enunciated by Hill[34] can be helpful in population-based studies but may still leave the clinician perplexed as to what was the specific cause of a stroke in an individual patient. Furthermore, the cerebral injury itself may cause some temporary cardiovascular changes. In addition, the long-term prognosis following a stroke may be influenced as much or more by concomitant cardiovascular disease than by cerebrovascular disease.

This review therefore discusses the cardiovascular associations of stroke under three areas. Firstly, preexisting cardiovascular factors which increase the risk of developing a stroke either as a primary or recurrent event will be discussed. Secondly, cardiovascular events which are unique to the stroke syndrome and are directly caused by the cerebral injury will be discussed. Thirdly, those cardiovascular events which may affect the prognosis and long-term recovery following the stroke will be discussed. Although it is not the purpose of this review to deal in detail with the treatment of cardiovascular disease, some guidelines for therapy of associated cardiovascular risk factors and events are given.

CARDIOVASCULAR CAUSES OF STROKE

In considering cardiovascular risk factors for stroke, it is important to consider not only the strength with which the risk factor is associated with the disease but also the commonness of that risk factor. Attributable risk combines both the strength and commonness of a risk factor within a population. Some cardiac risk factors, such as an infected or malfunctioning prosthetic valve, may have a high risk of causing a stroke, but because they are relatively uncommon, the attributable risk to the population is small. Conversely, if smoking and hypertension are common, then the attributable risk is high, and a New Zealand study suggested that one-third of all strokes may be attributed to raised blood pressure and one-third to smoking.[10]

Hypertension

Based on the concepts of attributable risk, hypertension is still the most important of all risk factors for stroke. In the Framingham study, hypertension was a major precursor for stroke in general and for each particular type of stroke, and this was true for men and women in all age groups.[96] Systolic pressure was just as strong a risk factor for stroke as diastolic blood pressure, even in the elderly.[41] Although the overall decline in stroke mortality was already decreasing before effective antihypertensive therapy became available, there is no doubt that efforts to control hypertension have contributed significantly to the reduced incidence of stroke. This has been shown in some of the major large trials of antihypertensive therapy in both borderline and severe hypertension, young and old patients, and isolated systolic hypertension.[23,24,89]

In the Framingham study, the initial casual measurement of systolic and diastolic pressure obtained by the physician on the first examination was found to accurately classify the patients according to the risk of an atherothrombotic cerebral infarct. Repeated blood pressure measurements including pulse pressure and mean arterial pressure, averages of pressures over time, estimates of the lability of pressure, or other indices of intra-arterial pressure appeared to provide little additional prognostic information.[41] Although the phenomenon of "white-coat hypertension" with physicians has more recently been recognized, the blood pressures obtained by a clinic nurse still appear to be reliable predictors of cardiovascular events. Every effort should therefore be made to smoothly control chronic elevations in arterial pressure using standard available hypotensive agents. The appropriate choice of an individual drug has been widely reviewed in the literature.

Cardiac Disease

Although "cardiac disease" often occurs secondary to elevations in blood pressure, the Framingham study was able to determine that, independent of blood pressure, patients with cardiac impairment of any sort, both symptomatic and asymptomatic, had increased risk of stroke. Cardiac impairment was determined by the presence of coronary artery disease, congestive heart failure, evidence of left ventricular hypertrophy by ECG or chest radiograph, or arrhythmias.[93] Similar findings were also obtained in the Honolulu Heart Program which followed 7,560 men for 12 years.[42] It has been estimated that three out of every four stroke victims have one or more of these cardiac impairments.[40] One study has suggested that 12.7% of patients who had a stroke had an associated acute myocardial infarction,[13] and conversely it has been estimated that 1.7% of patients who have an acute myocardial infarction will develop a stroke.[84]

In patients with a recent myocardial infarction, those who have had a large anteroseptal infarct are at greatest risk of developing mural thrombus. As a rule of thumb, based on a variety of epidemiologic studies, approximately one-third of patients with a large anteroseptal myocardial infarction will develop a mural thrombus, and approximately one-third of these are at risk of developing a systemic embolus. Not all of these may go to the brain, but that would be the most devastating consequence. Thus, several trials have considered both high- and low-dose anticoagulation for prophylaxis against stroke in patients with a recent large anteroseptal myocardial infarction.[77,89] It would certainly be prudent in such patients to consider an echocardiogram as a specific means of detecting those who should receive anticoagulants.

An autopsy study suggested that the incidence of systemic embolism is approximately 18% in patients who have heart failure.[28] Although placebo-controlled clinical trials in this area are lacking, patients with marked cardiomegaly, even if they are in sinus rhythm, should be considered for long-term anticoagulant therapy, though this can be low-dose with a prothrombin time adjusted to be between 14 and 16 seconds or with an INR (international normalized ratio) of 3.

Atrial Fibrillation

Lone atrial fibrillation is the presence of the arrhythmia in an otherwise normal heart and is associated with a significant incidence of systemic emboliza-tion.[35] In the Framingham study, chronic nonrheumatic atrial fibrillation was associated with a 5-fold increase in strokes, and if atrial fibrillation was present with rheumatic heart disease, the risk increased 17-fold.[95] Several recent prospective placebo-controlled clinical trials have shown that long-term anticoagulation for patients with chronic atrial fibrillation in the absence of rheumatic valvular disease significantly reduces the incidence of embolic complications such as stroke.[11,17,61,81] The benefit may be greater in those who are at the increased risk, such as those over the age of 60. In younger patients, who may have to stay on anticoagulants for longer, the possibility of hemorrhagic complications over a longer period of time may increase, and the results of an ongoing trial comparing the efficacy of aspirin versus anticoagulants in this age group are eagerly awaited. Patients with atrial fibrillation who have associated valvular disease, a past history of systemic embolism, history of hypertension, or recent congestive heart failure should be considered for anticoagulation.[82] The risk of a stroke occurring increases with the duration of the chronic atrial fibrillation, though there is a clustering of cerebral ischemic events at the onset of atrial fibrillation.[94]

Patients with nonrheumatic paroxysmal atrial fibrillation who are being considered for DC cardioversion probably do not require anticoagulation if it is well documented that the atrial fibrillation has only been of 2 to 3 days' duration or less. If there is doubt about the duration of the current episode of atrial fibrillation or if the patient has a large left atrium, then it may be safer to anticoagulate the patient for at least 1 week prior to attempted cardioversion.[3]

Sick Sinus Syndrome

Sick sinus syndrome generally presents as sinus bradycardia, sinus arrest, or sinoatrial block and is frequently associated with paroxysmal atrial tachyarrhythmias, when it is referred to as the "tachy-brady" syndrome. It is frequently a degenerative disorder which is common in older patients but may be associated with other forms of heart disease.

Fairfax et al.[26] followed 100 patients with sick sinus syndrome and compared them to 712 control subjects of similar age and sex who had chronic complete heart block. Systemic and cerebral embolism occurred in 16% of their study patients compared to 1.3% of control patients. All of the patients who developed systemic embolism were over 54 years old, the risk of embolism remained even if the tachy-brady syndrome was replaced by stable atrial fibrillation, and the authors concluded that paroxysmal supraventricular tachycardia also increased the risk of subsequent embolization. This latter concept is supported by another ambulatory ECG study of 68 consecutive patients with ischemic stroke, though this study was poorly controlled.[1] It remains unclear as to whether anticoagulation is appropriate in the absence of atrial fibrillation, though it could be considered in patients with recurrent emboli who have no other documented cause.

It should be noted in this context that cardiac arrhythmias such as paroxysmal tachycardias or atrioventricular disorders resulting in complete heart block generally cause significant reduction in cardiac output which is associated with syncopal or presyncopal symptoms and not focal neurologic signs. Reed et al.[67] followed 290 patients who received pacemakers for disturbances of cardiac rhythm or conduction, and only 4 had focal neurologic symptoms or signs and only 2 ($< 1\%$) had focal cerebral symptoms that could be related to a specific episode of cardiac dysfunction.

Valvular Heart Disease

Although the incidence of rheumatic heart disease has declined dramatically, the presence of significant valvular heart disease remains a significant cause of cerebral embolic infarct.

Mitral Stenosis. Cerebral embolism may be a presenting symptom of mild mitral stenosis, but generally the risk increases in parallel with the duration of mitral stenosis.[70,75] The thrombi occur most commonly in the left atria but may also occur on the left ventricular endocardium at the site of a jet lesion through a tight mitral valve. As noted previously, the Framingham study showed that the combination of rheumatic heart disease and chronic atrial fibrillation increased the risk of stroke 17-fold. Thus, all patients with mitral stenosis and atrial fibrillation should be anticoagulated.

Mitral stenosis can usually be diagnosed clinically by the presence of a loud first heart sound, an opening snap (which becomes closer to the second heart sound as the severity of mitral stenosis increases), and a mid-diastolic rumble. An echocardiogram is usually helpful to confirm the diagnosis, to assess the severity with increased accuracy (a mitral valve area of <1 cm^2/m^2 implies severe mitral stenosis), and to assess the size of the left atrium. In general, the larger the left atrium, the greater the risk of development of left atrial thrombus and atrial fibrillation. Occasionally, a past history of mitral stenosis can be misdiagnosed as chronic bronchitis, chronic obstructive pulmonary disease, or left ventricular failure. The presence of an enlarged left ventricle suggests that another valve lesion such as mitral incompetence or a cardiomyopathy may be the predominant problem.

Mitral Incompetence. This can be diagnosed clinically from an enlarged left ventricle on clinical examination and a pansystolic murmur loudest at the apex radiating into the axilla, and it is often associated with a third heart sound. When severe, the left ventricle would be enlarged on a posteroanterior or left lateral chest radiograph. On echocardiography, trivial mitral incompetence is not uncommon in an otherwise normal heart, but severe mitral incompetence will be associated with an enlarged left atrium and a dilated left ventricle. In severe mitral incompetence, atrial fibrillation frequently results, and occasionally a jet lesion occurs on the atrial endocardial surface. The incidence of embolic events in pure mitral incompetence is relatively low.[64] Mitral incompetence can occur as part of the natural history of mitral valve prolapse, as part of the degeneration of the mitral valve, or resulting from papillary muscle dysfunction or chordae tendineae rupture following myocardial infarction due to ischemic heart disease. It can also occur as part of a deformed rheumatic mitral valve.

Since the incidence of thromboembolism is relatively low, routine anticoagulation for isolated mitral incompetence is generally not indicated but should be considered if atrial fibrillation is also present or if the long-term volume effects of the mitral incompetence had caused a dilated cardiomyopathy.

Mitral Valve Prolapse. This clinical entity has been recognized for some time, but the incidence of its diagnosis has increased with the sensitive use of echocardiography. Clinically, it may be detected on auscultation of the heart as an isolated midsystolic click or as a click with a late systolic murmur best heard at the apex. It appears to be commoner in young women.[48] It has been associated with a wide variety of associated clinical symptoms such as palpitations and atypical chest pain. Patients with mitral valve prolapse are at risk of developing progressive mitral regurgitation and some patients can require mitral valve replacement, and they are also at risk of developing thrombus formation on the valve and bacterial endocarditis. Barnett[5] in 1974 pointed out the relationship between mitral valve prolapse and cerebral ischemia. However, specific treatment and prophylaxis of bacterial endocarditis or thromboembolism would not appear justified on the basis of an echocardiographic diagnosis alone and probably not on the basis of an isolated midsystolic click. Antibiotic prophylaxis against bacterial endocarditis is appropriate in the presence of an associated murmur of mitral regurgitation.

Barnett et al.[6] found that mitral valve prolapse was present in 40% of 60 patients under the age of 45 with cerebral ischemia, but in only 6.8% of 60 age- and sex-matched control subjects. In 141 patients older than 45 years, the incidence of mitral valve prolapse was 5.7% compared to 7.1% in age- and sex-matched controls. The risk of stroke in patients with mitral valve prolapse remains low, and it has been estimated to be 1 in 6,000/year.[33] However, cerebral and retinal ischemia can occur, especially in young patients.[38] Thus, the presence of mitral valve prolapse would not require anticoagulant therapy in an asymptomatic patient. However, in a young patient with cerebral or retinal ischemia who has no other risk factors, mitral valve prolapse should be considered. If clinically detectable, anticoagulation may be considered in selected patients. An echocardiographic diagnosis alone without evidence of thrombus on the valve and no clinical signs probably does not justify anticoagulation. Transesophageal echocardiography can be helpful to further refine the images of the mitral valve in cases where a high suspicion of thrombus on a prolapsing mitral valve continues to be entertained.

Antiplatelet therapy with aspirin (with or without dipyridamole) has been suggested as a reasonable initial treatment in patients with a prolapsing mitral valve and cerebral symptoms, to be interspersed with periods of anticoagulation if cerebral symptoms increase.[4] However, it should be remembered that this treatment is empirical at the present time, as no randomized clinical trials have been conducted.

Mitral Annulus Calcification. This disorder occurs more commonly in women and the elderly.[73] The first account of a stroke in a patient with mitral annulus calcification was by Rytand and Lipstich in 1946.[71] It may be an inadvertent finding on chest radiography or echocardiography but can be associated with both mitral stenosis and incompetence or the development of endocarditis or superimposed thrombus. It can also be associated with atrial arrhythmias and heart block.[8]

A long-term follow-up of 107 patients with mitral annulus calcification and 107 age- and sex-matched controls without mitral annulus calcification found cerebrovascular events occurred in 10% of patients with mitral annulus calcification and 2% of those without it over the course of approximately 4 years.[55] A recent report of 1,159 subjects in the Framingham study, whose echocardiograms could be assessed for mitral annular calcification and who had no history or current evidence of stroke at the index examination, found the prevalence of mitral annular calcification to be 10.3% in men and 15.8% in women.[8] Subsequent multivariate analysis demonstrated that the presence of mitral annular calcification was associated with a relative risk of stroke of 2.1. This incidence increased with worsening severity of the calcification. This increased risk persisted when patients with coronary heart disease or congestive heart failure were excluded from the analysis. However, the authors conclude that it remains difficult to know whether such calcification contributes causally to the risk of stroke or is merely a marker of increased risk because of its association with other precursors of stroke in an elderly population.

Two recent randomized controlled studies of patients with atrial fibrillation reached opposite conclusions with regards to whether mitral annulus calcification was associated with an increased risk of stroke.[11,80] Therefore, although the presence of mitral annular calcification may identify patients at increased risk of stroke, it is not clear that specific preventative therapy such as anticoagulation is justified since the emboli may be of calcium material which has broken off from the lesion rather than thromboembolic.

Calcific Aortic Stenosis. Calcium emboli to the retinal and cerebral circulations have been described in patients with calcific aortic stenosis, but the overall incidence of cerebral infarction in the absence of superimposed infective endocarditis is low,[4] and no specific prophylactic therapy would appear justified.

Hypotension

Johnson et al.[39] reported the incidence of postural hypotension in elderly patients in a geriatric unit. In four of the patients who had severe postural hypotension during life and came to autopsy, two had multiple infarcts, one had a massive left middle cerebral infarct, and the other did not have evidence of a specific cerebral infarct. It was not clear whether the cerebral infarcts had caused the postural hypotension or whether the postural hypotension might have resulted in the infarcts.

Hossmann and Zulch[37] reviewed the circadian variation of hemodynamics and stroke and concluded that circadian changes that have a beneficial effect on healthy subjects may endanger patients with cardiovascular disease, since they found that a majority of their patients who suffered a stroke between 5:00 and 9:00 AM developed neurologic symptoms shortly after getting up. However, they concluded that this hypothesis required testing in a large clinical trial.

Adams et al.[2] described 11 cases of prolonged systemic hypotension causing diffuse infarction in the "watershed" zone between the territories of two major cerebral arteries and additional smaller lesions in the cerebrum and cerebellum. However, watershed infarcts can also be caused by microemboli and by carotid occlusions, and some can be of unknown cause.[87] Although hypotension will generally cause syncope or presyncope, it is generally agreed that the abrupt inappropriate excessive lowering of blood pressure can precipitate a stroke.

The clinical testing of the carotid sinus by prolonged massage of the carotid artery has been associated with the development of a stroke on that side of the brain. It is believed that this incidence is extremely small, but it has been suggested that gentle massage should be given for a time not exceeding 5 seconds and should not be carried out in the presence of bilateral carotid occlusions. Prior to the maneuver, the carotid artery should be auscultated for murmurs, and the procedure should be carried out with caution in elderly patients over age 75 or those who have known cerebral vascular disease.[47]

Other Rare Cardiac Causes of Stroke

A stroke can be a rare complication of cardiac catheterization, open heart surgery, or prosthetic heart valves or cardiac transplantation. Endocarditis (either nonbacterial, thrombotic or infective), cardiac myxoma, paradoxical embolism, and congenital heart disease are other rare cardiovascular associations of stroke and may be considered in appropriate clinical situations.

Suspicion and Investigation of a Cardiac Cause of Recurrent Stroke

Barnett[4] has considered the role of cardiac causes in recurrent stroke in detail and has suggested that the following features should alert the physician to the possibility that the heart could be a primary cause for a stroke:

1. Symptoms and signs in the territory of more than one major cerebral artery.
2. A young patient.
3. A patient who has previously had diagnosed heart disease.
4. Heart disease which is detected on careful history, physical examination, and appropriate investigations.
5. Angiographic evidence of an occluded middle or posterior cerebral artery or the major branches without substantial evidence of concomitant atherosclerosis.
6. CT evidence of hemorrhagic infarction.
7. Evidence of other systemic emboli.
8. Stroke as an abrupt onset without warning.

These factors have been arranged in descending order of importance. Patients who have had a stroke and have the above features should be considered at increased risk of recurrent stroke during rehabilitation and should be considered for additional cardiovascular assessment and investigations.

With regards to investigations, Barnett[4] suggests the following:

1. Cardiac investigation including two-dimensional echocardiography in most younger patients with a stroke, in all patients with cardiac signs or symptoms, and in patients of all age groups in whom routine investigations produce no satisfactory cause for cerebral ischemia.

2. Two-dimensional echocardiography, 48 hours of Holter monitoring, and a search for a coagulation or platelet disorder in patients in any age group who have evidence of an occluded intracranial artery but lack convincing evidence of atherosclerosis in any of the appropriate extracranial or intracranial arteries.

3. Two-dimensional echocardiogram in patients with cerebral and retinal ischemia who have developmental skeletal abnormalities or familial neuromuscular disorders.

4. A cardiac physical examination and ambulatory ECG monitoring for recurrent syncope.

5. Ambulatory ECG monitoring in a patient with cerebral and retinal ischemia with a background history of recurrent unexplained syncopal episodes.

6. Remember that the presence of serious heart disease does not exclude the possibility that cerebral ischemia is of arterial origin.

These suggestions make sound clinical sense but should be ordered and interpreted in the context of the clinical scenario and with knowledge of the sensitivity and specificity of the test.

CARDIOVASCULAR CONSEQUENCES OF STROKE: ACUTE ASSOCIATIONS

Cardiac abnormalities may be found in up to 50% of stroke patients.[92] This is not surprising since cardiovascular and cerebrovascular disease often have a similar etiology and are likely to coexist in many patients. However, cardiac function, both chronotropic and inotropic, is regulated by the autonomic nervous system. Certain brain injuries may therefore result in significant changes in autonomic outflow to the heart with resultant cardiac findings which would generally be transient. Thus, cardiac consequences directly arising out of the stroke syndrome are generally recognized under the following categories: electrocardiographic changes, cardiac arrhythmias, changes in cardiac enzymes, changes in blood pressure, and "neurogenic" pulmonary edema.

Electrocardiographic Changes

ECG changes are more likely to occur with subarachnoid hemorrhage or a brainstem stroke and consist of prolonged QRS complex, prolonged QT interval, and prominent or inverted T-waves. These findings can frequently mimic an acute myocardial infarction.[12,48] Lavy et al.[44,45] used both standard 12-lead ECGs, in which they found an overall incidence of 68% for abnormalities, and cardiac monitoring. They suggested that their ECG changes were associated with poor prognosis. Cruickshank et al.[20] evaluated the prognostic significance of ECG changes in 40 patients with subarachnoid hemorrhage. There were 6 deaths, and 5 of these patients had consistently abnormal ECGs. The authors felt that the presence of either pathologic Q-wave or raised ST segment indicated a poor prognosis. They found a high incidence of peaked P-waves, short PR intervals, a long QTc, and tall U-waves in the ECGs of 6 patients who died, 15 patients with cerebral arterial spasm, and 7 patients who later developed cerebral arterial spasm. Three of the latter eventually died, in contrast to 1 death in the 22 patients who did not develop cerebral arterial spasm and had a low incidence of the above ECG changes. Cruickshank et al.[19] subsequently demonstrated that these ECG changes appear to be associated with increased endogenous catecholamine levels and suggested that this may be linked to the development and maintenance of cerebral arterial spasm.

Dimant and Grob[22] studied 100 consecutive patients with an acute cerebrovascular accident which was due to a cerebral thrombosis in 72, cerebral hemorrhage in 12, embolus in 6, and subarachnoid hemorrhage in 10 and found that 90 of these patients had ECG abnormalities during their first 3 days of admission compared to 50% in a control group of similar age and sex admitted for carcinoma of the colon. Patients with a stroke had a 7- to 10-fold higher incidence of ST segment depression, prolonged QTc interval and a 2- to 4-fold higher incidence of T-wave inversion and conduction defects. Those who died had a higher incidence of ECG evidence of a recent myocardial infarction, atrial fibrillation, or conduction defects.

ECG changes have been observed following manipulation of the circle of Willis during surgical procedures[65] and can be induced by surgical stimulation in animals of some areas of the central nervous system.[21,36,43,91] The ECG changes may therefore reflect a change in autonomic function in the brain. Prolongation of the QT interval is certainly associated with changes in autonomic balance.[74] However, alternative explanations have been suggested since there is an increase in catecholamine release and some evidence of myocardial damage (which will be discussed below), though the pathologic findings may not correlate well with the presence of the ECG changes.[31]

Since some of the ECG changes like the prolonged Q-T interval can be associated with sudden death[74] and since sudden death does occur in stroke,[63] there would be some concern that the ECG changes in acute stroke might be of importance in affecting outcome. However, it is not clear that the ECG changes are an independent predictor of poor outcome and may merely reflect significant brain damage which itself would be a predictor of poor outcome. Thus, they are more likely to be only a marker of poor outcome.

ECG changes can also occur in a transient ischemic attack, and Fujishima et al.[27] studied 30 patients within 24 hours of hospital admission. They found ST depression in 6 patients (5 showed nonspecific and 1 showed ischemic depression), and flattened T-waves with and without ST depression were noted in 3 and 1 patients, respectively. There was no obvious difference between patients having symptoms of hemispheric lesions and those with brainstem lesions. Price et al.[66] also studied 121 patients during an acute transient ischemic attack but do not comment on specific ECG changes other than some arrhythmias.

Most ECG changes during an acute stroke therefore do not require specific intervention, though they may be a marker of poor outcome. A patient with ECG changes that look similar to an acute myocardial infarction may not require further cardiac investigation if they have clearly had a large subarachnoid hemorrhage. In some circumstances where the diagnosis is unclear, an echocardiogram may be helpful to show if there is an associated wall motion abnormality suggestive of an acute myocardial infarction, which would then be treated in the normal way.

Cardiac Arrhythmias

Cardiac monitoring of patients with either acute hemorrhagic or ischemic stroke shows a high incidence of between 50 and 60% of most types of cardiac arrhythmias.[57,69] Arrhythmias can include isolated ventricular or atrial ectopics, atrial fibrillation, or other arrhythmias including sick sinus syndrome and supraventricular and ventricular tachycardias. Even when patients with an acute stroke are compared with a control group matched for age and the presence of heart disease, there still remains a preponderance of most types of arrhythmias in the stroke group.[52] However, the association between the strokes and arrhythmias appears to be loose, and arrhythmias appear to be nonspecific although their incidence is increased. In a review of deaths from stroke in Rochester, Minnesota, between 1955 and 1969, Phillips et al.[63] found that all of the instantaneous deaths and most of the deaths that occurred within 2 hours of onset of symptoms were from a subarachnoid hemorrhage and that most of the patients in their study had an intracerebral hemorrhage as the terminal event. It is therefore likely that even if arrhythmias are increased, the cause of death in an acute stroke is more likely to be a result of the cerebral lesion rather than an associated change in heart rhythm.

Increased Cardiac Enzymes

As previously noted, subarachnoid hemorrhage can be associated with striking ECG changes, though often the cardiac findings are normal. However, Wasserman et al.[90] in 1956 did report frank myocardial infarction occurring during a subarachnoid hemorrhage, and subsequently other changes of microscopic focal myocardial necrosis have been documented not only in subarachnoid hemorrhage[31] but also in ischemic stroke.[18] It has been suggested that these lesions may be due to excessive catecholamine release,[32,68] which may then cause changes similar to a pheochromocytoma. In 1964, Tomomatsu et al.[85] found elevated urinary catecholamine levels in patients who had an acute cerebrovascular event, and these levels were more marked in those who had had a subarachnoid hemorrhage. These results were confirmed by Peerless and Griffiths,[60] who found raised plasma norepinephrine levels in patients with subarachnoid hemorrhage, and by Benedict and Loach.[7] The rise in catecholamine levels is greater in hemorrhage stroke than in ischemic stroke.

Evidence for myocardial cell damage is also obtained from measurements of isoenzyme fractions of plasma CK levels. Norris et al.,[59] in a group of 230 patients with stroke, assayed CK-MB levels of 101 patients who had elevated total CK levels and showed 25 patients (11%) had specific CK-MB elevations. This small subgroup also was found to have an increased incidence of cardiac arrhythmias compared to patients without CK-MB elevations. One patient in this subgroup who died of an infarction to the brainstem was found at autopsy to have scattered focal myocytolysis throughout the myocardium and had ischemic-type ECG changes. The rise in CK-MB levels was slow and progressive up to the 4th day of the stroke, but in that study no enzyme levels were measured after this time. Anecdotally, the investigators report that in some individual cases, maximum values occurred by about the 6th day, usually not returning to normal until the 10th day,[58] and this pattern of enzyme rise is slower and distinct from that which occurs in acute myocardial infarction due to coronary thrombosis.

Blood Pressure Changes

Hypertension documented at the time of a stroke may represent preexisting chronic essential hypertension, a nonspecific acute stressful reaction, a secondary response to some swelling of the cerebral hemispheres, or a change in autonomic balance with increased sympathetic discharge (as has been discussed above). Acute accelerated malignant hypertension as a primary cause of a cerebral event may be more likely to cause global rather than focal cerebral findings. Hypertension resulting from a stroke may be more likely with a pontine hemorrhage.

Patients who are suspected of having accelerated hypertension and who have global cerebral signs with evidence of retinal flame hemorrhages and papilloedema should have their blood pressure treated immediately using the standard parenteral medications. Moderate elevations of blood pressure, if associated with CT evidence of a hemorrhagic infarct, could be associated as the etiologic event causing the stroke, but treatment to lower the pressure should be done cautiously as abrupt falls in blood pressure may reduce cerebral perfusion and aggravate ischemia. Mild elevations in blood pressure would generally be best observed and would rarely require acute intervention. In rare circumstances, mild or moderate elevations in blood pressure as a secondary manifestation of the stroke could aggravate heart failure in a patient with a severely compromised left ventricle, and careful clinical judgment would be required on an individual patient basis.

Price et al.[66] examined patients during an acute transient ischemic attack. They found some minimal increases in blood pressure, but only 3 of 121 patients had a notable increase. All 3 had carotid artery system transient ischemic attacks, but 1 also had evidence of acute glomerular nephritis and another had influenza and a fever. They concluded that most of the mild blood pressure changes they observed represented a nonspecific response to illness. Dimant and Grob[22] examined 100 patients with acute cerebral vascular accidents and 100 controlled patients admitted with carcinoma of the colon. Twelve of the control patients had a past history of hypertension, 18 had systolic hypertension on admission (>140 mm Hg), and 6 had diastolic hypertension on admission (>90 mm Hg). Forty-eight patients with stroke had a past history of hypertension, 65 had systolic hypertension on admission, and 43 had diastolic hypertension on admission. Therefore, hypertension is a common finding by history and on physical examination on admission in patients with acute cerebral vascular events.

Hypotension may occur as part of the clinical presentation of a large stroke, but generally it does not require specific intervention unless the patient has symptoms such as unstable angina.

Neurogenic Pulmonary Edema

It has been known for many years that severe head injury can be associated with severe and often fatal pulmonary edema.[53] This is considered to be neurogenic in origin since it is often not associated with previous cardiac disease, develops very rapidly after cerebral injury, and may be prevented experimentally by alpha-adrenergic blocking agents, suggesting that it may be sympathetic in origin.[83] It is more likely to occur with subarachnoidal and cerebral hemorrhage and is associated with catecholamine excess.[32]

When recognized, neurogenic pulmonary edema clearly is not likely to be helped by digoxin therapy. Alpha-adrenergic blocking agents may be helpful to reduce systemic vasoconstriction and prevent increases in pulmonary blood volume, hydrostatic pulmonary edema, and secondary local pulmonary blood vessel damage with increased capillary permeability. Patients may be treated with positive pressure ventilation, pulmonary vasodilators, and diuretics.

CARDIOVASCULAR COMPLICATIONS AFFECTING LONG-TERM PROGNOSIS AFTER STROKE

Acute mortality following stroke reflects the severity of the cerebral injury, and the overall acute mortality is in the region of 30% and increases with the age of the patient.[50] However, it is recognized that there has been an improvement in survival and this may reflect improved diagnosis and management.[30] It is also recognized that estimates of mortality vary greatly between different reported studies.[25]

Longer-term survival in stroke patients is also decreased compared to the general population and is greatly influenced by increasing age. However, the annual death rate remains almost constant irrespective of the time that has elapsed since the stroke and has been estimated as an average annual rate of 16% in males and 18% in females.[49] Thus, Marquardsen[49] concludes that the excess mortality of patients recovering from stroke is not so much due to the effect of the cerebral lesion but reflects the steady progression of an underlying vascular disease, with the most frequent causes of death being recurrent stroke, myocardial infarction, and congestive heart failure.[50] Other important causes of death include pneumonia, pulmonary embolism, and renal failure.[25]

Ischemic Heart Disease

The presence of any type of ECG abnormality has been estimated to reduce that patient's chance of surviving for 3 years by nearly 50%, though after that time the survival curves become nearly parallel.[50] It has also been found to be a major cause of death in patients with transient ischemic attacks or carotid bruits.[86] It therefore would appear reasonable that patients with ongoing symptomatic ischemia or a past history of myocardial infarction should receive therapy with aspirin.[29,99] A daily dose of enteric-coated aspirin, 325 mg orally once daily, would appear reasonable, though one baby aspirin per day may be sufficient. Therapy with aspirin should probably be continued indefinitely if side effects do not occur. Additional use of other drugs, such as a beta-blocker, calcium channel antagonist, long-acting nitrate (it is best to use nitrates in a dosing regimen which avoids 24-hour continuous dosing so that tolerance to the nitrate dose does not occur), or prophylactic sublingual nitroglycerin, is indicated to relieve symptoms. If the patient's pattern of angina is of increasing frequency or becomes unstable such that symptoms occur at rest, then consideration of heart catheterization or an interventional procedure such as balloon angioplasty or bypass surgery may be considered in appropriate patients.

In the setting of a recent Q-wave myocardial infarction, in addition to therapy with aspirin, a beta-blocker such as metoprolol (50–100 mg orally twice daily) or atenolol (50–100 mg orally once daily) is indicated.[98] Therapy should probably continue for at least 1 year and then be reevaluated. If the patient has had a recent non-Q-wave myocardial infarction, diltiazem for a period of at least 3 months in a dose of 60 to 90 mg orally four times daily would seem appropriate.[54] If the patient has had a recent large infarct with significant left ventricular systolic dysfunction such that the left ventricular ejection fraction is less than 40%, then therapy with captopril, 50 mg orally three times daily, is indicated.[62]

Asymptomatic patients with clear ECG evidence of ischemic heart disease require aspirin and possibly sublingual nitroglycerin if they become symptomatic.

If the ECG is abnormal but not believed to be caused by the stroke and not diagnostic for ischemic heart disease, consideration could be given to performing an echocardiogram to look for wall motion abnormality or a nuclear medicine myocardial perfusion study to look for evidence of myocardial ischemia. If the ECG is completely normal but the stroke is atherothrombotic in origin, a search should be made for other risk factors such as positive family history, hypertension, diabetes, or hyperlipidemia, and, if present, younger patients could be considered for further screening for ischemic heart disease such as an exercise treadmill test whenever their stroke rehabilitation allows. Their other risk factors should be addressed independently.

Hypertension

The presence of hypertension prior to the stroke is associated with increased mortality beyond 6 months.[49,72] A wide number of agents are available to treat blood pressure, and the choice of an individual agent depends on considerations of cost, side effects, and other concomitant illnesses or knowledge of side effects. Recently, it has been demonstrated that treatment of isolated systolic hypertension in the elderly reduces the risk of subsequent stroke.[76] If a patient surviving an acute stroke also has cardiac symptoms and hypertension, they have only a 25% chance of surviving 5 years. If one problem is present, survival is 50%, while if neither heart disease nor hypertension is present, there is a 75% chance of survival in 5 years.[50]

Congestive Heart Failure

Many recent advances have taken place in the treatment of congestive heart failure, and it is now evident that treatment with angiotensin-converting enzyme (ACE) inhibitors and combination vasodilator therapy can improve survival. All patients with symptomatic congestive heart failure should be considered for therapy with an ACE inhibitor such as captopril (25–50 mg orally three times daily), enalapril (10–20 mg orally twice daily), or lisinopril (10–20 mg orally once daily).[56,78] If patients cannot tolerate an ACE inhibitor, then combination therapy of hydralazine and nitrates can be considered.[15] There is now evidence that the ACE inhibitor treatment of asymptomatic left ventricular dysfunction can also reduce symptoms (SOLVD prevention arm)[78] and, when used in the setting of an acute myocardial infarction, can significantly reduce mortality (SAVE study).[62] Digoxin and diuretics can be added according to the symptom complex and severity of symptoms. Trials are currently underway to assess the influence of digoxin on survival (DIG study) and the use of combinations of ACE inhibitors and other vasodilators (e.g., PROFILE study, with flosequinan).

Pulmonary Embolism

Subcutaneous heparin can help to prevent deep venous thrombosis and pulmonary emboli and may produce a small improvement in survival.[51] If the patient is going to remain fairly immobile after a stroke, longer-term anticoagulation therapy may be considered at the discretion of the physician and with knowledge as to whether the original stroke was due to thrombosis or hemorrhage.

Hyperlipidemia

With our increasing understanding of the role of different lipoproteins in atherogenesis, patients with documented vascular disease should have a fasting plasma cholesterol (total, LDL, and HDL) measured. All patients should be encouraged to eat a low-fat, low-cholesterol diet. If the total cholesterol is above 7 mmol/L, then it is probable that drug therapy will be required if the patient has already demonstrated a thrombotic event on top of a severe vascular stenosis. If the initial cholesterol is less than 7 mmol/L, then drug therapy may be delayed and the patient strongly encouraged to stay on a low-fat diet and the cholesterol level checked 2 months later. If it is below 6 and if the HDL and LDL fractions are normal, then no drug therapy may be required. Total cholesterol levels persisting above 6 with elevated LDL fractions should be considered for drug therapy. Many patients do not tolerate bile acid sequestrants because of side effects. If triglycerides are also significantly elevated, then a medication such as gemfibrozil may be appropriate. In other patients, the HMG-CoA reductase inhibitors are well tolerated and can be predictably expected to reduce LDL cholesterol by approximately 30% when given in appropriate doses. Studies are ongoing to see if it is possible to achieve regression of coronary, carotid, and peripheral artery stenosis in patients treated with these agents and if the threshold for drug treatment should be lowered.

Diabetes and other risk factors which might increase vascular disease in individual patients should be treated appropriately. Peripheral vascular disease is also associated with poor outcome following a stroke.[79] Appropriate treatment of hyperlipidemia, hypertension, and diabetes will be necessary to improve peripheral vascular disease which presumably also mirrors disease in the coronary and cerebral vasculature.

A high hematocrit may increase blood viscosity and was shown to be associated with increased risk of stroke in the Framingham study and may need to be followed in patients at risk of vascular thrombosis.

CONCLUSION

Patients suffering a stroke are at risk of dying from that event acutely. If they survive the acute event, then they should have a careful cardiovascular evaluation by clinical history, physical examination, and appropriate investigations as guided by the initial assessment. The risk of recurrent stroke and mortality from other cardiovascular events can be estimated and appropriate interventions planned to reduce the high mortality that persists even during the rehabilitation phase. As the therapies improve to reduce cerebral damage and enhance functional recovery following a stroke, increased attention needs to be paid to those other cardiovascular risk factors which may also influence long-term outcome.

ACKNOWLEDGMENT

The author was supported by a Career Health Scientist award from the PMAC Health Research Foundation.

REFERENCES

1. Abdon NJ, Zettervall OCJ, Carlson J, et al: Is occult atrial disorder a frequent cause of nonhemorrhagic stroke? Long-term ECG in 86 patients. Stroke 13:832–837, 1982.
2. Adams JH, Brierley JB, Connor RCR, et al: The effects of systemic hypotension upon the human brain: Clinical and neuropathological observations in 11 cases. Brain 89:235, 1966.
3. Arnold AZ, Mick MJ, Mazurek RP, et al: Role of prophylactic anticoagulation for direct current cardioversion in patients with atrial fibrillation or atrial flutter. J Am Coll Cardiol 19:851–855, 1992.
4. Barnett HJM: Heart in ischemic stroke—A changing emphasis. Neurol Clin 1:291–315, 1983.

5. Barnett HJM: Transient cerebral ischemia: Pathogenesis, prognosis and management. Ann R Coll Phys Surg Can 7:153, 1974.
6. Barnett HJM, Boughner DR, Taylor WD, et al: Further evidence relating mitral-valve prolapse to cerebral ischemic events. N Engl J Med 302:139, 1980.
7. Benedict CR, Loach AB: Clinical significance of plasma adrenaline and noradrenaline concentrations in patients with subarachnoid hemorrhage. J Neurol Neurosurg Psychiatry 41:113, 1978.
8. Benjamin EJ, Plehn JF, D'Agostino RB, et al: Mitral annular calcification and the risk of stroke in an elderly cohort. N Engl J Med 327:374–379, 1992.
9. Bonita R, Scragg R, Stewart A, et al: Cigarette smoking and risk of premature stroke in men and women. BMJ 293:6–8, 1986.
10. Bonita R, Beaglehole R: Does treatment of hypertension explain the decline in mortality from stroke? BMJ 292:191–192, 1986.
11. Boston Area Anticoagulation Trial for Atrial Fibrillation Investigators: The effect of low-dose warfarin on the risk of stroke in patients with non-rheumatic atrial fibrillation. N Engl J Med 323:1505–1511, 1990.
12. Byer E, Ashman R, Toth LA: Electrocardiograms with large upright T waves and long Q-T intervals. Am Heart J 33:796, 1947.
13. Chin PL, Kaminski J, Rout M: Myocardial infarction coincident with cerebrovascular accident in the elderly. Age Ageing 6:29, 1977.
14. Cohn JN, Archibald DG, Ziesche S, et al: Effect of vasodilator therapy on mortality in chronic congestive heart failure: Results of a Veterans Administration Cooperative Study. N Engl J Med 314:1547–1552, 1986.
15. Cohn JN, Johnson G, Ziesche S, et al: A comparison of enalapril with hydralazine-isosorbide dinitrate in the treatment of chronic congestive heart failure. N Engl J Med 325:303–310, 1991.
16. Collins R, Peto R, MacMahon S, et al: Blood pressure, stroke and coronary heart disease: II. Short-term reductions in blood pressure: overview of randomised drug trials in their epidemiologic context. Lancet 335:827–838, 1990.
17. Connolly SJ, Laupacis A, Gent M, et al: Canadian Atrial Fibrillation Anticoagulation (CAFA) Study. J Am Coll Cardiol 18:349–355, 1991.
18. Connor RCR: Focal myocytolysis and fuchsinophilic degeneration of the myocardium of patients dying with various brain lesions. Ann NY Acad Sci 156:261, 1969.
19. Cruickshank JM, Neil-Dwyer G, Scott AW: Possible role of catecholamines, corticosteroids, and potassium in production of electrocardiographic abnormalities associated with subarachnoid haemorrhage. Br Heart J 36:697, 1974.
20. Cruickshank JM, Neil-Dwyer G, Brice J: Electrocardiographic changes and their prognostic significance in subarachnoid haemorrhage. J Neurol 37:755–759, 1974.
21. Dikshit BB: The production of cardiac irregularities by excitation of the hypothalmic centers. J Physiol 81:382–394, 1934.
22. Dimant J, Grob D: Electrocardiographic changes and myocardial damage in patients with acute cerebrovascular accidents. Stroke 8:448–455, 1977.
23. Doyle AE, Edmondson KW, Hunyor S: The Australian therapeutic trial in mild hypertension. Lancet 1:1261–1267, 1980.
24. Dunphy JE: Surgery's relevance to an understanding of basic biology: Tissue repair and cellular regeneration. JAMA 202:116–117, 1967.
25. Ebrahim S: Mortality after stroke. In Clinical Epidemiology of Stroke. Oxford University Press, 1990, pp 147–156.
26. Fairfax AJ, Lambert CD, Leatham A: Systemic embolism in chronic sinoatrial disorder. New Engl J Med 295:190–192, 1976.
27. Fujishima M, Tanaka K, Omae T: Electrocardiographic changes in cerebral transient ischemic attack. Angiology 24:310–315, 1973.
28. Fuster V, Gersh BJ, Guiliani ER, et al: The natural history of idiopathic dilated cardiomyopathy. Am J Cardiol 47:525–530, 1981.
29. Fuster V, Cohen M, Chesebro JH: Usefulness of aspirin for coronary artery disease. Am J Cardiol 61:637–640, 1988.
30. Garraway WM, Whisnant JP, Drury I, et al: The changing pattern of survival following stroke. Stroke 14:699–703, 1983.
31. Greenhoot JH, Reichenbach DD: Cardiac injury and subarachnoid hemorrhage: A clinical pathological and physiological correlation. J Neurosurg 30:521–531, 1969.
32. Hammermeister KE, Reichenbach DD: QRS changes, pulmonary edema, and myocardial necrosis associated with subarachnoid hemorrhage. Am Heart J 78:94, 1969.

33. Hart RG, Easton JD: Mitral valve prolapse and cerebral infarction (editorial). Stroke 13:429, 1982.
34. Hill AB: The environment and disease: Association or causation. Proc R Soc Med 58:295–300, 1965.
35. Hinton RC, Kistler JP, Fallon JT, et al: The influence of etiology of atrial fibrillation on incidence of systemic embolism. Am J Cardiol 40:509, 1977.
36. Hoff EC, Kell JF, Carrol MN: Effects on cortical stimulation and lesions on cardiovascular function. Physiol Rev 43:68–109, 1968.
37. Hossmann V, Zulch KJ: Circadian variations of hemodynamics and stroke. In Zulch KJ, Kaufmann W, Hossmann KA, Hossmann V (eds): Brain and Heart Infarct II. New York, Springer-Verlag, 1979, p 171.
38. Jackson AC, Boughner DR, Barnett HJM: Mitral valve prolapse and cerebral ischemic events in young patients. Neurology 34:784, 1984.
39. Johnson RH, Smith AC, Spalding JMK, et al: Effect of posture on blood-pressure in elderly patients. Lancet i:731–733, 1965.
40. Kannel WB, Wolf PA: Epidemiology of cerebral vascular disease. In Ross Russell RW (ed): Vascular Disease of the Central Nervous System, 2nd ed. New York, Churchill Livingstone, 1983, p 11.
41. Kannel WB, Dawber TR, Sorlie P, Wolf PA: Components of blood pressure and risk of atherothrombotic brain infarction: The Framingham Study. Stroke 7:327–331, 1976.
42. Knutsen R, Knutsen SF, Curb JD, et al: Predictive value of resting electrocardiograms for 12-year incidence of stroke in the Honolulu Heart Program. Stroke 19:555–559, 1988.
43. Korteweg GCJ, Boeles JTF, Ten Cate J: Influence of stimulation of some subcortical areas of the electrocardiogram. J Neurophysiol 20:100–107, 1957.
44. Lavy S, Stern S, Herishianu Y, et al: Electrocardiographic changes in ischemic stroke. J Neurol Sci 7:409, 1968.
45. Lavy S, Yaar I, Melamed E, et al: The effect of acute stroke on cardiac functions as observed in an intensive stroke care unit. Stroke 5:775, 1974.
46. Levine H: Non-specificity of the electrocardiogram associated with coronary artery disease. Am J Med 15:344, 1953.
47. Lown B, Levine SA: The carotid sinus: Clinical value of its stimulation. Circulation 23:766–789, 1961.
48. Markiewicz W, Stoner J, London E, et al: Mitral valve prolapse in one hundred presumably healthy young females. Circulation 53:464, 1976.
49. Marquardsen J: The natural history of acute cerebrovascular disease: A retrospective study of 769 patients. Acta Neurol Scand 45(suppl 38):1–192, 1969.
50. Marquardsen J: Natural history and prognosis of cerebrovascular disease. In Ross Russell RW (ed): Vascular Disease of the Central Nervous System, 2nd ed. London, Churchill-Livingstone, 1983, pp 25–40.
51. McCarthy ST, Robertson D, Turner JJ, et al: Low dose heparin as a prophylaxis against deep vein thrombosis after acute stroke. Lancet 2:800–801, 1977.
52. Meyers MG, Norris JW, Hachinski VC, et al: Cardiac sequelae of acute stroke. Stroke 13:838–842, 1982.
53. Moutier F: Hypertension et mort par oedeme pulmonaire aigu. Presse Med 26:108, 1918.
54. Multicentre Diltiazem Postinfarction Trial Research Group: The effects of diltiazem on mortality and reinfarction after acute myocardial infarction. N Engl J Med 319:385, 1988.
55. Nair CK, Thomson W, Ryschon K, et al: Long term follow-up of patients with echocardiographically detected mitral annular calcium and comparison with age- and sex-matched control subjects. Am J Cardiol 63:465–470, 1989.
56. Newman TJ, Maskin CS, Dennick LG, et al: Effects of captopril on survival in patients with heart failure. Am J Med 84(suppl 3A):140–144, 1988.
57. Norris JW, Froggatt GM, Hachinski VC: Cardiac arrhythmias in acute stroke. Stroke 9:392, 1978.
58. Norris JW: Effects of cerebrovascular lesions on the heart. Neurol Clin 1:87–101, 1983.
59. Norris JW, Hachinski VC, Myers MG, et al: Serum cardiac enzymes in stroke. Stroke 10:548, 1979.
60. Peerless SJ, Griffiths JC: Plasma catecholamines following subarachnoid hemorrhage. Ann R Coll Phys Surg Can 5:48, 1972.
61. Petersen P, Boysen G, Godtfredsen J, et al: Placebo-controlled, randomised trial of warfarin and aspirin for prevention of thromboembolic complications in chronic atrial fibrillation: The Copenhagen AFASAK study. Lancet i:175–179, 1989.

62. Pfeffer MA, Braunwald E, Moye LA, et al: Effect of captopril on mortality and morbidity in patients with left ventricular dysfunction after myocardial infarction: Results of the Survival and Ventricular Enlargement Trial. N Engl J Med 327:669–677, 1992.
63. Phillips LH, Whisnant JP, Reagan TJ: Sudden death from stroke. Stroke 8:392–395, 1977.
64. Pomerance A: Cardiac pathology and systemic murmurs in the elderly. Br Heart J 30:687, 1968.
65. Pool L: Vasocardiac effects of the circle of Willis. Arch Neurol Psych 78:355–367, 1957.
66. Price TR, Gotshall RA, Poskanzer DC, et al: Cooperative study of hospital frequency and character of transient ischemic attacks. JAMA 238:2512–2515, 1977.
67. Reed RL, Siekert RG, Merideth J: Rarity of transient focal cerebral ischemia in cardiac disrhythmia. JAMA 223:893–895, 1973.
68. Reichenbach DD, Benditt EP: Catecholamines and cardiomyopathy: The pathogenesis and potential importance of myofibrillar degeneration. Hum Pathol 1:125, 1970.
69. Reinstein L, Gracey JG, Kline JA, ct al: Cardiac monitoring in the acute stroke patient. Arch Phys Med Rehabil 53:311, 1972.
70. Rowe JC, Bland EF, Sprague HB, White PP: The course of mitral stenosis without surgery: Ten- and twenty-year perspectives. Ann Intern Med 52:741, 1960.
71. Rystand DA, Lipstich LS: Clinical aspects of calcification of the mitral annulus fibrosus. Arch Intern Med 78:544–564, 1946.
72. Sacco RL, Wolf PA, Kannel WB, McNamara PM: Survival and recurrence following stroke: The Framingham Study. Stroke 13:290–295, 1982.
73. Savage DD, Garrison RJ, Castelli WP, et al: Prevalence of submitral (annular) calcium and its correlates in a general population-based sample (the Framingham Study). Am J Cardiol 51:1375–1378, 1983.
74. Schwartz PJ, Periti M, Malliani A: Fundamentals of clinical cardiology: The long Q-T syndrome. Am Heart J 89:378–390, 1975.
75. Selzer A, Cohn KE: Natural history of mitral stenosis: A review. Circulation 45:878, 1972.
76. SHEP Cooperative Research Group: Prevention of stroke by antihypertensive drug treatment in older persons with isolated systolic hypertension. JAMA 265:3255–3264, 1991.
77. Smith P, Arnesen H, Holme I: The effect of warfarin on mortality and reinfarction after myocardial infarction. N Engl J Med 323:147–152, 1990.
78. SOLVD Investigators: Effect of enalapril on survival in patients with reduced left ventricular ejection fractions and congestive heart failure. N Engl J Med 325:293–302, 1991.
79. Solzi P, Ring H, Najenson T, et al: Hemiplegics after a first stroke: Late survival and risk factors. Stroke 14:703–709, 1983.
80. Stroke Prevention in Atrial Fibrillation Investigators: Predictors of thromboembolism in atrial fibrillation: II. Echocardiographic features of patients at risk. Ann Intern Med 116:6–12, 1992.
81. Stroke Prevention in Atrial Fibrillation Investigators: The Stroke Prevention in Atrial Fibrillation Study: Final results. Circulation 84:527–539, 1991.
82. Stroke Prevention in Atrial Fibrillation Investigators: Predictors of thromboembolism in atrial fibrillation: I. Clinical features of patients at risk. Ann Intern Med 116:1–5, 1992.
83. Theodore J, Robin ED: Pathogenesis of neurogenic pulmonary oedema. Lancet ii:749, 1975.
84. Thompson PL, Robinson JS: Stroke after a myocardial infarction: Relation to infarct size. BMJ 2:457, 1978.
85. Tomomatsu T, Ueba Y, Matsumoto T, et al: ECG observations and urinary excretion of catecholamines in cerebrovascular accidents. Jpn Circ J 28:905, 1964.
86. Toole JF, Janeway R, Choi K, et al: Transient ischemic attacks due to atherosclerosis: A prospective study of 160 patients. Arch Neurol 32:5–12, 1975.
87. Torvik A: The pathogenesis of watershed infarcts in the brain. Stroke 15:221–223, 1984.
88. Turpie AGG, Robinson JG, Doyle DJ, et al: Comparison of high-dose with low-dose subcutaneous heparin to prevent left ventricular mural thrombosis in patients with acute transmural anterior myocardial infarction. N Engl J Med 320:346–351, 1989.
89. Veterans Administration Cooperative Study Group on Antihypertensive Agents: Effects of treatment on morbidity in hypertension: II. Results in patients with diastolic blood pressure averaging 90 through 114 mmHg. JAMA 213:1143–1152, 1970.
90. Wasserman F, Choquette G, Cassinelli R, et al: Electrocardiographic observations in patients with cerebrovascular accidents. Am J Med Sci 231:502, 1956.
91. Weinberg SJ, Fuster JM: Electrocardiographic changes produced by localized hypothalamic simulations. Ann Intern Med 53:332–341, 1960.
92. Wilson G, Rupp C Jr, Riggs HE, et al: Factors influencing development of cerebral vascular accidents: Role of cardiocirculatory insufficiency. JAMA 145:1227–1229, 1951.

93. Wolf PA, Kannel WB, Verter J: Current status of risk factors for stroke. Neurol Clin 1:317–343, 1983.
94. Wolf PA, Kannel WB, McGee DL, et al: Duration of atrial fibrillation and imminence of stroke: The Framingham Study. Stroke 14:664, 1983.
95. Wolf PA, Dawber TR, Thomas HE Jr, et al: Epidemiologic assessment of chronic atrial fibrillation and risk of stroke: The Framingham Study. Neurology 23:973–977, 1978.
96. Wolf PA, Kannel WB, Dawber TR: Prospective investigations: The Framingham Study and the epidemiology of stroke. Adv Neurol 19:107–120, 1978.
97. Wolf PA, Kannel WB, McGee DL: Epidemiology of strokes in North America. In Barnett HJM, Mohr JP, Stein BM, Yatsu FM (eds): Stroke: Pathophysiology, Diagnosis and Management. Vol 1. New York, Churchill Livingstone, 1986, pp 19–29.
98. Yusuf S, Peto R, Lewis JA, et al: Beta-blockade during and after myocardial infarction: A review of the randomized trials. Prog Cardiovasc Dis 27:335, 1987.
99. Yusuf S, Wittes J, Friedman L: Overview of results of randomized clinical trials in heart disease: I. Treatments following myocardial infarctions. JAMA 260:2088–2093, 1988.

SAMUEL WIEBE-VELAZQUEZ, MD, FRCPC
WARREN T. BLUME, MD, FRCPC

5. SEIZURES

From the Department of Clinical
  Neurological Sciences
University Hospital
The University of Western Ontario
London, Ontario
Canada

Reprint requests to:
Dr. Samuel Wiebe-Velazquez
339 Windermere Road
London, Ontario N6A 5A5
Canada

The relationship between cerebral vascular disease and seizures has been recognized since the mid-19th century. John Hughlings Jackson[39] probably first recorded this association, stating in 1864 that "it is not very uncommon to find when a patient has recovered or is recovering from hemiplegia, the result of embolism of a middle cerebral artery, or some branch of this vessel, that he is attacked by convulsion beginning in some part of the paralysed region." William Gowers[29] reported 66 patients with hemiplegia and epilepsy and introduced the term *post-hemiplegic epilepsy.*

SCOPE OF THE PROBLEM
In industrialized countries, epilepsy is frequently viewed as an affliction of children and youth. However, the average age of patients with post-stroke seizures or epilepsy is 60 years across studies.[12,14,30,59,74,78] It has been repeatedly shown since the 1950s that vascular disease is the most common documentable etiology of seizures in this age group[46] (Table 1).

The incidence of post-stroke (including cerebral hemorrhage and infarction) seizures ranges from 7.7 to 42.8% depending on study design[5,16,17,38,50,56] (Table 2). Studies carried out prior to the era of CT and MRI relied on clinical or angiographic criteria for diagnosis and classification of strokes. Now, noninvasive, high-resolution imaging technology such as CT and MRI have improved the ability to localize and define the nature of a stroke. This will impact on future studies of post-stroke seizures.

TABLE 1. Etiology of Seizures in Older Patients*

	White et al.[86]	Ang & Utterback[1]	Hildick-Smith[37]	Seifer & Ignacio[72]	Schold et al.[71]
Age of patient (yrs)	>50	>40	>60	>40	>69
No. of patients	107	96	50	153	50
Cardiovascular (total)	49	46	22	26	15
Hypertension	6	5	—	—	—
Hemorrhage	—	6	—	8	2
Systemic/metabolic	2	7	4	—	5
Degenerative/atrophic	5	11	7	2	0
Tumor	21	4	5	26	1
Trauma	3	5	1	4	4
Other	2	6	4	10	0
Unknown	25	17	7	85	25

* From Lesser et al: Epileptic seizures due to thrombotic and embolic cerebrovascular disease in older patients. Epilepsia 26:622–630, 1985; with permission.

PATHOPHYSIOLOGY OF FOCAL EPILEPSY

Principles of cortical physiology and anatomy as applied to epilepsy can be gleaned from reviews in Kandel, Schwartz, and Jessell,[40] Engel,[20] and Blume.[6]

The two general classes of cortical neurons are pyramidal and stellate. Pyramidal cells are excitatory and play a major role in creating seizures and their propagation. Some stellate cells are excitatory, particularly those in neocortical layer IV. Inhibitory stellate cells likely synthesize and utilize gamma-amino butyric acid (GABA), an inhibitory transmitter.

Focal epileptogenesis, which is the type most commonly occurring in association with vascular disease, consists of high-frequency synchronous action potentials in large groups of cortical neurons. Underlying such "burst firing" is the paroxysmal depolarization shift (PDS) described by Matsumoto and Ajmone Marsan.[53] Such long-duration (100–200 ms) depolarization of groups of neurons associated with bursts of action potentials produces the "spike" of the electroencephalogram (EEG). PDSs have appeared in acute and chronic experimental epileptic foci and in humans.[63] Mechanisms responsible for the production of PDSs are not fully known. Many studies over the past 3 decades have focused on the relative roles of excitatory postsynaptic potentials (EPSPs) and intrinsic neuronal membrane bursting properties in generating PDSs.. Any factor such as an excitatory afferent impulse which depolarizes the membrane produces a larger

TABLE 2. Types of Seizures in Patients with Cerebrovascular Disease*

	Ang & Utterback[1]	Louis & McDowell[50]	Meyer et al.[56]	Schold et al.[71]	Cocito et al.[12]	Franck[25]	Decarolis et al.[15]	Total
Focal motor	14	34	14	27	11	13	2	115
Complex partial	—	—	—	1	2	3	—	6
Adversive	—	—	—	—	1	—	—	1
Focal with secondary generalization	15	—	—	—	4	—	16	35
Generalized only	17	26	4	22	4	1	—	74

* From Lesser et al. Epileptic seizures due to thrombotic and embolic cerebrovascular disease in older patients. Epilepsia 26:622–630, 1985; with permission.

change in membrane potential than do hyperpolarizing impulses of similar amplitude. Thus, depolarization may activate intrinsic membrane currents and thus increase the probability that the neuron will depolarize to the threshold to fire bursts of action potentials.[63]

Neurons with inherent bursting properties are those more likely to initiate burst firing in other neurons; these include some neurons of the hippocampus and the intrinsic bursting (IB) neurons of layers IV and V of the neocortex. Thus, development of an epileptogenic discharge may require a population of neurons with burst-generating properties; indeed, cortical epileptiform events appear to begin in areas where such neurons are found, such as layers IV and V.[63]

Fortunately, factors exist which terminate such burst firing. Thus, prolonged afterhyperpolarization (AHP) follows interictal PDSs.[53] The afterhyperpolarization corresponds to the EEG slow wave which follows an EEG spike. During the PDS, both sodium and calcium enter the cell. Such influx of calcium can cause an egress of potassium which is partially responsible for the afterhyperpolarization. Enhanced synaptic inhibition is also partially responsible.[64] Neurons in the region surrounding epileptic foci produce large hyperpolarizing membrane events without apparent preceding depolarization, and this has been termed the *inhibitory surround* by Prince and Wilder.[64] Not only does this inhibition surround the focus, but it occurs in the deeper cortical layers of any superficial excitatory focus.[18]

The transition from an interictal to an ictal state is characterized by a gradual decrease in the afterhyperpolarization which gradually becomes a prolonged depolarization.[54] This transition causes continuous bursts of action potentials at the axon hillock, leading to seizure activity. An epileptic discharge may spread locally and then can propagate along fiber tracts.

Pathologic processes can tip the excitation-inhibition balance toward excitation and thus lead to seizure activity. Inhibitory neurons of the cortex may be particularly vulnerable to cortical insults such as could result from hemorrhage or ischemia. Reorganization of excitatory circuits, distortion of neuronal soma and dendrites, and gliosis are pathologic changes which might produce seizures.[63] Among the many experimental models of partial seizures are iron or ferric chloride.[87] Hemosiderin deposits caused by hemoglobin breakdown might contribute to epileptogenesis after hemorrhage involving the cerebral cortex.

SEIZURE TYPES IN CEREBROVASCULAR DISEASE

A seizure can be defined as the clinical manifestation of excessive, hypersynchronous discharges of neurons in the cerebral cortex. The clinical phenomena vary according to the cerebral area involved, and frequently there is a progression of symptoms during any given seizure.[19]

The majority of stroke-related seizures are focal motor which may become secondarily generalized[46] (Table 2).

TIMING OF SEIZURE OCCURRENCE IN RELATION TO STROKE

In a prospective study, Black et al.[5] analyzed the incidence and timing of seizures in over 800 completed ischemic or hemorrhagic strokes. Eighty patients (10%) developed seizures. Thirty-nine percent of all seizures occurred in the first 24 hours, 57% in the first week, and 88% in the first year.[5] In a retrospective study of 90 men with seizures after ischemic but not hemorrhagic stroke, Gupta et al.[30] found that 30% occurred in the first 24 hours, 33% in the first week, and 73% in the first year. Up to 98% of all seizures occurred in the first 2 years.

Epilepsy Preceding Stroke

Epilepsy may precede a clinically apparent stroke[3]; a prospective case-control study in Britain has found the prevalence of epilepsy prior to the first known stroke to be 4.5%, compared to 0.6% in controls, the latter being within the known prevalence of epilepsy in similar age groups.[73] The prevalence rose to 9.3% in cases of recurrent stroke. The median duration of epilepsy before the first stroke was 9.5 years, and the median age of the patients was 60 years in this study.

What is the explanation for this phenomenon? Stroke is the commonest verifiable cause of epilepsy in the elderly.[1,37,46,71,72,86] Yet, many strokes are clinically silent as shown by necropsy studies[17] and CT scanning.[75] Thus, some of the late-onset epilepsies may be caused by clinically silent strokes. This is supported by the development of a hemiplegia in three of four patients with prior ipsilateral partial seizures in the British study.[73] Furthermore, a subset of patients from the British study shows that only those with prior seizures continued to have seizures during a follow-up period of 30 months.[74]

Although stroke may directly cause seizures, no common risk factors for both conditions—such as diabetes, atherosclerosis, hypertension, and cardiac arrhythmias—has ever been demonstrated.[12,16,46] This analysis has been done primarily from the point of view of stroke and not seizures, and no association has been found.[12,16,46] However, a case-control study of first seizures has recently shown by multiple logistic regression analysis that hypertension, a well-known stroke risk factor, also independently increases the risk of developing adult-onset seizures.[58]

All of this emphasizes the relevance of enquiring into the occurrence of seizures prior to stroke.

Seizures at Onset of Stroke

Almost 10% of strokes may be accompanied at onset by an epileptic seizure, which is usually focal motor.[3,12,14,22,50,66]

In such instances, De Rueck et al.[16] found that other possible etiologies for seizures were usually present, including renal failure, severe hypertension, and cerebral edema. Interestingly, in two other large studies,[12,22] such phenomena were found in five patients in association with transient ischemic attacks (TIAs) alone. Distinguishing Todd's postictal paralysis from vascular paralysis may be difficult in such circumstances.

The possibility of an ischemic event should always be considered when an individual at risk for stroke presents with new-onset seizures, whether single or in status epilepticus.[46] However, for a seizure to be considered "precursive," it should contain localizing focal features and be supported by clinical and/or radiologic evidence of vascular disease in the same area.

Early-Onset vs Late-Onset Seizures

Early-onset seizures may be defined as those occurring within the first 1 to 2 weeks after stroke.[12,14,30,33,42,46,74] The reported prevalence of early seizures ranges from 3 to 38%.[2,12,22,42] In the series of Black et al.,[5] up to 57% of all post-stroke seizures were of early onset. Lesser et al.[46] found a similar figure (57% of all cases) in their review of five series (97 patients) of ischemic stroke. Almost half of these were either sequential seizures or status epilepticus. As noted elsewhere in this chapter, at least 85% of all seizures in subarachnoid hemorrhage are early seizures.[77]

The risk of epilepsy in patients with early-onset seizures depends on length of follow-up. Gupta et al.[30] found no difference in risk of recurrence with early vs late-onset seizures after a follow-up period of only 30 months. However, Hauser et al.[33] found the cumulative risk at 6 years post-stroke to be 19%. This risk increased 22-fold in patients with early-onset seizures.

Most studies agree that early-onset seizures are not associated with a higher mortality or a worse functional outcome.[32,42,73,74,77]

Epilepsy After Stroke

Epilepsy can be defined as a condition characterized by a tendency for recurrent seizures which are not caused by an immediately preceding insult. This excludes childhood febrile convulsions and seizures due to an acute metabolic derangement or an acute insult to the brain.[19,34]

Retrospective studies looking at all stroke types have consistently found the prevalence of post-stroke epilepsy to be below 10%.[2,22,50,52,66] Olsen et al.[59] prospectively followed a group of 61 patients with supratentorial stroke for 2 to 4 years. Seven patients (9%) developed epilepsy, most of them within 6 to 12 months.

The long-term risk of post-stroke epilepsy has been analyzed prospectively using the life-table method in a Swedish cohort of 409 stroke patients followed for 3.5 to 7 years.[83] The cumulative risk was 3% at 1 year and 5% at 5 years, which is in keeping with the known prevalence rates of 6 to 10%. The annual incidence was highest in the first year (3%) and thereafter it decreased to 0.4% per year (Fig. 1).

Hauser et al.,[33] in a prospective study of 206 patients hospitalized for ischemic stroke, found a cumulative risk for epilepsy of 19% at 6 years, a figure four times higher than in the Swedish study.[83] The risk increased to 56% in those with a history of seizures prior to stroke, as has been suggested in other studies.[74] However, a history of previous cerebrovascular disease did not increase the risk of epilepsy above that of the whole group.

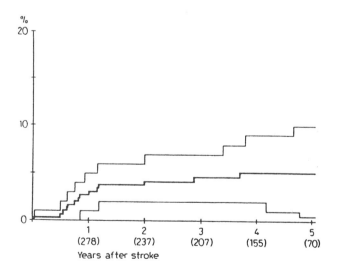

FIGURE 1. Risk of epilepsy in a cohort of 345 stroke patients surviving 1 month and analyzed by life-table technique. The bold line indicates mean; fine lines, 95% confidence intervals. From Vitanen M, Eriksson S, Apslund K: Risk of recurrent stroke, myocardial infarction and epilepsy during long-term follow-up after stroke. Eur Neurol 28:227–231, 1988; with permission.

In the Olsen et al. study,[59] seizures were focal motor or generalized and were easily controlled with antiepileptic drugs. The patients at highest risk for epilepsy in that study were those with persistent hemiparesis (6 with seizures out of 7) and cortical involvement (6 out of 7), regardless of the nature of the stroke.

Several studies have analyzed the EEG features of post-stroke epilepsy. Focal delta or theta has been found in most, and epileptiform activity in some of the series. However, the EEG does not help to determine the risk of developing epilepsy after stroke.[22,50,52,59]

STROKE TYPES AND SEIZURES

Thrombotic vs Embolic Stroke

Early studies support the notion that seizures are more common with embolic than with thrombic infarcts.[38,56,57,66] However, several more recent studies fail to support these observations,[5,42,59,74] particularly because these entities may be indistinguishable clinically, radiologically, and even pathologically.[39]

In the prospective study of Black et al,[5] a potential source of cardiac embolism was found in 32 (38%) patients with seizures following stroke, compared with 200 (27%) in patients with stroke and no seizures; the difference was not statistically significant. Similarly, Shinto et al.,[74] in a case-control study, found no difference in the frequency of seizures after either embolic, thrombotic, or hemorrhagic stroke.

More recently, Kilpatrick et al.[42] prospectively studied 1,000 patients with TIA or stroke of all types and locations in the brain. Early seizures occurred in 44 patients (4.4%). No difference in incidence of seizures was found between embolic and thrombotic stroke.

The prospective study of Olsen et al.[59] found no difference in seizure incidence among thrombotic, embolic, or hemorrhagic stroke; however, heart failure and recent myocardial infarction, both risk factors for embolic stroke, were among the many exclusion criteria. This study found that a lesion involving the cerebral cortex, irrespective of size as determined by CT, is a prerequisite for the development of epilepsy, regardless of the nature of the stroke (embolic, thrombotic, or hemorrhagic) as shown in previous clinicopathologic studies.[66] Supporting this is the complete lack of seizures among Kilpatrick et al.'s 1,000 patients with subcortical vascular lesions, regardless of their nature.[42]

Intracerebral Hemorrhage

Intracerebral hemorrhage is the third most frequent cause of stroke after infarction and embolism. The major causes of hemorrhage are vascular malformations, hypertension, bleeding disorders, and, in the elderly, amyloid angiopathy.

The reported incidence of seizures following intracerebral hemorrhage ranges from 2 to 17%. Table 3 highlights the features of 11 studies addressing this issue, summarized by Sung and Chu.[78] Despite the widely held belief that seizures occur more commonly with intracerebral hemorrhage than with ischemic stroke, there is no consensus in the literature in this regard, with some studies showing evidence in favor of[2,42,57] and others against[5,59,74] this notion.

As with ischemic stroke, cortical involvement appears to be a prerequisite for the development of seizures in intracerebral hemorrhage, as deep-seated hemorrhages rarely cause seizures.[42,59,78]

TABLE 3. Reports on Seizures in Patients with Intracerebral Hemorrhage*

Author	Year	Diagnostic Method	Number of Patients	Study Period	Patients w/Seizure	Incidence of Seizure (%)
Aring & Merritt[2]	1935	Autopsy	116	Admission	16	13.8
Richardson & Dodge[66]	1954	Autopsy	23	Admission	1	4.3
Schaafsma[68]	1968	Autopsy	42	Admission	1	2.0
Fentz[22]	1971	Chart review	23	Acute stage	2	6.0
Fentz[22]	1971	Chart review	12	Late stage	2	17.0
Mohr et al.[57]	1978	Prospective, Clinical diagnosis	115	Acute stage	7	6.0
Harrison[31]	1980	CT	62	Acute stage	4	6.0
Kase et al.[41]	1985	CT and autopsy	24	Acute stage	3	12.5
Lipton et al.[49]	1987	CT	112	Acute stage	19	17.0
Berger et al.[4]	1988	CT	112	Acute stage	19	17.0
Sung & Chu[78]	1989	CT	1402	Acute & late stage	64	4.6

* From Sung C-Y, Chu N-S: Epileptic seizures in intracranial hemorrhage. J Neurol Neurosurg Psychiatry 52:1273–1276, 1989; with permission.

It has been proposed that intracerebral hemorrhage is more frequently associated with late-onset than with early-onset seizures, in contradistinction to other stroke types.[46] However, in a recent series of 1402 patients with primary intracerebral hemorrhage, Sung and Chu[78] found that 64 patients (4.6%) had seizures whose timing was very similar to that reported for other stroke entities; 19 (30%) occurred in the first 24 hours, 38 (60%) in the first 2 weeks, and 58 (90%) by the first year post-intracerebral hemorrhage. Seizure phenomena were similar to those seen in other stroke types. Epilepsy occurred in 37 (58%) of patients with seizures, and there was a marked prevalence in the group with late-onset (>2 weeks) seizures.

Subarachnoid Hemorrhage

This section is devoted to seizures occurring in spontaneous, nontraumatic subarachnoid hemorrhage (SAH) caused by aneurysms. This type of intracranial hemorrhage accounts for approximately 10% of all strokes.[36,82] The frequency, time of onset, and consequences of seizures in SAH have not been systematically studied, and the available data are controversial.[23]

Several difficulties are encountered in the analysis of such data. For example, alteration of consciousness at onset is a prominent feature of SAH; such occurs transiently in up to 45% of patients, while 21% are comatose at onset.[85] Seizures in these patients may be subtle. Likewise, intracranial pressure may acutely increase, producing episodes of decerebrate posturing which may be mistaken for seizures.[79]

Sundaram and Chow[77] retrospectively studied 131 consecutive cases of spontaneous SAH with a highly disciplined protocol; prior epilepsy, decerebrate posturing, and vague "blackouts" were excluded, and an accurate seizure description was sought. Seizure incidence was 24%. Eighty-four percent of these took place in the first 2 weeks of SAH, mostly within the first few hours or minutes of initial bleeding or rebleeding (Table 4). Late-onset (>2 weeks) seizures occurred in 4% of all patients and 16% of those with seizures. In more than 60% of the cases, seizures were multiple with a range of two to four seizures per patient over a 2-year period. As in other recent studies, there was no evidence

TABLE 4. Time of Seizures in Relation to Subarachnoid Hemorrhage*

Early seizures (within the first 2 wks)	26 (20%)
<24 hrs of bleeding	19
24 to 48 hrs	2
48 hrs to 1 wk	3
1 to 2 wks	2
Delayed seizures	5 (4%)
(1st seizure > 2 wks after hemorrhage)	

* From Sundaram and Chow: Seizures associated with spontaneous subarachnoid hemorrhage. Can J Neurol Sci 13:229–231, 1986; with permission.

that SAH patients with seizures have a higher mortality or rebleeding rate than those without seizures. Half of all seizures were partial with or without secondary generalization, and half appeared to be primarily generalized although an occult focus was likely present. Importantly, partial seizure phenomena did not correlate with location of the aneurysm.

Hart et al.[32] retrospectively analyzed 100 consecutive cases of aneurysmal SAH from two centers and found a similar seizure incidence of 26%. More than half of all attacks happened within the first 12 hours of hemorrhage, and the great majority of those occurring after 12 hours were related to acute rebleeding as documented by new blood in the cerebrospinal fluid. All seizures were easily controlled with anticonvulsants and had no relationship with mortality or short-term prognosis. Most recent studies concur that seizures are easily controlled and that long-term prophylactic anticonvulsants are probably not indicated.

Seizures have been reported to occur at some point during the acute period of SAH in 3 to 26% of patients.[2,9,32,35,42,67,77,84,85,88] After recovery from SAH, 4 to 10% of these patients continue to have seizures.[32,67,77,84,85,88]

Vascular Malformations and Epilepsy

Most of the data presented below concern arteriovenous malformations. The incidence of seizures among series of patients with such lesions ranges from 23 to 58%.[8,26,60,61] In the Crawford et al. study,[13] seizures were more likely to occur among younger patients, in those with large arteriovenous malformations, and among those with involvement of the cerebral cortex. In two studies, the risk of a subsequent bleed fell from 36 to 67% among patients presenting with hemorrhage to 22 to 27% in those manifesting with seizures.[13,26] However, two other studies found no difference.[8,60].

Crawford et al.[13] found that an average of 10 years elapsed before an arteriovenous malformation was discovered as the cause of epilepsy; this would likely be shortened with even greater access to neuroimaging.

We are aware of only one study relating seizure origin to arteriovenous malformation location. In addition to seizures arising from the vicinity of the arteriovenous malformation, Yeh and Privitera[90] found remote foci in 8 of 27 patients, all ipsilateral mesial temporal in location.

Cerebral Venous Thrombosis

Cerebral venous thrombosis can involve the cerebral cortical or deep veins, the dural venous sinuses, or, more often, a combination of these. The clinical neurologic features are related to the production of increased intracranial pressure, hemorrhagic infarct, intracerebral hemorrhage, subarachnoid hemorrhage, or seizures.

As opposed to most cerebrovascular conditions associated with epilepsy, cerebral venous thrombosis frequently affects young adults and children with conditions such as meningitis, otitis, dehydration, systemic malignancy, hypercoagulable states, pregnancy, postpartum, and use of oral contraceptives.[27]

Seizures occur in about one-half of patients with cerebral venous thrombosis, particularly those with cortical vein and superior sagittal sinus thrombosis. Most paroxysmal events occur at the onset; they may be focal or generalized, and repeated seizures or status epilepticus at onset are said to be characteristic. Seizures may be followed by a worsening hemiparesis.[10] Cerebral venous thrombosis is one of the few vascular diseases in which seizures may originate in a multifocal manner.[10] Most seizures respond to antiepileptic monotherapy.

STROKE IN CHILDREN

Seizures with Pediatric Vascular Disease

Lanska et al.[44] studied the clinical profile of 42 children with stroke. Infants with strokes in the first few days of life almost always presented with seizures, as a cortically originating neurologic deficit is usually not apparent at that age. Other authors found a similar presentation at this age.[11,24,47,76,80] In contrast, infants with strokes identified later in the first year of life usually presented with an early hand preference but without a history of ictus. Strokes in older children most commonly presented as a sudden hemiparesis or hemiplegia, occasionally associated with seizures. The incidence of late seizures in childhood stroke has varied among studies from 11 to 49%.[44] Possible risk factors for epilepsy following childhood stroke include seizures at stroke onset, epileptiform activity in the EEG, early age of stroke onset, cortical involvement, and residual motor deficit.

Among children with arteriovenous malformations, between 12 and 18% will present with seizure disorder.[28,43] Surgical excision of the arteriovenous malformation and associated epileptogenic regions relieved seizures in over 70% of patients in various series.[43,45,89]

One specific condition which involves stroke and seizures is mitochondrial encephalomyopathy, lactic acidosis, and stroke-like episodes (MELAS).[51] This syndrome may become clinically apparent from age 2 years to young adulthood. Such patients are of short stature and have partial or generalized seizures. Episodic headaches with vomiting afflict some of these children. In association with such headaches or seizures, stroke-like episodes may develop. Unfortunately, such episodes of cerebral infarction may lead to a progressive loss of cognitive function, alternating hemiparesis with bilateral upper motor neuron signs, cortical deafness, and visual impairment. Muscle weakness and atrophy occur in a minority of such patients. The seizure disorder may be moderately resistant to therapy because of its multifocality.

DIFFERENTIAL DIAGNOSIS OF SEIZURES WITH STROKE

In the patient with cerebrovascular disease, associated neurologic conditions that resemble epileptic seizures may occur.

Syncope

Syncope is the most common neurologic condition of systemic origin that is confused with epilepsy. The common mechanism for the several types of syncope is cerebral hypoxia. Syncope is characterized by attacks of loss of consciousness with loss of motor tone. Tonic spasms and some clonic movements may occur after the fall, whereas in epileptic seizures the tonic component begins first and causes the fall. Sphincter incontinence is more common with seizures but may occur with syncope. The duration of syncope is usually less than a minute, and afterwards the patient arouses promptly, fatigued but not confused. Cardiac arrhythmia and postural hypotension, spontaneous or precipitated by antihypertensive therapy, are common causes of syncope in the elderly.[21,46]

Transient Ischemic Attacks

Both TIAs and partial seizures may produce intermittent, focal neurologic deficits. TIAs usually consist of "negative" phenomena such as paresis, visual or sensory deficit, and aphasia, whereas partial seizures tend to have "positive" phenomena such as jerking or stiffening of a limb which may spread rapidly over seconds to engage other parts.

Todd's paralysis refers to temporary focal weakness reflecting postictal cerebral dysfunction but not resulting from a new lesion. Transient sensory, visual, auditory, and language cerebral dysfunctions may also occur after a seizure. Distinguishing such dysfunction from TIA may be very difficult in the presence of cerebrovascular disease, but Todd's paralysis without a motor seizure is most unusual.

Other Abnormal Movements and Posture

In comatose patients, decerebrate posturing and intermittent muscle spasms should not be mistaken for epileptic seizures. They occur in subarachnoid hemorrhage or in parenchymal hemorrhages and infarcts with severe intracranial hypertension.

Axial and multifocal myoclonus may be present in hypoxic-ischemic encephalopathy, especially after cardiac arrest, and entails a poor prognosis.

Finally, hemiballismus or flailing movements of the limbs may occur after a stroke in the contralateral subthalamic nucleus or its connections.

TREATMENT

Controlling seizures related to vascular disease is usually relatively easy to attain, as it is with most unifocal nonprogressive lesions. However, seizures may become medically refractory in the following circumstances.

1. Intercurrent Illness Lowering the Seizure Threshold. Many intercurrent illnesses impair the quality of sleep, which augments a seizure tendency. Metabolic disorders, such as diabetes, may fluctuate creating a varying seizure threshold. Seizures in such instances may result from hypoglycemia, hyponatremia, and other metabolic aberrations. Therapy for associated illnesses may enhance the seizure tendency; well known in this respect are theophylline for asthma and cyclosporine. Finally, therapy for intercurrent illnesses may lead to polypharmacy and therefore to drug interactions.

2. Impaired Compliance. This aspect may have many causes, including an unwillingness or inability to follow physician's instructions or the bewilderment with which the elderly patient may regard his or her medications, particularly if they are multiple.

3. Progressive Vascular and Other Lesions. Multiple infarcts or enlarging arteriovenous malformations fall into this category. Unexpected refractoriness to medical therapy should raise suspicion of a progressive lesion such as a primary or secondary brain tumor.

4. Lesions in Very Epileptogenic Areas. This includes the hippocampus, Rolandic cortex, and calcarine cortex of the occipital lobe.

Need for Antiepileptic Medication

Faced with a patient with a history of one or more seizures, the physician should always consider whether the condition warrants antiepileptic medication. A single, brief seizure associated with a correctable cause may not require therapy. Epilepsia partialis continua (reviewed by Blume[6]) is a persistent stereotyped focal motor seizure disorder which has minimal to no tendency to propagate and is usually refractory to medical management. Therapy for such patients may be limited to low-dose antiepileptic medication to prevent rare spread.

A spontaneously improving epileptic tendency may require only temporary medication; this occurs if excitatory factors gradually dissipate.

Monotherapy

Most seizure disorders are as effectively managed with single antiepileptic medications as with multiple drugs.[55,65,69,70] Many patients with vascular disease are elderly and already take multiple medications. They may have less than average comprehension of medication regimes and may be constrained by limited financial resources. Monotherapy will be associated with fewer drug interactions, and the effectiveness of an antiepileptic medication can be more accurately assessed.

Choice of Medication

As vascular-related epilepsy almost always originates focally, antiepileptic medication appropriate for this type of epilepsy is preferred. In order of preference, carbamazepine and phenytoin are the most effective.

Procedure

Excepting phenytoin, therapy with all antiepileptic medications should be begun slowly at about one-fifth to one-quarter of the ultimate dose, ascending by about 25% every 4 to 7 days until the plateau is reached. This prevents early clinical toxicity, allowing the hepatic microsomal system to adjust to its task. Phenytoin can be started at about 150% of the ultimate dose for about 2 days to bring the serum level rapidly to the therapeutic range.

Therapeutic Range

The *therapeutic range* is that distribution of antiepileptic drug serum values for a population of patients within which the drug is effective yet unwanted effects are minimal. Patients differ with respect to the severity of their seizure disorders and their threshold for noticing side effects. Therefore, the particular circumstances of a patient delimits his or her individual therapeutic range. For example, if an antiepileptic drug fully controls seizures at a level in the low part of the general therapeutic range or below it, no dosage change is necessary. If seizures persist and the antiepileptic drug serum level is low, a 20 to 25% daily dosage increase may be tolerated. In contrast, if the level is midrange, more than a minimal increase may cause subtle or overt clinical toxicity.

TABLE 5.   Symptoms and Signs of Possible Drug Excess

Impaired cognition, manifested by:	Lethargy
Lower school, job performance	Daytime sleepiness
Forgetfulness, due to:	Depression
Impaired memory or inattention	Nystagmus
Irritability due to:	Incoordination
Disrupted wake-sleep cycle	Ataxia
Drug-induced anemia	
Direct side effect	

Pharmacokinetics of each antiepileptic drug also determine degree of dosage adjustments.[48] For comparative purposes, serum levels should always be determined at the same hour, preferably as morning predose trough levels. Total drug levels usually provide clinically reliable data. Free fractions are helpful in situations which might affect protein binding, such as renal disease, or in the presence of multiple drugs, antiepileptic or other.

Further discussion of therapeutic range and antiepileptic drugs management strategies is available in the reviews of Blume or Troupin.[7,81]

Management of Outcomes

One of three outcomes may ensue:

1. No Seizures Occur and the Patient Feels Asymptomatic. In this instance, antiepileptic blood levels could be determined 1 and 2 months after attaining the initial dosage plateau. Even if the level is below the therapeutic range, increasing the antiepileptic medication is normally not necessary, as its purpose has already been accomplished.

2. Continued Seizures. In this circumstance, symptoms and signs of medication toxicity should be sought via functional enquiry and neurologic examination (Table 5). One or more antiepileptic serum levels should be determined to see whether the free and/or total fractions are below the therapeutic range or within the lower part of the usual therapeutic range. If so, the antiepileptic drug dosage could be increased by about 25%. If the level is in the higher part of the therapeutic range, it may be necessary to change to a second antiepileptic drug.

3. Signs and/or Symptoms of Medication Excess but No Seizures. After determining an antiepileptic drug level to verify that the total or free fraction level is high within the therapeutic range or exceeds it (Table 5), lowering the total daily dose by 20 to 25% will likely improve the symptoms without causing seizure recurrence. As phenytoin obeys zero-order kinetics, slight (approximately 10%) adjustments may alter the serum level markedly. Other common antiepileptic drugs do not share this characteristic.

Metabolic Rate

Metabolic clearance rates of many antiepileptic drugs peak in childhood and gradually decline with age.[48,62] Thus, the elderly usually require fewer daily dosages and lower total doses.

ACKNOWLEDGMENT

We wish to thank Mrs. Maria Raffa for the typing of this chapter.

REFERENCES

1. Ang RT, Utterbach RA: Seizures with onset after forty years of age: Role of cerebrovascular disease. South Med J 59:1404–1408, 1966.
2. Aring CC, Merritt HH: Differential diagnosis between cerebral hemorrhage and cerebral thrombosis: Clinical and pathologic study of 245 cases. Arch Intern Med 56:435–456, 1935.
3. Barolin GS: The cerebrovascular epilepsies. Electroencephalogr Clin Neurophysiol 35(suppl):287–295, 1982.
4. Berger AR, Lipton RB, Lesser ML, et al: Early seizures following intracerebral haemorrhage: Implications for therapy. Neurology 38:1363–1365, 1988.
5. Black SE, Norris JW, Hachinski VC: Post-stroke seizures. Stroke 14:134, 1983.
6. Blume WT: Motor cortex: Anatomy, physiology, and epileptogenesis. In Wyllie E (ed): The Treatment of Epilepsy. Malvern, PA, Lea & Febiger, 1992, pp 590–599.
7. Blume WT: Managing intractable seizure disorders. In Hachinski V (ed): Challenges in Neurology. Philadelphia, FA Davis Co., 1992, pp 135–148.
8. Brown RD, Wiebers DO, Forbes G, et al: The natural history of unruptured intracranial arteriovenous malformations. J Neurosurg 68:352–357, 1988.
9. Cabral RJ, King TT, Scott DF: Epilepsy after two different neurosurgical approaches to the treatment of ruptured intracranial aneurysms. J Neurol Neurosurg Psychiatry 39:1052–1056, 1976.
10. Chopra JS, Banerjee AK: Primary intracranial sinovenous occlusions in youth and pregnancy. In Vinken PJ, Bruyn GW, Klawans HL (eds): Handbook of Clinical Neurology, vol 54. New York, Elsevier Publ Co, 1989, pp 425–452.
11. Clancy R, Malin S, Laraque D, et al: Focal motor seizures heralding stroke in full-term neonates. Am J Dis Child 139:601 606, 1985.
12. Cocito L, Favale E, Reni L: Epileptic seizures in cerebral arterial occlusive disease. Stroke 13:189–195, 1982.
13. Crawford PM, West CR, Shaw MDM, Chadwick DW: Cerebral arteriovenous malformations and epilepsy: Factors in the development of epilepsy. Epilepsia 27:270–275, 1986.
14. Daniele O, Mattaliano A, Tassinari CA, et al: Epileptic seizures and cerebrovascular disease. Acta Neurol Scand 80:17–22, 1989.
15. DeCarolis P, D'Alessandro R, Ferrara R, et al: Late seizures in patients with internal carotid and middle cerebral artery occlusive disease following ischemic events. J Neurol Neurosurg Psychiatry 47:1345–1347, 1984.
16. De Rueck J, Krahel N, Sieben G, et al: Epilepsy in patients with cerebral infarcts. J Neurol 224:101–109, 1980.
17. Dodge PR, Richardson EP, Victor M: Recurrent convulsive seizures as a sequel to cerebral infarction: A clinical and pathological study. Brain 77:610–638, 1954.
18. Elger CE, Speckmann EJ: Penicillin induced epileptic foci in the motor cortex: Vertical inhibition. Electroencephalogr Clin Neurophysiol 56:604–622, 1983.
19. Engel JP Jr: Terminology and classification. In Seizures and Epilepsy. Philadelphia, FA Davis Co, 1989, pp 3–10.
20. Engel JP Jr: Mechanisms of neuronal excitation and synchronization. In Seizures and Epilepsy. Philadelphia, FA Davis Co, 1989, pp 41–70.
21. Engel JP Jr: Differential diagnosis. In Seizures and Epilepsy. Philadelphia, FA Davis Co, 1989, pp 340–379.
22. Fentz V: Epileptic seizures in patients with cerebrovascular accidents (abstract). Nordisk Med 86:1023–1025, 1971.
23. Ferguson GG: Intracranial arterial aneurysms: A surgical perspective. In Vinken PJ, Bruyn GW, Klawans HL (eds): Handbook of Clinical Neurology, vol 55. New York, Elsevier Publ Co, 1989, pp 41–88.
24. Filipek PA, Krishnamoorthy KS, Davis KR, Kuehnle K: Focal cerebral infarction in the newborn: A distinct entity. Pediatr Neurol 3:141–147, 1987.
25. Franck G: Border zone ("watershed area") cerebral ischemia. Electroencephalogr Clin Neurophysiol 35(suppl):297–306, 1982.
26. Fults D, Kelly DL: Natural history of arteriovenous malformations of the brain: A clinical study. Neurosurgery 15:658–662, 1984.
27. Gates PC, Barnett HJM: Venous disease: Cortical veins and sinuses. In Barnett HJM, Stein BM, Mohr JP, Yatsu FM (eds): Stroke: Pathophysiology, Diagnosis and Management. New York, Churchill Livingstone, 1986, pp 731–743.
28. Gerosa MA, Cappellotto P, Licata C, et al: Cerebral arteriovenous malformations in children (56 cases). Childs Brain 8:356–371, 1981.

29. Gowers WR: Epilepsy and Other Chronic Convulsive Disorders. New York, Dover, 1964, p 104.
30. Gupta SR, Naheedy MH, Elias D, et al: Post infarction seizures: A clinical study. Stroke 19:1477–1481, 1988.
31. Harrison MJG: Clinical distinction of cerebral haemorrhage and cerebral infarction. Postgrad Med J 56:629–632, 1980.
32. Hart RG, Byer JA, Slaughter JR, et al: Occurrence and implications of seizures in subarachnoid hemorrhage due to ruptured intracranial aneurysms. Neurosurgery 8:417–421, 1981.
33. Hauser WA, Ramirez-Lassepas M, Rosenstein R: Risk for seizures and epilepsy following cerebrovascular insults. Epilepsia 25:666, 1984.
34. Hauser WA: Incidence and prevalence. In Hauser WA, Hesdorffer DC (eds): Epilepsy: Frequency, Causes and Consequences. New York, Demos, 1990, pp 2–3.
35. Heidrich R: Subarachnoid hemorrhage. In Vinken PJ, Bruyn GW (eds): Handbook of Clinical Neurology, vol 12. New York, American Elsevier, 1972, pp 68–204.
36. Heros RC, Zervas NT: Subarachnoid hemorrhage. Annu Rev Med 34:367–375, 1983.
37. Hildick-Smith M: Epilepsy in the elderly. Age Aging 3:203–208, 1974.
38. Holmes GL: The electroencephalogram as a predictor of seizures following cerebral infarction. Clin Electroencephalogr 11:83–86, 1980.
39. Jackson JH: Epileptiform convulsions from cerebral disease. In Taylor J, Holmes G, Walshe FMR (eds): Selected Writings of John Hughlings Jackson on Epilepsy and Epileptiform Convulsions, vol 1. London, Hodder and Stoughton Ltd, 1931, pp 330–340.
40. Kandel ER, Schwartz JH, Jessell TM: Principles of Neural Science: Hypothalamus, Limbic System, and Cerebral Cortex: Homeostasis and Arousal, 3rd ed. New York, Elsevier, 1991, p 732.
41. Kase CS, Williams JP, Wyatt DA, Mohr JP: Lobar intracerebral haematomas: Clinical and CT analysis of 22 cases. Neurology 32:1146–1150, 1982.
42. Kilpatrick CJ, Davis SM, Tress BM, et al: Epileptic seizures in acute stroke. Arch Neurol 47:157–160, 1990.
43. Kondziolka D, Humphreys RP, Hoffman JH, et al: Arteriovenous malformations of the brain in children: A forty year experience. Can J Neurol Sci 19:40–45, 1992.
44. Lanska MJ, Lanska DJ, Horwitz SJ, Aram DM: Presentation, clinical course, and outcome of childhood stroke. Pediatr Neurol 7:333–341, 1991.
45. Leblanc R, Feindel W, Ethier R: Epilepsy from cerebral arteriovenous malformations. Can J Neurol Sci 10:91–95, 1983.
46. Lesser RP, Lüders H, Dinner DS, Morris HH: Epileptic seizures due to thrombotic and embolic cerebrovascular disease in older patients. Epilepsia 26:622–630, 1985.
47. Levy SR, Abroms IF, Marshall PC, Rosquete EE: Seizures and cerebral infarction in the full-term newborn. Ann Neurol 17:366–370, 1985.
48. Levy RH, Unadkat JD: General principles: Drug absorption, distribution, and elimination. In Levy R, Mattson R, Meldrum B, et al (eds): Antiepileptic Drugs, 3rd ed. New York, Raven Press, 1989, p 16.
49. Lipton RB, Berger AR, Lesser ML, et al: Lobar vs thalamic and basal ganglion haemorrhage: Clinical and radiographic features. J Neurol 234:86–90, 1987.
50. Louis S, McDowell F: Epileptic seizures in non-embolic cerebral infarction. Arch Neurol 17:414–418, 1967.
51. Maertens P, Dyken PR: Inborn errors of metabolism: I. Neurologic degenerative diseases. In David RB (ed): Pediatric Neurology for the Clinician. Norwalk, CT, Appleton & Lange, 1992, pp 303–362.
52. Marquardsen J: The Natural History of Acute Cerebrovascular Disease. Copenhagen, Munksgaard, 1969, pp 1–192.
53. Matsumoto H, Ajmone Marsan C: Cortical cellular phenomena in experimental epilepsy: Interictal manifestations. Exp Neurol 9:286–304, 1964.
54. Matsumoto H, Ajmone Marsan C: Cortical cellular phenomena in experimental epilepsy: Ictal manifestations. Exp Neurol 9:305–326, 1964.
55. Mattson RH, Cramer JA, Collins JF, et al: Comparison of carbamazepine, phenobarbital, phenytoin, and primidone in partial and secondarily generalized tonic-clonic seizures. N Engl J Med 313:145–151, 1985.
56. Meyer JS, Charney JZ, Rivera VM, Mathew NT: Cerebral embolization: Prospective clinical analysis of 42 cases. Stroke 2:541–554, 1971.
57. Mohr JP, Caplan LR, Melski JW, et al: The Harvard cooperative stroke registry: A prospective registry. Neurology 28:754–762, 1978.
58. Ng SA, Hauser WA, Brust JCM, et al: Risk factors for adult onset first seizures. Ann Neurol 18:153, 1985.

59. Olsen TS, Hogenhaven H, Thage O: Epilepsy after stroke. Neurology 37:1209–1211, 1987.
60. Ondra SL, Troupp H, George ED, Schwab K: The natural history of arteriovenous malformations of the brain. Presented at the annual meeting of the Congress of Neurologic Surgeons, 1988.
61. Perret G, Nishioka H: Arteriovenous malformations: An analysis of 545 cases of cranio-cerebral arteriovenous malformations and fistulae reported to the Co-operative Study. J Neurosurg 25:467–490, 1966.
62. Perucca E, Richens A: General principles: Biotransformation. In Levy R, Mattson R, Meldrum B, et al (eds): Antiepileptic Drugs, 3rd ed. New York, Raven Press, 1989, p 30.
63. Prince DA, Connors BW: Mechanisms of interictal epileptogenesis. In Delgado-Escueta AV, Ward AA Jr, Woodbury DM, Porter RJ (eds): Advances in Neurology, vol 44. New York, Raven Press, 1986.
64. Prince DA, Wilder BJ: Control mechanisms in cortical epileptogenic foci: "Surround" inhibition. Arch Neurol 16:194–202, 1967.
65. Reynolds EH, Shorvon SD: Monotherapy or polytherapy for epilepsy. Epilepsia 22:1–10, 1981.
66. Richardson EP, Dodge PR: Epilepsy in cerebral vascular disease. Epilepsia 3:49–74, 1954.
67. Rose FC, Sarner M: Epilepsy after ruptured intracranial aneurysm. BMJ 1:18–21, 1965.
68. Schaafsma S: On the differential diagnosis between cerebral haemorrhage and infarction. J Neurol Sci 7:83–95, 1968.
69. Schmidt D: Two antiepileptic drugs for intractable epilepsy with complex-partial seizures. J Neurol Neurosurg Psychiatry 45:1119–1124, 1982.
70. Schmidt D: Reduction of two-drug therapy in intractable epilepsy. Epilepsia 24:368–376, 1983.
71. Schold C, Yaruell PR, Earnest MP: Origin of seizures in elderly patients. JAMA 238:1177–1178, 1977.
72. Seifer FP, Ignacio OJ: Seizures in patients over the age of 40: A general hospital study. J Ky Med Assoc 72:371–373, 1974.
73. Shinton RA, Zekulka AV, Gill GS, Beevers DG: The frequency of epilepsy preceding stroke: Case-control study in 230 patients. Lancet i:11–13, 1987.
74. Shinton RA, Gill JS, Melnick SC, et al: The frequency, characteristics and prognosis of epileptic seizures at the onset of stroke. J Neurol Neurosurg Psychiatry 51:273–276, 1988.
75. Shorvon SD, Gilliat RW, Cox TCS, Yu YL: Evidence of vascular disease from CT scanning in late onset epilepsy. J Neurol Neurosurg Psychiatry 47:225–230, 1984.
76. Sran SK, Baumann RJ: Outcome of neonatal strokes. Am J Dis Child 142:1086–1088, 1988.
77. Sundaram MBM, Chow F: Seizures associated with spontaneous subarachnoid hemorrhage. Can J Neurol Sci 13:229–231, 1986.
78. Sung C-Y, Chu N-S: Epileptic seizures in intracerebral hemorrhage. J Neurol Neurosurg Psychiatry 52:1273–1276, 1989.
79. Toole JF, Robinson MK, Mercuri M: Primary subarachnoid hemorrhage. In Vinken PJ, Bruyn GW, Klawans HL (eds): Handbook of Clinical Neurology, vol 55. New York, Elsevier Publ Co, 1989, pp 1–40.
80. Trauner DA, Mannino FL: Neurodevelopmental outcome after neonatal cerebrovascular accident. J Pediatr 108:459–461, 1986.
81. Troupin AS: Practical pharmacokinetics. In Robb JP (ed): Epilepsy Updated: Causes and Treatment. Chicago, Year Book, 1980, pp 101–117.
82. Uttley D: Subarachnoid hemorrhage. Br J Hosp Med 19:138–154, 1978.
83. Viitanen M, Eriksson S, Asplund K: Risk of recurrent stroke, myocardial infarction and epilepsy during long-term follow-up after stroke. Eur Neurol 28:227–231, 1988.
84. Walton JN: The electroencephalographic sequelae of spontaneous subarachnoid hemorrhage. Electroencephalogr Clin Neurophysiol 5:41–52, 1953.
85. Walton JN: Subarachnoid Hemorrhage. New York, Churchill Livingstone, 1956, p 59.
86. White PT, Bailey AA, Bickford RG: Epileptic disorders in the aged. Neurology 3:674–678, 1953.
87. Wilson CL, Isokawa-Akesson M, Babb TL, et al: A comparative view of local and interhemispheric limbic pathways in humans: An evoked potential analysis. In Engel J Jr, Ojemann GA, Luders HO, Williamson PD (eds): Fundamental Mechanisms of Human Brain Function. New York, Raven Press, 1987, pp 27–38.
88. Winn HR, Richardson AE, O'Brien W, Jane JA: The long term prognosis in untreated cerebral aneurysms: II. Late morbidity and mortality. Ann Neurol 4:418–426, 1978.
89. Yeh HS, Kashiwagi S, Tew JM, et al: Surgical management of epilepsy associated with cerebral arteriovenous malformations. J Neurosurg 72:216–223, 1990.
90. Yeh HS, Privitera M: Secondary epileptogenesis in humans with cerebral arteriovenous malformations. Epilepsia 30:683, 1989.

ROBERT W. TEASELL, MD, FRCPC
HILLEL M. FINESTONE, MDCM, FRCPC
LINDA GREENE-FINESTONE, MSc, RPDt

6. DYSPHAGIA AND NUTRITION FOLLOWING STROKE

From the University of
  Western Ontario
  and
Department of Physical Medicine
  and Rehabilitation
  and
Clinical Nutrition Services
University Hospital
London, Ontario
Canada

Reprint requests to:
Dr. Robert W. Teasell
University Hospital
339 Windermere Road
London, Ontario N6A 5A5
Canada

Problems with dysphagia and nutrition following stroke are being increasingly recognized. Although swallowing and nutritional deficits are more prominent in the early stages following a stroke, they can extend into that period of time when rehabilitation efforts are over and the patient has returned home. Early recognition of these difficulties allows treating clinicians to intervene to significantly reduce future morbidity.

DYSPHAGIA/ASPIRATION FOLLOWING STROKE

Dysphagia is simply defined as difficulty with swallowing. The incidence of dysphagia following acute stroke ranges from 25%[20] to 45%[19] and is higher among elderly stroke victims.[7,19] It can occur following brainstem, bilateral, and even unilateral hemispheric lesions.[11,45] Of those patients with dysphagia following stroke, approximately one-third will aspirate. Of those stroke patients who aspirate, 40% will be silent aspirators.[27,30] Pneumonia is a common sequelae of aspiration and contributes significantly to morbidity and mortality.[30,45] Hence, detection of aspiration, both silent and audible, is very important in the prevention of pneumonia, malnutrition, and dehydration.[18,27,34,44]

Normal Swallowing Mechanism

According to Bach et al.,[5] swallowing involves a series of complex events which reflect oral and pharyngeal anatomical structures,[13] multiple neural mechanisms,[35] features of the food bolus,[12] and specific patient-related factors. Normal swallowing consists of three stages: the oral, pharyngeal, and esophageal stages. Food is first manipulated in the mouth, masticated if necessary, and pulled together into a cohesive bolus before swallowing.[45] The **oral stage** is voluntary. In the oral phase, the tongue propels food posteriorly until the swallowing reflex is triggered as the bolus passes the anterior faucial arches.[45] The pharyngeal and esophageal stages are involuntary. In the **pharyngeal phase,** the swallow reflex is triggered and moves the material through the pharynx.[45] This is a rapid process, lasting approximately 1 second, which provides protection for the airway and propulsion of the bolus into the esophagus.[34] Pharyngeal peristalsis carries the bolus through the pharynx to the cricopharyngeal sphincter. Elevation, anterior displacement, and closure of the larynx prevent food from entering the airway. The cricopharyngeal sphincter then relaxes, and food passes from the pharynx into esophagus.[18] In the **esophageal phase,** esophageal peristalsis moves the food bolus into the stomach.[45] The cricopharyngeus muscle again contracts to prevent reflux.[18]

Pathophysiology

Aspiration occurs in approximately one-third of stroke patients with dysphagia. Contrary to popular opinion, aspiration is not confined to brainstem or bilateral hemispheric cerebral lesions.[27] This erroneous concept arose because of the bilateral upper neuron innervation of the lower cranial nerves involved in swallowing; it was felt that the bilateral innervation would allow sufficient compensation to occur following a unilateral cerebral hemispheric lesion. However, recent studies have clearly shown that dysphagia and aspiration can occur in unilateral cerebral hemispheric lesions.[1,6,11,19,40,45] Alberts et al.[1] showed that even small-vessel (lacunar) strokes can lead to swallowing problems. Teasell et al.[43] have even suggested that the higher incidence of dysphagia/aspiration in bilateral strokes is the result of the cumulative effects of two unilateral lesions and may not be a unique complication of bilateral lesions. These studies suggest that swallowing function may be distributed throughout the brain.[1]

Most swallowing problems are due to dysfunction in the pharyngeal phase of swallowing, with a delayed swallowing reflex being the most common abnormality. Pharyngeal stasis is seen in the valleculae or pyriform sinuses and may relate to pharyngeal paresis, reduced pharyngeal peristalsis, or unilateral pharyngeal paralysis.[11] Aspiration is defined as "entry of material into the airway below the level of the true vocal cords." Aspiration most often results from a functional disturbance in the pharyngeal phase of swallowing related to reduced laryngeal closure or pharyngeal paresis.

Diagnosis of Dysphagia/Aspiration

In making the diagnosis of dysphagia/aspiration, it is important to maintain a high level of suspicion. The diagnosis of aspiration should be suspected when the patient has a subjective complaint of trouble swallowing, an abnormal chest radiograph, congested voice quality, delay in voluntary initiation of the swallow reflex, and coughing during or after swallowing.[27] Where aspiration is suspected, video fluoroscopic modified barium swallow (VMBS) is considered the "gold standard" test in confirming the diagnosis.[42] The VMBS not only establishes the presence and extent of aspiration but also may establish the etiology or mechanism of the swallowing disorder.

VMBS and Silent Aspiration

The VMBS examines the oral and pharyngeal phases of swallowing. The patient must have sufficient cognitive and physical skills to undergo testing.[5] The patient is placed in the sitting position in a chair designed to simulate the typical mealtime posture.[5] Radiopaque materials of various consistencies are tried; thin and thick liquid barium and barium-impregnated pudding, mashed potatoes, and cookies are routinely used.[5] Various aspects of oral, laryngeal, and pharyngeal involvement are noted during the radiographic examination (Table 1).[5] The VMBS is followed by a chest radiograph to document any barium which may have been aspirated into the tracheobronchial tree.[5]

Splaingard and Hutchins[42] studied 107 patients, the majority of whom had suffered strokes, who were admitted to a rehabilitation center and subsequently referred for swallowing evaluation. Each patient underwent a careful clinical bedside assessment including a standardized diagnostic feeding routine. Aspiration was suspected if during feeding the clinician noted signs of respiratory distress, choking, cough, food-tinged secretions in patients with tracheostomy, wet-hoarse vocal quality, or the appearance of wet-hoarse vocal quality. Patients were then studied within 72 hours of clinical examination by VMBS performed by individuals blinded to the results of the clinical assessment. Of the total patient population, 43 (40%) aspirated at least one consistency of food during VMBS. Bedside evaluation identified only 18 (42%) of those patients who aspirated on VMBS. Of the 25 patients who aspirated on VMBS but were not reported to be aspirators on bedside clinical assessment, 21 (or 20% of the entire sample) did not cough or change clinically at the time aspiration was noted during VMBS. The patients were felt to be "silent aspirators." Horner and Massey[27] and Logemann[30] also found that VMBS identified "silent aspirators" in 38% and 40%, respectively, of clinically dysphagic stroke patients.

Silent aspiration is defined as "penetration of food below the level of the true vocal cords, without cough or any outward sign of difficulty."[29] It should be

TABLE 1.   Radiologic Evaluation During VMBS*

Oral Phase
  Lips: closure
  Tongue: anterior and posterior motion with consonants; motion and coordination during
    transport, and manipulation of bolus
  Soft palate: evaluation and retraction with consonants
  Jaw: motion
  Oral cavity: pocketing

Pharyngeal Phase
  Swallow: delay, absence
  Peristalsis: residue in valleculae, pyriform sinuses, nasopharyngeal regurgitation

Laryngeal Function
  Elevation of larynx
  Penetration into laryngeal vestibule
  Aspiration
  Cough: presence, delay, effectiveness
  Vocal cord function

Post-Examination Chest Radiograph
  Chronic changes
  Presence of barium in valleculae, pyriform sinuses, tracheobroncheal tree, lungs

* From Bach DB, Pouget S, Belle K, et al: An integrated team approach to the management of patients. J Allied Health (Fall):459–468, 1989; with permission.

suspected in the stroke patient with recurrent lower respiratory infections, chronic congestion, low-grade fever, or leukocytosis.[14]

What is apparent from these studies and clinical impressions is that the VMBS is the only accurate means of assessing the pharyngeal phase of swallowing and the presence or absence of aspiration. As such it represents the "gold standard" of diagnosis. At the present time there are no data in the literature which indicate how long "silent aspirators" continue to aspirate or whether it leads to significant future complications.

Clinical Studies

There are numerous studies looking at dysphagia and/or aspiration in patients who have suffered a cerebrovascular insult. They demonstrate a great deal of variability in their clinical findings.

Veis and Logemann[45] studied 38 cerebrovascular accident patients referred for VMBS. The majority were seen less than 1 month following their stroke, and all were seen no later than 4 months following their stroke. Eighteen of the 38 had prior strokes. Eighty-two percent of the patients studied had delayed triggering of the swallowing reflex, 58% had reduced pharyngeal peristalsis, and 50% had reduced lingual control. Thirty-two percent of patients aspirated on VMBS because of disorders in the pharyngeal phase of swallowing, most notably a delayed swallowing reflex.

Gordon et al.[19] looked at dysphagia in an unselected group of 91 consecutive patients who had suffered an acute stroke. VMBS was not performed, and dysphagia, defined as an inability to drink 15 mL of water or choking more than once while attempting to drink 15 mL of water on two occasions, was found in 41 of the 91 acute stroke patients (45%). Patients with dysphagia were significantly older than those without. Dysphagia in those patients who survived the stroke lasted a mean of only 8.5 days. No attempt was made to look at aspiration apart from noting dysphagic patients did not experience a significant increase in chest infections when compared to the nondysphagic patients.

Barer[7] found that after evaluation of 357 patients within 48 hours of the onset of their stroke, 30% had swallowing impairments. Patients were evaluated using a subjective scale measuring the difficulty a patient had swallowing 10 mL of water. Barer determined that at 1 month, only 6 of 277 (2.2%) patients had swallowing problems and at 6 months, only 1 of 248 (0.4%) patients had difficulty. In this study VMBS was not used, and therefore cases of "silent aspiration" were likely missed. Some of the strokes were likely "minor" and these patients would be less likely to aspirate. What is notable about this study is that the author looked at all cases diagnosed as "stroke" and not just those selected out through their referral for swallowing assessment. However, even with that taken into account, the number of patients with reported dysphagia still appears to be quite low.

Chen et al.[11] studied 46 consecutive patients with cerebrovascular disease who were referred for VMBS assessment of swallowing because of concerns about dysphagia/aspiration. All VMBS assessments were conducted within 1 month of the stroke onset. All patients had some swallowing difficulties on VMBS, although only 11% were felt to have severe dysfunction. Twenty-four of 46 patients (52%) aspirated during VMBS testing. Many of the patients had unilateral cortical or subcortical strokes. Pharyngeal stasis in the valleculae or pyriform sinuses was noted in the majority of patients, but there was no pattern, i.e., asymmetric stasis, which correlated with the site or side of the cerebral lesion. Unfortunately, this study does not indicate the population (number and severity) of stroke patients from which the 46 patients were drawn.

Teasell et al.[43] performed a retrospective study of stroke patients admitted to a tertiary care rehabilitation unit. Of 255 patients with strokes severe enough to require admission to the rehab unit, 54 patients underwent VMBS because of concern about aspiration. Forty-two of these patients demonstrated evidence of aspiration of thin liquids on VMBS, which was performed an average of 5 weeks following the onset of the stroke. Of the 42 patients who demonstrated VMBS-documented aspiration, 7 demonstrated recovery on the follow-up VMBS, while 11 were felt to have recovered significantly clinically to not require a repeat VMBS. Therefore, on average 6 weeks after the initial VMBS, 43% of patients with aspiration improved. Also significant is the fact that at least 23 patients were still aspirating (out of the total of 255 patients) at least thin liquids on VMBS an average of 2.5 months after their stroke.

Aspiration and Stroke Location

As mentioned previously, dysphagia and aspiration post-stroke have generally been associated with brainstem, unilateral, and bilateral hemispheric strokes. The studies of Teasell,[43] Veis,[45] Gordon,[19] and Barer[6] all reported a higher incidence of dysphagia/aspiration among left hemispheric patients when compared to right, although in none of these studies was this difference considered significant. Interestingly, in the study of Teasell et al.,[43] 6 of 25 (24%) of bilateral stroke patients aspirated, suggesting that the effects of bilateral strokes may simply be the additive effects of two unilateral events (i.e., 9.9% left + 12.1% right = 22% vs. 24% for bilateral events). Unfortunately, the fact that only those patients suspected of aspirating underwent VMBS assessment and not the entire cohort makes this conclusion suspect. Brainstem strokes demonstrated a much higher incidence of stroke, i.e., 15 of 38 (39.5%).

MANAGEMENT OF DYSPHAGIA/ASPIRATION

On VMBS those patients who aspirate over 10% of the test bolus[30] or who have severe oral and/or pharyngeal motility problems[34] are considered at high risk of aspiration and subsequent pneumonia. Treatment of high-risk aspirators involves nonoral or tube (NG, G, or J tube) feedings. The goal is prevention of aspiration pneumonia and maintenance of adequate nutrition and hydration. The VMBS is repeated in 3 to 6 months if there is continuing concern about aspiration.

Those patients who aspirate less than 10% of the test bolus on VMBS or who have difficulty with only high volumes of thin liquids are considered at mild to moderate risk of aspiration.[30] In these cases, oral feedings may be appropriate. Before deciding on oral feedings, other factors must also be taken into consideration such as the patient's respiratory status, the effectiveness of airway clearance, along with the type and amount of aspiration.[5]

Unfortunately, the literature does not provide a clear indication on how serious the risks of aspiration are. Such a study may well prove to be unethical. Although aspirating more than 10% of the test bolus is considered an indication for non-oral feeding, we have no clear idea on the actual risks present with oral feedings for this group of patients. There is some evidence that dietary modification can affect the incidence of aspiration pneumonia,[21] although this has not been established in a properly controlled trial; again, such a study may well be unethical.

Many stroke patients, especially those with right hemispheric lesions, are very impulsive and may attempt to eat and swallow at too fast a rate. Therefore, close supervision with frequent cuing is necessary in these cases.[34] Special techniques, such as compensatory head and neck postures,[30] double swallowing, or coughing after swallowing[27] may help to prevent aspiration. Therapy may be recommended to improve the oral strength and functioning of the oral and laryngeal structures.[5] Heimlich[23] anecdotally reported successful rehabilitation of swallowing in 7 patients following stroke. All patients had been on tube-feedings for between 5 months to 3.9 years. A normal diet was restored in 5 patients, and 2 patients improved but were not able to resume a regular diet due to their underlying condition. Wood and Ehrforth[48] reported that 15 of 27 (55.6%) patients treated by a dysphagia rehabilitation team became independent feeders, although there was no control group.

Long-term Consequences

The immediate consequences of dysphagia/aspiration in stroke patients are more apparent then the long-term consequences. Teasell et al.[43] reported that a minimum 23 of 255 patients admitted to a stroke rehabilitation unit showed evidence of aspiration on a second VMBS performed an average of 11 weeks post-stroke onset. Data regarding dysphagia/aspiration 1 to 2 years post-stroke are not available, in part because of the ethics of performing VMBS studies, which impose a relatively high dose of radiation to the head and neck region, in a large cohort of clinically asymptomatic patients.

There are certain groups who remain at high risk of aspiration post-stroke. These include those with large brainstem and significant bilateral hemispheric (pseudobulbar palsy) strokes. It is these groups who are likely to have the greatest degree of difficulty maintaining adequate nutrition and hydration and avoiding aspiration pneumonia. The latter problem is particularly true if the patient has significant diabetes with immunocompromization or if he or she has underlying lung problems such as chronic obstructive pulmonary disease. These patients may not tolerate even small amounts of aspirate without problems.

In those cases where the patient is having obvious problems maintaining adequate nutrition and hydration, where concern is expressed regarding frequent choking while eating, or in the case of recurrent respiratory infection, a VMBS should be performed. Other factors such as a new stroke, depression and lung cancer, or unrelated respiratory infections must also be considered. Where the VMBS shows swallowing difficulties, a change to nonoral feedings or a more manageable oral diet should be made. Dysphagia diets and nonoral feeding are discussed later in the chapter.

NUTRITION

Scope of the Problem

Protein-calorie malnutrition has been reported to occur commonly in municipal hospitals on both medical and surgical services.[10,26] It is well accepted that various disease processes and physiological stress can lead to malnutrition.[9] Protein-calorie malnutrition is a major cause of acquired immune dysfunction[36] and has been implicated as a contributory factor in cardiac insufficiency[39] and poor wound healing.

Newmark et al.[37] studied 49 consecutive patients admitted to a general rehabilitation ward. They collected data that included mean calorie and protein intake, weight change, alterations in appetite, feeding problems, anthropometric data, and laboratory data which included serum albumin and antigen skin tests. Fifteen of the 49 patients were diagnosed with a cerebral vascular accident. Five of these stroke patients were of normal nutritional status, 3 were obese, and 9 had significant malnutrition in the form of kwashiorkor (protein malnutrition) or marasmus (protein-calorie malnutrition). Only 15 of all 49 patients assessed were of normal nutritional status at the time of the rehabilitation admission to the acute care hospital.

Other studies have looked exclusively at the nutritional status of stroke patients.[3,4] Poor nutritional status was evident in 16% of the patients on admission to an acute care hospital. Changes in nutritional status did occur and were partly age-related; male stroke patients over the age of 74 experienced a greater deterioration in nutritional status over a 4-week period than did younger patients. The medical factor most closely associated with poor nutritional status during the stay in hospital was infection; the close relationship between undernutrition, impaired cell-mediated immune response, and clinically manifested infections is well recognized.[33] In those patients whose hospital stay was greater than 20 days, the development of undernutrition was most closely related to low self-care performance during the first week in hospital, poor nutritional status on admission, and the male sex.[4] A higher proportion of patients with right-arm motor deficits than patients with left-arm motor deficits suffered from poor nutritional status 3 weeks after admission.

There are no long-term studies describing patients' nutritional status following a stroke. Anecdotal experience, along with evidence on acute stroke patients cited,[3,4] suggests that malnutrition, occurring months to years after a stroke has occurred, is a potential problem. Studies of the head-injured population indicate that in the acute phase, metabolic rates are increased to a mean of 140% of the predicted energy expenditure for noninjured patients. Protein degradation exceeds protein synthesis, and in severe cases, approximately 25% of available protein contributes to energy expenditure.[49] Developing a nutritional assessment and treatment strategy for the stroke patient must be considered an important component of acute rehabilitation and long-term care of the stroke patient.

Factors Contributing to Eating Difficulties and Nutritional Impairment in the Stroke Patient

Various stroke syndromes produce neurologic deficits which, as outlined in other chapters, can include diminished level of consciousness, alteration in mentation, a reduced swallowing or gag reflex, paresis or paralysis of the extremities, disorientation, apraxia, agnosia, right and left disorientation, and neglect. Any number of these deficits, along with other medical, social, psychological, and aging factors, may have a negative impact on the ability of the patient to feed him or herself and thus meeting his or her nutritional needs may be difficult to achieve. These potential problems concerning the act of eating are shown in Table 2.

Nutritional Assessment of the Stroke Patient

In a nutritional assessment, nutritional deficiencies or excesses can be identified and an interventional strategy planned. This is particularly important in stroke patients with concurrent health problems that require dietary modifications such as diabetes mellitus, hypertension, renal or cardiac disease.[41]

TABLE 2.   Factors Contributing to Eating Difficulties in the Stroke Patient

Deficits or Factors	Comments
Hemiplegia or paresis	If dominant hand affected, eating may be tedious. Problems with chewing and swallowing.
Hemisensory abnormalities	Limited ability to adequately visualize and eat meals. Pocketing of food in oral cavity.
Dysphagia	See text.
Motor apraxia	Difficulty performing learned tasks can include inability to feed oneself.
Altered mental status	May affect food intake of dietary selection.
Depression	Common complication of stroke.[47] Leads to anorexia, weight loss and changed eating habits.
Medications	Nonsteroidal antiinflammatory drugs lead to nausea/heartburn. Anticholinergics (antidepressants and oxybutinin) lead to anorexia, nausea and dry mouth.
Aging	Decreased sense of smell and taste.[2] Diminished saliva production. Loss of teeth. Improperly fitting dentures (frequent occurrence following stroke). Elderly may resort to less nutritious soft meals.[46]
Social	Lack of socialization may lead to less oral intake (meals often social events). Embarrassment of eating post-stroke may lead to diminished oral intake.

Anthropometric measures such as height, weight, skin-fold thicknesses, and midarm circumference are used to estimate fat and protein stores. Biochemical measures such as albumin, tranferrin, and the urine creatinine height index can help identify visceral and somatic protein undernutrition. Total lymphocyte count and the less-routine delayed cutaneous hypersensitivity can assess immunocompetence, a factor which is adversely affected by malnutrition. Measurements of nutritional status are most effective when used in combination.[17] Dietary intake can be measured by means of calorie counts, direct observation, or 24-hour recalls. They may reveal deficits in intakes when compared to the US Recommended Dietary Allowances (RDA)[15] or the Canadian Recommended Nutrient Intakes (RNI).[22]

Several aspects of the nutritional assessment of the stroke patient have already been described in an earlier issue of *Physical Medicine & Rehabilitation: State of the Art Reviews*[41] and are comprehensively described in texts such as that of Gibson.[17] Each test has its limitations and indications for use. While there are differing opinions regarding which combinations of tests should make up the nutritional assessment,[17] the assessment provides the dietitian with a measurement of the baseline nutritional status and a means to evaluate the efficiency of nutritional support.[5]

Nutritional Intervention

Diet after Stroke.   The diet must meet the nutritional needs of the patient and take into account the patient's medical condition as well as preexisting disease requiring dietary modification. Food preferences, ethnic background, and activity level must also be considered. During the initial phase of the stroke, fluid may need to be administered intravenously for adequate hydration. However, the standard 5% dextrose solution provides minimal nutrition (only 340 kcal/2 L), and enteral feeding in the form of oral and/or tube feedings with liquid complete nutritional formulas should begin as soon as possible.[16] Weight loss may result from the dietary interruption for diagnostic tests. A study by Baugh[8] revealed that calories lost due to diagnostic tests were not replaced in 90% of patients on a rehabilitation ward.

Dysphagia Diet. In tertiary care centers, a swallowing team may be available to assess the stroke patient. Based on the team's recommendations, the dietitian arranges for the appropriate dysphagia diet. In smaller centers, the implementation of the dysphagia diet should be done in consultation with the dietitian. Special dysphagia diets are based upon three distinct consistencies: soft, pureed, and thick fluids. A dysphagia soft diet excludes all hard, small, and stringy food particles, and there are four consistencies of meat in the soft diet: soft, chopped, minced, and ground.[5] A pureed diet has the consistency of pudding and is generally the easiest to swallow.[45] A thick fluid diet eliminates all thin liquids. Alternatives to thin liquids such as jelled water or liquids may be required. High-energy, high-protein foods are frequently recommended, as oral intake is often limited.[38]

Suggested complete nutritional formulas include those that are high in protein and fiber. In this regime, food textures and consistencies are modified. Liquids may have to be "thickened" with various commercial products for safe swallowing. The dysphagia evaluation should be repeated, and as the patient either improves or deteriorates, the dysphagia diet is then altered accordingly.[5] Food with a firmer texture is easier to move around the mouth and swallow.[16,50] The dietitian can recommend appropriate food choices.

Liquid nutritional supplements (i.e., Osmolite HN, Jevity) can be used as between-meal nourishments or meal replacements. Eating six small "meals" can be less fatiguing for a patient than three large ones. It is extremely important to counsel the stroke patient's family that adequate time to eat or be fed be provided. Dyspraxia, poor motivation, and depression, even in the presence of good motor power, can lead to slowness in initiating eating. Guidelines for the dysphagia diet are found in Table 3.

Non Oral or Tube-Feeding. As mentioned previously, if a patient aspirates more than 10% of food swallowed of all consistencies, then he or she is not appropriate for oral feeding.[30] As well, if the oral and pharyngeal stage of swallowing (radiographic study or larynx moving up in the throat indicates completion) cannot be completed in 10 seconds for every consistency of food tried, then the patient will probably tire easily and not receive adequate oral nutrition. In the latter case, patients may still feed by mouth, but nonoral feeding may be needed to supplement the oral intake.[30]

TABLE 3. Dysphagia Diet: General Guidelines for the Patient*

---

1. Follow American or Canadian Dietetic Association guidelines for food selection.
2. Determine, with the therapist, the best head and body posture for swallowing.
3. Sit upright during food ingestions and do not lie down for at least 15–30 minutes afterwards.
4. Put food in the middle of the mouth or on the unaffected side, if applicable.
5. Concentrate and chew food slowly. Ingest foods in small mouthfulls (½ to 1 teaspoon).
6. Avoid washing food down with liquids.
7. Use liquid thickeners if thin liquids are to be avoided. The dietitian can advise on this.
8. Check the form of medication being used (e.g., liquid, crushed, or whole pills) to ensure that it complies with the swallowing regimen.

---

* Data from ODA–OHA.[38]

In our institution, gastrojejunostomy tubes (GJ-tubes) inserted percutaneously are very effective. They prevent regurgitation and aspiration and present few management problems. Commercial formulas, easy to handle and bacteriologically safe, will provide adequate protein, vitamins, minerals, and even fiber through the tube.[16] The GJ-tube can periodically become blocked. Regular flushing of tubes with 25 to 50 mL of warm water and ensuring that medications are adequately crushed or prepared prior to entering the tube is the first step in reducing the frequency of blocking. We have found that a solution of one tablet of sodium bicarbonate (300 mg) and one capsule of pancrealipase works well to unblock the GJ-tube when blockage does occur.[31] Local infection is occasionally a problem and is managed by increased dressing changes and the use of antibiotic ointment. Peritonitis or other associated problems are rare except at the time when the tube is initially inserted.

Tube-feeds may be administered either continuously over 24 hours, by bolus, or, the authors' preference, by intermittent schedule. Tube feeding at night offers the advantages of not interfering with the patients' therapy schedule early in rehabilitation or with general lifestyle after discharge. There is evidence that energy from feeds administered continuously are used more efficiently than those administered by bolus.[24,25] However, continuous 24-hour/day feeds are time-consuming and would mainly be recommended over bolus for the patient with severe gastrointestinal motility disorder, the diabetic with severe gastroparesis, and the malnourished comatose patient with hypertonic feeding demands.

If the repeat dysphagia evaluation reveals that some swallowing is possible in a patient who has previously been on tube-feedings, then the tube-feeding should only be removed when it is demonstrated by calorie counts that the patient is orally consuming sufficient quantities of foods to meet the RNI[22] or RDA[15] or the requirements for special needs.

In those patients who must remain on nonoral feeding, we have had considerable success discharging them home. GJ-tube feedings can be managed by the patients or their caregivers with some practice. A public health nurse or home care worker can initially monitor the patient at home. Several of our stroke patients have successfully managed feeding pumps at home for 2 or more years.

CONCLUSIONS

Dysphagia is a common consequence of stroke. Dysphagia is associated with a variety of complications including aspiration pneumonia and malnutrition/dehydration. Aspiration, which is often clinically "silent," can be reliably detected using VMBS studies. For those patients who are felt to be at high risk of aspiration, special diets and specific compensatory feeding techniques or non-oral tube feedings may be necessary.

Malnutrition has been identified as a potential problem in the stroke patient. The treating physician must be able to identify the wide-ranging physical and cognitive factors which can contribute to nutritional impairment. The performance of a nutritional assessment includes the collection of appropriate dietary, biochemical and anthropometric measures as well as evaluation of swallowing status. Subsequent diet therapy for the stroke patient may include modification of food consistencies and/or enteral feeding. While some issues apply particularly to the acute stroke patient, principles apply for months and years after the initial stroke event.

REFERENCES

1. Alberts MJ, Horner J, Gray L, Brazer SR: Aspiration after stroke: Lesion analysis by brain MRI. Dysphagia 7:170–173, 1992.
2. Arey LB, Tremaine MJ, Monzingo FL: The numerical and topographical relations of taste buds to human circumvallate papillae throughout the lifespan. Anat Rec 64:9, 1935.
3. Axelsson K, Asplund K, Norberg A, Alafuzoff I: Nutritional status in patients with acute stroke. Acta Med Scand 224:217–224, 1988.
4. Axelsson K, Asplund K, Norberg A, Eriksson S: Eating problems and nutritional status during hospital stay of patients with severe stroke. J Am Diet Assoc 89:1092–1096, 1989.
5. Bach DB, Pouget S, Belle K, et al: An integrated team approach to the management of patients. J Allied Health (Fall):459–468, 1989.
6. Barer DH: Lower cranial nerve motor function in unilateral vascular lesions of the cerebral hemisphere. BMJ 289:1622, 1984.
7. Barer DH: The natural history and functional consequences of dysphagia after hemispheric stroke. J Neurol Neurosurg Psychiatry 52:236–241, 1989.
8. Baugh E: Actions to improve nutrition care on a general rehabilitation unit. J Am Diet Assoc 85:1632–1634, 1985.
9. Bernard MA, Jacobs DO, Rombeau JL: Nutritional Assessment in Nutritional and Metabolic Support of Hospitalized Patients. Philadelphia, WB Saunders Co., 1986.
10. Bistrian BR, Blackburn GL, Vitale J, et al: Prevalence of malnutrition in general medical patients. JAMA 235:1567–1570, 1976.
11. Chen MYM, Ott DJ, Peele VN, Gelfand DW: Oropharynx in patients with cerebrovascular disease: Evaluation with videofluoroscopy. Radiology 176:641–643, 1990.
12. Coster ST, Schwarz WH: Rheology and the swallow-safe bolus. Dysphagia 1(3):113–118, 1987.
13. Donner MW, Bosma JF, Robertson DL: Anatomy and physiology of the pharynx. Gastrointest Radiol 10:196–212, 1985.
14. Elliott J: Swallowing disorders in the elderly: A guide to diagnosis and treatment. Geriatrics 43:95, 1988.
15. Food and Nutrition Board, National Research Council: Recommended Dietary Allowances, 10th ed. Washington, DC, National Academy Press, 1989.
16. Gastineau CF: Nutrition and the stroke patient. In Dialogues in Nutrition. Bloomfield, NJ, Health Learning Systems Inc., 1979.
17. Gibson R: Principles of Nutritional Assessment. New York, Oxford University Press, 1990.
18. Glickstein J (ed): Feeding and swallowing problems in the elderly: An interdisciplinary approach. Focus Geriatr Care Rehabil 2:1989.
19. Gordon C, Hewer RL, Wade DT: Dysphagia in acute stroke. BMJ 295:411–414, 1987.
20. Groher ME, Bukatman R: The prevalence of swallowing disorders in two teaching hospitals. Dysphagia 1:3–6, 1986.
21. Groher ME: Bolus management and aspiration pneumonia in patients with pseudobulbar dysphagia. Dysphagia 1:215–216, 1987.
22. Health and Welfare Canada: Nutrition Recommendations, Supply and Services Canada, 1990.
23. Heimlich HJ: Rehabilitation of swallowing after stroke. Ann Otol Rhinol Laryngol 92:357–359, 1983.
24. Heymsfield S, Hill J, Evert M, et al: Energy expenditure during continuous intragastric infusion of fuel. Am J Clin Nutr 45:526, 1987.
25. Heymsfield S, Casper K: Continuous nasogastric feeding: Bioenergetic and metabolic response during recovery from semistarvation. Am J Clin Nutr 97:900, 1988.
26. Hill GL, Blackett RL, Pickford I, et al: Malnutrition in surgical patients: An unrecognized problem. Lancet i:689, 1977.
27. Horner J, Massey EW: Silent aspiration following stroke. Neurology 38:317–319, 1988.
28. Johnson ER, McKenzie SW, Rosenquist CJ, et al: Dysphagia following stroke: Quantitative evaluation of pharyngeal transit times. Arch Phys Med Rehabil 73:419–423, 1992.
29. Linden P, Siebens AA:: Dysphagia: Predicting laryngeal penetration. Arch Phys Med Rehabil 64:281–284, 1983.
30. Logemann JA: Evaluation and Treatment of Swallowing Disorders. San Diego, CA, College-Hill Press, 1983.
31. Marcuard SP, Stegall KL, Trogdon S: Clearing obstructed feeding tubes. J Parent Enteral Nutr 31:81–83, 1989.
32. Meadows JC: Dysphagia in unilateral cerebral lesions. J Neurol Neurosurg Psychiatry 36:853–860, 1973.
33. Meakins JL, Pietsch JB, Bubenick O, et al: Delayed hypersensitivity: Indicator of acquired failure of host defense in sepsis and trauma. Ann Surg 186:241–250, 1970.

34. Milazzo LS, Bouchard J, Lund DA: The swallowing process: Effects of aging and stroke. Phys Med Rehabil State Art Rev 3:489–499, 1989.

35. Miller AJ: Neurophysiological basis of swallowing. Dysphagia 1:91–100, 1986.

36. Mullin TJ, Kirkpatrick JR: The effect of nutritional support on immune competency in patients suffering from trauma, sepsis, or malignant disease. Surgery 610–615, 1981.

37. Newmark SR, Sublett D, Black J, Gelles R: Nutritional assessment in a rehabilitation unit. Arch Phys Med Rehabil 62:279–282, 1981.

38. Ontario Dietetic Association and Ontario Hospital Association: Oral-Pharyngeal Dysphagia Diet in Nutritional Care Manual. Toronto, Ontario Hospital Association, 1989, pp 483–487.

39. Pittman JG, Cohen P: The pathogenesis of cardiac cachexia. N Engl J Med 271:403, 1964.

40. Robbins J, Levine RL: Swallowing after unilateral stroke of the cerebral cortex: Preliminary experience. Dysphagia 3:11–17, 1988.

41. Signore J, Erickson RV: Nutritional assessment of the stroke patient. Phys Med Rehabil State Art Rev 3:501–518, 1989.

42. Splaingard ML, Hutchins B, Sulton LD, Chaudhuri G: Aspiration in rehabilitation patients: Videofluoroscopy vs bedside clinical assessment. Arch Phys Med Rehab 69:637–640, 1988.

43. Teasell R, Bach D, MacRae M: Prevalence and recovery of aspiration post stroke: A retrospective analysis. Dysphagia (in press).

44. Tobin MJ: Aspiration pneumonia. In Dantzker DR (ed): Cardiopulmonary Critical Care. New York, Grune & Stratton, 1986.

45. Veis S, Logemann J: Swallowing disorders in persons with cerebrovascular accidents. Arch Phys Med Rehabil 66:373–374, 1985.

46. Wayler AH: Effects of age and dentition status on measures of food acceptability. J Gerontol 37:294–299, 1982.

47. Weintraub RJ, Karamouz N, Askinazi C, Finkelstein S: Antidepressant treatment of depressed stroke patients and the implications for rehabilitation. Arch Phys Med Rehabil 65:618, 1984.

48. Wood PL, Ehrforth JW: Systemic management of neurogenic dysphagia within a comprehensive rehabilitation setting. Arch Phys Med Rehabil 65:661, 1984.

49. Young B, Ott L, Norton J, et al: Metabolic and nutritional sequelae in the non-steroid treated head injury patient. J Neurosurg 17:784–791, 1985.

50. Zimmerman JE, Oder LA: Swallowing dysfunction in acutely ill patients. Phys Ther 61:1755–1763, 1981.

MICHAEL JOHN BORRIE, MBCHB, FRCPC

7. URINARY INCONTINENCE AFTER STROKE

From the Division of Geriatric
   Medicine
Department of Medicine
University of Western Ontario
   and
Continence Clinic and Continence
   Outreach Program
Regional Geriatric Program
Parkwood Hospital

Reprint requests to:
Michael John Borrie, MBChB,
   FRCPC
Division of Geriatric Medicine
Parkwood Hospital
801 Commissioners Road East
London, Ontario N6C 5J1
Canada

Urinary incontinence following stroke is common and compounds the physical and psychological insult of the neurologic deficit. It has a negative impact on morale and self-esteem. When incontinence persists, it compromises rehabilitation, will influence discharge location, and places undue stress on caregivers at home.[18] Remaining or becoming dry is an important positive predictor of discharge within 6 months after stroke.[3] Incontinence following stroke receives varying attention[5,22,32] or may be ignored.[7]

Following stroke, 51 to 60% of patients will have urinary incontinence.[10,13] Of these, 17 to 22% will have premorbid urinary incontinence.[5,10] At 1 month and 6 months, 29% and 14% will have urinary incontinence, respectively.[2] It is important to recognize that incontinence from any cause including stroke may be resolved, improved, or better managed in almost all cases. One should never assume that the incontinence is entirely a consequence of the stroke. A clear understanding of the etiology and a thorough assessment of incontinence are critical to successful management.

NORMAL BLADDER AND URETHRA

Normal bladder and urethral function is dependent on neurologic, urologic, psychologic, and mobility factors. A detailed discussion of the neurologic reflexes and pathways is beyond the scope of this chapter and is well reviewed elsewhere.[6,12,30] In brief, bladder (detrusor) and urethral functions are coordinated for storage and emptying of urine. The sympathetic nervous system promotes storage of urine by relaxing the detrusor smooth muscle to accommodate urine as it is formed. The internal urethral sphincter closure pressure is sustained by stimulation of sympathetic alpha-adrenergic receptors located at the internal sphincter. During bladder emptying, sympathetic closure of the internal urethral sphincter is inhibited and parasympathetic acetylcholine-mediated detrusor contraction occurs. The pelvic floor, including the external urethral sphincter and external anal sphincter, has somatic innervation via the pudendal nerve and is under voluntary control. The sacral reflex arc promoting emptying is facilitated by the pontine micturition center. The pontine micturition center is consciously inhibited at a cerebral cortical level. This cortical inhibition of micturition is a learned behavior, usually acquired at a young age, and allows an individual to postpone micturition until the appropriate moment.

ETIOLOGY

Cortical lesions, particularly from stroke, can cause an unstable detrusor.[10,20] Unstable detrusor contractions occur with little warning, giving symptoms of urinary urgency and urge incontinence. The bladder volume at which unstable bladder contractions occur can be quite variable. It is usually lower than the volume at which a person would normally have a strong sensation to void. In addition to bladder volume, stimuli such as movement, standing, or anxiety can provoke unstable bladder contractions. The term for the unstable bladder due to a neurologic lesion is *detrusor hyperreflexia.*[23] Whether or not a person develops detrusor hyperreflexia following a stroke depends on the site, size, and number of lesions, as well as the time elapsed since the stroke, and is not an invariable consequence of a stroke.[10,20] Theoretically, brainstem strokes below the pons, which are uncommon, could cause a loss of synchronization of the detrusor contraction and relaxation of the external urethral sphincter. This so-called *detrusor external urethral dyssynergia* is well recognized in individuals with spinal cord injuries. Since little has been written about this condition after stroke, it will not be discussed further.

Urologic conditions such as urethral strictures in men or women may cause incomplete bladder emptying. These may predate the stroke or occur secondary to an indwelling catheter used during the management of the acute stroke. Benign or malignant prostatic obstruction in older men may predate the stroke and, in combination with immobility following a stroke, contribute to urinary retention. Immobility and/or fecal impaction may precipitate urinary retention in the acute phase following a stroke. Pelvic floor weakness in women may predate the stroke and will be an additional etiologic factor to consider when assessing the incontinence.

Post-stroke incontinence will invariably occur if the neurologic deficit is large with consequent immobility and altered level of unconsciousness. Aphasia will contribute to incontinence because of the person's inability to convey if he or she is aware of bladder fullness and need to void. Physical restraints for "protection" from post-stroke confusion compromises continence by reducing independence for toileting, particularly if the person is aware of the need to void. Post-stroke depression and amotivation are very real phenomena. Incontinence may contribute to the person's depressed affect or be a consequence of the feeling of hopelessness. For more severe strokes, indwelling urethral catheters are often inserted within the first 24 hours to monitor the fluid output and to manage incontinence when regular transferring to a commode or bedpan is unrealistic. Urinary retention with overflow urinary incontinence may occur if the catheter is removed or "falls out" before the person is ready physically or psychologically for a toileting program. Factors contributing to prestroke incontinence can improve or be eliminated in the acute hospital setting. Poorly controlled diabetes with osmotic diuresis, alcohol-induced antidiuretic hormone inhibition, and/or the weak diuretic effect of caffeine-excess are such factors.

ASSESSMENT

The history of the incontinence and related urinary symptoms is the key part of the assessment that is often overlooked. Corroboration by a relative will determine if factors predating the stroke are important. The history of present symptoms from patient or primary nurse history should categorize the incontinence into the following types: urge, stress, incomplete emptying, mixed stress/urge, functional, and iatrogenic. Prestroke urinary urgency and urge incontinence in men or women may reflect a previous stroke or other neurologic lesion with subsequent detrusor hyperreflexia. The same symptoms could also suggest idiopathic detrusor instability in an older individual or, alternatively, sensory urgency with a stable detrusor. In women, loss of urine with stress maneuvers such as coughing, laughing, sneezing, walking, or jumping, usually without urgency, predating the stroke, suggests genuine stress incontinence due to internal sphincter incompetence. In men, these symptoms are rare unless they have had prostatic surgery with internal sphincter damage. In women or men, prestroke symptoms of hesitancy, reduced stream, straining, or postmicturition dribbling suggest possible outlet obstruction due to urethral stricture or prostatic obstruction in men.

Nursing or patient observations of frequent often small voids or loss of urine when moving in the bed could indicate urinary retention. The fact that a person is voiding some urine does not rule out urinary retention. A history of indwelling catheter post-stroke may raise the possibility of post-stroke urethral stricture.

In previously continent patients, who now have no warning of urinary loss while awake or asleep, post-stroke detrusor hyperreflexia is the likely cause.

Examination

The neurologic signs of the stroke will be evident and not discussed further here. Ability to transfer on and off a bedpan with or without assistance every 2 hours is a critical level of mobility. It would be one indication of when an indwelling catheter could be removed. Assessment of affect and the patient's expectations for recovery of motor function and continence are important. Post-stroke depression causing amotivation may not be evident until some weeks or months after the stroke. This is well reviewed by Koenig and Studenski and by others.[26] Antidepressant drugs can affect bladder and urethral function and can be used for added advantage when treating depression if the patient is also incontinent.

Memory and cognitive function can be assessed using a screening tool such as the Mini-Mental State Examination (MMSE).[21] The interpretation of score on the MMSE is limited in patients with aphasia, since it is a very verbal test. Physical findings of urogenital prolapse in women may be relevant if prestroke stress incontinence was present and will influence the final choice of treatment. Perianal sensation is usually intact unless there is a history of long-standing diabetes with sacral neuropathy. If sensation is absent, impaired sacral parasympathetic innervation of the detrusor muscle may cause incomplete bladder emptying due to a poorly contractile or noncontractile detrusor. Rectal examination should easily rule out fecal impaction, but it is often not done.

Bladder Residual Urine

A true post-void residual urine test is critical to determine if bladder emptying is complete. The patient must have voided under optimal circumstances in a private location and in an appropriate position. The in/out urethral catheterization to test for the "residual" urine would then be considered valid. A sterile culture result from the catheter specimen would rule out urinary tract infection. Two consecutive residual urines of greater than 150 mL suggest a significant degree of incomplete bladder emptying, and outlet obstruction should be ruled out by urologic assessment with possible flexible cystoscopy. There is no consensus as to what residual urine volume is definitely abnormal. Most would regard greater than 150 mL as abnormal, but it depends to some degree on the volume of urine voided before catheterization.

The core evaluation findings from the history and physical examination and residual urine presented in Table 1 will establish a working diagnosis for subsequent management. A trial of intervention would be appropriate without further detailed investigations in those patients with a straightforward clinical picture and a low residual urine volume. This approach is consistent with that stated in the National Institutes of Health consensus panel on urinary incontinence in adults.[19]

MANAGEMENT

The assessment and management to this point can be accomplished by trained nurses or physicians who are aware of the need for a thorough assessment of incontinence. A team approach can be an effective and rewarding way to deal with incontinence. Philosophically, an approach that emphasizes behavioral interventions that are reversible and without side effects, as a first step, is in the patient's best interests. Drug therapy is reversible but often has side effects, and surgical intervention is irreversible.[9] If the patient's goal is realistic for regaining

TABLE 1. Types of Incontinence (Based on History, Examination, and Post-Void Residual Urine)

History	Findings (may be present)	Residual	Pathophysiology (confirmed by urodynamics)
Urgency	Signs consistent with specific neurologic disease	Low	Detrusor instability
Stress	Demonstrate stress	Low	(Genuine) stress incontinence
Overflow/incomplete emptying	Palpable bladder Prostate enlarged Urethral stricture Anal sphincter tone reduced Sacral sensation reduced	High	Outlet obstruction or Poorly contractile detrusor or Both
Mixed	Variable	Variable	Mixed
Functional	Mobility impaired Mental state impaired Environmental factors	Low	Functional
Iatrogenic	Drugs Restraints	Variable	Iatrogenic (depending on medication)

continence, it should be communicated and understood by family, nurses, and physicians so that there is a common purpose towards a successful outcome. Differing expectations will undermine the team effort.

Fluids

The total measurable fluid intake should be on the order of 1500 to 1800 mL/ 24 hours. Food contains fluid and will increase the total fluid intake. There is a common misconception by patients, nurses, and physicians that the patient should drink 6 to 8 glasses (1500 to 2000 mL) of water, in addition to everything else they drink. The justification of this is that there is a need to "flush the kidneys" and it will reduce the likelihood of urinary tract infection. Some medications, such as the sulfa-containing antibiotics, do require a higher fluid intake to prevent renal sulfa crystal deposition, but usually these medications are time limited. If a person is receiving intravenous or nasogastric fluid because of dysphagia following the stroke or intravenous antibiotics, fluid loads greater than 2 L/24 hours will compromise successful bladder management. For those who are not able to transfer frequently with assistance, an indwelling per-urethral catheter is a reasonable measure until the fluid intake can be reduced to a reasonable level and ability to transfer has improved. This strategy may preserve morale rather than overwhelm the patient with too broad a rehabilitation focus. The alternatives to per-urethral catheterization would include intermittent catheterization or suprapubic catheterization. For men who have an unstable bladder but are not in urinary retention, an external condom catheter will at least keep them dry until a toileting program can be initiated.

Bladder Charts

If incontinence persists after the patient can transfer with assistance, is catheter-free, and urinary infection has been ruled out, then a baseline bladder chart should be initiated. A bladder chart should record incontinent (wet) events and voiding frequency over 1 week, fluid intake for 72 hours, and, when possible, voided urinary volumes for 72 hours. Three days of complete information by the primary bedside nurse, patient, or caregiver at home is of more value than many incomplete days. Compliance with subsequent recording requests is more likely to occur.

From the baseline bladder chart, mean wet events and voids per 24 hours can be established for later comparison to determine improvement. The particular pattern of incontinence, such as night or daytime incontinence, may be evident by reviewing the times of wet events across a whole week.

Habit Training

Habit training follows a set schedule of voiding every 2 to 4 hours regardless of sensation of bladder fullness. Such a program needs reinforcement. Normally people are conditioned to void when their bladder is full, i.e., when they need to go. Following a stroke, the cortical awareness of bladder fullness is often reduced. Initiation of toileting in response to urgency may not allow sufficient time to void successfully. This is particularly so if post-stroke mobility is limited.

At the awareness of urgency, the detrusor muscle is often already contracting. Nurses will ask patients every 2 hours, "Do you need to void?" and the patients may say, "No," as they have no sense of bladder fullness or urgency. Voiding preventively before the bladder volume reaches the threshold at which it is more likely to reflexively contract is the logical objective. This is surprisingly difficult for patients to follow consistently. For cognitively impaired patients, "prompted" regular 2-hourly voiding is necessary with more direct cuing such as "Now is the time to go to the toilet" and the appropriate level of supervision or physical assistance provided.

Repeat bladder charts will guide habit training with more frequent voids at times of consistent wet events. Bladder training, on the other hand, allows for a gradual increase in the voiding interval as the patient becomes consistently dry.[15]

Pelvic Floor Exercises

Techniques to suppress the urge to void can be taught to men and women who are compliant and cognitively intact. Pelvic floor exercises attributed to Kegel[25] are useful, not only for stress incontinence (for which they were originally intended) but also to suppress urgency. Teaching how to identify and contract the pelvic floor muscles takes time.[14] Asking patients to contract the anal sphincter as though they are trying to prevent the passage of gas or a bowel movement is one technique. Secondly, stopping or slowing the stream of urine, by contracting the external urethral sphincter, which is part of the pelvic floor muscles, may be successful. Some patients are not able to successfully slow the stream of urine, let alone stop it. Sometimes patients misunderstand the instructions and try to stop the urine stream every time they void. This is counterproductive, as it may promote incomplete bladder emptying.

A third technique in women is for them to insert a finger into the vagina and feel the circumvaginal muscle contraction during pelvic floor contractions. Pelvic floor contractions can be sustained for 3 to 5 seconds. Pelvic floor relaxation for a count of 3 is equally as important.

Initially, a set of 5 contractions, five times per day, is a reasonable starting point. A goal of 100 contractions/day is not always obtainable and it is not clear what is the optimal number of contractions per day. Incorporating pelvic floor exercises after voiding as part of the toileting routine is a strategy that helps patients to remember to do the exercises.

Urge Suppression

When patients can do effective pelvic floor contractions and they experience urgency, a series of rapid pelvic floor contractions can be effective to suppress the "urgency wave" of the reflex bladder contraction.[14] Resisting the temptation to "rush" to the toilet in response to the urgency is important, as the sudden movement may reinforce the reflex bladder contraction. Once the sensation of urgency has temporarily subsided, toileting can occur and is more likely to be successful without incontinence.

Distraction is another technique whereby patients, experiencing a sense of urgency, think of thoughts unrelated to voiding until the urge subsides.

Biofeedback

In subjects with persisting incontinence who have not responded to the above conservative measures, biofeedback offers a further effective but time-intensive intervention. Audio and visual biofeedback has been used effectively for a number of years for urinary incontinence.[15,16,28] Patients have to be cognitively intact to retain learning between training sessions as well as keep accurate records.

Middaugh et al.[28] reported on four subjects with post-stroke incontinence of 8 months' to 10 years' duration. Visual biofeedback was used during sequential filling of the bladder by a catheter with 20-mL increments of sterile water. The subjects were aware of bladder sensations and monitored the visual display of bladder pressure. With a pressure rise indicating detrusor contraction, they contracted their external anal and urinary sphincter (pelvic floor contraction) and observed the effect of reflex inhibition of the detrusor contraction. At the same time, they were relaxed and avoided general skeletal muscle tensing or breath-holding.

During biofeedback sessions, all of the subjects demonstrated unstable detrusor contractions at low bladder filling volumes. Secondly, they had impaired bladder sensation of fullness, with little time between the first sensation of urgency and detrusor contraction. Thirdly, they had poor urge control, being unable to stop the stream of urine. A particularly interesting observation in one patient was that increased spasticity caused by standing resulted in an uninhibited detrusor contraction at a volume of 300 mL. When lying relaxed, uninhibited contractions were not evident up to 600 mL. This observation confirmed that spasticity contributes to detrusor instability. The four subjects regained continence after biofeedback sessions every 2 to 4 weeks over a 3-month period and they remained continent at 12 months.

Biofeedback did not alter the physiologic parameters of the bladder, such as first sensation of fullness, or maximal cystometric bladder capacity. Biofeedback did heighten the awareness of bladder sensation and helped identify early bladder sensations as a cue to void. It also facilitated use of external sphincter contractions to inhibit voiding reflexes.

Urinary Retention

Urinary retention with overflow incontinence may occur following a stroke, usually in the acute phase. Immobility, fecal impaction, anticholinergic action of medications, and outlet obstruction may also contribute. These can be addressed through the combined-team rehabilitation efforts by improving mobility, an appropriate bowel routine, reviewing medications, and ruling out bladder outlet obstruction. Teaching the credé maneuver combined with pelvic floor relaxation may improve bladder emptying for persisting incontinence due to urinary retention.

Intermittent catheterization, either by the patient, relative, or health professional can be taught using a sterile technique in a hospital or, alternatively, a clean (nonsterile) routine for the home environment. Projection slide tape programs are available[33] for instructions of patients or next of kin. The frequency of catheterization should be monitored and adjusted. An algorithm to determine the appropriate frequency of catheterization, based on the premise that a residual urine of greater than 100 mL is abnormal and total bladder capacity should not exceed 600 mL, can be a useful guide.[8] The frequency of catheterization can be reduced as the residual urine decreases.

Stress Incontinence

Prestroke stress incontinence due to sphincter incompetence may be worsened. Kegel pelvic floor exercises, as described earlier, would be a first-line approach. Strengthening the pelvic floor and external urethral sphincter by conscientious repeated sets of pelvic floor exercises each day should resolve or reduce stress incontinence. If resolution using pelvic floor exercises and the above conservative measures are unsuccessful, further investigation could include combined video fluoroscopy and urodynamic studies by a gynecologist or urologist to determine if surgery is appropriate.[17]

CYSTOMETRY

Persisting incontinence despite improved mobility and a trial of behavioral interventions requires further investigation. Cystometry using per-urethral pressure transducers measures the intravesical pressure as the bladder is filled with carbon dioxide or water. The rate of filling with water may be slow, medium, or rapid, i.e., 10 mL, 50 mL, or more than 100 mL/minute, respectively.[23] Dual-channel water cystometry with simultaneous bladder and rectal transducer pressure recordings during filling allows subtraction of intra-abdominal pressure. This yields true intravesical pressure in response to bladder filling and allows detection of lower amplitude unstable bladder contractions. The detrusor response during cystometry in normal healthy volunteers is well described.[1] Water cystometry has the added advantage of demonstrating water leakage during filling due to sphincter incompetence in the absence of detrusor contractions, and this can confirm the diagnosis of genuine stress incontinence. As filling progresses detrusor instability may also be detected, confirming combined detrusor instability and genuine stress incontinence. The traditional International Continence Society (ICS) definition of detrusor instability is a contraction of greater than 15 cm of water, though it is recognized that unstable detrusor contractions may generate lower pressures.[23]

The volume at which an unstable detrusor contraction occurs and the magnitude of the detrusor pressure rise (measured in cm of water) will reflect the severity of the detrusor instability and contractility of detrusor muscle, respectively. Sensory urgency with a stable detrusor can be confirmed when the first sensation of fullness and urgency is reported at a lower volume but filling proceeds to 500 to 600 mL without subsequent detrusor contraction despite provocative maneuvers such as standing or coughing. Confirming sensory urgency might encourage persistence with behavioral interventions rather than adding medications.

A combined cystometrogram and electromyogram can provide additional information about the pelvic floor muscles, including the external urethral sphincter. This investigation would only be indicated in the occasional patient in whom detrusor external urethral sphincter dyssynergia is suspected.

PHARMACOLOGIC THERAPY

Prescribing Principles

In most instances, drugs should be considered as an adjunct therapy, only to be implemented after an adequate trial of behavioral interventions. The main drawbacks of drugs are their side effect profiles, which are often underestimated, particularly in the elderly. Following stroke, the potential for adverse effects is increased, particularly in those who are on multiple medications or who have cognitive impairment following a stroke. The potential for side effects is a strong justification for cystometric confirmation of detrusor hyperreflexia before commencing medication.

The common medications used for post-stroke detrusor hyperreflexia have varying degrees of anticholinergic action and include flavoxate, oxybutynin, propantheline, and imipramine. There is no advantage to commencing with the maximum dose regardless of age, and the disadvantage, from the probable side effects, is the patient's loss of confidence that medication can help. Gradual titration over 4 to 6 weeks, increasing the dose each week, allows patient comfort and confidence to prevail and arrival at the lowest dose with the optimal effect and least side effects. With any upward titration of medication, once an optimal drug effect occurs, there is no need to continue increasing the dose. Likewise, if an increased dose results in intolerable side effects, the drug dose should be reduced to where the desired action occurred without intolerable side effect. If at that point the desired effect is not present, the medication should be stopped.

Even after reaching an optimal dose, after 6 months at that dose, stepwise titration back down is worth trying. Continued recovery from the stroke and continued reinforcement of behavioral intervention may negate any benefit from the drug. If symptoms of detrusor hyperreflexia reappear at a lower dose, the indication for continuing the drug is confirmed. Close monitoring with bladder charts provides objective information to determine if the drug is having this desired effect. Establishing the new baseline reflecting the effect of behavioral interventions is important before commencing medication. It gives the physician a clear idea if further significant improvement has occurred in response to medication.

Before starting medications, the acceptable endpoints should be defined. The anticholinergic effect, when optimal, on the unstable detrusor decreases detrusor contractility and symptoms of urgency and frequency of voiding and allows greater postponement of voiding. Common side effects include excessive dry mouth, confusion, postural hypotension, urinary retention, constipation, blurred vision, and nausea. Patients may also note a reduction in the strength of the urinary stream. For the medication to be effective, it is preferable that patients have some awareness of bladder sensations. For the cognitively impaired, the potential for increased confusion from the central anticholinergic action of medications far outweighs any perceived beneficial effect on incontinence, and anticholinergic medications are not recommended. There are a few double-blind trials of the use of anticholinergic drugs for detrusor instability due to various disorders but none in patients who exclusively have detrusor hyperreflexia following stroke.[31]

Drug Doses and Choices

Flavoxate, which is proported to have a direct smooth muscle relaxing action and little anticholinergic effect, may be worth trying first because of lower potential for anticholinergic side effects. It could be started with 200 mg daily and increased by 200 mg/day each week to 200 mg four times daily at week 4. A higher maximum dose of 400 mg three times daily has been shown to be well tolerated.[29] If there is no response to flavoxate, oxybutynin or propantheline can be tried instead. The absorption of propantheline, a quaternary ammonium compound, is variable between individuals. It is said not to cross the blood-brain barrier, which is a theoretical advantage in those who have potential for confusion. It is significantly cheaper than oxybutynin or flavoxate. Propantheline can be titrated beginning with 7.5 mg twice daily up to 30 mg three times daily and a maximum over 6 weeks using 15-mg increments each week. Alternatively, oxybutynin can be titrated by 2.5 mg (one-half tablet) each week, up to a maximum of 5 mg three times daily by week 6.

Imipramine is a more complex drug with anticholinergic alpha-agonist and antidepressant properties. Given this profile, theoretically, imipramine might be most useful for persisting post-stroke incontinence in a patient with detrusor hyperreflexia, depression, and some genuine stress incontinence. It should be avoided in male patients with incipient urinary retention due to prostatic obstruction. Imipramine could be titrated over 6 weeks beginning at 10 mg/day and increasing by 10 mg/day each week up to 20 mg three times daily. Post-stroke depression has been treated successfully with nortriptyline, though delirium did occur in some subjects.[27] If symptomatic detrusor hyperreflexia is present as well, amitriptyline may have an additional advantage since it has a strong anticholinergic effect compared to nortriptyline. Again titration of amitriptyline by 10 mg/week would be a reasonable frequency of increase in the young and by 10 mg every other week up to a maximum dose of 70 mg in the elderly.

For patients with poorly contractile detrusor due to partial bladder denervation and atonic decompensated bladders, bethanechol may improve detrusor contractility. Most experience is anecdotal, and the effectiveness of bethanechol is controversial.[34] Bethanechol, 10 mg three times daily and increasing by 10 mg each week up to 50 mg three times daily maximum, would be a reasonable trial. This would usually be used as an adjunct to intermittent catheterization. Failure of the residual to decrease, excessive sweating, asthmatic attacks, or abdominal cramps would all be reasons to discontinue the bethanechol.

CONTAINMENT

Aids to voiding are many and include a variety of male and female urinals, slipper pans, commodes, and adaptions to the toilet itself, such as raised toilet seats and bars.

Resolution of incontinence will not be a realistic goal for every post-stroke patient. Degree of mobility, cognitive impairment, awareness of bladder sensation, and severity of detrusor instability are likely the most important factors contributing to persistent incontinence. The range of incontinence products for containment is extensive. Pads range in size, absorbency, construction, cost, and availability and are disposable or reusable. Pads that will contain small volumes of urine are more commonly disposable, but increasingly small reusable pads are becoming available, usually at medical supply stores. Larger reusable bed pads or diapers for large daytime or nighttime incontinent episodes are available in reusable or disposable forms. Some reusable bed sheets with very high absorbency draw urine away from the skin and allow undisturbed sleep. Reusable products are more environmentally friendly despite laundering and are more cost-effective over the long term.

Cost of incontinence within the community and institutions can be substantial, and maintaining mobility is potentially one way to reduce costs.[10] When transfers are difficult, male external condom catheters for day or night or for 24-hour use are worth trying, depending on the patient preference and whether they will leave the external catheter attached. Skin care must be meticulous for this to be successful. Female external catheters are being developed. Long-term indwelling catheters are only indicated with significant persisting retention where attempts for resolution of incontinence have failed and intermittent catheterization is impractical. The patient or relatives need to be involved in the decision and aware of the risks of chronic urinary bacteriuria, bladder spasms, leakage around the catheter, and bladder stones/catheter balloon calcification. Catheter care protocol should be followed with regular changes. Latex catheters are cheaper, but if allergy to latex rubber is a problem, the more expensive inert silicon could be used.

OUTCOMES

Incontinence as a predictor following stroke has been associated with a poor outcome.[25,35] In a more positive light, continence, either remaining dry or regaining continence, has been reported as a positive predictor for survival, recovery, and final discharge.[2] Barer[2] reported that of those who were continent at day 1, only 3% died in the first month. Those who regained continence in the first month were most likely to be home within 6 months of the stroke. This relationship between continence and a good outcome was independent of age or gender. Barer[2] suggested that a return of continence preceded other areas of functional improvement and that it may be linked to other prognostic factors such as motivation and self-respect.

This raises the possibility that more rapid return of continence may facilitate return of other functions, possibly through improved motivation and self-esteem. To determine the effect of a well-coordinated post-stroke continence program, a large well-designed controlled trial would be required. This approach could be compared to "regular continence care" with endpoints relating to continence, other parameters of function, motivation, self-esteem, quality of life, and impact of incontinence.[36] Who will accept this challenge?

CONCLUSIONS

Urinary incontinence following stroke is common. It is not necessarily a consequence of the stroke. In virtually all patients, incontinence can be resolved, improved, or better contained. An accurate history, physical examination, and residual urine volume testing will determine the prestroke and post-stroke factors contributing to incontinence. Detrusor instability is the most common bladder abnormality after a stroke.

Management of persisting incontinence, once mobility is not a limiting factor, should focus firstly on reversible behavioral interventions which do not have other side effects. This could include fluid management, bladder charts, habit training, pelvic floor exercises, urge suppression techniques, and biofeedback. Anticholinergic medications for detrusor instability should be used as an adjunct to behavioral interventions. Medication doses should be titrated gradually to obtain the lowest possible dose with the maximum effect and least side effects. Persisting stress incontinence, not responding to behavioral interventions, should be evaluated further with urodynamic studies to determine if surgery is appropriate. Urinary retention can be managed with sterile or clean intermittent catheterization, and bethanechol may have an adjunct role. The range of incontinence products for containment is extensive, and careful consideration should be given to style, size, absorbency, time of use, and reusable versus disposable items.

Improving incontinence will improve morale, and it may well facilitate rehabilitation and reduce time to discharge from hospital.

REFERENCES

1. Bagley NA, O'Shaughnessy EJ: Urodynamic evaluation of voluntary detrusor response in healthy subjects. Arch Phys Med Rehabil 66:160–163, 1985.
2. Barer DH: Continence after stroke: Useful predictor or goal of therapy? Age Ageing 18:183–191, 1989.
3. Barer DH, Mitchell JRA: Predicting the outcome of acute stroke: Do multivariate models help? Q J Med [New Series] 70(261):27–39, 1989.
4. Bates P, Bradley WE, Glen E, et al: The standardization of terminology of lower urinary tract function. J Urol 121:551–554, 1979.

5. Benbow S, Sangster G, Barer D: Incontinence after stroke. Lancet ii(338):1602–1603, 1991.
6. Blaivas JG: The neurophysiology of micturition: A clinical study of 550 patients. J Urol 127:958, 1982.
7. Bliss MR: Incontinence after stroke. Lancet i(339):1113, 1992.
8. Borrie MJ, Foster PM, Reilly A: Intermittent catheterization: An algorithm for managing frequency of catheterization based on the residual urine and voided volume. Clin Invest Med 12(4):82, 1989.
9. Borrie MJ, Bawden ME, Kartha AS, Kerr PS: A nurse/physician continence clinic triage approach for urinary incontinence: A 25 week randomized trial. Neurourol Urodyn 11:364–365, 1992.
10. Borrie MJ, Campbell AJ, Caradoc-Davies TH, Spears GFS: Urinary incontinence after stroke: A prospective study. Age Ageing 15:177–181, 1986.
11. Borrie MJ, Davidson HA: Incontinence in institutions: Costs and contributing factors. Can Med Assoc J 147:322–328, 1992.
12. Bradley WE, Rockswold GL, Timm GW, Scott FB: Neurology of micturition. J Urol 115:481, 1976.
13. Brocklehurst JC, Andrews K, Richards B, Laycock PJ: Incidence and correlates of incontinence in stroke patients. J Am Geriatr Soc 33:540–542, 1985.
14. Burgio KL, Pearch K, Lulco AJ: Staying Dry. Baltimore, Johns Hopkins University Press, 1989, p 80.
15. Burgio KL, Burgio LD: Behavior therapies for urinary incontinence in the elderly. Clin Geriatr Med 2:809–827, 1986.
16. Burgio KL, Whitehead WE, Engel BT: Urinary incontinence in the elderly: Bladder-sphincter biofeedback and toileting skills training. Ann Intern Med 104:507–515, 1985.
17. Chancellor MB, Blaivas JG: Diagnostic evaluation of incontinence in patients with neurological disorders. Comp Ther 17(2):37–43, 1991.
18. Ebrahim S, Nouri F: Caring for stroke patients at home. Int Rehabil Med 8:171–173, 1987.
19. Elliott JM: Urinary incontinence in adults. JAMA 261:2685–2690, 1989.
20. Feder M, Heller L, Tadmor R, et al: Urinary continence after stroke: Association with cystometric profile and computerised tomography findings. Eur Neurol 27:101–105, 1987.
21. Folstein MF, Folstein SE, McHugh PR: Mini-mental state: A practical method for grading the cognitive state of patients for the clinician. J Psych Res 12:189–198, 1975.
22. Henriksen T: Incontinence after stroke. Lancet ii(338):1335, 1991.
23. International Continence Society Committee on Standardization of Terminology: Standardization of terminology of the lower urinary tract function. Fourth report: Neuromuscular function. Urology 17:618–620, 1981.
24. Jongbloed L: Prediction of function after stroke: A critical review. Stroke 17:765–776, 1986.
25. Kegel AH: Progressive resistance exercises in the functional restoration of the perineal muscles. Am J Obstet Gynecol 56:238–248, 1948.
26. Koenig JG, Studenski S: Post-stroke depression in the elderly. J Gen Intern Med 3:508–517, 1988.
27. Lipsey JR, Robinson RG, Pearlson GD, et al: Nortriptyline treatment of post-stroke depression: A double blind study. Lancet i:297–300, 1984.
28. Middaugh SJ, Whitehead WE, Burgio KL, Engel BT: Biofeedback in treatment of urinary incontinence in stroke patients. Biofeedback Self-Regul 14:3–19, 1989.
29. Milani R, Scalambrino S, Carrera S, et al: Comparison of flavoxate hydrochloride in daily dosages of 600 versus 1200 mg for the treatment of urgency and urge incontinence. J Intern Med Res 16:244–248, 1988.
30. Opitz JL, Thorsteinsson G, Schutt AH, et al: Neurogenic bladder and bowel. In DeLisa JA (ed): Rehabilitation Medicine: Principles & Practice. Philadelphia, JB Lippincott Co, 1988, p 492.
31. Ouslander JG, Sier HC: Drug therapy for geriatric urinary incontinence. Clin Geriatr Med 2:789–807, 1986.
32. Silbert PL, Stewart-Wynne EG: Incontinence after stroke. Lancet i(339):1602, 1992.
33. Skelly J, Worral J, Campbell-Spooner L, et al: Intermittent Self-Catheterization. Hamilton, ON, St. Joseph's Hosp Foundation, 1984.
34. Sondra LP, Gershon C, Diokno AC, Lapides J: Urological neurology and urodynamics—Further observations on the cystometric and uroflowmetric effects of bethanechol chloride on the human bladder. J Urol 122:775–777, 1979.
35. Wade DT, Hewer RL: Functional abilities after stroke: Measurement, natural history and prognosis. J Neurol Neurosurg Psychiatry 50:177–182, 1987.
36. Wyman JF, Harkins SW, Choi SC, et al: Psychosocial impact of urinary incontinence in women. Obstet Gynecol 70:378–381, 1987.

KAREN L. HARBURN, PhD
PATRICK J. POTTER, MD, FRCPC

8. SPASTICITY AND CONTRACTURES

From the Departments of
    Occupational and
    Physical Therapy
Elborn College
The University of Western
    Ontario (KLH)
        and
Department of Physical Medicine
    and Rehabilitation
The University of Western Ontario
    and Victoria Hospital
    Corporation (PP)
London, Ontario
Canada

Reprint requests to:
Karen L. Harburn, PhD
Department of Occupational
    Therapy
Elborn College
The University of Western Ontario
London, Ontario N6G 1H1
Canada

Spasticity often presents as a problem following stroke. Chronic spasticity is probably always associated with some degree of contracture, which often complicates the clinical picture by causing joint restrictions, thereby compromising functional activities. Yet, the true relationship of spasticity to functional outcome is unclear,[24,59] partly due to the inaccuracy of commonly used outcome measures (e.g., functional level).[95] It is certain, however, that long-term survival following stroke is becoming more common, with the consequence of an increasing incidence of disability.

This chapter introduces the topics of spasticity and contracture separately. Each section begins with a definition that precedes a critical review of relevant clinical and physiological literature. The two sections are followed by medical and rehabilitative approaches for both spasticity and contractures.

WHAT IS SPASTICITY?

Clinical Definition

Spasticity is a term commonly used by patients, allied health professionals, and medical staff to describe the increase in muscle tone often experienced following stroke. Clinically, spasticity is defined as "a motor disorder characterized by a velocity-dependent increase in tonic stretch reflexes [of muscles] with exaggerated tendon jerks, resulting from hyperexcitability of the stretch reflex as one component of the upper motor neuron syndrome."[68] *Muscle tone* is often, though in error, used synonymously with the term *spasticity*. Muscle tone is more accurately defined as "the resistance of muscle to being passively lengthened, or stretched."[46] Indeed, the clinical assessment of *spasticity* is most often a measure of a component or components of *muscle tone* and may have little to do with actual neurophysiologic spasticity. This concept will be discussed further in the section entitled Muscle Tone and Stiffness.

Neurophysiological Mechanisms

The exact neurophysiological mechanisms related to cerebral spasticity, and accounting for the clinical features exhibited by patients with spasticity, are not fully known. There are, however, three basic neurophysiological hypotheses that alone, or more likely in some combination, may explain spasticity:

1. The muscle stretch receptors are hyperactive, and this is related to the increased activity of the muscle spindle innervation fibers called gamma;
2. The alpha-motoneurons innervating the affected muscle(s) are hyperactive, with possible contribution by weakened Renshaw cell inhibition; and
3. There is a lack of normally acting presynaptic inhibition of the motoneurons that innervate the affected muscle(s). This third mechanism may include other abnormalities in interneuronal activity, such as abnormal cutaneous input integration and reciprocal inhibition of antagonist muscles.

Recent animal[73] and human[50] research suggests that hyperactivity of muscle stretch receptors is more than likely *not* involved in spasticity, even though tendon reflexes are enhanced. It may, however, be explained by a decrease in threshold for the stretch reflex.[62,72,91] Recurrent Renshaw cell inhibition, normally acting on the alpha-motoneurons innervating the affected muscle(s), is abnormal in stroke patients during active movements but not during passive movements or at rest, and it cannot account for the hyperexcitability of the stretch reflex seen in these patients.[27,32,61] There is some suggestion that there are alterations in the excitability of both alpha-motoneurons innervating the affected muscle[108] as well as specific interneurons such as those mediating flexor reflex afferent effects and reciprocal inhibition.[47] An attractive hypothesis, and one that has received much support,[62] is the idea that presynaptic inhibition, via spindle and flexor reflex afferents, is abnormal in stroke-related spasticity.[10,29,31,54,78]

To summarize, spasticity is caused by the hyperexcitability of the dynamic stretch reflex due to altered supraspinal modulation of specific spinal circuitry. Strong evidence exists for the idea of faulty presynaptic inhibition via the muscle stretch receptors and possibly via flexor reflex afferents terminals,[54] and reduced reciprocal inhibition during movement. There is some evidence for reduced Renshaw cell inhibition of alpha-motoneurons. Therefore, the neurophysiological picture probably involves several variables that together, or in some combination, account for spasticity related to stroke.[22]

Physiologic Characteristics of Spastic Muscles

In the event of muscle disuse after cerebral damage, the normally very active antigravity muscles are often profoundly affected.[37,55,113] These slow-twitch muscles, such as soleus, rapidly atrophy as a response to the lack of innervation,[44] with the resulting expanded usage of fast-twitch motor units. Reductions in strength and size of skeletal muscle also have more widespread implications. For example, a loss or lessening of muscular function would cause the atrophy of other components of the musculoskeletal system such as bone, ligaments, and tendon.

These problems complicate an already compromised musculoskeletal system and can lead to additional medical problems, such as an increased potential for bone fracture.

Process of Motor Recovery and the Development of Spasticity

Generally, spasticity of cerebral origin tends to develop slowly. However fast-developing spasticity may occur following high brainstem lesions.[28] It should be noted that the extent of spasticity exhibited by a stroke patient appears not to be directly related to the size or location of the lesion(s)[20] (Matheson and Harburn, unpublished observations). Although animal research has shown the precentral (especially motor) cortex,[79] premotor cortex,[119] supplementary area,[114] and postcentral cortex[67] to contribute to spasticity, the findings cannot be directly applied to the human situation since the lesioning technique in the animal studies employs ablation.[81]

The lengthy recovery following stroke suggests an adaptation process, which has been described in greater detail by Burke.[22] A portion of the recovery is related to the resolution of local edema and tissue damage,[8] but long-term functional recovery is more closely associated with neural and soft-tissue factors[56] that may continue to change for months or even years.[117] Evidence points to the plasticity of the central nervous system with the eventual level of recovery being related to both the reparative neural process[22] and to the functional demands which include specific rehabilitation procedures designed to optimize functional return.[8,95] The two neurophysiological mechanisms thought to underlie functional recovery in stroke are neural pathway unmasking and neuronal collateral sprouting.[8,22] However, the older the patient, the worse the prognosis is for functional recovery since central nervous system plasticity is affected by aging.[95]

The stages of motor recovery involve a general pattern,[21,115] although this pattern is not followed in all cases of stroke (for more detail, refer to Ryerson[95]). Initially, there is a complete loss of voluntary movement and a reduction in the tendon reflexes. Resistance to passive movement is often decreased, with low tone or flaccidity presenting.[21] It is thought that the longer the flaccidity lasts, the poorer the prognosis of functional return.[49]

Forty-eight hours following stroke, the tendon reflexes become more pronounced on the affected side and resistance to passive movements begins to increase.[8] The development of spasticity occurs in the arm, leg, head, neck, and trunk[95] with the physiological flexors being most prominently affected; these include the adductors and flexors in the upper limb and the adductors and extensors in the lower limb. As spasticity increases, clonus becomes apparent.[8,95] Several days (6 to 38[115]) after the onset of hemiplegia, voluntary movements are seen, initially in the spinal extensors and the shoulder and pelvic complex elevators,[21,95] and these are the muscles also seen to be first affected by spasticity.[95] Bach-y-Rita[8] described the return of an upper limb flexor synergy which includes the shoulder, elbow, wrist, and fingers and produces the typical "mass" flexion pattern.[95] Very soon afterward, an extensor synergy develops.[8] As voluntary control of shoulder and elbow flexion increases, spasticity is reduced and may disappear with complete resumption of voluntary control. It should be noted that initial voluntary motor control involves abnormally slow movement and motor relaxation times; greater movement velocities and control are achievable when the patient directly observes his or her own limbs.[8] Indeed, Bach-y-Rita[8] describes the important role of vision, since without it, ataxia, tremor, and less dextrous movements occurred as stroke patients attempted activities.

The lower limb mimics the upper limb in the development first of flexor followed by extensor synergies.[8] A positive effect of the extensor synergy in the lower limb is that of splinting the extremity to assist in producing a stilt-like gait. This may help increase venous return and maintenance of muscle mass. There appear to be more adverse effects of muscle tone in the upper limb where spasticity is often felt to be a detriment to function, since it may cause difficulty with the more controlled movements required of the upper extremities. The relationship of voluntary movement to spasticity has not yet been clearly defined. However, clinical observation indicates that synergistic movement and spasticity decrease as volitional movement increases.[96]

Muscle Tone and Stiffness Contributions to Spasticity

The amount of "muscle tone" is typical of what is clinically assessed by passively moving a joint, but relative muscle tautness can also be assessed by palpation.[46] To see this more clearly, one can compare a flaccid muscle to a normal one. The flaccid muscle hangs due to its inability to resist gravity.[46] It is considered less stiff when one considers its elastic tension,[100] whereas the opposite occurs as contracture develops. Indeed, Gordon[46] considers contracture a form of hypertonus.

Physiologically, muscle tone includes the intrinsic elastic properties of muscle, tendon, and connective tissue as well as the two components of active contraction—reflexes and voluntary motor control.[46] Under resting conditions, healthy and spastic muscles are electrically silent.[69] Therefore, normal tone results entirely from the intrinsic stiffness of muscles and tendons.[46,98,112] Since aging is related to an increase in connective tissue in muscle, aged muscles have been shown to be stiffer.[6] This aging factor would contribute to the stiffness in the muscles of stroke patients who are typically in the older age range. Stiffness in the intrinsic components has been noted to increase following stroke and is thought to be related to the increased development, over time, of connective tissue.[56]

Reflex contribution to tone comes mainly from the stretch reflexes, which produce a "neural" stiffness or a tendency to resist muscle lengthening.[82] Due to the mediation of muscles spindles, the velocity sensitivity of the stretch reflex implies that it contributes to viscous (i.e., dynamic) stiffness. Voluntary muscle contraction may also contribute to muscle resistance during passive elongation. The stiffness of a muscle increases with higher levels of contraction, but even more so in stroke.[59,99] This voluntary activation of muscles increases the gain of spinal stretch reflexes[45]; therefore, the ability to modulate stiffness during voluntary activities is an extremely important function and is probably hampered following a stroke.

Limb inertia[62] is another factor that may affect the muscle's response to passive stretch. In line with this idea is the possibility that functional activity produces greater passive tension in spastic versus healthy muscles.[111] Certainly, it has been suggested that certain reflexes, which would normally be modulated during functional movement, are not as easily modulated by stroke subjects.[99]

Abnormal tone takes the form of hypo- or hypertonus. Following stroke, hypotonus usually results from a reduction in reflexes and/or a diminution in alpha-motoneuron excitability.[46] Within a few days, the muscles lose most of their intrinsic elasticity, hence their softness on palpation and the limp appearance of the limbs. During recovery following stroke, stretch reflexes appear first, yet the muscles may still appear flaccid. Gordon[46] suggested this reflects a lag between the appearance of neural versus intrinsic stiffness. Loss of strength due to peripheral or central weakness contributes to the hypotonus. As the recovery proceeds, spasticity often ensues with the characteristic resistance of muscles to passive stretch, particularly when a particular critical velocity is reached. In addition, there may be an increase in static stiffness (also called elastic stiffness) as spasticity and the development of additional connective tissue progress.[56] These recovery components may cause a large degree of the increase in muscle tone seen.

Biomechanical Basis of Muscle Tone

Muscles resist length changes and are thought to behave like springs,[46] which produce a resisting force during passive lengthening; this can be referred to as **elastic stiffness.** Since mechanical stiffness can be defined as the change in tension associated with change in length, the slope of this relationship describes the relative stiffness (see Gordon[46] for additional detail). This relationship is slightly curvilinear such that stiffness increases more so as length increases. A muscle also exhibits a point of zero resistance, called **zero length,** or that length below which it does not resist lengthening. This zero position, or resting length, can be appreciated by moving a limb in a plane without gravitational effects. Gordon[46] suggests that tension felt in a muscle depends on both its stiffness and resting length.

A muscle differs from a spring by virtue of its dynamic or **viscous stiffness.** Indeed, muscle exhibits increased resistance with increasing speeds of passive lengthening, and Gordon[46] describes this relationship as similar to the resistance one feels when trying to rapidly close a door equipped with a hydraulic damper. Viscous stiffness also exhibits a velocity of stretching below which no tension is felt, i.e., **zero velocity.**

MEASUREMENT OF SPASTICITY

Current Clinical Measurement of Muscle Tone

Current clinical measures cannot assess all the known components of neuro-physiological spasticity.[54,62] Therefore, the clinical neurological assessment of spasticity following stroke (for historical overview of clinical assessments, see Worley et al.[122]) typically assesses a component or components of "muscle tone." The most common clinical assessment of tone consists of a subjective five-point scale (i.e., ranging from no increase in tone, (0) to affected part(s) rigid in flexion or extension, (4) of limb resistance to passive movement while the patient is relaxed in the supine position.[7] The Ashworth scale has exhibited high interrater reliability for the upper extremity[17]; however, it tends to lack sensitivity since the score range is so narrow. The Ashworth assessment's reliability relies on the clinician's ability to maintain a slow, constant speed of limb movement since speed of stretch is related to the amplitude of the muscle spindle's response. The speed of limb movement is not indicated in the literature on the Ashworth assessment. Notably, the score is related to the whole body position of the patient.[54] Therefore, a patient whose functional upright gait may be severely affected by spasticity may exhibit little or no spasticity in the supine testing position. In addition to body position, several other important factors affect level of spasticity, including speed of limb movement, whether the movement is passive or active (see Muscle Tone and Stiffness Contributions to Spasticity above for more detail), resting joint position, "state" of the patient (e.g., level of anxiety), and soft-tissue alterations. These factors are problematic and certainly contribute to a rather imprecise clinical description of muscle tone when using many of the available clinical measures. Often a functional movement assessment[41,74] or an additional passive limb movement test is done by a therapist. These contribute to the quality of the measure.

Suggested Clinical Measurement of Muscle Tone

Gordon[46] has suggested that clinical evaluations of muscle tone should measure four different biomechanical components, as described above, after the clinician first determines if contracture exists. The first is **elastic stiffness,** or the relative resistance of muscles to passive length change, which can be assessed by slowly stretching the muscle to different lengths and evaluating the amount of tension "felt" at each position with the limb held in the gravity-eliminated plane of movement. It is important to first ascertain resting[122] or **zero length** (i.e., length below which tension is zero) as a reference point. When measuring elastic stiffness, it is imperative that the stretch reflex, which contributes to viscous stiffness, not be evoked. Hufschmidt and Mauritz[56] suggested that movements below approximately 20° per second would not evoke stretch reflexes in most stroke patients.

Viscous stiffness is determined by stretching the muscle by equal amounts but at different velocities and feeling the amount of tension at each velocity. A metronome would be useful in this procedure to more precisely time movement throughout a specified range, thereby allowing more consistant and quantifiable control of velocity of the limb within the specified range. **Zero velocity** is the final biomechanical component that should be measured as the rate of length change below which no tension can be ascertained. Individuals with abnormal tone have been shown to exhibit selective alterations in one or more of these four parameters.[46]

The fact that muscle tone varies under such a wide variety of conditions should not deter clinicians from measuring it.[122] Understanding the contribution of the abovementioned factors to the production of muscle tone permits the clinician to better control the testing situation, creating the potential for increasing the reliability and validity of these measures for assessment of treatment efficacy.

Laboratory Measurement

Several techniques have been developed for determining the amount or level of neurophysiological spasticity. However, problems with methodologies and samples studied have made difficult the interpretation of the data.

Some have recorded torque of a displaced limb and/or the electromyographic (EMG) responses of the limbs' muscles to electrically or mechanically evoked responses.[54,75] Others have recorded the EMG and mechanical responses to passive muscle stretch through flexion and extension of joints[53,77]; or recorded the level of reflex inhibition during muscle vibration[83]; or recorded EMG and torque during muscle stretch and voluntary stretch responses[19]; or measured torque during isokinetic movements.[16,64] Functional movements have also been studied as indicators of spasticity, for example, as a gross indication of spasticity during gait[64,65] or bicycle pedalling.[12]

Emerging from the studies are the following clinically related issues:

1. Spasticity affects the supposedly "normal" side's muscular function in stroke;[77,111]
2. There are soft-tissue changes in long-standing spastic limbs that affect joint stiffness;[19,35,56,62,108]
3. Slow, passive movement measurements have been shown to be more related to the clinical assessment of spasticity[10,19]; however, it is thought by some that effects on spastic muscle in tests of passive movement cannot be expected to explain all the effects on functional ability that result from the disorganized control of movement;[12,64]
4. "State" of the patient during testing procedures is crucial for accurate and reliable measurements of spasticity severity (*state* refers to level of anxiety, bladder filling, positioning, acclimitization response, and noise level effects[75,85]).

CONTRACTURES

What Are Contractures?

Joint contractures are periarticular impairments which typically result in loss of movement range and occur as secondary sequelae of other disease processes or injuries. A direct relationship between the duration of immobility and the time period for recovery of range of movement (ROM) has been reported.[4,34,87] However, other factors that have been shown to contribute to the development of contractures include local edema, trauma, and aging.

Immobility and spasticity, two of the major sequelae of stroke, are prominent among the causes of contractures. In addition to these, the commonly associated peripheral edema, hemiplegic pain, and trauma caused by sensory impairment and neglect predispose stroke patients to the development of contractures. An association between aging and decreased ROM has also been demonstrated.[57] Since stroke typically affects those beyond middle-age, these individuals probably have preexisting restriction of joint movement prior to the onset of their stroke.

Pathophysiology of Contractures

As contractures develop, the initial tissue changes are due to shortening of the connective tissue within muscle,[104] whereas ligament, tendon, capsule, and fascia have similar but later-developing connective tissue responses to immobility.[4] Following enforced immobilization, significant losses of water, soluble collagen, hyaluronic acid, and other glycosaminoglycans (GAG) were found in each of these tissues,[3] with the reduction in total hyaluronic acid content exhibiting a significant correlation with stiffness of the related joints.[123] In contrast, the total amount of collagen present was unchanged.[123]

Akeson et al.[3] suggested that the mechanism for contracture, occurring in these tissues, related to a change in the nature of the collagen, in contrast to a previous study which reported a role for increased collagen synthesis in the formation of contractures.[86] Akeson et al.[3] postulated that the difference seen may have been due to heterogeneity of the connective tissue, since the biopsy samples in Peacock's[86] study were taken from only one site and precision of the location of rebiopsy is difficult to control. Stolov and Hardy[103] have also shown that there is no significant change in the total amount of collagen following immobilization.

In the Woo et al.[123] study of immobilized rabbit knees, the solubility of collagen changed, suggesting the possibility of increased crosslinks or a change in the type of collagen within the 9-week period of immobilization. During stiffness testing of the tissue, there was a large reduction in resistance to movement between the first torque applied to the contracted tissue and the next stress applied. The suggested mechanism for this difference was the disruption of collagen crosslinks or adhesions.

Changes in connective tissue resistance to stress are postulated to be due to the crimped nature of collagen. When normal tendon is stressed, there is a sliding action between fibers which allows an initially low strain,[42] and it is likely that with the loss of other connective tissue elements, this crimping is compromised and increased crosslinking between collagen occurs.[5] Radin and Paul[92] postulated that hyaluronic acid may have an important role in lubricating soft tissues around joints, thereby preventing such crosslinking.[5] The physical forces of stress and motion stimulate fibroblasts to control the amount of proteoglycans and lubrication present. A critical interfiber distance may thus be created which would potentially prevent further crosslinking.[123] Therefore, on a molecular level, changes in collagen appear significant in the process of formation of contractures.

Permysial collagen comprises the majority of muscle collagen by dry weight, and collagen changes during immobilization probably involve this type to the greatest extent. Initially, type 1 collagen replaces type 3 collagen.[58] Contracture occurs secondary to the connective tissue of skeletal muscle shortening, rather than shortening of the tendon.[51] At later stages of immobilization in the shortened position, sarcomere loss of up to 40% has been documented.[102,104] The more permanent change related to sarcomere loss, in addition to the long-term sequelae of fibrous adhesions between cartilage surfaces and breakdown in joint cartilage, resulted in relatively irreversible changes. Comparisons of the contribution by capsule and muscle to flexion contractures induced in rats have shown that while contracture of both muscle and capsule occurs, the shortening of muscle appears to have a more significant restricting effect on joint movement.[34] These studies were done on rat knees immobilized for up to 90 days. Studies of contractures due to immobility for longer periods suggested that the involvement of periarticular connective tissue becomes a more significant factor.[33,123]

In reviewing a population of active elderly individuals who did not feel handicapped by restricted joint motion, James and Parker[57] were able to demonstrate decreasing ROM with increasing age from 70 to 90 years in all joints of the lower extremities. Those joints spanned by muscles crossing two joints were more severely restricted. Hip abduction, a movement less likely to require full range during functional movements in the elderly, was the most restricted. Muscle fiber loss and a relative increase in the proportion of connective tissue have been demonstrated in the elderly,[18,80] with these ideas leading to speculation that they play a role in the decreased ROM seen by James and Parker.[57]

Alterations in Cartilage

Finsterbush and Friedman[36] reported degenerative changes in the knee joints of rabbits immobilized in a neutral position for 2 and 6 weeks, then remobilized for periods up to 8 months. After 2 weeks of immobilization, partial limitation was seen initially, but this resolved completely within 2 months of remobilization. Grossly, the joints appeared normal, but histologically, empty lacunae and fissuring of the cellular column suggested that the cartilage had not returned to normal. Immobilization for 6 weeks resulted in marked reduction of knee ROM. Recovery occurred only within the first 4 months and joints which did not recover full ROM within this time period remained restricted. Joints in which ROM was residually restricted were found to have intra-articular adhesions. Replacement of areas of cartilage with fibrocartilage and proliferation of chondrocytes were seen with the longer periods of immobilization. Fibrous adhesions between cartilage surfaces and fissuring with replacement by fibrous tissue, rather than normal cartilage, have also been observed by other researchers.[5,33,34,52,70] Rigid immobilization is not essential to produce these structural changes. Evans et al.[34] noted structural changes around and within a joint and adhesions between adjacent cartilage surfaces when slight joint movements were allowed.

The duration of immobilization appears to be more significant in producing these changes than the type of immobilization used. Enneking and Horowitz[33] noted that the final outcome was the same histologically, regardless of the etiology. They examined human cadaver knees that had in vivo been immobilized for a long period of time. Static compression between constantly apposed cartilage is felt to be a major determinant in chondrocyte death and cartilage degeneration.[110] This finding has far-reaching implications regarding the long-term "slow-onset effects" of immobilization and contractures. Joints which have a mechanically inferior surface would be expected to undergo degenerative arthritic changes sooner.[101]

Immobility and Loss of Muscle Strength

Strength is related to immobilization. Elbows splinted in a 90°-flexed position resulted in a significant decrease in flexor strength but not in extensor strength.[116] Since the flexors are expected to be stronger than the extensors,[60] it follows that in a weakened condition, they may not be able to counteract the extensors during functional activities, thereby compromising joint integrity.[82] Certainly, this loss of strength may be related to the development of contractures since the propensity for muscle imbalance and therefore joint range imbalance are increased.

Commonly Affected Sites

Due to the period of immobility and the prominent role of spasticity in the early stages of stroke recovery, contractures in hemiplegic limbs would be inevitable if no treatment was provided to those hemiplegic patients who did not recover spontaneously in the first month. Only 10% of stroke patients have such rapid recovery without residual loss.[49]

The common areas of contracture in the upper limb are restriction in shoulder movement in all planes, elbow flexion contractures, wrist flexion contractures, and finger intrinsics contractures. The pattern of contractures follows the flexion, adduction, and internal rotation pattern of an upper motor neuron lesion affecting the pyramidal tracts. Shoulder contractures may possibly be associated with trauma to the rotator cuff caused by shoulder subluxation. Elbow flexion contractures occur due to the spastic contraction of the elbow flexors unopposed by the triceps, particularly during the recovery stage during which flexor synergy is present. Similarly, contracture of the long flexors of the fingers and of the hand intrinsics result in finger and wrist flexion deformities due to persistent flexed position of the wrist and fingers secondary to spasticity. Edema over the dorsum of the hand often compromises active dorsiflexion of the fingers.

Flexion contractures in the lower extremities also follow the initial patterns of upper motor neuron recovery. Hip flexion, knee flexion, and ankle plantar flexion and inversion are the common positions of contracted lower extremity joints.

Muscles which span two joints are biomechanically more prone to develop contractures due to the ability to adjust to decreased length by compensatory movements of the two joints spanned. This effect is seen in the hamstring muscles, where hip extension can be used to allow full knee extension in spite of shortened hamstring muscle length. Therefore, in trying to restore full ROM or prevent loss of range, joints must be positioned to allow full physiologic stretch of the muscle groups involved. This principle also applies to the testing of ROM during which the muscle should be positioned at its full length to determine if tightening is present. Other two-joint muscle groups in which contractures are often seen are the intrinsic muscles of the hands, gastrocnemius, tensor fascia latae, and the long heads of biceps brachii and triceps.

Disability and Movement Efficiency

Impairments in the neuromusculoskeletal system often result in decreased movement efficiency. During normal ambulation and standing, movement or postural inefficiency is most apparent when an impairment occurs which changes lower limb function.[38] For example, in persons who are able to stand in a relaxed posture with their knees fully extended, the gravity force line from the body's center of mass is anterior to the axis of flexion-extension of the knee joint[66] (Fig. 1). In this position, the ankle plantar flexors (e.g., gastrocnemius and soleus) are active, while the knee extensors do not need to contract to maintain stance.[11] Standing in a knee-flexed or crouched position (i.e., similar to that adapted with knee flexor contractures) requires active knee extension, as the knee extensors counteract the flexion moment that exists because gravity acts through a force line behind the knee axis in this position.[89] Consequently, during standing activities requiring support by the antigravity muscles of the lower extremities, an increase in muscle activity is required.

Ralston[93] studied the effects of complete immobilization by simulating contractures on selected joints of the lower extremities. Immobilizing one ankle resulted in a 6% increase in energy consumption, and immobilizing both ankles resulted in a 9% increase when subjects walked at a speed of approximately 73 m/min, which had been their self-selected walking speed prior to joint immobilization. He further found that a knee immobilized at 15° and 45° short of full extension increased the energy expenditure of walking by 10% and 37%, respectively. With the knee immobilized in full extension, a 13% increase in energy expenditure occurred. At the same speed of ambulation, hip immobilization at full extension and 30° flexion resulted in increases of 13% and 6%, respectively. Immobilization of the arms had no effect on energy consumption, and immobilization of the torso increased energy costs by 10%. However, these simulated contractures involved complete fixation of the joint, rather than a freely swinging joint through a restricted range of movement, which would be the usual case encountered with joint contractures of the lower extremities where complete loss of ROM is a rare occurrence.

Waters et al.[118] ascertained that oxygen cost increased by 32% following arthrodesis of one hip at an average angle of 21°. After arthrodesis of the ankle joint only, the oxygen consumption associated with walking increased by 3%. Campbell et al.[23] studied 20 young, able-bodied women using simulated knee-flexion contractures

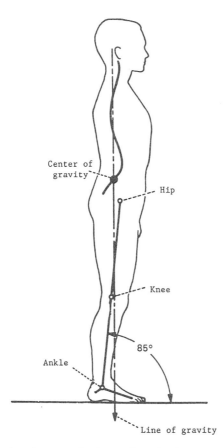

FIGURE 1. In a relaxed stance, the force-of-gravity line falls in front of the knee joint (Adapted from Lehmkuhl LD, Smith LK: Brunnstrom's Clinical Kinesiology. Philadelphia, FA Davis, 1985, p 363; with permission).

of 15°, 20°, and 25°; oxygen uptake increased and the velocity of walking and stride length decreased at flexion limitations of 20° or greater. In their model, the knee was restricted in extension only. Similarly, restrictions in joint ROM have been found to affect movements other than walking. Fleckenstein et al.[39] found that simulated knee-extension contractures significantly increased the hip torque necessary to stand from sitting. In general, hemiplegic individuals have been found to expend 41% more energy per meter traveled.[9,30] Combine these findings with the loss of muscle strength following immobilization, and the potential for compromise of functional impairment is increased.

Standing with Contractures

Approximations of the extension force needed to stabilize the flexed knee during weight-bearing have been calculated.[88] When the knee was flexed 15°, the force to maintain standing was approximately 75% of body weight (i.e., load) on the femoral head, 210% at 30° of knee flexion, and 410% at 60°. The measured quadriceps torque was approximately 20% of maximum quadriceps strength at

15° and 50% at 30°. Potter and Kirby[89] found that due to the high torques produced in the 60° flexed position, standing with this degree of bilateral simulated contracture resulted in cessation of standing in less than 2 minutes. This was related to marked muscle fatigue. Standing with 60° of unilateral contracture, would likely result in a marked or entire weight shift to the unaffected side,[90] reducing the energy consumption required.

MEDICAL AND REHABILITATIVE MANAGEMENT OF SPASTICITY AND CONTRACTURES

Pharmacologic Treatment of Spasticity Related to Stroke

Pharmacologic treatment is sometimes used in the acute phase of spasticity development. Of the drugs commonly available, the four medications most commonly used in the past decade have been baclofen, diazepam, dantrolene sodium, and barbiturates.[95,124] More recently employed drugs include clonidine, cyproheptadine, tizanidine, and ketazolam, since the aforementioned caused negative side effects such as drowsiness, weakness, and fatigue. In addition, some success has been found with the use of intramuscular neurolysis (e.g., phenol or procaine blocks) (Table 1).

The development and study of pharmacological treatments for spasticity are limited by the difficulties experienced in measuring outcome and differentiating between the components of disability caused by "negative" and "positive" symptoms. For example, a too-aggressive approach may reduce spasticity in the lower extremities to a dysfunctional level during gait.[95,109] Neurophysiologic measurement techniques may eventually be useful in screening patients prior to therapy. For instance, those patients with near-normal vibratory inhibition would presumably be less likely to respond to drugs which facilitate vibratory inhibition.

Baclofen, diazepam, and dantrolene remain the most commonly used agents but are limited by side effects. Clonidine, cyproheptadine, tizanidine, and ketazolam are potential alternatives in the pharmacologic management of spasticity; however, the available literature does not allow the establishment of a general protocol for choosing the most appropriate medication.

Neurorehabilitative Treatment of Spasticity

The relationship between functional outcome and the level of spasticity exhibited in limbs is unknown. Burke[22] has suggested that the major deficits in function, from cerebral stroke, are weakness and loss of dexterity. It can be suggested that a certain level of spasticity in the lower extremity appears to be useful in facilitating weight-bearing during gait when acting as a limb-splinting mechanism. This may somewhat compensate for the loss of strength exhibited by the muscles following stroke. The upper extremity often presents differently since any spasticity is probably a detriment to function, particularly with respect to dexterity. Therefore, the medical and rehabilitative management of spasticity is, at present, extremely controversial, with some clinicians believing that all spasticity is dysfunctional, while others suggest that certain levels of spasticity, in specific limbs, are helpful. Certainly, several neurorehabilitative treatment approaches have evolved for neurologic disorders such as stroke under the philosophy that muscle tone must be normalized or reduced for optimal functioning.[14,21,63,94] Current rehabilitation practice often utilizes a more functional rehabilitation approach which is employed alone or in combination with pure or eclectic neurorehabilitation

TABLE 1. Pharmacological Treatment Approaches to Spasticity in Stroke

Treatment	Hypothesized Mechanism of Action	Side Effects	Comments
Diazepam	Spinal action Increases presynaptic inhibition of muscle spindles	Sedation, light-headedness Habituation	A second choice to baclofen
Baclofen	Suppresses release of excitory transmitters (e.g., substance P) Possible post-synaptic action	Reaction with other drugs (e.g., some anti-depressants) Sedation, ataxia, respiratory and cardiovascular depression Decreases seizure threshold Confusion	More success in treating spasticity when compared to diazepam
Pantrolene sodium	Interrupts excitation-contraction coupling of skeletal muscle	Drowsiness, weakness, fatigue Hepatotoxicity Precipitates seizures Lymphocytic lymphoma	Reduces spasticity in 60–80% of patients Useful in nonambulatory patients
Barbiturates	Central action Depresses lateral reticular formation	Depresses entire nervous system (e.g., drowsiness, lethargy)	Widely used
Clonidine	Central action Facilitates the alpha-2 agonists	Side effects not consistently seen Major ones seem to be hypotension, lethargy, dizziness, insomnia	Evolving as an important primary and adjunctive approach to spasticity treatment
Tizanidine*	Central action Facilitates alpha-2 receptors Increases muscle spindle presynaptic inhibition	Insomnia Side effects not consistently seen	More study required
Ketazolam	Benzodiazepam	Some drowsiness, lightheadedness More study required	Fewer side effects than diazepam
Procaine block (intramuscular neurolysis)	Selectively inhibits small gamma fibers, resulting in relaxation of intrafusal muscle fibers	None known	Transient effect
5–7% Phenol	Destroys small intramuscular mixed nerve branch	Tissue toxicity Possible pain complication	Found to decrease spasticity when followed by intensive therapy

* Not currently available in North America

approaches when treating stroke-related spasticity. In addition, a relatively new task-specific treatment style, based on the motor-learning research of human movement, has been developed and is a promising new treatment approach that does not attempt to reduce spasticity in stroke patients.[25,26]

Until the time arrives when spasticity can be sensitively, validly, and reliably measured, it will be difficult to measure the efficacy of treatment approaches designed to reduce spasticity. Since many clinicians strongly believe, from countless clinical observations, that neurorehabilitative treatment approaches such as the neurodevelopmental approach[14] do reduce spasticity, these authors do not suggest that these treatment approaches be abandoned. Rather, use of the treatment or treatment approaches that the clinician believes to be efficacious are appropriate.

Treatment of Contractures

In relation to musculoskeletal contractures, anticipation of this secondary problem associated with stroke and stroke-related spasticity is necessary to avoid complications. When a muscle shortens relative to contracture, the stretch reflex will be evoked earlier in the movement range since, for any joint angle, the muscle will be stretched more than normal. Ada and Canning[1] suggested this problem establishes a vicious cycle, since spasticity causes contracture and the shortened muscles then facilitate spasticity. Therefore, proper positioning within the bed or wheelchair, appropriate splinting, and passive mobilization are mainstays of treatment in the prevention of the two major stroke-related factors that interfere with function, i.e., a decrease in muscle length and an increase in stiffness.[1] Certainly, a shorter, stiffer calf muscle will affect standing and will require stronger muscles to overcome its passive stiffness during active or passive lengthening.[1] In addition, the treatment of local pain, edema, and spasticity may be necessary as part of the adjunctive treatment of contractures, if these problems are present.

Mobilization and passive stretching techniques for the avoidance of muscle shortening have been described in detail by Ada and Canning.[1] Daily half-hour periods of muscle stretch have been shown to prevent both sarcomere loss and connective tissue remodeling,[121] with these factors being associated with contracture development.

As an example of passive mobilization for the lower extremities, lying in the prone position will result in partial stretching of the hip flexors. However, usually only 155° of hip extension is attained compared to standing normal hip extension of 170°.[66] Hip extension is facilitated during normal standing by the extension torque produced due to the line of gravity falling behind the axis of rotation of the hip. Standing with the knees in full extension provides a moderate stretch to both the gastrocnemius and soleus, as well as to the hamstrings muscles. Therefore, patients should be encouraged to stand as soon as possible following stroke. Indeed, preventative contracture treatment should employ active motor training to facilitate the regaining of voluntary movement control, with more passive strategies being implemented when voluntary movement is slow or unlikely to return, when contractures are already present, or when spasticity limits active practice.[1] In this regard, biofeedback has been useful in helping stroke patients train appropriate muscle activity for certain tasks.[71,95]

Treatments which utilize maximal contractions are thought to exacerbate spasticity and contribute to muscle contractures.[1] These maximal contractions were found to interfere with the patient's ability to turn off muscle activity once initiated.[96] However, it is important to differentiate between an involuntary contraction which interferes with task performance and a controlled contraction of the same muscle group.[1] It has been suggested that employing the motor-learning approach[25] with the specific training of muscles at risk for the development of spasticity has been helpful in eliminating unnecessary muscle activity.

The mainstay of treatment, once a contracture is present, is prolonged stretching of the contracted tissue to provide tissue deformation, thereby producing definitive changes in the collagen of connective tissue involved. It is felt that the minimal treatment for contractures is a sustained stretch greater than 30 minutes.[43,66] Less-used treatments are progressive serial splinting and progressive serial casting. While successful use of casts to reduce contractures in the neurologically impaired has been demonstrated,[2,106,107] the muscle immobilization research in animals indicates deleterious secondary effects of casting, particularly on those muscles casted in the shortened position (see Goldspink and Williams[44] for detailed discussion). The better approach may be serial splinting, rather than permanent stretching or casting, which would prevent muscle atrophy in patients. Unfortunately, the critical amount of stretch and its duration during splinting to produce appropriate results is unknown.[44] For long-standing contractures (i.e., >6 months), it is likely that surgical release is necessary due to the sarcomere loss which has occurred. This may include surgical approaches like tendon lengthening, reposition, osteotomy, or joint replacement.

The choice of treatment of joint contractures should be based on their etiology and the availability of orthotic devices and therapy. The duration and extent of the contractures are critical in the decision process, and longstanding contractures in the face of spasticity may not be successfully treated by conservative management.

General Goal of Medical and Rehabilitative Management

The facilitation of an optimal functional outcome in stroke recoverers is of primary importance. To this end, the rehabilitation team should endeavor to employ those treatment approaches they feel are worthy, while simultaneously empowering the patient toward the goal of achieving the highest level of functional recovery attainable (see Teasell[109] for review of medical treatment approaches in hemiplegia). The affect of psychosocial variables in this regard cannot be underestimated. Certainly, most clinicians have noticed that those patients with strong motivation and supportive environments learn to function, often despite extreme disabilities. The in-depth understanding of psychosocial factors and their influence on functional outcome following stroke requires further research.

CONCLUSION

Longevity following stroke provides motivation for health professionals to increase their understanding of the often-observed effects of stroke (i.e., spasticity and contractures) in order to provide the most efficacious medical and rehabilitative treatment of these disorders. Physiologically, both spasticity and contracture are multidimensional and provide health professionals with formidable challenges with regards to choosing the most appropriate treatments. In this respect, it would be imperative to measure spasticity and monitor the development of contractures in order to evaluate treatments. Since spasticity can only be measured in the clinic by quantitatively assessing muscle tone, a new clinical technique for muscle tone and contracture measurement has been described and scientifically rationalized. Pharmacologic treatment of spasticity was briefly described as well as the current medical and rehabilitative treatment approaches to dealing with spasticity and contractures. An in-depth understanding of the psychosocial factors related to optimal functional outcome following stroke, despite disability related to spasticity and contractures, requires future research.

REFERENCES

1. Ada L, Canning C: Anticipating and avoiding muscle shortening. In Ada L, Canning C (eds): Physiotherapy: Foundations for Practice—Key Issues in Neurological Physiotherapy. London, Heinemann Medical, 1990.
2. Ada L, Scott D: Use of inhibitory weight-bearing plasters to increase movement in the presence of spasticity. Aust J Physiother 26:257, 1980.
3.. Akeson WH, Amiel D, LaViolette D: The connective tissue response to immobility: A study of chondroitin-4 and -6 sulfate and dermatin sulfate changes in the periarticular connective tissue in the control and immobilized knees of dogs. Clin Orthop 51:183–197, 1967.

4. Akeson WH, Woo SL-Y, Amiel D, et al: The connective tissue response to immobility: Biochemical changes in periarticular connective tissue of the immobilized rat knee. Clin Orthop 93:356–362, 1973.
5. Akeson WH, Amiel D, Woo SL-Y: Immobility effects on synovial joints—The pathomechanics of joint contracture. Biorheology 17:95–110, 1980.
6. Alnaqueeb MA, Alzaid NS, Goldspink G: Connective tissue changes and physical properties of developing and aging skeletal muscle. J Anat 139:677–689, 1984.
7. Ashworth B: Preliminary trial of carisoprodal in multiple sclerosis. Practitioner 192:540–542, 1964.
8. Bach-y-Rita P: Process of recovery from stroke. In Brandstater ME, Basmajian JV (eds): Stroke Rehabilitation. Baltimore, Williams & Wilkins, 1987, pp 80–108.
9. Bard G, Ralston JH: Measurement of energy expenditure during ambulation with special reference to evaluation of assistive devices. Arch Phys Med Rehabil 40:415–420, 1959.
10. Barolat-Romana G, Davis R: Neurophysiological mechanisms in abnormal reflex activities in cerebral palsy and spinal spasticity. J Neurol Neurosurg Psychiatry 43:333–342, 1980.
11. Basmajian JV, DeLuca C: Muscles Alive. Baltimore, Williams & Wilkins, 1985.
12. Benecke R, Conrad B, Meinck HH, Hohne J: Electromyographic analysis of bicycling on an ergometer for evaluation of spasticity of lower limbs in man. In Desmedt JE (ed): Motor Control Mechanisms in Health and Disease. New York, Raven Press, 1983.
13. Bisch L, Semenciw R, Wilkins K: Temporal and spatial patterns in stroke mortality and morbidity among the Canadian elderly. Chronic Dis Can 10:63–67, 1989.
14. Bobath B: Adult Hemiplegia. Oxford, Heinemann, 1989.
15. Bohannon RW: Variability and reliability of the pendulum test for spasticity using a Cybex II isokinetic dynamometer. Phys Ther 67:659–661, 1987.
16. Bohannon RW, Larkin PA: Cybex II isokinetic dynamometer for the documentation of spasticity. Phys Ther 65:46–47, 1985.
17. Bohannon RW, Smith MB: Interrater reliability of a modified Ashworth scale of muscle spasticity. Phys Ther 67:206–207, 1987.
18. Bonner CD: Rehabilitation instead of bed rest? Geriatrics 24:109–118, 1969.
19. Broberg C, Grimby G: Measurement of torque during passive and active ankle movements in patients with muscle hypertonia—A methodological study. Scand J Rehabil Med (suppl)9:108–117, 1983.
20. Brodal A: Neurological Anatomy: In Relation to Clinical Medicine, 3rd ed. New York, Oxford, 1981, pp 845–847.
21. Brunnstrom S: Movement Therapy in Hemiplegia. New York, Harper & Row, 1970.
22. Burke D: Spasticity as an adaptation to pyramidal tract injury. In Waxman SG (ed): Advances in Neurology, vol 47: Functional Recovery in Neurological Diseases. New York, Raven Press, 1988, pp 401–423.
23. Campbell J, Waters RL, Thomas L, et al: Simulated knee flexion contracture: Demands of walking (abstract). Phys Ther 64:715, 1984.
24. Carr JH, Shepherd RB: Physiotherapy in Disorders of the Brain: A Clinical Guide. London, Heinemann, 1980.
25. Carr JH, Shepherd RB: A Motor Relearning Programme for Stroke, 2nd ed. Oxford, Heinemann Medical, 1987.
26. Carr JH, Shepherd RD (eds): Movement Science: Foundations for Physical Therapy in Rehabilitation. Rockville, MD, Aspen, 1987.
27. Chaco J, Blank A, Ferber I, Gonnen MDB: Recurrent inhibition in spastic hemiplegia. Electromyogr Clin Neurophysiol 24:571–576, 1984.
28. Chapman CE, Wiesendanger M: Recovery of function following unilateral lesions of bulbar pyramid in the monkey. Electroencephalogr Clin Neurophysiol 53:374–387, 1982.
29. Chapman CE, Wiesendanger M: The physiological and anatomical basis of spasticity: A review. Physiother Can 34:125–135, 1982.
30. Corcoran PJ, Brengelmann GL: Oxygen uptake in normal and handicapped subjects, in relation to speed of walking beside velocity-controlled cart. Arch Phys Med Rehabil 51:78–87, 1970.
31. Delwaide PJ: Human monosynaptic reflexes and presynaptic inhibition. In Desmedt JE (ed): New Developments in Electromyography and Clinical Neurophysiology, vol 3. Basel, Karger, 1973, pp 508–522.
32. Delwaide PJ: Electrophysiological testing of spastic patients: Its potential usefulness and limitations. In Delwaide PJ, Young RR (eds): Clinical Neurophysiology in Spasticity. Amsterdam, Elsevier, 1985.
33. Enneking WF, Horowitz M: The intra-articular effects of immobilization on the human knee. J Bone Joint Surg 54A:973–985, 1972.

34. Evans EB, Eggers GWN, Butler JK, Blumel J: Experimental immobilization and remobilization of rat knee joints. J Bone Joint Surg 42A:737–758, 1960.
35. Fellows SJ, Ross HF, Thilmann AF: Mechanical alterations in the flexibility of spastic human ankle joint. J Physiol 420:83P, 1990.
36. Finsterbush A, Friedman B: Early changes in immobilized rabbits knee joint. Clin Orthop 131:279, 1972.
37. Fischback GD, Robbins N: Changes in contractile properties of disused soleus muscles. J Physiol (Lond) 201:305, 1969.
38. Fisher SV, Gullickson G: Energy cost of ambulation in health and disability: A literature review. Arch Phys Med Rehabil 59:124–133, 1978.
39. Fleckenstein SJ, Kirby RL, MacLeod DA: Effect of limited knee-flexion range on peak hip joint moments of force in humans transferring from sitting to standing. J Biomech 21:915–918, 1988.
40. Folger WN: Epidemiology of cerebrovascular disease. In Brandstater ME, Basmajian JV (eds): Stroke Rehabilitation. Baltimore, Williams & Wilkins, 1987, pp 1–35.
41. Fugl-Meyer AR, Jaasko L, Leyman I, et al: The post-stroke hemiplegic patient: 1. A method of evaluation of physical performance. Scand J Rehabil Med 7:13–31, 1975.
42. Fung YCB: The elasticity of soft tissues in simple elongation. Am J Physiol 213:1532–1544, 1967.
43. Goldspink DF: The influence of immobilization and stretch on protein turnover in rat skeletal muscle. J Physiol 264:267–282, 1977.
44. Goldspink G, Williams P: Muscle fibre and connective tissue changes associated with use and disuse. In Ada L, Canning C (eds): Physiotherapy: Foundations for Practice—Key Issues in Neurological Physiotherapy. Oxford, Butterworth Heinemann, 1990, pp 197–218..
45. Goodwin GM, Hoffman D, Luschei ES: The strength of the reflex response to sinusoidal stretch of monkey jaw closing muscles during voluntary contraction. J Physiol 279:81, 1978.
46. Gordon J: Disorders of motor control. In Ada L, Canning C (eds): Physiotherapy: Foundations for Practice—Key Issues in Neurological Physiotherapy. Oxford, Butterworth Heinemann, 1990, pp 25–50.
47. Gottlieb GL, Myklebust BM, Stefoski D, et al: Evaluation of cervical stimulation for chronic treatment of spasticity. Neurology 35:699–704, 1985.
48. Grimm RJ: Program disorders of movement. In Desmedt JE (ed): Advances in Neurology—Motor Control Mechanisms in Health and Disease. New York, Raven Press, 1983.
49. Hachinski V, Norris JW: The Acute Stroke. Philadelphia, FA Davis, 1985, p 87.
50. Hagbarth KE, Wallin G, Lofstedt L: Muscle spindle responses to stretch in normal and spastic subjects. Scand J Rehabil Med 5:156–159, 1973.
51. Halar EM, Bell KR: Contracture and other deleterious effects of immobility. In Delisa JA (ed): Rehabilitation Medicine: Principles and Practice. Philadelphia, JB Lippincott, 1988, pp 448–462.
52. Hall MC: Cartilage changes after experimental immobilization of the knee joint of the young rat. J Bone Joint Surg 45A:36–44, 1963.
53. Halpern D, Beck R, Nesse D: Myotonometry—A quantitative technique to measure muscular hypertonia. Minn Med 63:565–604, 1980.
54. Harburn KL, Hill KM, Vandervoort AA, et al: Spasticity measurement in stroke: A pilot study. Can J Public Health (in press).
55. Hnik P, Vejsada R, Goldspink DF, et al: Quantitative evaluation of electromyogram activity in rat extensor and flexor muscles immobilized at different lengths. Exp Neurol 88:515, 1985.
56. Hufschmidt A, Mauritz KH: Chronic transformation of muscle in spasticity: A peripheral contribution to tone. J Neurol Neurosurg Psychiatry 48:676–685, 1985.
57. James B, Parker AW: Active and passive mobility of lower limb joints in elderly men and women. Am J Phys Med Rehabil 68:162–167, 1989.
58. Jimenez SA: The connective tissues: Structure, function, and metabolism. In Schumacher HR, Klippel JH, Robinson DR (eds): Primer on the Rheumatic Diseases. Atlanta, Arthritis Foundation, 1988.
59. Johnstone M: Restoration of Motor Function in the Stroke Patient: A Physiotherapist's Approach. Edinburgh, Churchill Livingstone, 1983.
60. Kapandji IA: The Physiology of the Joints: Upper Extremity. London, Churchill Livingstone, 1979.
61. Katz R, Pierrot-Deseilligny E: Recurrent inhibition of alpha-motoneurons in patients with upper motor neuron lesions. Brain 105:103–124, 1982.
62. Katz RT, Rymer WZ: Spastic hypertonia: Mechanisms and measurement. Arch Phys Med Rehabil 70:144–155, 1989.
63. Knott M, Voss DE: Proprioceptive Neuromuscular Facilitation. New York, Harper & Row, 1968.

64. Knutsson E: Analysis of gait and isokinetic movements for evaluation of antispastic drugs or physical therapies. In Desmedt JE (ed): Motor Control Mechanisms in Health and Disease. New York, Raven Press, 1983.

65. Knutsson E: Studies of gait control in patients with spastic paresis. In Delwaide PJ, Young RR (eds): Clinical Neurophysiology in Spasticity. Amsterdam, Elsevier, 1985, pp 175–184.

66. Kottke FJ, Pauley DL, Park RA: The rationale for prolonged stretching for correction of shortening of connective tissue. Arch Phys Med Rehabil 47:345–352, 1966.

67. Kruger L, Porter P: A behavioral study of the functions of the rolandic cortex in the monkey. J Comp Neurol 109:439–469, 1958.

68. Lance JW: Pathophysiology of spasticity and clinical experience with baclofen. In Feldman RG, Young RR, Koella WP (eds): Spasticity—Disordered Motor Control. Chicago, Yearbook, 1980, pp 185–203.

69. Lance JW, McLeod JG: A Physiological Approach to Clinical Neurology. London, Butterworths, 1981.

70. Langenskiold A, Michelsson J-E, Videman T: Osteoarthritis of the knee in the rabbit produced by immobilization. Acta Orthop Scand 50:1–14, 1979.

71. LeCraw D: Biofeedback in stroke rehabilitation. In Basmajian JV (ed): Biofeedback—Principles and Practice for Clinicians. Baltimore, Williams & Wilkins, 1989.

72. Lee WA, Boughton A, Rymer WZ: Absence of stretch reflex gain enhancement in voluntarily activated spastic muscle. Exp Neurol 98:317–335, 1987.

73. Liebermann JS: Physiological correlates of clinically observed changes in posture and tone following lesions of the central nervous system. Int Rehabil Med 4:195–199, 1982.

74. Mahoney FI, Barthel DW: Functional evaluation: The Barthel index. Maryland St Med J 14:61–65, 1965.

75. Mai J: Adrenergic influences on spasticity studies on the influence of alpha and beta adrenergic blockage on proprioceptive reflex parameters in spastic patients. Acta Neurol Scand 63(suppl 85):6–143, 1981.

76. Matheson JE: Neuroanatomical Localization of Spasticity in Stroke, Via MRI: A Descriptive Study (Thesis). London, ON, The University of Western Ontario, 1992, 66 pp.

77. McPherson JJ, Mathiowetz V, Strachota E, et al: Muscle tone: Objective evaluation of the static component at the wrist. Arch Phys Med Rehabil 66:670–674, 1985.

78. Meinck HM, Benecke R, Conrad B: Spasticity and the flexor reflex. In Delwaide PJ, Young RR (eds): Clinical Neurophysiology in Spasticity. Amsterdam, Elsevier, 1985.

79. Mettler FA: Extensive unilateral cerebral removals in the primate: Physiologic effects and resultant degeneration. J Comp Neurol 79:185–245, 1943.

80. Miller MG: Iatrogenic and neurogenic effects of prolonged immobilization of the ill aged. J Am Geriatr Soc 23:360–369, 1975.

81. Molinari FG: Experimental models of ischemic stroke. In Barnett HJM, Mohr JP, Stein BM, Yatsu FM (eds): Stroke: Pathophysiology, Diagnosis and Management. New York, Churchill Livingstone, 1986, pp 57–74.

82. Norkin CC, Levangie PK: Joint Structure and Function: A Comprehensive Analysis. Philadelphia, FA Davis, 1992, p 119.

83. Ongerboer de Visser BW, Bour LJ, et al: Cumulative vibratory indices and the H/M ratio of the soleus H-reflex: A quantitative study in control and spastic subjects. Electroencephalogr Clin Neurophysiol 73:162–166, 1989.

84. Ostfeld A: A review of stroke epidemiology. Epidemiol Rev 2:136–152, 1980.

85. Otis JC, Root L, Pamilla JR, Kroll MA: Biomechanical measurement of spastic plantar flexors. Dev Med Child Neurol 25:60–66, 1983.

86. Peacock EE: Some biomechanical and biophysical aspects of joint stiffness: Role of collagen synthesis as opposed to altered molecular bonding. Ann Surg 164:1–12, 1966.

87. Perkins G: Rest and movement. J Bone Joint Surg 25B:521–539, 1953.

88. Perry J, Antonelli MS, Ford W: Analysis of knee joint forces during flexed-knee stance. J Bone Joint Surg 57A:961–967, 1975.

89. Potter PJ, Kirby RL: Relationship between electromyographic activity of the vastus lateralis while standing and the extent of bilateral simulated knee-flexion contractures. Am J Phys Med Rehabil 70:301–305, 1991.

90. Potter PJ, Kirby RL, Macleod DA: The effects of simulated knee-flexion contractures on standing balance. Am J Phys Med Rehabil 69:144–147, 1990.

91. Powers RK, Marder-Meyer J, Rymer J: Quantitative relations between hypertonia and stretch reflex threshold in spastic hemiparesis. Ann Neurol 23:115–124, 1988.

92. Radin EL, Paul IL: A consolidated concept of joint lubrication. J Bone Joint Surg 54A:607–616, 1972.

93. Ralston HJ: Effects of immobilization of various body segments on energy cost of human locomotion. Ergonomics 7(suppl):53–60, 1964.
94. Rood M: Neurophysiological mechanisms utilized in the treatment of neuromuscular dysfunction. Am J Occup Ther 10:220–225, 1956.
95. Ryerson S: Hemiplegia resulting from vascular insult or disease. In Umphred DA (ed): Neurological Rehabilitation. St. Louis, Mosby, 1990, pp 619–659.
96. Sahrmann S, Norton BJ: The relationship of voluntary movement to spasticity in the upper motor neuron system. Ann Neurol 2:460, 1977.
97. Schoenberg BS: Epidemiology of cerebrovascular disease. South Med J 72:31, 1979.
98. Sinkjaer T, Toft E, Andreassen S, Hornemann BC: Muscle stiffness in human ankle dorsiflexors: Intrinsic and reflex components. J Neurophysiol 60:1110–1121, 1988.
99. Sinkjaer T, Magnussen I: Reflex stiffness within normal range in spastic patients with hemiparesis. In Wollacott M, Horak F (eds): Posture and Gait: Control Mechanisms 1992, XIth International Symposium of the Society for Postural and Gait Research. Portland, OR, University of Oregon, 1992, pp 31–34.
100. Soderberg GL: Kinesiology—Application to Pathological Motion. Baltimore, Williams & Wilkins, 1986, p 73.
101. Sokoloff L, Hough AJ: Pathology of Osteoarthritis. In McCarty DJ (ed): Arthritis and Allied Conditions. Philadelphia, Lea & Febiger, 1985, pp 1377–1399.
102. Spector SA, Simard CP, Fournier SM, et al: Architectural alterations of rat hind limb skeletal muscle immobilized at different lengths. Exp Neurol 76:94–110, 1982.
103. Stolov WC, Hardy RW: Muscle contracture: Growth and immobilization (abstract). Arch Phys Med Rehabil 57:562–563, 1976.
104. Tabary JC, Tabary C, Tardieu C, et al: Physiological and structural changes in the cat's soleus muscle due to immobilization at different lengths by plaster casts. J Physiol 224:231–244, 1972.
105. Tabary J-C, Tardieu C, Tardieu G, Tabary C: Experimental rapid sarcomere loss with concomitant hypoextensibility. Muscle Nerve 4:198–203, 1981.
106. Tardieu C, Tardieu G, Colbeau-Justin P, et al: Trophic muscle regulation in children with congenital cerebral lesions. J Neurol Sci 42:357, 1979.
107. Tardieu C, Huet de la Tour E, Bret MD, et al: Muscle hypoextensibility in children with cerebral palsy: I. Clinical and experimental observations. Arch Phys Med Rehabil 63:97, 1982.
108. Taylor S, Ashby P, Verrier M: Neurophysiological changes following traumatic spinal lesions in man. J Neurol Neurosurg Psychiatry 47:1102–1108, 1984.
109. Teasell R: Musculoskeletal complications of hemiplegia following stroke. Semin Arthritis Rheum 20:385–395, 1991.
110. Thaxter TH, Mann RA, Anderson CE: Degeneration of immobilized knee joints in rats. J Bone Joint Surg 47A:567–585, 1965.
111. Thilmann AF, Fellows SJ, Garms E: Pathological stretch reflexes on the "good" side of hemiparetic patients. J Neurol Neurosurg Psychiatry 53:208–214, 1990.
112. Toft E, Sinkjaer T, Andreassen S, Larsen K: Mechanical and electromyographic responses to stretch of the human ankle extensors. J Neurophysiol 65:1402–1410, 1991.
113. Tomanek RJ, Lund DD: Degeneration of different types of skeletal muscle fibres: II. Immobilization. J Anat 118:531, 1974.
114. Travis AM: Neurological deficiencies following supplementary motor area lesions in *Macaca mulatta*. Brain 78:174–198, 1955.
115. Twitchell TE: The restoration of motor function following hemiplegia in man. Brain 73:443–480, 1951.
116. Vaughan VA: Effects of upper limb immobilization on isometric muscle strength, movement time, and triphasic electromyographic characteristics. Phys Ther 69:119–129, 1989.
117. Wall JC, Ashburn A: Assessment of gait disability in hemiplegics. Scand J Rehabil Med 11:95, 1979.
118. Waters RL, Barnes G, Husseri T, et al: Comparable energy expenditure after arthrodesis of the hip and ankle. J Bone Joint Surg 70A:1032–1037, 1988.
119. Welch WK, Kennard MA: Relation of cerebral cortex to spasticity and flaccidity. J Neurophysiol 7:255–268, 1944.
120. Wilkins K, Morris S, Lane R: Mortality and morbidity of Canada's elderly population: A historical perspective. Chronic Dis Can 9:79–84, 1988.
121. Williams PE: Use of intermittent stretch in the prevention of serial sarcomere loss in immobilized muscles. Ann Rheum Dis 49:316, 1990.

122. Worley JS, Bennet W, Miller G, et al: Reliability of three clinical measures of muscle tone in the shoulder and wrists of post stroke patients. Am J Occup Ther 45:50–58, 1991.
123. Woo SL-Y, Mathews JV, Akeson WH, et al: Connective tissue response to immobility: Correlative study of biomechanical and biochemical measurements of normal and immobilized rabbit knees. Arthritis Rheum 18:257–264, 1975.
124. Young RR, Delwaide PJ: Drug therapy: Spasticity. N Engl J Med 304:28–33 and 96–99, 1981.

SUGGESTED READINGS

Ada L, Canning C (eds): Physiotherapy: Foundations for Practice—Key Issues in Neurological Physiotherapy. Oxford, Heinemann Medical, 1990.
Brandstater ME, Basmajian JV (eds): Stroke Rehabilitation. Baltimore, Williams & Wilkins, 1987.
Delwaide PJ, Young RR (eds): Clinical Neurophysiology in Spasticity: Restorative Neurology, vol 1. New York, Elsevier, 1985.
Montgomery PC, Connolly BH (eds): Motor Control and Physical Therapy—Theoretical Framework and Practical Applications. Hixson, TN, Chattanooga Group, 1991.

ROBERT W. TEASELL, MD, FRCPC
MARTIN GILLEN, MD, FRCPC

9. UPPER EXTREMITY DISORDERS AND PAIN FOLLOWING STROKE

From the Department of Physical
    Medicine and Rehabilitation
University of Western Ontario
    and
University Hospital
London, Ontario (RWT)
    and the
Department of Medicine
Division of Physical Medicine
    and Rehabilitation
University of Ottawa
    Rehabilitation Centre
Ottawa, Ontario, Canada (MG)

Reprint requests to:
Robert W. Teasell, MD, FRCPC
Chief
Department of Physical Medicine
    and Rehabilitation
University Hospital
339 Windermere Road
London, Ontario N6A 5A5
Canada

RECOVERY OF THE UPPER EXTREMITY POST STROKE

The various problems affecting the arm following a stroke are either directly or indirectly related to the degree of paresis and spasticity. As a result, the majority of upper extremity complications are seen following a middle cerebral artery stroke where the upper extremity is typically more involved, where recovery is not as complete, and where distal functions involving wrist and hand movements are the last to return. Given the fact that complex, coordinated hand activities require a high degree of neurologic recovery and that such activity is required in order to have an effectively functioning upper extremity, it is not too surprising that functional recovery is the exception, rather than the rule, following hemiplegia. It is against this background of incomplete neurologic recovery that problems affecting the arm occur.

Full recovery of voluntary motion may occur in up to 40% of stroke patients. However, full functional recovery is less likely to occur, as sensory recovery frequently lags behind motor recovery, interfering with coordination and dexterity of the hand. Indeed, the chance of functional recovery may be only 4 to 5%.[41,50] Stroke patients who have regained full recovery are usually exhibiting some functional return within the first 2 weeks.[6,24] Measurable recovery continues until the end of the third month and in some cases does continue after 3 months.[114]

In the majority of paretic upper extremities following stroke, the hemiplegic posture develops with the onset of increased tone and disinhibition of primitive reflexes. Flexor tone predominates as scapular retraction and depression, internal rotation and adduction of the shoulder, pronation of the forearm, and flexion of elbow, wrist, and fingers.[112] Complications in these patients are common, thereby reducing even further the degree of recovery and having a significant negative impact on the stroke patient's overall quality of life (Table 1). Anticipation of potential problems leading to a preventative program, as well as early diagnosis and intervention where complications do arise, remains crucial to minimizing their adverse impact on the stroke patient.

UPPER EXTREMITY DISORDERS

Shoulder Pain

Shoulder pain is a frequent complaint among stroke victims with hemiplegia.[42,95,113] Shoulder pain is most common early on following the onset of hemiplegia but may develop at any time during the first year following the stroke.[30] The two most reliable prospective studies have noted that 55 to 72% of hemiparetic stroke patients will develop shoulder pain in the affected limb within the first 6 to 12 months after a stroke.[18,113] However, Parker et al.[86] noted that at 3 months 74% and at 6 months 80% of patients with acute stroke had no pain. However, only 25% of their patients had moderate to severe paralysis while 75% had mild or no paralysis. It would appear that there is a relationship between the degree of paralysis and the risk of developing shoulder pain.

Possible causes of shoulder pain include glenohumeral subluxation,[14,80,97,99] restricted shoulder range of motion,[9,37,43,44,93] spasticity,[20,23,77] reflex sympathetic dystrophy,[26,29,87] and rotator cuff disorders[80,82] or disorders of the subacromial region.[51] Shoulder pain and associated restriction of range of motion interfere with achievement of optimal upper extremity function. Because each of these disorders affecting the shoulder region following hemiplegia may have pain as a presenting feature, it is oftentimes difficult to sort out the underlying cause of the shoulder pain.

Shoulder Subluxation

Subluxation of the head of the humerus in relation to the glenoid fossa may be noted not only in the flaccid stage of hemiplegia but also in the early or later spastic stage. Shoulder subluxation may be noted in hemiplegic patients with or without sensory impairment and may be painless. Although it is frequently associated with pain in the shoulder region,[30,99,113] it is controversial as to whether it is the cause of pain[10,37,51,61,87,88,105] Subluxation of the glenohumeral joint is a common problem following hemiplegia after stroke, with an overall prevalence of 30 to 50%.[79,95]

TABLE 1. Pain in the Hemiplegic Arm

Shoulder–hand syndrome	Hand and forearm pain
Shoulder pain	Hand and wrist contractures
Shoulder contracture	Wrist fracture
Glenohumeral subluxation	Peripheral nerve entrapment
Humeral fracture	Brachial plexus neuropathy
Rotator cuff disorder	Central pain states
Bicipital tendinitis	
Acromioclavicular joint disorder	

The diagnosis of subluxation is a clinical one where a palpable gap between the acromion and the humeral head on the affected side is more apparent than on the unaffected side.[39] Recent work has also suggested this can be quantified by radiographic comparison of the V-shaped space.[5] Subluxation most likely occurs as a result of a combination of contributing factors. The most important factor appears to be the supraspinatus and deltoid muscles, which are flaccid immediately after a stroke and can no longer serve to oppose the downward pull of the weight of the unsupported arm, or inappropriate pulling on the arm during transfers. The shoulder capsule and rotator cuff muscles may become elongated, allowing downward and lateral subluxation to occur[20,25] (Fig. 1). Scapular depression and

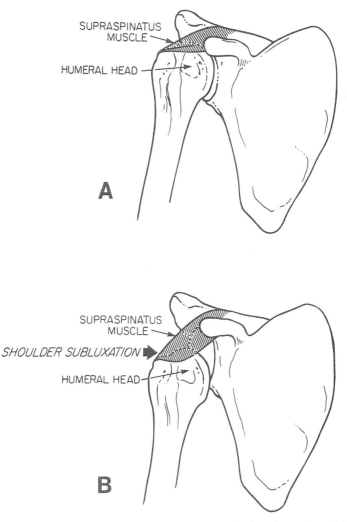

FIGURE 1. *A,* **Normal shoulder.** The humeral head is maintained in the glenoid fossa by the rotator cuff (supraspinatus muscles). *B,* **Shoulder subluxation.** During the initial phase of hemiplegia, the supraspinatus muscle is flaccid. The weight of the unsupported arm can cause the humeral head to sublux downward out of the glenoid fossa.

rotation causing changes in the angulation of the glenoid fossa may also promote subluxation,[20] although this has not been conclusively demonstrated.[89] Given these underlying dynamics, activities such as improper positioning of the arm in supine and upright positions or pulling on the flaccid hemiplegic arm during transfers may lead to glenohumeral subluxation.[105]

Management of shoulder subluxation consists initially of optimizing the position of the hemiplegic upper extremity in bed. In the seated position the use of a forearm trough or a clear acrylic lapboard can help prevent subluxation. The arm is positioned in slight elbow flexion, forearm pronation, wrist and finger extension, and thumb abduction. A protective elbow pad may also be required.[39] Arm trough and lapboards allow the shoulder to be positioned in less adduction and internal rotation, thereby reducing contractures.[19] Seating positions relative to humeral length are also important to avoid excessive downward drag on the humeral head or a functional scoliosis if the trough or tray are too low; relative humeral head impaction may occur if the trough is too high.

The use of slings remains controversial[20] in that they may not mechanically reposition the humeral head into the glenoid fossa and may encourage flexor synergy by maintaining the arm in a flexed position thereby inhibiting extension. Excessive use of slings may promote contractures if used continuously without a regular ranging/mobilization program. A sling appears to be useful when supporting a flaccid arm while the patient is ambulating in order to translate the majority of the weightbearing of the limb to the back of the neck.[56] Brooke et al.[19] used x-ray measurements in 10 stroke patients to obtain objective measurement of shoulder subluxation in relation to different shoulder supports. A Harris hemisling provided consistent correction of shoulder subluxation in hemiplegia compatible with the uninvolved shoulder. On the other hand, the Bobath sling did not correct vertical subluxation as well as it tended to distract the glenohumeral joint horizontally when compared to the uninvolved shoulder. An arm trough or lapboard tended to overcorrect the vertical subluxation without distracting the joint horizontally.[19] Fit, comfort, and ease of donning of the sling are important considerations.[39] Basmajian[7] has reported success in decreasing and often eliminating subluxation by using myoelectric biofeedback from upper trapezius (for shoulder elevation), middle deltoid (for shoulder abduction), and anterior deltoid (for shoulder flexion) muscles.

Contracture or Frozen Shoulder

A contracture is characterized by stiffness associated with loss of elasticity and fixed shortening of involved soft tissues, resulting in loss of motion of the surrounding joints.[13] Some loss of motion in the shoulder region is common, even in stroke patients experiencing full recovery.[20] Spasticity can contribute to contracture, and it may be difficult to differentiate clinically between the two. Other factors that can contribute to contracture formation are paralysis, muscle imbalance in flexion and extension synergies, poor positioning, excessive use of slings or splints, failure to perform regular range of motion exercises, and pain.[105] Muscular and periarticular contracture occurs with thickening of the capsule.[20] Rizk et al.[93] found 23 of 30 patients with hemiplegic shoulder pain had reduced joint volume on arthroscopy. There is a clinical impression that the incidence of painful contractures is much less today than two or three decades ago when daily range of motion exercises were not as routinely employed.[56]

Management initially consists of prevention by avoiding or minimizing those previously mentioned contributing factors which are correctable. Once a shoulder contracture develops, treatment with local heat and analgesics followed by progressive range of motion exercises can be used. In some cases, local or systemic corticosteroids can be tried.[95] In later stages of the process, surgical manipulation or even operative treatment may be occasionally required.[95] In the flaccid or spastic hemiplegic arm, improved shoulder range of motion is required not only for pain control but also to maintain axillary skin integrity and hygiene.

Other musculoskeletal conditions affecting the shoulder need to be considered, as they generally present as a painful shoulder and may ultimately lead to more generalized complications such as a frozen shoulder. These include supraspinatus and bicipital tendinitis as well as partial or complete tears of the rotator cuff musculotendinous unit.[80,82] However, although there is an incidence of 33 to 40% of rotator cuff tears on arthrography in stroke patients with shoulder pain, it may be no different than the incidence of tears in the contralateral shoulder[44] or in the general population. Another cause of shoulder pain may be an acromioclavicular lesion where pain and tenderness are localized to this site. Crepitation can be felt on movement of the joint. In the hemiplegic patient demonstrating partial or incomplete recovery, the acromioclavicular joint is stressed because of the compensatory "shrugging" due to limited glenohumeral movement or attempted arm movement.[20] Management is by local anesthetic injection.

Reflex Sympathetic Dystrophy/Shoulder–Hand Syndrome

Reflex sympathetic dystrophy (RSD) is a term used to describe a clinical condition characterized by distal limb pain, edema, and vasomotor instability[57–59]; hyperalgesia and/or allodynia are regarded as characteristic clinical findings necessary to make a diagnosis[103] (Table 2). RSD has long been regarded as a consequence of a disordered sympathetic nervous system based largely on the vasomotor instability and frequent response of this condition to sympathetic blockade. However, the role of the sympathetic nervous system in RSD is not clear. Campbell et al.[22] have pointed out that in patients with a clinical picture of RSD, the pain may or may not be dependent on the sympathetic nervous system. This has led to terms such as sympathetically maintained pain.[94] Campbell et al.[22] have gone so far as to define sympathetically maintained pain on the basis of whether the pain is eliminated by blockade or sympathetic efferent innervation of the painful area, i.e., sympathetic-dependent and -independent pain.

Incidence of RSD Following Hemiplegic Stroke. Shoulder–hand syndrome (SHS) usually has its onset between 1 to 3 months but has been reported as late as 5 months post stroke.[29] Davis et al.[29] performed a retrospective study of hemiplegic patients with thromboembolic middle cerebral artery infarcts. Of 540 patients, 68 (12.5%) were diagnosed clinically as having SHS. Most patients developed signs and symptoms between 1 to 4 months post stroke. Tepperman et al.[108] studied consecutive post-stroke hemiplegic patients. Each patient underwent a three-phase technetium bone scan within 72 hours of admission to a rehabilitation

TABLE 2.   Clinical Criteria for RSD Diagnosis*

Definite	Probable	Possible
Pain in an extremity	Pain and tenderness in	Vasomotor instability
Vasomotor instability	an extremity	Edematous extremity
Edematous extremity	Vasomotor instability	
Dystrophic skin changes	Extremity swelling	

* Data from Kozin et al.[57–59] and Teasell.[106]

unit. Twenty-one (25%) of the 85 patients had abnormal bone scans, with increased uptake in the hemiplegic wrist, metacarpal-phalangeal and interphalangeal joints on delayed scan. Fourteen of the 21 patients met diagnostic criteria for definite and probable RSD, while 4 more patients had unexplained metacarpal-phalangeal joint tenderness. Of the 3 patients who were diagnosed as "normal" on clinical examination but had positive bone scans, 2 went on to develop the clinical picture of RSD within 2 weeks while only 1 patient remained asymptomatic. All 18 symptomatic patients had positive bone scans.[108] Van Onwenaller et al.[113] similarly reported a SHS incidence of 23% following hemiplegic stroke. However, this incidence appears to be dropping.[55]

Clinical Presentation. SHS is characterized by the development of the clinical picture of RSD in the upper extremity in the absence of obvious peripheral trauma.[31] It commonly occurs in association with hemiplegia following stroke.[29,108,113] The degree of distal limb pain and distal edema is variable. In the majority of cases, there is moderate to marked swelling of the back of the wrist and hand with a fusiform swelling of the fingers. Tepperman et al.[108] found that metacarpal-phalangeal joint tenderness or hyperalgesia was characteristic of RSD in hemiplegics, while wrist and hand swelling was so common in "normal" hemiplegics it was not a useful clinical sign. Redness or discoloration, when present, is generally diffuse, and the hand is drier and warmer than usual. Allodynia is frequently not present. RSD is often associated with a sore and stiff shoulder[101] while the elbow is generally spared, hence the name shoulder–hand syndrome. In some cases, shoulder–hand syndrome may begin with shoulder pain. Osteoporosis in the affected limb develops over time and is greater than what one would expect on the basis of disuse alone.

Pathophysiology of RSD Post Stroke. There is increasing evidence supporting the concept of reduced sympathetic outflow in RSD, leading to peripheral α_1-adrenoceptor hypersensitivity presumably through an upregulation mechanism.[4,22,32] It has been hypothesized that the former results in swelling, edema, and discoloration, while the latter results in hyperalgesia and allodynia.[4] It has been shown that the abnormalities of RSD are not confined to the involved limb but also involve the contralateral "unaffected" limb[4,8]; however, in the early stages of RSD post hemiplegia, bilaterality may not be a feature.[108]

SHS does not have its onset after the central nervous system has stabilized, generally 3 to 6 months post stroke. The initial CNS changes following a hemiplegic stroke have been shown to cause autonomic dysfunction in the paretic limbs.[55] Korpelainen et al.[55] noted hyperhydrosis in hemiparetic patients following acute hemispheral brain infarction. This was felt to reflect autonomic dysfunction which was attributed to loss of reputed sympathoinhibitory pathways controlling sweating.

SHS may onset as a result of this CNS and autonomic instability seen following a stroke with or without a painful peripheral stimulus (generally from the shoulder) eventually producing the clinical picture of SHS. Tepperman et al.[108] found that shoulder pain was only present in one-third of patients who developed bone scan evidence of RSD shortly after the onset of hemiplegia, casting doubt on the necessity for a painful peripheral stimulus. The incidence of SHS has been anecdotally noted to be reduced by careful upper limb care. The development of α_1-adrenoceptor hypersensitivity is thought to somehow stimulate nociceptors in a yet undefined manner to produce the characteristic hyperalgesia in the distal upper extremity.[4,22,90]

Diagnosis. The primary signs and symptoms of RSD are distal pain, swelling, stiffness, and discoloration, and these must be present to make a presumptive diagnosis. The secondary signs and symptoms include osteoporosis, sudomotor, trophic and temperature changes, and vasomotor instability. Some, but not all, of the secondary symptoms must be present. The clinical presentation remains highly variable, depending on the severity of primary signs and symptoms and the combination of presenting secondary signs and symptoms. Technetium diphosphonate bone scan demonstrating periarticular uptake in the wrist and metacarpal-phalangeal joints of the involved limb is the most specific diagnostic test[105]; however, RSD remains a clinical diagnosis. Regional sympathetic blockade resulting in variable-term resolution of symptoms can be both diagnostic and therapeutic.

Management. Treatment of SHS involves a variety of options. Early intervention yields better outcomes. The cornerstone of any treatment program is physiotherapy designed to maintain range of motion of the involved limb. Emphasis is on mobilization of the involved limb, optimal positioning of the joints, and reduction of noxious stimuli to the limb. A short course of oral high-dose steroids[59] or alternatively stellate ganglion blocks may be used in more severe or disabling cases. Response to steroids has been shown to be much better in those patients with positive bone scans.[59]

It has been our experience that early aggressive treatment with corticosteroids is the best treatment when medical intervention seems to be warranted. Those patients who are untreated or respond incompletely to therapy are often left with varying degrees of pain in the upper extremity and significant upper extremity contractures, while a significant number improve spontaneously. In those individuals who develop a well-established SHS, adjunctive hand therapy including mobilization and splinting is important to optimize functional outcome.[48] Adjunctive use of heat and transcutaneous electrical nerve stimulation (TENS) may assist mobilization. Analgesics or NSAIDs can be used for pain control. We generally avoid use of sympathectomy in this subset of RSD. Surgical sympathectomy is generally considered if definite benefit has occurred (albeit temporarily) following sympathetic blocks. However, the efficacy of sympathectomy has never been established. Many stroke patients are elderly with associated cardiac abnormalities, which should lead to a reluctance to use α-adrenergic blockers such as oral phenoxybenzamine,[40] guanethidine[45,46,49] or phentolamine[3,90] to diagnose or treat SHS.

Brachial Plexus Injury

Traction injury to the brachial plexus can present as shoulder pain and should be suspected when there is atypical return of function distally before proximal functional return, segmental muscle flaccidity and atrophy, extension rather than flexion contracture of the fingers (in the absence of other RSD manifestations), and electromyographic changes demonstrating lower motor neuron involvement in a pattern consistent with a brachial plexus lesion, as opposed to a random, nonsegmental pattern which may be seen in post-stroke limbs.[33,52] Traction injury may occur when the patient moves or is moved while the shoulder and arm are still flaccid, as may occur from improper positioning or transfer techniques. Treatment is basically directed at preventing or minimizing traction forces at the brachial plexus.

Forearm and Hand Disorders

The spastic forearm and hand with flexion deformities are a common problem in patients who have suffered a stroke with involvement of the contralateral upper extremity.[105] Flexion contractures of the hand and wrist may be painful, thereby increasing spasticity (Fig. 2A); the presence of contracture and increased spasticity will prevent return of optimal functional recovery in the involved upper extremity. Distal radius fracture after a fall are not common but may be a source of pain. Painful entrapment of peripheral nerves may occur if the paralyzed limb is improperly positioned.[53]

The key to treating long-term complications of hemiplegic stroke in the forearm and hand is prevention. Contractures may be, at least in part, avoided through range of motion exercises and resting splints; the wrist is maintained in 20° to 30° of extension, the so-called functional position[17] (Fig. 2B). Resting splints are designed to maintain a gentle stretch on flexor muscles to counteract the tendency towards increased flexor tone and postures in the upper extremity (Fig. 2C). It is important that the splint not be painful.[21] Upper extremity splints are discussed in more detail in the chapter on orthotics.

Kraft et al.[60] assessed the effectiveness of three treatment techniques in improving function of the arm and hand in chronic hemiplegia (more than 6 months). The numbers in each group were small. Subjects were treated with either (1) electromyographically-initiated electrical stimulation of wrist extensors, (2) low-intensity electrical stimulation of wrist extensors combined with voluntary contraction, (3) proprioceptive neuromuscular facilitation (PNF) exercises, or (4) no treatment. Fugl-Meyer post-stroke motor recovery score improved by 42% in the first group, 25% in the second, and 18% in the third. Aggregate improvement of the Fugl-Meyer and grip-strength scores was significant from pretreatment to post-treatment and was maintained at 9 months follow-up. In contrast, the control group showed no improvement.[60] This study shows that treatment of the chronic hemiplegic upper extremity can result in functional gains.

PAIN OF CENTRAL ORIGIN

Pathophysiology

Contrary to popular misconceptions, central pain following stroke (excluding reflex sympathetic dystrophy) is rare, occurring in less than 2% of cases.[78,84,91,104] Central pain resulting from a stroke is often mistakenly referred to as thalamic pain, despite the fact that in many patients with central post-stroke pain (CPSP) the thalamus is not affected.[1,15,35,38,62,68] Central pain states have been shown to occur following lower brainstem, thalamic, and suprathalamic cerebrovascular events. When the thalamus is involved, generally the lesion involves the posterolateral or posterior thalamus.[71] However, involvement of this area does not necessarily lead to central pain (the analgic thalamic syndrome).[71]

The pathophysiology of central pain remains unknown. The most widely accepted explanation is that there is loss of inhibitory influences upon somatosensory pathways or systems,[85] although the mechanism of this action remains controversial.[62,85] Mauguiere and Demedt[71] point out that "central pain is often believed to reflect some alteration of lemniscal control over nociceptive inputs."[2,27,85] Their study suggested that larger lesions in the thalamus leading to complete interruption of lemniscal transmission through the ventroposterolateral thalamic nucleus up to the parietal cortex did not necessarily lead to central pain. Smaller lesions in the same area seemed to be at higher risk.[71] To add to the complexity, there appear to be individual idiosyncrasies, as patients with identical lesions often do not go on to develop central pain.[71,104]

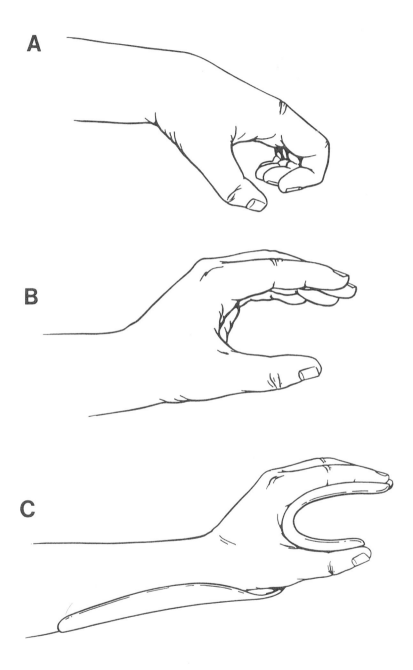

FIGURE 2. *A*, **The hemiplegic hand.** The wrist and fingers are in the flexed position while the thumb is adducted. *B*, **Functional hand position.** The wrist is extended at 15 to 20°, while the fingers are slightly flexed. *C*, **A volar wrist splint.** This holds the hemiplegic wrist in the functional hand position to prevent contractures (straps not shown).

Clinical Picture

Central pain is often described as a "burning" sensation in association with an unpleasant sensation of tingling, pins and needles, or numbness[104]; however, central pain is also described in terms such as ripping, tearing, pressing, twisting, aching, pricking, and lacerating.[11,62,104] Leijon et al.[62] studied 23 patients with CPSP following a known cerebrovascular lesion and reported little difference in the character of the pain in relation to the site of the lesion. An exception was the "burning" pain which was more commonly described following brainstem and suprathalamic lesions, while "lacerating" pain was seen more often with thalamic lesions. The pain is generally constant with spontaneous paroxysms of pain,[11,62,104] which is consistent with other central pain states. Like other central pain states, the pain may be exacerbated by physical movement, emotional stress, loud noises or voices, changes in the weather, cold, and light touch.[11,62,104]

Patients with CPSP frequently report spontaneous or evoked paresthesias and/or dysesthesias.[62] Spontaneous dysesthesias occur in the majority of CPSP patients, and almost all demonstrate some hypersensitivity to an external somatic stimuli.[62] Mauguiere and Demedt[71] found that hyperpathic overreactions to touch was a common feature in vascular thalamic pain syndromes. The spontaneous pain seen in central pain states are frequently accompanied by further unpleasant effects induced by somatosensory stimuli known as hyperesthesia, hyperpathia, and allodynia.[71,111] The presence of hyperpathia, hyperaesthesia, and allodynia and the demonstration of central mediation of reflex sympathetic dystrophy due to other causes have led to speculation that many of these cases may have a component of sympathetic mediated pain.[107] Patients with CPSP generally have some kind of sensory abnormality on the affected side,[62] although in some cases loss of sensation is not present.[71] Leijon et al.[62] found that 52% of 27 patients with CPSP were left with no paresis, 37% had moderate paresis, and only 11% had severe paresis. Hemiataxia occurred in well over half the patients, while choreoathetoid movements were uncommon.[62]

Treatment

Central pain is generally intractable to therapeutic interventions. Narcotic and nonnarcotic analgesics fail to provide adequate pain relief.[83] Tricyclic antidepressant medications have been shown in general to have a beneficial effect on central pain states.[54,110] Amitriptyline in a controlled study was shown to reduce pain in CPSP patients.[55] Phenothiazines (chlorpromazine[69,83]) and anticonvulsants (phenytoin[23,75] and carbamazepine[63]) are minimally effective in reducing pain.[15] Apomorphine has been reported to be effective but is associated with significant adverse effects and a tendency to lose its effectiveness over time.[74] Transcutaneous electrical nerve stimulation is effective in some CPSP patients.[64] Sympathetic blockade in the form of stellate ganglion and lumbar sympathetic blocks or local venous guanethidine blocks may provide some temporary relief of pain.[68] A variety of operative treatments have been tried for central pain states. These include neurosurgical brain lesions,[28,70,81,115] brain stimulation,[73,102] and even stereotaxic chemical hypophysectomy.[66] Overall neurosurgical ablative procedures have demonstrated a 25% effectiveness in permanently relieving central pain states but are associated with a significant risk of brain injury.[84] Interestingly, Soria and Fine[100] reported on a case of central pain syndrome secondary to a thalamic infarct being cured by a second small stroke in the ipsilateral corona radiata.

CONCLUSION

Pain following stroke, especially where spastic hemiplegia results, is very common in the upper extremity. Most cases of pain are due to a peripheral mechanism and are generally associated with spastic paralysis and/or joint contractures. Shoulder pain is particularly common and has been reported to occur in up to 84% of hemiplegic patients. Shoulder-hand syndrome is a frequent source of upper limb pain in hemiplegics and represents a form of reflex sympathetic dystrophy. Pain may also originate centrally, although central post-stroke pain occurs in less than 2% of stroke patients. It is almost always intractable to treatment. For many stroke patients, pain in the upper extremity is a common consequence of the stroke which significantly adds to their burden of suffering and disability.

REFERENCES

1. Agnew DS, Shetter AG, Segall HD, Flom RA: Thalamic pain. Adv Pain Res Ther 5:941–946, 1983.
2. Albe-Fessard D, Berkley KJ, Kruger L, et al: Diencephalic mechanisms of pain sensation. Brain Res Rev 9:217–296, 1985.
3. Arner S: Intravenous phentolamine test: Diagnostic and prognostic use in reflex sympathetic dystrophy. Pain 46:17–22, 1991.
4. Arnold JM, Teasell R, MacLeod AR, et al: Altered venous alpha-adrenoceptor responsiveness in patients with reflex sympathetic dystrophy. Ann Intern Med (In press).
5. Arsenault AB, Bilodeau M, Antil E, et al: Clinical significance of U-shaped space in the subluxed shoulder of hemiplegic stroke 22:867–871, 1991.
6. Bard G, Hirschberg GG: Recovery of voluntary motion in upper extremity following hemiplegia. Arch Phys Med Rehabil 46:567–572, 1965.
7. Basmajian JV: Muscles Alive: Their Functions Revealed by Electromyography, 4th ed. Baltimore, Williams & Wilkins, 1979, p 6.
8. Bej MD, Schwartzman RJ: Abnormalities of cutaneous blood flow regulation in patients with reflex sympathetic dystrophy as measured by laser Doppler fluxmetry. Arch Neurol 48:912–915, 1991.
9. Bohannon RW, Larkin PA, Smith MB, Horton MG: Shoulder pain in hemiplegia: Statistical relationship with five variables. Arch Phys Med Rehabil 67:514–516, 1986.
10. Bohannon RW, Andrews AW: Shoulder subluxation and pain in stroke patients. Am J Occup Ther 44:507, 1990.
11. Boivie J, Leijon G, Johansson I: Abnormalities in sensibility accompanying central post-stroke pain. Pain (suppl 4):5405, 1987.
12. Boivie J, Leijon G, Johansson I: Central post-stroke pain—A study of the mechanisms through analyses of the sensory abnormalities. Pain 37:173–185, 1989.
13. Botte MJ, Waters RC, Keenan M, et al: Orthopedic management of the stroke patient: Part II. Treating deformities of the upper and lower extremities. Orthop Rev 17:891–910, 1988.
14. Bowsher D, Lahuerta J, Brock L: Twelve cases of central pain, only three with thalamic lesion. Pain (suppl 2):583, 1984.
15. Bowsher D, Laheuerta J: Central pain in 22 patients: Clinical features, somatosensory changes and CT scan findings. J Neurol 232:297, 1985.
16. Braun RM, West F, Mooney V, et al: Surgical treatment of painful shoulder contracture in the stroke patient. J Bone Joint Surg 53A:1307–1312, 1971.
17. Brennan J: Response to stretch of hypertonic muscle groups in hemiplegia. BMJ 1:1504–1507, 1959.
18. Brocklehurst JC, Andrews K, Richards B, et al: How much physical therapy for patients with stroke? BMJ 1:1307–1310, 1978.
19. Brooke MM, deLateur BJ, Diane-Rigby GC, Questad KA: Shoulder subluxation in hemiplegia: Effects of three different supports. Arch Phys Med Rehabil 72:582–586, 1991.
20. Cailliet R: The Shoulder in Hemiplegia. Philadelphia, F.A. Davis Co., 1980.
21. Caldwell CB, Wilson DJ, Brown RM: Evaluation and treatment of the upper extremity in the hemiplegic stroke patient. Clin Orthop 63:69–93, 1969.
22. Campbell JN, Meyer RA, Raja SN: Is nociceptor activation by alpha-1 adrenoceptors the culprit in sympathetically maintained pain? Am Pain Soc J 1:3–11, 1992.

23. Cantor FK: Phenytoin treatment of thalamic pain. BMJ 4:590, 1972.
24. Carroll D: Hand function in hemiplegia. J Chronic Dis 18:493–500, 1965.
25. Chaco J, Wolf I: Subluxation of the glenohumeral joint in hemiplegia. Arch J Phys Med 50:139–143, 1971.
26. Chu DS, Petrillo C, Davis SW, Eichberg R: Shoulder-hand syndrome: Importance of early diagnosis and treatment. J Am Geriatr Soc 29:58–60, 1981.
27. Craig AD, Burton H: Spinal and medullary lamina I cells projecting to medial and/or lateral thalamus: A possible pain center. J Neurophysiol 45:443–466, 1981.
28. Davis RA, Stokes JW: Neurosurgical attempts to relieve thalamic pain. Surg Gynecol Obstet 123:371–384, 1966.
29. Davis SW, Pestrillo CR, Eischberg RD, Chu DS: Shoulder-hand syndrome in a hemiplegic population: A 5-year retrospective study. Arch Phys Med Rehabil 58:353–355, 1977.
30. Poulin de Courval LP, Barsauskas A, Berenbaum B, et al: Painful shoulder in the hemiplegia and unilateral neglect. Arch Phys Med Rehabil 71:673–676, 1990.
31. Dimitru D: Reflex sympathetic dystrophy. Phys Med Rehab State Art Rev 5:89–102, 1991.
32. Drummond PM, Finch PM, Smythe GA: Reflex sympathetic dystrophy: The significance of differing catecholamine concentration in affected and unaffected limbs. Brain 114:2025–2036, 1991.
33. Estape R, Ferel D, Barth R: Brachial plexus lesions in hemiplegics. Acta Neurol Belg 79:444, 1979.
34. Eto F, Yoshikawa M, Ueda S, Hirai S: Post-hemiplegic shoulder-hand syndrome with special reference to cerebral localization. J Am Geriatr Soc 28:13–17, 1980.
35. Fields HL, Adams JE: Pain after cortical injury relieved by electrical stimulation of the internal capsule. Brain 97:169–178, 1974.
36. Fitzgerald-Finch OP, Gibson I: Subluxation of shoulder in hemiplegia. Age Aging 4:16, 1975.
37. Fugl-Meyer AR, Jaasko L, Leyman I, et al: Post-stroke hemiplegic patient: I. Method for evaluation of physical performance. Scand J Rehab Med 7:13–31, 1975.
38. Garcin R, Lapresle J: Incoordination cerebelleuse du membre inferieur par lesion localisee dans la region intern du thalamus control-lateral. Rev Neurol (Paris) 120:5, 1969.
39. Garrison SJ, Rolak LA, Dodaro RR, O'Callaghan AJ: Rehabilitation of the stroke patient. In Delisa JA (ed): Rehabilitation Medicine: Principles and Practice. Philadelphia, JB Lippincott, 1988, pp 565–584.
40. Ghostine SY, Comair YG, Turner DM, et al: Phenoxybenzamine in the treatment of causalgia. J Neurosurg 60:1263–1268, 1984.
41. Gowland C: Recovery of motor function following stroke: Profile and predictors. Physiother Canada 34:77–88, 1982.
42. Griffin J, Reddin G: Shoulder pain in patients with hemiplegia: A literature review. Phys Ther 61:1041–1045, 1981.
43. Grossens-Sills J, Schenkman M: Analysis of shoulder pain, range of motion, and subluxation in patients with hemiplegia. Phys Ther 65:731, 1985.
44. Hakuno A, Sashika H, Ohkawa T, Itoh R: Arthrographic findings in hemiplegic shoulders. Arch Phys Med Rehabil 65:706–711, 1984.
45. Hannington-Kiff JG: Intravenous regional sympathetic blockade with guanethidine. Lancet i:1019–1020, 1974.
46. Hannington-Kiff JG: Relief of Sudek's atrophy by regional intravenous guanethidine. Lancet i:1132–1133, 1977.
47. Heller A, Wade DT, Wood VA, et al: Arm function after stroke: Measurement and recovery over the first three months. J Neurol Neurosurg Psychiatry 50:714–719, 1987.
48. Hunter JM, Schneida LH, Mackin EJ, et al: Rehabilitation of the Hand, 2nd ed. St. Louis, CV Mosby, 1984, ch 47.
49. Jaeger SH, Singer DI, Whitenack SH: Nerve injury complications: Management of neurogenic pain syndromes. Hand Clin 2:217–236, 1986.
50. Joshi J, Singh N, Varma SK: Residual motor deficits in adult hemiplegic patients. In Proceedings of the World Conference Physical Ther, 7th International Conference, Montreal, June 1974.
51. Joynt RL: The source of shoulder pain in hemiplegia. Arch Phys Med Rehabil 73:409–413, 1992.
52. Kaplan PE, Meredith J, Taft G, Betts HB: Stroke and brachial plexus injury: A difficult problem. Arch Phys Med Rehabil 38:415, 1977.
53. Kellner WS, Felsenthal G, Anderson JM, et al: Carpal tunnel syndrome in the nonparetic hands of hemiplegics, stress-induced by ambulatory assistive devices. Orthop Rev 15:608–611, 1986.
54. Koppel BS: Amitriptyline in the treatment of thalamic pain. South Med J 79:759–761, 1986.

55. Korpelainen JT, Sotaiemi KA, Myllyla VV: Hyperhidrosis as a reflection of autonomic failure in patients with acute hemispheral brain infarction: An evaporimetric study. Stroke 23:1271–1275, 1992.
56. Kottke FJ, Lehman JF: Krusen's Handbook of Physical Medicine and Rehabilitation, 4th ed. Philadelphia, WB Saunders, 1990, ch 30.
57. Kozin F, McCarty DJ, Sims JE, Genant HK: The reflex sympathetic dystrophy syndrome: I. Clinical and histologic studies: Evidence of bilaterality, accentuation of periarticular regions and predictable response to corticosteroids. Am J Med 60:321–331, 1976.
58. Kozin F, Genant HK, Bekerman C, McCarty DJ: The reflex sympathetic dystrophy syndrome: II. Roentgenographic and scintigraphic evidence of bilaterality and of periarticular accentuation. Am J Med 60:332–338, 1976.
59. Kozin F, Ryan LM, Carerra GF, et al: The reflex sympathetic dystrophy syndrome (RSDS): III. Scintigraphic studies, further evidence for the therapeutic efficacy of systemic corticosteroids and proposed diagnostic criteria. Am J Med 70:23–30, 1981.
60. Kraft GH, Fitts SS, Hammond MC: Techniques to improve function of the arm and hand in chronic hemiplegia. Arch Phys Med Rehabil 73:220–227, 1992.
61. Kumar R, Metter EJ, Mehta AJ, Chew T: Shoulder pain in hemiplegia: The role of exercise. Am J Phys Med Rehabil 69:205–208, 1990.
62. Leijon G, Boivie J, Johansson I: Central post-stroke pain—Neurological symptoms and pain characteristics. Pain 36:13–225, 1989.
63. Leijon G, Boivie J: Central post-stroke pain—A controlled study of amitriptyline and carbamazepine. Pain 36:27–36, 1989.
64. Leijon G, Boivie J: Central post-stroke pain—The effect of high and low frequency TENS. Pain 38:187–191, 1989.
65. Leijon G, Boivie J, Johansson I: A clinical investigation of central post-stroke pain. Pain (suppl 4):5404, 1987.
66. Levin AB, Ramirez LF, Katz J: The use of stereotaxic chemical hypophysectomy in the treatment of thalamic pain syndrome. J Neurosurg 59:1002–1006, 1983.
67. Lieberman JS: Hemiplegia: Rehabilitation of the upper extremity. In Kaplan PE, Cerullo LJ (eds): Stroke Rehabilitation. Stoneham, MA, Butterworth Publishers, 1986, pp 95–117.
68. Loh L, Nathan PW, Schott GD: Pain due to lesions of central nervous system removed by sympathetic block. BMJ 282:1026–1028, 1981.
69. Margolis LH, Gianascol AJ: Chlorpromazine in thalamic pain syndrome. Neurology 6:302, 1956.
70. Mark VH, Ervin FR, Yakolev PI: Correlation of pain relief sensory loss and anatomical lesion sites in pain patients treated by stereotactic thalamotomy. Trans Ann Neurol Assoc 86:86, 1961.
71. Mauguiere F, Demedt JE: Thalamic pain syndrome of Dejerine-Roussy. Arch Neurol 45:1312–1320, 1988.
72. Melzack R, Wall PD: Pain mechanisms: A new theory. Science 150:971–979, 1965.
73. Meyerson BA: "European" study on deep brain stimulation. In Third European Workshop on Electrical Neurostimulation, Megeve, France, March 30–31, 1979.
74. Miley DP, Abrams AA, Atkinson JH, Janowsky DS: Successful treatment of thalamic pain with apomorphine. Am J Psychiatry 135:1230–1232, 1978.
75. Mladinich EK: Diphenylhydantoin in the Wallenberg syndrome. JAMA 230:372–373, 1974.
76. Moskowitz E, Porter JI: Peripheral nerve lesions in the upper extremity in hemiplegic patients. N Engl J Med 269:776–778, 1963.
77. Moskowitz E: Complications in rehabilitation of hemiplegic patients. Med Clin North Am 53:541–559, 1969.
78. Mucke L, Maciewicz R: Clinical management of neuropathic pain. Neurol Clin 5:649–663, 1987.
79. Najenson T, Pikielmi SS: Malalignment of glenohumeral joint following hemiplegia: A review of 500 cases. Ann Phys Med 8:96–99, 1965.
80. Najenson T, Yacubovich E, Pikelini S: Rotator cuff injury in hemiplegic patients. Scand J Rehabil Med 3:131–137, 1971.
81. Nashold BS, Wilson WP, Slaughter DG: Stereotaxic midbrain lesions for central dysesthesia and phantom pain: Preliminary report. J Neurosurg 30:116–126, 1969.
82. Nepomuceno CS, Miller JM III: Shoulder arthrography in hemiplegic patients. Arch Phys Med Rehabil 55:49–51, 1974.
83. Nuzzo J, Warfield C: Thalamic pain syndrome. Hosp Pract (Aug 15):32c–32j, 1985.
84. Pagni CA: Central pain and painful anaesthesia. Prog Neurol Surg 8:132–257, 1977.
85. Pagni CA: Central pain due to spinal cord and brainstem damage. In Wall PD, Melzack R (eds): Textbook of Pain. New York, Churchill Livingstone, 1984, pp 481–495.

86. Parker VM, Wade DT, Langton-Hewer R: Loss of arm function after stroke: Measurement, frequency and recovery. Int Rehabil Med 8(2):67–73, 1986.
87. Perrigot M, Bussel B, Pierrot Deseilligny E, Held JP: L'epaule de l'hemiplegique. Ann Med Phys 18:175–187, 1975.
88. Peszczynski M, Rardin TE: The incidence of painful shoulder in hemiplegia. Bull Pol Med Sci Hist 8:21–23, 1965.
89. Prevost R, Arsenault AB, Antil E, et al: Rotation of the scapula and shoulder subluxation in hemiplegia. Arch Phys Med Rehabil 68:786–790, 1987.
90. Raja SN, Treede R-D, Davis KD, Campbell JN: Systemic alpha-adrenergic blockade with phentolamine: A diagnostic test for sympathetically mediated pain. Anesthesiology 74:691–698, 1991.
91. Reding MJ, McDowell F: Stroke rehabilitation. Neurol Clin 5:601–630, 1987.
92. Riddoch G: The clinical features of central pain. Lancet 234:1093–1098, 1150–1156, 1205–1209, 1938.
93. Rizk TE, Christopher RP, Pinals RS, et al: Arthrographic studies in painful hemiplegic shoulders. Arch Phys Med Rehabil 65:254–255, 1984.
94. Roberts WJ, Elardo SM: Sympathetic activation of unmyelinated mechanoreceptors in cat skin. Brain Res 339:123–125, 1985.
95. Roy CW: Shoulder pain in hemiplegia: A literature review. Clin Rehabil 2:35–44, 1986.
96. Salter BS: Textbook of Disorders and Injuries of the Musculoskeletal System, 2nd ed. Baltimore, Williams & Wilkins, 1983, ch 11.
97. Savage R, Robertson L: Relationship between adult hemiplegic shoulder pain and depression. Physiother Can 34:86–90, 1982.
98. Shahani BT, Kelly EB, Glasser S: Hemiplegic shoulder subluxation. Arch Phys Med Rehabil 62:519, 1981.
99. Shai G, Ring H, Costeff H, Solzi P: Glenohumeral malalignment in hemiplegic shoulder. Scand J Rehabil Med 16:133–136, 1984.
100. Soria ED, Fine EJ: Disappearance of thalamic pain after parietal subcortical stroke. Pain 44:285–288, 1991.
101. Subbaro J, Stillwell GK: Reflex sympathetic dystrophy syndrome of the upper extremity: Analysis of total outcome of management of 125 cases. Arch Phys Med Rehabil 62:549–554, 1981.
102. Sweet WH: Intracerebral electrical stimulation for the relief of chronic pain. In Youmans JR (ed): Neurological Surgery, 2nd ed. Philadelphia, WB Saunders, 1982, pp 3739–3748.
103. Tahmoush AJ: Causalgia: Redefinition as a clinical pain syndrome. Pain 10:187–197, 1981.
104. Tasker RR: Pain resulting from central nervous system pathology (central pain). In Bonica JJ (ed): The Management of Pain, vol I, 2nd ed. Malvern, PA, Lea & Febiger, 1990, pp 264–283.
105. Teasell R: Musculoskeletal complications of hemiplegic stroke. Semin Arthritis Rheum 20:385–395, 1991.
106. Teasell R: Pain following stroke. Crit Rev Phys Med Rehabil 3:205–217, 1992.
107. Teasell R, Arnold JMO: Reflex sympathetic dystrophy: A unifying hypothesis of centrally-mediated diminished sympathetic outflow. (unpublished).
108. Tepperman PS, Greyson ND, Hilbert L, Williams JI: Reflex sympathetic dystrophy in hemiplegia. Arch Phys Med Rehabil 62:549–554, 1981.
109. Tobis JS: Posthemiplegic shoulder pain. NY State J Med 57:1377–1380, 1957.
110. Tourian AY: Narcotic responsive "thalamic" pain treatment with propanolol and tricyclic antidepressant. Pain (suppl 4):S411, 1987.
111. Turk DC, Salovey P: Chronic pain as a variant of depressive disease: A critical reappraisal. J Nerv Ment Dis 172:398–404, 1984.
112. Twitchell TE: The restoration of motor function following hemiplegia. Brain 74:443–480, 1951.
113. Van Onwenaller C, LaPlace PM, Chantraine A: Painful shoulder in hemiplegia. Arch Phys Med Rehabil 67:23–26, 1985.
114. Wade RL, Langton-Hewer R, Wood VA, et al: The hemiplegic arm after stroke: Measurement and recovery. J Neurol Neurosurg Psychiatry 46:521–524, 1983.
115. White JC, Sweet WH: Pain and the Neurosurgeon: A Forty-Year Experience. Springfield, IL, Charles C Thomas, 1969, pp 386–406.

PATRICK J. POTTER, MD, FRCPC

10. LOWER EXTREMITY DISORDERS

From the
Department of Physical Medicine
and Rehabilitation
Victoria Hospital
University of Western Ontario
London, Ontario
Canada

Reprint requests to:
Dr. P.J. Potter
Victoria Hospital
800 Commissioners Road East
London, Ontario N6A 4G5
Canada

In understanding the long-term consequences of the stroke-affected lower extremity, difficulties arise in separating this area of body function from the whole. The residual effects of stroke are generally not restricted to a single limb. Cognitive and visual-perceptual deficits further disable the stroke patient over and above the usually obvious disability due to the residual hemiparesis and hemisensory deficits. Assessment of patients who have suffered a cerebrovascular accident resulting in residual deficits in the lower extremity should take into account the concepts of impairment, disability, and handicap.[62] An approach which encompasses these three areas steers one away from the "go home and live with it" syndrome.[33] This is particularly relevant when one considers that 90% of patients who have survived a stroke will have impairments which do not resolve.[54] Disability may be modifiable with aids and adaptive devices, while handicap may be altered by modification of the social environment; therefore, quality of life after a cerebrovascular accident may be improved without changing the basic residual deficits.

UNIQUE FEATURES OF LOWER EXTREMITY FUNCTIONING

Most of the unique features of lower extremity deficits are a result of the functional use of the lower extremity. Relative to the upper extremity, in which there is a large geographic representation in each hemisphere for hand function, in the lower extremity the homunculus is much more evenly distributed. Whereas upper extremity function revolves around fine hand function and control requiring moderate sensory input and motor control, in the lower extremity the necessary functions are those of locomotion.

Because lower extremity tasks are considered more gross tasks in terms of what is necessary for independent movement, less neurologic recovery is required to perform the tasks adequately. As a result the affected lower limb may be supplemented with the use of aids and orthotics with greater success than what is achieved with upper limb orthotics. Residual recovery of a small percentage of functioning CNS tracts innervating the lower extremity will allow adequate ambulation. It is noted that this is a minimal requirement and does not represent complete recovery. More significantly complex functions such as running or climbing ladders require extensive neurologic recovery.

A parallel example of what can be accomplished on a functional basis, in spite of decreased control of the lower extremity, may be drawn from the amputee population. For the upper extremity amputee, a high-above-elbow amputation results in the need for a prosthesis which has controls that are often too cumbersome to provide useful function. It therefore may be used for cosmesis only. In the lower extremity amputee, a high-above-knee amputation can be successfully fitted, and the person can establish a useful gait pattern using only the proximal musculature and alignment of the center pressure during gait to control weight support through the joints of the prosthesis. Similarly, weight-bearing in the paretic limb may be supplemented by orthotic support and training.

The early return of primitive reflexes which allow the extensor pattern of foot plantar flexion, knee extension, and hip extension during standing, in combination with increased extensor tone, results in a locking effect at the knee and hip joints. This occurs because the center of gravity is anterior to the axis of rotation of the knee and posterior to that of the hip, as shown in Figure 1.[49] Where neurologic recovery is moderately impaired, this method of compensation may still allow for adequate support in the upright position.

ENERGY COSTS

Other features unique to the lower extremity are the effect of residual impairments on energy expenditure during gait. This is best explained by examining the six determinants of gait described by Saunders et al.[50] Within these determinants of gait, the body's center of gravity maintains a sinusoidal curve both in the vertical and horizontal planes. This sinusoidal distribution of the body movement is kept to a minimum by the defined determinants of gait which are (1) pelvic rotation; (2) pelvic tilt; (3) knee flexion; (4) ankle flexion; (5) coordination of ankle and knee motion; and (6) lateral pelvic rotation.[50] Any increase in the amplitude of the sinusoidal pattern increases the kinetic energy necessary to move the center of gravity and therefore increases the energy expenditure within the system.

The average metabolic cost per meter (E/m) of normal walking at a self-selected speed has been described as between 0.00076 and 0.00083 kcal/m/kg body weight.[14,21] In accommodating to neurologic deficits which result in a higher energy consumption per meter per kilogram, patients have been shown to self-select a speed of ambulation which is less than that of normal ambulation. The energy consumption per unit time is therefore lower and approximates normal, although the energy cost per meter may be increased up to 200%.[14,21] The average energy cost of walking without braces is 51 to 62%.[14] The use of a below-knee brace of either molded plastic or double metal upright construction decreases this energy cost by 10 to 20%.

The consequences on energy expenditure are explained as a result of moderately different gait patterns following cerebrovascular accident.[6,38] Patients

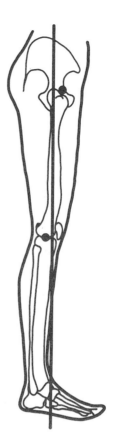

FIGURE 1. The center of gravity during normal standing falls posterior to the axis rotation of the hip and anterior to the axis of rotation of the knee, thereby allowing normal standing to occur with only active contraction in the gastrocsoleus necessary.

lose selective muscle control.[48] In a normal person, selected muscle contraction through all aspects of gait allows for eccentric and concentric contractions of the muscles of the lower extremity to provide both acceleration and deceleration to optimize energy expenditure. In the hemiplegic patient, co-contraction with spasticity and loss of selective muscle control are present.[18,36,47] This results in inefficient muscle contraction and therefore inefficient gait.

LESION SPECIFICITY

The effect on the lower extremity of a stroke is very much dependent on the site of the stroke. The portion of the homunculus which provides motor function to the lower extremity is supplied primarily by the anterior cerebral artery with partial supply by the middle cerebral artery. Therefore, in a typical middle-cerebral-artery stroke, there is greater impairment of the upper extremity than the lower extremity.[33] In the same light, an infarct in the anterior cerebral artery territory will result in moderate motor and sensory deficits in the lower extremity.[33] Anterior cerebral artery infarcts account for only 3% of strokes, with the majority involving the middle cerebral artery territory. Anatomical diagnoses by imaging modalities do not always correlate with clinical findings.[53]

Often, enough residual recovery is achieved to allow partial to complete independence in functions basic to the lower extremities.[16,22] Although motor recovery is a major factor in useful functional recovery of the lower extremity, neglect, visual-perceptual, and sensory (proprioceptive) losses may result in a nonfunctional limb.[19] This is particularly true in the insensate, neglected limb, as cognitive "control" of weight-bearing is often not possible. Internal capsule infarcts often present as primarily motor impairment with sensory and cognitive functions relatively intact. The limitations imposed by sensory, perceptual, and cognitive deficits may hamper rehabilitation of patients following stroke. Guidelines for deciding which patients will preferentially benefit from rehabilitation are not as well defined as likely exclusion criteria.[33] In this regard, predictors of poor outcome have been shown to include perceptual deficits, bladder and bowel incontinence, age, and poor premorbid health.[31] For rehabilitation intervention to proceed, cognitive functioning should allow retention of information and the ability to follow two stage commands.

Lesions involving the brainstem result in moderate spasticity with involvement of the pyramidal tracts and ataxia depending on the extent of involvement of the cerebellum. Recovery is more gradual, continuing for a longer period of time before plateauing. Patients with involvement of the brainstem alone lack the cognitive problems frequently seen with hemisphere lesions.

ASSESSMENT

Assessing the lower extremity of a patient with upper motor neuron deficits is a difficult task. Limited correlation between the Medical Research Council (MRC) scale[1] (Table 1) of measurement and the ability to walk has been shown, although this scale may be useful as a simple measure.[46] The ability to do repetitive movements in the lower extremity and to maintain standing balance are also useful predictors of gait performance.[6] Difficulty occurs in separating those movements which are the result of a return of primitive reflexes from those due to return of active motor control. Similarly, it is difficult to measure the extent to which movements are compromised by lack of proprioception, spasticity, and co-contraction of antagonist muscles. Strength measurement and tone assessment are also compromised by the change in motor control which occurs with changes in position. For example, an extensor reflex of the lower extremity may be present in the standing position and provide adequate hip extension, knee extension, and plantar flexion, whereas this may be lacking in a lying or sitting position. Fatigue and time of day may also influence findings on assessment.

In this regard, the usual MRC scale of 1 to 5 for motor testing is not as useful as looking at the functional abilities of the limb with a scale which encompasses the effects of primitive reflexes, spasticity, and active motor control outside of patterned movement. Such a scale was initially developed by Brunnstrom in

TABLE 1.   UK Medical Research Council Motor Testing Scale*

0	No contraction
1	Flicker or trace of contraction
2	Active movement with gravity eliminated
3	Active movement against gravity
4	Active movement against gravity and resistance
5	Normal power

* From Aids to the Examination of the Peripheral Nervous System. Toronto, Bailliere Tindall, 1986, pp 1–2, with permission.

TABLE 2. Definitions of the Stages of Motor Impairment*

Stage 1	Presynergy. Muscle (i.e., phasic) strength reflexes are absent or hypoactive. No resistance to passive movement (i.e., tonic stretch reflex) is felt. No active movement can be elicited either reflexively by a facilitatory stimulus or volitionally.
Stage 2	Resistance to passive movement is felt. No voluntary movement is present, but active movement can be elicited reflexively by a facilitatory stimulus or volitionally.
Stage 3	Spasticity is marked. Voluntary movement occurs in synergies (i.e., stereotyped patterns of flexion and extension). Movement results from higher center facilitation of associated reactions or spinal or brain stem reflexes.
Stage 4	Spasticity decreases. Synergy patterns can be reversed if the pattern occurs first in the weakest synergy. Movements combining antagonist synergies can be performed if the strong components act as prime movers. The synergies lose their dominance, the spinal and brain stem reflexes commence being modified and integrated by higher centers utilizing more complex neutral networks.
Stage 5	Spasticity wanes. Synergy patterns can be reversed even if movement occurs first in the direction of the stronger synergy. Movements utilizing the weak components of the synergies acting as prime movers can be performed (i.e., difficult extensor and flexor synergy movements can be mixed). Spinal and brain stem reflexes become modified and integrated into a more complex network. Most movements become environmentally specific.
Stage 6	Coordination and patterns of movement are near normal. Spasticity as demonstrated by resistance to passive movement is no longer present. A large variety of environmentally specific patterns of movement are now possible. Abnormal patterns of movement with faulty timing emerge when rapid (ballistic) or complex (ramp) targeted movements are requested.
Stage 7	Normal

* From Gowland CA: Staging motor impairment after stroke. Stroke 21(suppl 2):19–21, 1990; with permission of the American Heart Association.

1970,[10] standardized by Fugl-Meyer et al.,[23] and continues to be revised and tested (Table 2).[26–28] This type of functional testing allows a standardized description of motor recovery from the point of view of a movement pattern rather than individual joint movements. Increasing complexity of the motor task is taken into account, and the description process basically follows the usual pattern of recovery from an upper motor neuron lesion with a series of stages acting as an analogue scale. Further description of these stages may be found in the previously noted references, with the expectation of further publication on the validity of such measurement tools.

Other methods of functional assessment of the lower extremity include basic gait studies in which one describes the degree of assistance needed from no assistance to maximum assistance by one to two persons. A commonly used scale is that of no assistance, standby assistance, minimal assistance, moderate assistance, and maximum assistance. Similarly, the degree of need for aids may also act as a functional assessment for evaluation of the recovery of the lower extremity—i.e., whether or not the patient is able to stand, whether the patient is able to ambulate or stand between parallel bars, or what other aid is necessary (e.g., quad cane vs single-point cane). The speed and distance of gait may be useful parameters for measurement.[5] Although the speed a patient walks is an indication of ability, their safety is an important aspect of the observation process. The maximum distance of walking may be a function of both central fatigue,[3] that due to the moderate energy expenditure,[14] and what may be described as peripheral fatigue (in which as the patient fatigues, co-contraction of lower limb musculature and spasticity results in incoordination, therefore increasing mental and physical energy expenditure). A number of functional indexes, e.g., Barthels, Pulses, and FIM, have been developed. Usually these also encompass other aspects of patient's abilities and are therefore not restricted to lower limb function. More specific indexes of lower extremity function useful for isolated lower extremity evaluation are under review.[6,28,46]

TREATMENT

Treating upper motor neuron lesions involves separating neurologic from functional recovery. Neurologic recovery is postulated to occur on the basis of decreasing edema, collateral circulation, and brain plasticity. This includes both sprouting and unmasking as the common current theories of brain plasticity.[2,20,44] Neurologic recovery is difficult to define in terms of the anatomical lesion seen. Often small infarcts, placed in eloquent and important areas such as the internal capsule, may not be easily visualized but may result in moderate functional impairments.[53] Residual neurologic deficits and alterations to quality of life are not directly proportional. Modifying the disability may allow a patient who has minimal motor and sensory recovery in the lower extremity to walk with the aid of a spouse, quad cane, and below-knee brace. Long-term utilization of ankle-foot orthoses (AFO) has been documented, with approximately 80% of patients wearing their AFO a minimum of 7 hours/day.[55] This same person with minimal neurologic recovery in the lower extremity may have the social handicap reduced by returning to a work environment which does not require ambulation. Access to accommodating transportation allows for returning to work and avocational activities. These modifications in the environment allow for functional recovery but do not alter the neurologic impairment.

There are several theoretical schools of therapeutic exercises for neurologic recovery. These include the approaches of Brunnstrom, Rood, Bobath, and proprioceptive neuromuscular facilitation as described by Kabat, Knott, and Voss.[24] Often, therapy approaches are combined using whatever form of stimulation and training is necessary to provide a positive result.

Bed mobility is the initial stage of the retraining process. The patient's ability to roll in bed and to sit up in bed is a major accomplishment in the early stages following a cerebrovascular accident. Coordination between the upper and lower extremities is required. The ability to transfer and weight-shift on to the affected lower extremity is the next important step. Walking begins once appropriate weight-shift and postural control have been achieved. Initial walking is done with the therapist controlling the limb to provide proprioceptive feedback to the patient.

The process of recovery is a relearning process for the patient, as weakness is due to dysfunction in motor control rather than true muscle weakness. As part of the process of stimulating recovery, electrical stimulation and biofeedback modalities have been used successfully in the retraining process.[15,61] Biofeedback has been found to be more effective in the lower extremity than the upper.[61] Biofeedback may be given through an electromyographic signal or by positional biofeedback, which is still in the experimental stages.[39] Progressive resisted exercises are not done unless there has been almost normal recovery. In the early stage a progressive resisted exercise program will result in increased co-contraction of the antagonist muscles and spasticity. In this regard, isokinetic equipment is less useful in the upper motor neuron lesions of the lower extremity. Such equipment strengthens isolated movements rather then providing resistance to movement of the limbs as a whole. The walking or climbing pattern is better modelled by a resistance machine, such as the Kinetron (Cybex, Ronkonkoma, NY), which allows resistance to a pattern of movement rather than an isolated movement.

Techniques for reducing spasticity include limb positioning, concentration and relaxation on the part of the patient and may also include the use of hydrotherapy techniques. Medications have a controversial role in stroke recovery. Medications are not usually effective in the treatment of hemisphere lesions. Spasticity is usually treated with dantrolene sodium which works at the neuromuscular junction.[35] Early intervention with dantrolene sodium to prevent spasticity has not been effective.[34] Other medications, such as lioresal, clonidine, and diazepam, used for spasticity tend to be more effective if the CNS lesion is at the spinal cord level, and they are therefore often not useful in spasticity due to stroke. If spasticity is being used by the patient to support the paretic limb, then treating the spasticity may result in decreased functional ability.

Treatment of pain and contractures is important. Lower extremity pain due to premorbid osteoarthritis or other musculoskeletal conditions will, by reflex action, often increase spasticity and result in antalgic inhibition of the pattern of movement attempted. Stroke recovery has been postulated to be improved by CNS stimulants such as noradrenergic and cholinergic agents.[25]

LONG-TERM COMPLICATIONS

Hip Contracture

One of the major complications seen after stroke is contractures, often a preventable problem. Hip flexion contractures result in the need for moderately active hip extension in order to weight-bear through the affected extremity as the center of gravity falls anterior to the hip axis of rotation, increasing the hip flexion moment present.[49] With early hip flexion contracture, an aggressive stretching routine may be effective in reducing the extent of contracture present. Hip flexion contractures greater than 30° and present for several months result in prolonged disability which may not respond to conservative management. Anterior surgical release may be required.[32] Adductor spasticity decreases the width of the base of support. Although often present, this is rarely a serious problem and may be successfully treated with obturator nerve blocks or motor point blocks. Adductor releases have been described but are rarely necessary.

Genu Recurvatum

Plantar flexion spasticity and lack of knee control, producing genu recurvatum, is a well-known complication. Genu recurvatum is posterior bowing of the knee, which occurs due to tensile stress through the posterior capsule and posterior tendon support of the knee (Fig. 2). It occurs due to decreased knee and ankle control which result in excessive foot plantar flexion and knee extension moments, therefore resulting in loss of the passive restriction to knee extension normally present. Genu recurvatum often results in moderate knee pain due to the tensile forces in the posterior capsule, as well as degenerative changes within the knee joint due to the change in weight-bearing surfaces within the knee joint. This problem occurs over an extended period of time, as repetitive knee extension over a long period such as several months is necessary to result in the deformity seen. Due to the difficulty in tissue recovery from this biomechanical derangement, once present, genu recurvatum has long-term consequences. This may be prevented by

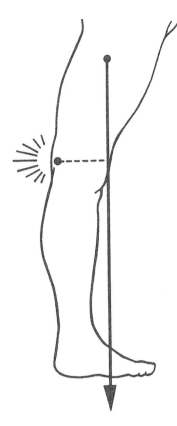

FIGURE 2. With absent knee and ankle control, the knee extensor moment may result in excessive tensile stress to the posterior capsule, resulting in genu recurvatum and posterior knee pain.

early intervention with training of knee control and appropriate fitting of an AFO. An AFO with a plantar flexion stop will decrease the knee extensor moment.

Knee Flexion Contractures

Similarly, knee flexion contractures are a significant complication when present following stroke. Knee flexion contractures occur due to lack of active knee extension by the patient, as well as due to the increased withdrawal reflex which may be present after stroke. Knee flexion contractures are often worsened by bed positioning with pillows under the knee while the patient is lying supine and with excessive lying in the fetal position during the initial stages of recovery after stroke. Knee flexion contractures exceeding 15° dramatically increase the quadriceps muscle activity necessary to stabilize the knee when standing.[49]

Equinovarus Deformity

The common extensor reflex pattern of the lower extremity following upper motor neuron insult includes active plantar flexion and inversion of the foot. On this basis, due to the increased tone present, a moderate plantar flexion/equinus deformity may result. This contributes to genu recurvatum due to the extensor moment placed on the knee by the plantar flexion deformity. Treatment should emphasize prevention; however, surgical treatment after occurrence includes Achilles' and posterior tibial tendon releases and split anterior tibial tendon transfer.[7,60] Bracing at an early stage, before spasticity becomes a major factor, may also be of benefit in preventing this type of deformity.[38,60] Bracing after spasticity is present may control the extent of deformity present.

Lateral Foot Pain

Equinovarus deformities of the ankle resulting in moderate foot inversion will cause the patient to walk on the anterolateral aspect of the foot. Stress fractures may result, and even without stress fracture, local foot pain from persistent trauma and pressure over a small weight-bearing area may become significant. This may be a major limiting factor in gait. This can be successfully treated by below-knee bracing and, in less severe presentations, by lateral outflares and lateral wedging of the patient's footwear. The medial and lateral stability which can be provided in either a double upright metal brace or a molded AFP can provide better heel and medial foot contact.

Fractures

Fractures in the lower extremity occur more often on the hemiplegic side and in elderly individuals.[43] There is often osteopenia present due to the decreased weight-bearing through the affected side. Hip fractures are thought to occur equally in both right and left hemiplegic patients.[43] This suggests that perceptual deficits, including left-sided neglect, do not play a major role in this problem. Fracture of the lower extremity, because of the antalgic inhibition and because of the reflex CNS stimulation caused by the fracture, often results in a moderate increase in spasticity. This may result in a significant decrease in the functional capacity to use the limb for extended periods of time, in the order of 4 to 6 months after the fracture, provided successful union occurs.

Heterotopic Ossification

Heterotopic ossification is commonly seen following head injury, spinal cord injury, burns, or direct trauma. It has been reported following stroke but is a rare occurrence.[29] Heterotopic ossification is diagnosed clinically by pain and restricted range of movement occurring around the large joints of the lower extremity. The hip is most commonly affected. The usual presentation is pain, tenderness, and warmth with decreased range of movement. This can be further appreciated by bone scan and elevated sedimentation rate. Treatment for heterotopic ossification involves maintaining the passive range of movement, as contractures along with the heterotopic ossification will result in a moderately impaired limb. Surgical removal is performed only when there has been full maturation of the ossified tissue. This is best determined by decreased activity on bone scan. The prophylactic effect of indomethacin, ibuprofen, and etidronate sodium in these stroke patients with respect to heterotopic ossification is unknown, although these have been shown to be effective in the spinal cord, head injury, and trauma populations.

Arthritis

Osteoarthritis on the affected side is often aggravated by the stroke. Similarly, on the unaffected side, because of increased mechanical demands due to contralateral weakness, there is exacerbation of pain in the large joints. Premorbid inflammatory arthritis will often be relieved in the affected lower extremity.[56]

Deep Venous Thrombosis

Deep venous thrombosis (DVT) is a common consequence of immobility and, as such, is a significant cause of morbidity after stroke. The reported incidence of DVT following stroke varies depending on the type of patient studied, the interval since the stroke, and the method used to screen for DVT. Brandstater et al.[8] have estimated an incidence of 50% based on the summation of data from a group of studies using ^{125}I fibrinogen scanning to detect DVT. After the initial recovery period, the occurrence of DVT decreases[17] but is still present in 29 to 31% as detected by venography or ^{125}I fibrinogen.[13,42] Although the velocity of blood flow in the hemiparetic lower limb has been measured as approximately 50% of the unaffected extremity,[37] DVT has been reported in up to 13% in the "unaffected" lower extremity.[51]

Venous insufficiency following DVT is important; however, of major concern is the incidence of pulmonary embolism secondary to DVT which has been estimated to be around 10 to 20%.[8,58] Approximately 10% of pulmonary emboli occurring following stroke are fatal.[58]

Profound weakness and reduced ambulatory status increase the risk of DVT.[9,51] The relative risk of deep venous complication after stroke was five times greater in the nonambulatory population and further improved when the patients could walk greater than 50 feet with a cane.[9] Although the long-term risk of DVT in the hemiparetic limb is not yet reported, in an extensive review of the literature, Brandstater et al.[8] suggest that the relative risk of DVT varies according to the patients' residual deficits.

Standard prophylaxis for DVT following stroke is subcutaneous heparin, usually given in 5,000 IU subcutaneously every 12 hours for 14 days.[41] Relative contraindications are hemorrhagic stroke or recent intracranial surgery. The risk of DVT in patients on prophylaxis is reduced to approximately 20%.[41] Extended prophylaxis is suggested until the patient has reached ambulatory status.[45]

OUTCOME

The majority of neurologic recovery in the lower extremity occurs in the first 3–6 months.[11,40] A small percentage of patients will show continued recovery for the first year. Statistics suggest that greater than 50% of patients are able to walk unassisted within 6 months,[12] although this ambulation may be limited (in the majority) to within the home only.[52] In patients who were discharged to independent living, generally within their own home, only minor decrements occurred in the patient's functional capacity after 12 months. Ninety-nine percent continued to walk indoors, and 92 to 95% could climb a staircase.[57] Approximately 10% of stroke patients recover normal function, 40% have mild impairments, 40% have moderate impairments but are able to continue basic functions in spite of those, and 10% of stroke patients are severely impaired and require long-term care.[54] Individuals most likely to return to work have a short rehabilitation length of stay, are not aphasic, consume few alcoholic beverages, have higher Barthel's indexes, and are younger.[4] In general, outcome predictors are multifactorial in nature, as functional outcome following stroke in itself is multifactorial.

APPROACH TO FOLLOW-UP

Patients treated in a neurological rehabilitation program should be seen 6 weeks to 3 months after discharge. At this point, it is common for patients to have had a further plateauing of their abilities.[11,30,33,40] It is also possible to screen out those patients who have had detrimental loss in their function due to decreased activity or lack of supports at home. The common problems seen after discharge are loss of ambulation ability due to deconditioning, loss of confidence related to falls, and joint pain and contractures. In the stroke patient, these are common but preventable problems.

REFERENCES

1. Aids to the Examination of the Peripheral Nervous System. Toronto, Bailliere Tindall, 1986, pp 1–2.
2. Bach-y-Rita P: Brain plasticity as a basis of the development of rehabilitation procedures for hemiplegia. Scand J Rehabil Med 13:73–83, 1981.
3. Baker CA: Activity tolerance in the geriatric stroke patient. Rehabil Nurs 16:337–343, 1991.
4. Black-Schaffer RM, Osberg JS: Return to work after stroke: Development of a predictive model. Arch Phys Med Rehabil 71:285–290, 1990.
5. Bohannon RW: Gait performance of hemiparetic stroke patients: Selected variables. Arch Phys Med Rehabil 68:777–781, 1987.
6. Bohannon RW: Strength deficits also predict gait performance in patients with stroke. Percet Mot Skills 73:146, 1991.
7. Botte MJ, Waters RL, Keenan M, et al: Orthopaedic management of the stroke patient: Part II. Treating deformities of the upper and lower extremities. Orthop Rev 17:891–910, 1988.
8. Brandstater ME, Roth EJ, Siebens HC: Venous thromboembolism in stroke: Literature review and implications for clinical practice. Arch Phys Med Rehabil 73(suppl):379–391, 1992.
9. Bromfield EB, Reding MJ: Relative risk of deep venous thrombosis or pulmonary embolism post-stroke based on ambulatory status. J Neurol Rehab 2:51–57, 1988.
10. Brunnstrom S: Recovery stages and evaluation procedures. In Brunnstrom S (ed): Movement Therapy in Hemiplegia. New York, Harper & Row, 1970, pp 34–55.
11. Carroll D: The disability in hemiplegia caused by cerebrovascular disease: Serial study of 98 cases. J Chron Dis 15:179–188, 1962.
12. Chin PL, Rosie A, Irving M, Smith R: Studies in hemiplegic gait. In Clifford Rose F (ed): Advances in Stroke Therapy. New York, Raven Press, 1982, pp 197–211.
13. Cope C, Reyes TM, Skversky MJ: Phlebographic analysis of the incidence of thrombosis in hemiplegia. Radiology 109:581–584, 1973.
14. Corcoran PJ, Jebsen RH, Brengelmann GL, Simons BC: Effects of plastic and metal leg braces on speed and energy cost of hemiparetic ambulation. Arch Phys Med Rehabil 51:69–77, 1970.
15. Cozean CD, Pease WS, Hubbell SL: Biofeedback and functional electrical stimulation in stroke rehabilitation. Arch Phys Med Rehabil 69:401–405, 1988.
16. Davidoff GN, Kerren O, Solzi P: Acute stroke patients: Long-term effects of rehabilitation and maintenance of gains. Arch Phys Med Rehabil 72:869–873, 1991.
17. Desmukh M, Bisignani M, Landau P, Orchard TJ: Deep vein thrombosis in rehabilitation stroke patients: Incidence, risk factors, and prophylaxis. Am J Phys Med Rehabil 70:313–316, 1991.
18. Dimitrijevic MR, Faganel J, Sherwood AM, McKay WB: Activation of paralysed leg flexors and extensors during gait in patients after stroke. Scan J Rehabil Med 13:109–115, 1981.
19. Dobato JL, Villanueva JA, Gimenez-Roldan S: Sensory ataxic hemiparesis in thalamic hemorrhage. Stroke 21:1749–1753, 1990.
20. Fisher CM: Concerning the mechanism of recovery in stroke hemiplegia. Can J Neurol Sci 19:57–63, 1992.
21. Fisher SV, Gullickson G: Energy cost of ambulation in health and disability: A literature review. Arch Phys Med Rehabil 59:124–133, 1978.
22. Friedman PJ: Gait recovery after hemiplegic stroke. Int Disabil Stud 12:119–122, 1990.
23. Fugl-Meyer AR, Jaasko L, Leyman I, et al: Post-stroke hemiplegic patient: I. Method for evaluation of physical performance. Scand J Rehabil Med 7:13–31, 1975.
24. Garrison SJ, Rolak LA, Dodaro RR, O'Callaghan AJ: Rehabilitation of the stroke patient. In Delisa JA (ed): Rehabilitation Medicine: Principles and Practice. Philadelphia, J.B. Lippincott, 1985, pp 565–584.
25. Goldstein LB: Pharmacology of recovery after stroke. Stroke 21:139–142, 1990.

26. Gowland C: Predicting sensorimotor recovery following stroke rehabilitation. Phys Can 36:313–320, 1984.

27. Gowland C, Torresin W, Stratford P, et al: Chedoke-McMaster stroke assessment: A comprehensive clinical and research measure. In Proceedings of the World Confederation for Physical Therapy, 11th International Congress, London, England, 1991, p P-033.

28. Gowland CA: Staging motor impairment after stroke. Stroke 21(suppl II):19–21, 1990.

29. Hajek VE: Heterotopic ossification in hemiplegia following stroke. Arch Phys Med Rehabil 68:313–314, 1987.

30. Hier DB, Mondlock J, Caplan LR: Recovery of behavioral abnormalities after right hemisphere stroke. Neurology 33:345–350, 1983.

31. Jongbloed L: Prediction of function after stroke: A critical review. Stroke 17:765–776, 1986.

32. Jordan C, Waters RL: Stroke. In Nickle VL (ed): Orthopaedic Rehabilitation. New York, Churchill Livingstone, 1982, pp 277–291.

33. Kaplan PE: Hemiplegia: Rehabilitation of the lower extremity. In Kaplan PE, Cerullo LJ (eds): Stroke Rehabilitation, Stoneham, MA, Butterworth, 1986, pp 119–146.

34. Katrak PH, Cole AMD, Poulos CJ, McCauley JCK: Objective assessment of spasticity, strength and function with early exhibition of dantrolene sodium after cerebrovascular accident: A randomized double-blind study. Arch Phys Med Rehabil 73:4–9, 1992.

35. Ketel WB, Kolb ME: Long term treatment with dantrolene sodium of stroke patients with spasticity limiting the return of function. Curr Med Res Opin 9:161–169, 1984.

36. Knuttsson E: Gait control in hemiparesis. Scand J Rehabil Med 13:101–108, 1981.

37. Laban MM, Johnson EW: Velocity of blood flow in the saphenous vein of hemiplegic patients. Arch Phys Med Rehabil 3:245–249, 1965.

38. Lehmann JF, Condon SM, Price R, deLateur BJ: Gait abnormalities in hemiplegia: Their correction by ankle-foot orthoses. Arch Phys Med Rehabil 68:763–771, 1987.

39. Mandel AR, Nymark JR, Balmer SJ, et al: Electromyographic versus rhythmic positional biofeedback in computerized gait retraining with stroke patients. Arch Phys Med Rehabil 71:649–654, 1990.

40. Mayo NE, Korner-Bitensky NA, Becker R: Recovery time of independent function post-stroke. Am J Phys Med Rehabil 70:5–12, 1991.

41. McCarthy ST, Turner J: Low-dose subcutaneous heparin in the prevention of deep-vein thrombosis and pulmonary emboli following acute stroke. Age Aging 15:84–88, 1986.

42. Miyamoto AT, Miller LS: Pulmonary embolism in stroke: Prevention by early heparinization of venous thrombosis detected by iodine-125 fibrinogen leg scans. Arch Phys Med Rehabil 61:584–587, 1980.

43. Mulley G, Esply AJ: Hip fracture after hemiplegia. Postgrad Med J 55:264–265, 1979.

44. Murray C, Parsons J, Rush PJ: The role of neurological rehabilitation in stroke recovery. Mod Med Can 45:862–868, 1990.

45. Office of Medical Applications of Research, NIH. Consensus conference: Prevention of venous thrombosis and pulmonary embolism. JAMA 256:744–749, 1986.

46. Olsen TS: Arm and leg paresis as outcome predictors in stroke rehabilitation. Stroke 21:247–251, 1990.

47. Peat M, Dubo HIC, Winter DA, et al: Electromyographic temporal analysis of gait: Hemiplegic locomotion. Arch Phys Med Rehabil 57:421–425, 1976.

48. Perry J, Waters RL, Perrin T: Electromyographic analysis of equinovarus following stroke. Clin Orthop 131:47–53, 1978.

49. Potter PJ, Kirby RL: Relationship between electromyographic activity of the vastus lateralis while standing and the extent of bilateral simulated knee-flexion contractures. Am J Phys Med Rehabil 70:301–305, 1991.

50. Saunders JB, Inman VT, Eberhart HD: Major determinants in normal and pathological gait. J Bone Joint Surg 35A:543–558, 1953.

51. Sioson ER, Crowe WE, Dawson NV: Occult proximal deep vein thrombosis: Its prevalence among patients admitted to a rehabilitation hospital. Arch Phys Med Rehabil 69:183–185, 1988.

52. Skilbeck CE, Wade DT, Langont Hewer R, Wood VA: Recovery after stroke. J Neurol Neurosurg Psychiatry 46:5–8, 1983.

53. Sotaniemi KA, Pyhtinen J, Myllyla VV: Correlation of clinical and computed tomographic findings in stroke patients. Stroke 21:1562–1566, 1990.

54. Stallones RA, Dyken ML, Fang HCH, et al: Epidemiology for stroke facilities planning. Stroke 3:360–371, 1972.

55. Sullivan MJL, Heisel B, Lemaire E, et al: Utilization of orthotic devices in stroke patients: A comparison of out-reach and institution based services. Can J Rehabil 4:47–50, 1990.

56. Thompson M, Bywaters EGL: Unilateral rheumatoid arthritis following hemiplegia. Ann Rheum Dis 21:370–377, 1962.
57. Thorngren M, Westling B, Norrving B: Outcome after stroke in patients discharged to independent living. Stroke 2:236–240, 1990.
58. Warlow C, Ogston D, Douglas AS: Deep venous thrombosis of the legs after strokes. BMJ 1:1178–1183, 1976.
59. Waters RL, Montgomery J: Lower extremity management of hemiparesis. Clin Orthop 102:102–113, 1974.
60. Waters RL, Penny J, Garland DE: Surgical correction of gait abnormalities following stroke. Clin Orthop 131:54 63, 1978.
61. Wolf SL, Baker MP, Kelly JL: EMG biofeedback in stroke: Effect of patient characteristics. Arch Phys Med Rehabil 60:96–102, 1979.
62. World Health Organization: International Classification of Impairments, Disabilities, and Handicaps: A Manual of Classification Relating to the Consequences of Disease. Geneva, World Health Organization, 1980.

DOUGLAS K. DITTMER, MD, FRCPC
DAWN E. MacARTHUR-TURNER, BSc, CO(C)
IAN C. JONES, BM, MA

11. ORTHOTICS IN STROKE

From the
Orthotics Clinic
Department of Physical Medicine
  and Rehabilitation
Victoria Hospital and
University of Western Ontario
  (DKD, ICJ)
            and
Custom Orthotics of London, Inc.
  (DEMT)
London, Ontario
Canada

Reprint requests to:
Douglas K. Dittmer, MD, FRCPC
Victoria Hospital
800 Commissioners Road East
London, Ontario N6A 4G5
Canada

An orthosis can be defined as an externally applied device used to modify structural and functional characteristics of the neuromuscular system in order to support, correct, or protect the body part. Previously, the term *orthosis* would refer to a brace or splint, an external device that assisted or restricted motion of body parts for a defined purpose. The scope of orthotics now covers the wide range of the theory and practice of designing, casting, fabricating, and fitting an orthosis followed by a suitable clinical trial.

This state-of-the-art review, however, is not intended to cover the whole field of orthotics; that topic was the subject of a previous issue in this series (vol. 1, no. 1, February 1987). Rather, this discussion refers to the use of orthotics in hemiplegic patients as the result of a cerebrovascular accident. Traditional, including conventional (metal), as well as newer, thermoplastic, combination types and functional electrical stimulation orthoses are described. A description of materials, clinical and laboratory analyses of gait, and gait training will follow. While those in the field of rehabilitation are generally aware of various types of orthoses in stroke and their applications, it is hoped that this review will cover some of the newer techniques in a rapidly changing field.

The stroke patient provides a rehabilitation challenge in terms of the wide range of clinical recovery that occurs following the acute event. An orthosis that may be most appropriate during the in-hospital stay may be rendered obsolete with subsequent neurologic recovery. Many of these patients are elderly and present additional problems in terms of decreased skin tolerance to external pressure, peripheral vascular disease, and other concomitant diseases such as coronary artery disease, congestive heart failure, and diabetes. The benefits gained in the biomechanics of gait may be offset by the energy (oxygen consumption) requirements of placing a weighted object at the end of a long lever such as a leg. The patient must also be able to don and doff the orthosis in a reasonable period of time; otherwise, it will not be used and will adorn the closet. Finally, the financial constraints of purchasing, repairing, and/or replacing the device can be considerable. These issues are particularly relevant for the disabled and retired elderly patient.

A typical regional or tertiary level orthotics clinic is comprised of at least four people: the physiatrist, certified orthotist, physiotherapist, and occupational therapist. This form of "one-stop shopping," which is becoming more prevalent, is economical for the patient and the rehabilitation team in terms of time and effort. Those who provide "on-call" consultation include the social worker (for funding issues), chiropodist, and gait lab kinesiologist.

STROKE ASSESSMENT AND CLINICAL ANALYSIS OF GAIT

Under normal circumstances, walking is an automatic activity, requiring mere thought for the CNS centers to initiate and guide gait. Following nervous system injury, however, these patterns no longer are accessible and the individual must develop new strategies using alternate pathways. Brunnstrom[7] described these as the "basic limb synergies" (Table 1). Various components of the synergies had different strengths. It was felt that these various synergies changed in a predictable fashion through a series of stages (Table 2).

Most patients are at least at a Brunnstrom recovery stage 3 before successful ambulation can be attempted. Brandstater et al.[5] showed that of 11 selected

TABLE 1.   Basic Limb Synergies

The flexion synergy of the upper arm consists of:
    Flexion of the elbow to an acute angle
    Full range supination of the forearm
    Abduction of the shoulder to 90°
    External rotation of the shoulder
    Retraction and/or elevation of the shoulder girdle

The extension synergy of the upper limb consists of:
    Extension of the elbow
    Full range pronation of the forearm
    Adduction of the arm in front of the body
    Internal rotation of the arm
    Fixation of the shoulder girdle in a somewhat protracted position

The flexion synergy of the lower limb consists of:
    Dorsiflexion of the toes
    Dorsiflexion and inversion of the ankle
    Flexion of the knee to about 90°
    Flexion of the hip
    Abduction and external rotation of the hip

The extension synergy of the lower limb consists of:
    Plantar flexion of the toes
    Plantar flexion and inversion of the ankle
    Extension of the knee
    Extension of the hip
    Abduction and internal rotation of the hip

TABLE 2. Stages of Motor Recovery

1	Flaccidity.
2	Early spasticity with some voluntary control of the synergies.
3	Severe spasticity.
4	Spasticity declines
5	More difficult movement combinations are learned as the basic limb synergies lose their dominance over motor acts.
6	Spasticity disappears, individual joint movements have become possible, and coordination has approached normal.
7	Normal function is restored.

temporal and distance variables, 2 in particular—walking speed and symmetry of swing phases—were significantly related to motor recovery as classified according to defined stages. However, it was felt that the clinical classification of motor recovery stages, while useful, was not precise enough. Keenan et al.[16] found that balance was the most significant factor correlating with the patient's ability to ambulate at the time of discharge. Motor control, motor planning, proprioception, and sensory integration were also found to be significantly correlated with ambulation ability. Yet of the 90 patients studied, a mere 50% regained sufficient function to permit a community level of ambulation while 17% remained totally unable to ambulate.

Examination of the Patient

Determining at what point during the gait cycle an orthosis may be helpful is an important part of the physical examination. However, one must first examine the musculoskeletal, neurologic, and peripheral vascular systems.

The lower extremity examination includes examining for hip, knee, and ankle range of motion and determining the presence or absence of any contractures about these joints. Knee and ankle-foot stability is tested, and muscle tone is examined by passive joint movement. Direct leg length measurements are made by measuring the distances from the anterior superior iliac spine to the medial malleoli, and indirect measurements from the umbilicus to the medial malleoli. Muscle tone is examined by passive joint motion, and excessive spasticity (i.e., >4 beats of clonus) is recorded. Muscle strength is tested using the Medical Research Council (MRC) scale (Table 3).

Sensory determination of touch, pinprick, vibration sense, and position sense is important as the insensate foot may preclude certain braces. Ataxia is not an indication for a brace.

Clinical gait analysis is part of the physical examination and is comprised of two phases: stance and swing. The stance phase consists of heel strike (weight

TABLE 3. Muscle Strength Testing Using the MRC Scale

5	Normal strength.
4	Muscle is weak but moves the joint against a combination of gravity and resistance.
3	Muscle moves the joint against gravity but not a combination of gravity and resistance.
2	Muscle moves the joint when gravity is eliminated.
1	A flicker of movement is seen or felt in the muscle.

acceptance), midstance, and push-off. The swing phase consists of acceleration, midswing, and deceleration periods. The lower limb muscles function in groups during the gait cycle[14]:

1. The anterior leg muscles are active during swing phase and contract eccentrically at heel strike.
2. The plantar flexors are active exclusively during the stance phase, initially contracting eccentrically and later concentrically.
3. Inversion/eversion of the foot is controlled by the peroneals and tibialis posterior. These muscles contribute during the stance phase by transferring weight from the medial to the lateral half of the foot and during the swing phase by controlling the medial lateral position of the foot in the air.
4. The quadriceps are active eccentrically from heel strike to midstance, providing knee stability during the loading period, and are active concentrically during early swing acceleration.
5. The hamstrings are active during the swing stance transition by contracting eccentrically during the latter part of swing and concentrically during heel strike, contributing to hip and knee extension.
6. The hip muscles are active both concentrically and eccentrically to maintain hip stability.

A full review of the gait parameters and biomechanics is provided by Kottke.[17]

MEASURING ORTHOTIC EFFECTIVENESS

The use of orthoses to improve the gait of hemiplegic patients is a common rehabilitation practice. New materials used for orthotics have made dramatic changes in orthoses design and subsequently the need to monitor the effectiveness of the new designs. An Electrodynogram system (EDG—The Langer Biomechanics Group, Deer Park, NY) has been used to measure the temporal aspects of gait and the pressure on specific areas of the foot as a result of two types of ankle-foot orthoses.[12] EDG data are collected in a portable wrist-pack worn by the subject that is connected to the sensors attached to the subject's feet (Figs. 1 and 2). Data are transferred via a serial connection to a computer system for analysis after collection. This system and other portable "in-shoe" pressure measurement systems have the advantage over fixed collection systems in that the person being analyzed is not restricted to striking a specific target with their foot during gait.

The improvement in walking speed has been indicated by Mizrahi et al.[26,27] as the most effective method to monitor improvements in the gait of hemiplegic patients. An effective orthosis would allow greater cadence (number of steps per minute) than one of an inferior design. Cadence data can be easily acquired by the researcher or clinician with a simple stopwatch. To calculate walking velocity, some known linear distance must be used as a reference. Temporal descriptive measures can also be derived from the use of foot switches, instrumented walkways, and videography or cinematography. These systems can provide more information than that of a stop-watch and calibrated walking distance, but they are also substantially more expensive.

One goal of rehabilitation of hemiplegia due to a cerebrovascular accident is to reduce asymmetrical movements during gait.[40] Normal gait is energy-efficient, symmetrical by nature, and relatively safe. Any evaluation of the effectiveness of an orthotic in correcting hemiparetic gait must be based on improvements from the "normal" hemiparetic gait. Biomechanical research has shown that hemiparetic

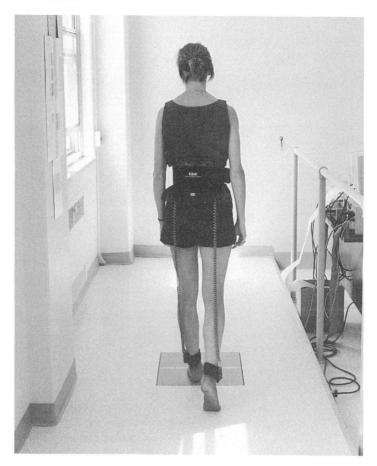

FIGURE 1.   Gait analysis incorporating a triaxial force platform and electrodynogram.

gait is characterized by several temporal, kinematic, and kinetic patterns which differ distinctly from normal gait. A shorter step length, longer stance duration, and consequently shorter swing phase, on the affected side as compared to the unaffected side, are the temporal aspects that differ from normals. Greater hip flexion during midstance, knee extension, and plantar flexion on the affected side may relate to the difficulty in advancing the total body center of mass during the stance phase. Circumduction of the affected limb is necessary during the swing phase to avoid toe drag, because of less than normal knee flexion and less ankle dorsiflexion.[20] The forces transmitted through the affected side, when measured under the feet, have been shown to be less than those on the unaffected side.[1] The abnormalities present in these parameters of gait create a pattern that is very slow and uncoordinated.

Gait kinematic data, the time-space branch of gait mechanics, provide information as to how the body moves in space. Consequently, kinematic data are often used to quantify the effectiveness of an orthotic. Accelerometers, specialized goniometers, and cine and video analyses are among the most common methods of collecting kinematic data. A disadvantage of some of these instruments is

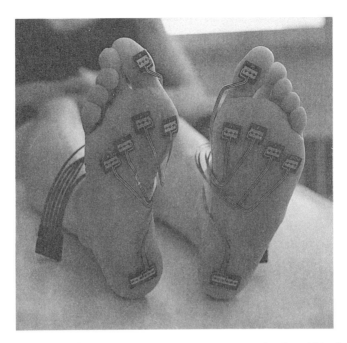

FIGURE 2.   Electrodynogram sensors adhere to the feet, allowing for within-shoe surface pressure and temporal measures.

derived from the subject's having to wear specific apparatus, such as the goniometer, fasteners for the accelerometer, or reflective markers or light-emitting diodes for cine and video analysis. Each of these "intrusions" can affect the gait pattern of the person wearing the apparatus. Data gathered from cinematographic and videographic methods can be manually analyzed, relieving the patient of the necessity of wearing markers; however, this type of analysis is more labor-intensive and time-consuming than the automated methods requiring markers.

Electromyographic (EMG) data derived from surface electrodes can provide clinicians and researchers information indicative of the neurologic control of the superficial musculature used in gait. This information may assist in determining the type of orthosis that would be most beneficial to the patient. Intramuscular electrodes must be used if the function of deep muscles is to be analyzed. The size, type, shape, and location of the electrodes all affect the magnitude and content of the EMG signal.[41]

A heel-to-toe walking pattern is not normally elicited on the affected side because of greater than normal ankle plantar flexion and less knee flexion. Ankle-foot orthotics (AFO) attempt to restore the natural heel-to-toe weight transference. Many gait laboratories use triaxial force platforms to test the effectiveness of AFOs by measuring the forces transmitted to the platform during locomotion (Fig. 1). The ground reaction forces that are collected when a person walks across the platform reflect the vertical and horizontal (shear) forces that are acting on the platform. The platform can be used to monitor the transfer of weight through both the affected and unaffected limbs. Because the platform is a fixed instrument, consideration must be given to the difficulty, experienced by some persons, in successfully striking the platform without altering their normal gait pattern.

ORTHOTIC MATERIALS

Some of the factors affecting the hemiplegic gait pattern are spasticity, edema, decreased sensation, decreased range of motion, decreased voluntary muscle control, and instability of the ankle and knee joint.[12] The rehabilitation team is faced with deciding on the appropriate orthotic device which will address these factors and at the same time minimize the energy consumption required for ambulation.

Historically, the orthotist would fit the hemiplegic with a double metal upright AFO fixed to a leather-soled oxford shoe. In the 1960s, higher temperature thermoplastic materials became available. Corcoran et al.[8] concluded that energy consumption decreased while wearing an AFO. There was no significant difference in energy consumption between thermoplastic and conventional orthoses.

Recently, there has been an emphasis on different types of thermoplastic materials. Polypropylene is the most routinely used sheet plastic in the orthotic and prosthetic industry. Its durable and rigid characteristics are essential for vacuum-forming custom orthoses. Copolymer is more rigid after the forming process, so some practitioners feel it is the appropriate choice. There is no right or wrong answer in determining the plastic type.[36] Thermoplastic Elastomer (TPE— American Plastics) is a new type of sheet material which combines both rubber and polypropylene. This combination provides a superior "flex" life when it is used in both directional or torsional stress applications. As new materials are developed the combinations for fabricating various orthoses become endless.

LOWER EXTREMITY ORTHOSES

The role of the lower limb orthotic device includes the stabilization of an unstable joint (to maintain alignment or prevent total collapse of a joint with weak musculature), to complement the activity of a weak muscle (as in the use of a spring to assist in ankle dorsiflexion), to prevent contractures, or to enhance sensory feedback in patients with impaired proprioceptive sense in the leg.

When prescribing an orthotic device for a stroke patient, the physiatrist needs to consider questions such as which device is most appropriate and when the device should be introduced and subsequently used. Other factors include the degree of spasticity, ataxia, organic mental changes, hemisensory defect, visual disturbances, and the stage of motor recovery. In general, most recovery occurs within the first 3 to 6 months. Usually, there is sufficient motor power in the hip for weight-bearing and forward progression, sufficient power or extensor tone at the knee, and little or no function at the ankle. There is a tendency for knee hyperextension, and the gait is usually slow, halting, and stiff. There is a short step on the paretic side, with a tendency to plant the foot flat rather than in a heel-toe pattern. It is also characteristic to have the foot in equinovarus during swing phase. The loss of the heel-toe gait, the shift in body weight to above the foot at the moment the foot hits the ground, the lateral trunk movement, and the reduced perception of spatial orientation result in greater instability. Given all of these factors, the patient who must rely on a knee-ankle-foot orthosis (KAFO) to maintain upright posture will likely not be a functional ambulator. Hopefully, the use of a KAFO can be limited to the early recovery phase if needed and can be abandoned later.

Ankle-Foot Orthoses

A wide variety of AFOs have been described by Lehmann et al.[19-21] The conventional double metal upright AFO is attached to the shoe by a stirrup affixed under the heel. Conventional AFOs can comprise a Klenzak dorsiflexion assist with an anterior spring or limited motion with a plantar flexion or posterior stop. Bicaal joints can incorporate both stops and springs. Springs are avoided in cases of excessive spasticity. Medial lateral stability is provided with a firm oxford shoe, and if required, a T-strap can be added. The plastic, usually polypropylene, of the AFO may be trimmed posterior or anterior to the malleoli, providing greater flexibility in the former and greater stability in the latter. As plastic AFOs tend to limit plantar flexion, there is the potential for knee instability during heel strike. The greater the resistance to plantar flexion (as in the anterior trimline model), the greater the potential for knee bending at heel strike. The knee flexion moment is also significantly increased with the AFO in 5° of dorsiflexion but not in 5° of plantar flexion. Shoe modifications, such as medial and lateral flares and heels of differing densities, also contribute to stability. Rocker-bottom soles can smooth the heel-toe phase, especially with rigid AFOs. A smoother gait pattern can also be achieved by utilizing an articulated AFO (Fig. 3).

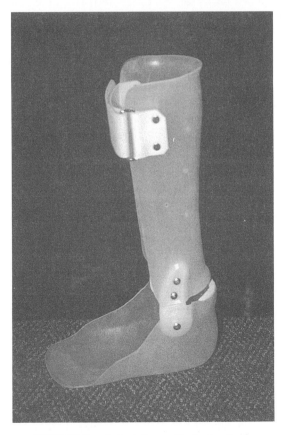

FIGURE 3. Articulating ankle-foot orthosis.

In general, the advantages of the plastic AFOs over the metal AFOs are better cosmetics, light weight, and transferability from shoe to shoe. However, the presence of insensate skin, intermittent or fluctuating edema, and increased clonus at the ankle may favor the metal braces. Overall, the main benefits of AFOs may be to increase walking speed and normalize the heel-strike duration through use of an optimally adjusted plantar-flexion stop.[21] Exaggerated knee flexion moment causes knee instability. AFOs allow safe ambulation by improving mediolateral stability during stance and toe clearance during swing. Past problems with conventional orthoses included a lack of total contact fit, poor ankle position, and pressure sores.

In contrast to posterior-type braces, a low thermoplastic anterior AFO has been reported in a recent clinical trial by Wong et al.[42] to improve gait in stroke patients and to be comparable in performance to a posterior trimline AFO.

Tone-Inhibiting Ankle-Foot Orthoses

Historically, we have described gait through sagittal plane movements and position of the ankle. Lately, there has been an interest in neurodevelopmental techniques in both physiotherapy and orthotic fittings.[8] Cussick et al.[9] utilized these techniques to improve foot and proximal alignment, to improve weight-transfer control of abnormal reflexes, and to increase the base of support. These techniques are well accepted with children.[12] Combined with these neurodevelopmental techniques, it appears clinically that tone-inhibiting ankle-foot orthoses (TIAFO) lead to appropriate patterns of muscle coordination (Fig. 4).

The neurophysiologic principles for inhibiting excessive muscle tone have been well documented in the literature relating to pediatric populations but less so in hemiplegic populations. These principles are as follows[8,12,13,22,31,36]:

1. Prolonged stretch of plantar flexions and long toe flexors
2. Pressure on long toe flexor tendons
3. Decreased reflexes produced by tactile stimulation
4. Weight-bearing in proper alignment which induces proprioceptors
5. Altered muscle length
6. Improved recruitment and sequence of muscle activity

It is very hard to evaluate the effectiveness of the TIAFOs across the adult hemiplegic population because of the variability in the severity of the stroke. We need research to document the effectiveness of the orthoses and how they relate to foot-loading patterns. There are different ways to fabricate the TIAFO. Each patient's unique situation must be analyzed to determine which method is most effective. A hybrid-style AFO (Fig. 4), consisting of an inner polyethylene shell in conjunction with an exterior polypropylene shell, is becoming more popular in clinical practice. The inner shell maintains the foot in a proper alignment, maximizing the neurophysiologic principles.

Occasionally, the rehabilitation team is faced with a patient who exhibits a crouch-style gait pattern caused by weak quadriceps. With this gait pattern, the patient can be fitted with a ground reaction or anterior AFO. This allows the orthotist to position the ankle in the appropriate neutral position, thus positioning the knee in a stable "nonflexed" position.

Tubular-Style Ankle-Foot Orthoses

Our clinical experience has shown a tubular-style AFO is beneficial for patients exhibiting a fixed equinovarus deformity. The orthosis allows the patient

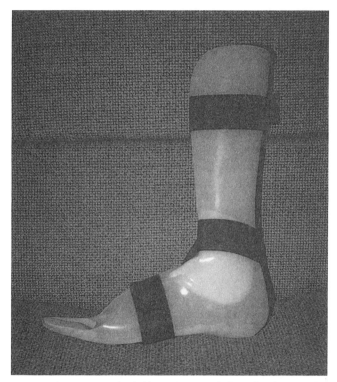

FIGURE 4. A hybrid-style tone-inhibiting AFO consisting of an inner polyethylene shell with an outer polypropylene shell.

to obtain a plantigrade position, which will enable a heel-to-toe gait pattern. The orthosis consists of an inner calfhide sleeve, padded with Plastizote. The sleeve is built up in such a manner with Plastizote so that a neutral position is achieved prior to vacuum forming with copolymer. The tubular orthosis is bulky; however, it enables the patient to achieve a plantigrade (neutral) position and a more stable foot position in the brace.

Knee-Ankle-Foot Orthoses

The use of a knee-ankle-foot orthosis (KAFO) by hemiplegic patients requires a large energy expenditure. As a result, the use of a KAFO is often limited to the early recovery phases, while the patient is learning the gait patterns, and is replaced with an AFO later in the treatment program. Some Japanese rehabilitation centers routinely use KAFOs in the early recovery stages.[28,29]

Indications for prescribing a KAFO include a Brunnstrom recovery stage 2 in a patient with an unstable walk, patients exhibiting a genu recurvatum, and patients with an equinovarus deformity. The principal objective in using the KAFO is to support and control the patient's knee and ankle simultaneously, thus leading to an improved gait pattern.[28,29]

Fitting a patient with a KAFO that will be discarded later in the treatment program may seem to be an unwise use of resources unless it decreases length of stay in hospital. However, from a morbidity viewpoint recent literature has indicated that a 17.6 odds ratio for developing venous thromboembolism existed for patients bedridden or wheelchair bound at the time of admission. The odds ratio dropped to 0.06 if the patients were walking with or without aids at the time of admission.[32] This may suggest that some consideration should be given to mobilizing these patients as quickly as possible when instituting a lower extremity exercise program.

UPPER EXTREMITY ORTHOSES

Occupational and physical therapists most commonly use the functional position resting hand splint for achieving improvements in positioning and tone as well as protection of the joints for stroke patients with low levels of motor recovery. For patients with distal hypotonus, or those who are at risk of traumatizing the affected hand due to moderate-to-severe neglect, a splint may be used to protect the joints and prevent contractures. More commonly, the functional resting position splints are used to manage distal hypertonicity. In this situation, the splint is used to maintain a passive stretch in the functional hand position in an attempt to decrease tone and prevent contractures from developing or progressing.

Types of Splints

Resting hand and wrist splints are usually custom made to achieve the most desirable results. Sansplint is the material of choice for many therapists, but other splinting materials can be used. Some therapists use preformed splints when only minimal adjustments are required, saving both time and money (Fig. 5).

Wearing schedules vary depending on the individual patient's needs. Typically, however, patients with moderate-to-severe increased tone will wear the splint for 2 hours on, 0.5 hours off; and patients with minimal-to-moderate increased tone will wear the splint for 2 hours on, 2 hours off. Education of the patient, family, and staff regarding the purpose of the splint, the wearing schedule, and the need for passive or assisted range of motion exercises to all of the joints immobilized by the splint when it is off should be an integral component of the overall splinting approach.

Another method of addressing the problem of hypertonia in the upper limb is the **tone-reducing wrist-hand orthosis**. The high-temperature thermoplastic brace was tried in 18 patients who wore their brace for a minimum of 4 hours and up to 16 to 22 hours/day. The result was a dramatic improvement in independence in hygiene and in reduction in pain in those patients who used the brace.[34]

Other types of splints used include variations of the foam finger-spreader, dorsal splints, and cone splints.[3,25] **Finger-spreader splints** made out of Plastizote have been successful in reducing tone and edema in some patients. Skin integrity must always be monitored with the use of any splint and especially with finger-spreaders. The increased tone in combination with the greater skin–splint contact area can contribute to skin breakdown if not fitted properly or removed as scheduled.

Dorsal forearm troughs with volar palm pans and **cone splints** are used by some therapists to manage increased tone distally. These tend to be more time-consuming and difficult to custom-make and, as a result, are not usually the first choice by most therapists. **Cock-up wrist splints** are sometimes used to assist with the reduction of hand edema.[11] This type of splint can help to improve venous drainage by maintaining the wrist in dorsiflexion and preventing sustained extension of the metacarpophalangeal joints.[11]

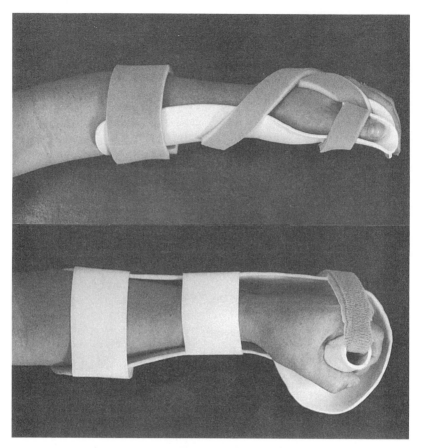

FIGURE 5. Preformed resting hand and wrist splints: forearm trough and cone.

The use of **slings** with stroke patients remains a point of controversy in the literature. Slings are most commonly used to prevent trauma to the flaccid shoulder or arm during early mobilization and transfers. A double-cuff-style sling is often used because of its simple design and ease of application. There are numerous sling designs to choose from (e.g., Harris hemisling, Bobath sling), although very few, including the Harris hemisling, have been proven effective in correcting subluxation.[4,6] Most therapists agree that careful active treatment and correct handling and positioning achieve the best prevention and/or reduction of shoulder pain and subluxation commonly associated with hemiplegia, and therefore they limit their use of slings.

Functional Electrical Stimulation

Electrical stimulation for the rehabilitation of paralyzed limbs dates back as far as 1975,[39] when it was used for treatment of peripheral lesions. In 1962, Moe and Part[39] coined the name *functional electrical stimulation* (FES). Since then, FES-orthotic systems have been designed and used with some success following spinal cord injuries and cerebrovascular accidents.[2,30] The FES system has been able to provide some active movement at specific joints; however, it is limited in its ability to duplicate normal muscle function.[30] Electrical stimulation is used by therapists as an adjunct to other forms of clinical treatment of musculoskeletal and neuromuscular problems. The purpose of electrical stimulation is to prevent atrophy of peripherally denervated muscles, maintain or increase range of movement, strengthen muscles, inhibit spasticity, facilitate voluntary motor function, and facilitate orthotic training.[18]

Studies on the use of FES with patients in the acute stage of stroke have been contradictory at best.[23,24,35,39] Results have either shown no significant differences between FES and other forms of therapy or have left a question as to how much improvement was due to spontaneous recovery or to the FES. However, a recent study[18] has shown that FES may work with patients in the chronic (longer than 6 months) stage post stroke. The results of this study did find that for maximal functional gain in the wrist, FES and voluntary muscle contractions should be used together, instead of FES or proprioceptive neuromuscular facilitation alone.

Documentation of the use of FES in the lower extremities for ambulation has been well documented for patients with spinal cord injury.[30,33,37] Three new systems documented in 1988[30] have shown success for both victims of a spinal cord injury or stroke. The first is a system for walking and standing involving FES and minimal bracing. The second is for standing using mechanical support and FES for antigravity muscles, and the third system trains muscles using FES and a garment of electrodes.

The use of FES to maintain or improve the function of individuals after spinal cord injury and cerebrovascular accident is an exciting field that requires more research and development. Despite the current controversy that surrounds the effectiveness of FES, the prospect that patients may be able to ambulate or function at a greater level of independence will spur therapists, orthotists, and physicians to continue to expand on this area of treatment.

GAIT TRAINING FOLLOWING ORTHOTIC PRESCRIPTION

The primary goals of gait training are to reduce asymmetry and to encourage normal selective movement. The training not only involves reciprocal lower extremity motion but also encompasses total body movement. The result of a stroke is hemiplegia or hemiparesis with altered sensation, postural reflexes and tone, and possible visual deficits, cognitive loss, and perceptual dysfunction. The magnitude of each of these deficits must be considered in the design of a treatment program.

To improve abnormal gait, attention in treatment must focus on regaining trunk and limb control, proprioception, and balance. Proximal control may be facilitated if the foot is held in correct alignment with an orthosis. The proper orthosis can assist in achieving heel contact at the end of the swing phase and thus increase the safety and efficiency of ambulation.[15] Maximum benefit can be derived from an orthosis when used in conjunction with well-fitted and -constructed, supportive footwear. A well-fitted shoe has adequate length for the foot, adequate forefoot width and depth, and a firm heel counter. The body weight should be evenly distributed over the foot. This can be achieved with either good running shoes or low-heel leather shoes.

In the initial stage of a gait training program following a stroke, the patient stands facing a mirror, within parallel bars, holding one bar with the strong hand to assist balance. The mirror is useful for perceptual feedback provided such deficits are minimal. Overbed tables or grocery carts provide mobile support if a tendency to overcompensate exists when using parallel bars.

Correct standing posture with trunk alignment and feet parallel, but 20 cm apart, is taught first. The maintenance of correct posture is encouraged at all times. Forward weight-shifting teaches proper weight transference, from heel to toe, on the affected side (Fig. 6). Progression is as follows: step stance, walking forward, walking backward, turns, ascending and descending one small step. When these tasks have been mastered, instruction is provided for ambulation with an appropriate walking aid. Additional activities in sitting or four-point kneeling are provided if necessary. Kinetic training devices such as the Kinetron II (Cybex, Ronkonkoma, NY) are incorporated into the gait training program (Fig. 7). The Kinetron II is a bilateral reciprocal multijoint unit. It provides end-loaded compressive forces to the lower extremities. It assists in preparation for gait by

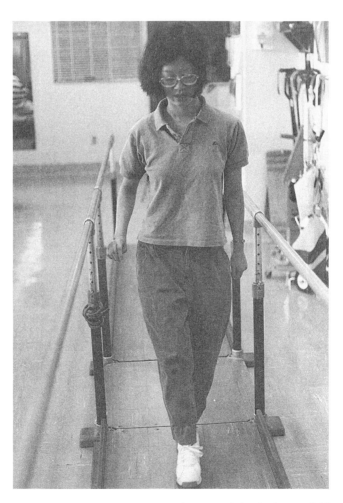

FIGURE 6.   Heel-to-toe weight-transference training in the parallel bars.

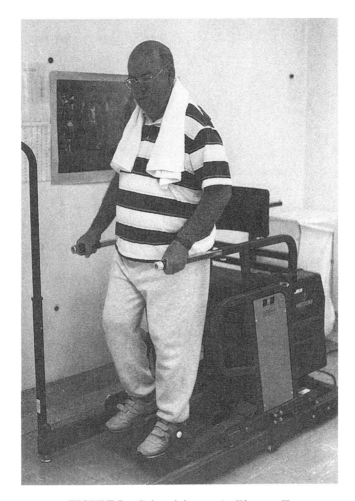

FIGURE 7.   Gait training on the Kinetron II.

maximizing unilateral force control accuracy and bilateral weight-transfer motor-coordination skills.[10]

Upon discharge, the patient should be able to ambulate independently with the appropriate walking aid on smooth and rough ground and on inclines and should be able to ascend and descend stairs. Gait training following a stroke has changed in conjunction with different neurologic approaches (i.e., Bobath and Brunnstrom), but the basic physical elements have remained consistent over time.

FUTURE TRENDS

Orthotics is a major component of rehabilitation and continues to undergo development. Newer materials, such as lightweight carbon filaments and shape-memory alloys, will continue to improve existing designs. For complex requirements, the orthotics team requires the physiatrist, orthotist, physiotherapist, and occupational therapist. According to an Ottawa study, 80% of stroke patients reported wearing their orthosis at least 7 hours/day,[38] but further research into consumer needs and preferences is required. Gait analysis will become more portable and user friendly. The orthosis in stroke, however, will remain an adjunct to specialized gait training and strengthening exercises, stretching and mobilizing, or corrective surgery.

ACKNOWLEDGMENTS

The authors wish to thank Irene Weigl, Ruth King-Roeb, Heather Frosst McCallum, and Cathy Ferguson, from the Departments of Physical Therapy and Occupational Therapy at Victoria Hospital, for their valuable input to this chapter. We also wish to thank Heather Charlton for her assistance in preparing the manuscript.

REFERENCES

1. Arcan M, Brull MA, Najenson T, Solzi P: FGP assessment of postural disorders during process of rehabilitation. Scand J Rehabil Med 9:165–168, 1977.
2. Bajd T, Andrews BJ, Kralj A, et al: Restoration of walking in patients with incomplete spinal cord injuries by use of surface electrical stimulation: Preliminary results. Clin Prosthet Orthotics 10(3):111–114, 1986.
3. Bobath B: Adult Hemiplegia: Evaluation and Treatment, 2nd ed. London, Spottiswoode Ballantyne Ltd., 1978.
4. Boyd G: Shoulder supports with stroke patients: A survey. Can J Occup Ther 53:61–68, 1986.
5. Brandstater ME, deBruin H, Gowland C, Clark B: Hemiplegic gait: Analysis of temporal variables. Arch Phys Med Rehabil 64:583–587, 1983.
6. Brooke MM, deLateur BJ, Diana-Figby GC, et al: Shoulder subluxation and hemiplegia: Effects of three different supports. Arch Phys Med Rehabil 72:582–586, 1991.
7. Brunnstrom S: Movement Therapy in Hemiplegia: A Neurophysiological Approach. New York, Harper & Row, 1970, pp 583–587.
8. Corcoran PJ, Jebsen RH, Brengelmann GL, Simons BC: Effects of plastic and metal braces on speed and energy cost of hemiparetic ambulation. Arch Phys Med Rehabil 51:69–77, 1970.
9. Cussick, et al: Progressive Casting and Splinting for Lower Extremity Deformities in Children with Neuromotor Dysfunction. Tucson, AZ, Therapy Skill Builders, 1990.
10. Cybex: A Handbook for Using the Kinetron II exercise and Training System. New York, Cybex, 1985, pp 1–17.
11. Davies PM: Steps to Follow: A Guide to the Treatment of Adult Hemiplegia. New York, Springer-Verlag, 1985.
12. Diamond MF, Ottenbacher KJ: Effect of a tone-inhibiting dynamic ankle-foot orthosis on stride characteristics of an adult with hemiparesis. Phys Ther 70:423–430, 1990.
13. Haberman L: Thera-step and the hypertonic lower leg. J Prosthet Orthotics 2(1):59–67, 1989.
14. Halar E, Cardenas D: Ankle foot orthoses, prescription and design. Phys Med Rehabil State Art Rev 1:45–66, 1987.
15. Hunt GC: Physical Therapy of the Foot and Ankle. New York, Churchill Livingstone, 1988, pp 109–131.
16. Keenan M, Perry J, Jordan C: Factors affecting balance and ambulation following stroke. Clin Orthop 182:165–171, 1984.
17. Kottke FJ, Lehmann JF: Krusen's Handbook of Physical Medicine and Rehabilitation, 4th ed. Philadelphia, W.B. Saunders Co., 1990.
18. Kraft GH, Fitts SS, Hammond MC: Techniques to improve function of the arm and hand in chronic hemiplegia. Arch Phys Med Rehabil 73:220–277, 1991.
19. Lehmann JF: Biomechanics of ankle foot orthoses, prescription and design. Arch Phys Med Rehabil 60:200–207, 1979.
20. Lehmann JF, Condon SM, Price R, de Lateur BJ: Gait abnormalities in hemiplegia: Their correction by ankle-foot orthoses. Arch Phys Med Rehabil 68:763–771, 1987.
21. Lehmann JF, Esselman PC, Ko MJ, et al: Plastic ankle foot orthoses: Evaluation of function. Arch Phys Med Rehabil 64:402–407, 1983.
22. Lin R, Gage J: The neurological control system for normal gait. J Prosthet Orthotics 2(1):1–13, 1989.
23. Logigian MK, Sanuels MA, Falconer J, et al: Clinical exercise trial for stroke patients. Arch Phys Med Rehabil 64:364–367, 1983.

24. Lord JP, Hall K: Neuromuscular re-education versus traditional programs for stroke rehabilitation. Arch Phys Med Rehabil 67:88–91, 1986.
25. Mathiowetz V, Bokding DJ, Trombly CA: Immediate effects of positioning devices on the normal and spastic hand measured by electromyography. Am J Occup Ther 37(4): 1983.
26. Mizrahi J, Susak Z, Heller L, Najenson T: Variation of time-distance parameters of the stride as related to clinical gait improvements in hemiplegics. Scand J Rehabil Med 14:133–140, 1982.
27. Mizrahi J, Susak Z, Heller L, Najenson T: Objective expression of gait improvement of hemiplegics during rehabilitation by time-distance parameters of the stride. Med Biol Eng Comput 20:628–634, 1982.
28. Morinaka Y, Matsuo Y, Nojima M, Morinaka S: Clinical evaluation of a knee ankle foot orthosis for hemiplegic patients. Prosthet Orthot Int 6:111–115, 1982.
29. Morinaka Y, Matsuo Y, Nojima M, et al: Biomechanical study of a knee ankle foot orthosis for hemiplegic patients. Prosthet Orthot Int 8:97–99, 1984.
30. Muccia P, Andrews B, Byron-Marsolais E: Electronic orthoses: Technology, prototypes and practices. J Prosthet Orthotics 1(1):3–17, 1988.
31. Mueller K, Cornwall M, McPhoil T, et al: Effect of a tone-inhibiting dynamic ankle-foot orthosis on the foot loading pattern of a hemiplegic adult: A preliminary study. J Prosthet Orthotics 4:86–92, 1990.
32. Oczkowski WJ, Ginsberg JS, Shin A, Panju A: Venous thromboembolism in patients undergoing rehabilitation for stroke. Arch Phys Med Rehabil 73:712–716, 1992.
33. Phillips CA: Functional electrical stimulation and lower extremity bracing for ambulation exercises of the spinal cord injured individual. Phys Ther 69:842–849, 1989.
34. Scherling E, Johnson H: A tone reducing wrist hand orthosis. Am J Occup Ther 43:609–611, 1989.
35. Shomp J: Neurophysiologic orthotic designs in the treatment of central nervous system disorders. J Prosthet Orthotics 2:14–32, 1989.
36. Showers D, Strunck M: Sheet plastics and their applications in orthotics and prosthetics. Orthotics Prosthet 38(4):41–48, 1984.
37. Solomonow M, Baratta R: The RGO Generation: II. Muscle stimulation powered orthosis as a practical Walking System for thoracic paraplegics. Orthopedics 12:1309–1315, 1989.
38. Sullivan MJL, Heisel B, Lemaire E, et al: Utilization of orthotic devices in stroke patients: A comparison of out-reach and institution based services. Can J Rehabil 4:47–50, 1990.
39. Trnkoczy A: Functional electrical stimulation of extremities: Its basis, technology and role in rehabilitation. Automedica 2:59–100, 1978.
40. Wall JC, Ashburn A: Assessment of gait disability in hemiplegics. Scand J Rehabil Med 11:95–103, 1979.
41. Winter DA: The Biomechanics and Motor Control of Human Gait: Normal, Elderly and Pathological, 2nd ed. Waterloo, University of Waterloo Press, 1991.
42. Wong AMK, Tang FT, Wu SH, Chen CM: Clinical trial of a low-temperature plastic anterior ankle foot orthosis. Am J Phys Med Rehabil 71:41–43, 1992.

LEORA SWARTZMAN, PhD
ROBERT W. TEASELL, MD, FRCPC

12. PSYCHOLOGICAL CONSEQUENCES OF STROKE

From the Departments of
Psychology (LS) and
Medicine (RWT)
University of Western Ontario
and the
Department of Physical Medicine
and Rehabilitation (RWT)
University Hospital
London, Ontario
Canada

Reprint requests to:
Leora Swartzman, PhD
Department of Psychology
Faculty of Social Science
University of Western Ontario
London, Ontario N6A 5C2
Canada

A stroke is a significant and traumatic event in an individual's life, affecting the well-being of not only the stroke victim but also the immediate family.[72] The subsequent impairments and disabilities are invariably accompanied by significant psychosocial consequences, though these psychosocial sequelae of stroke may be downplayed and even ignored by health care professionals.[18] Current medical care is focused primarily on the acute and recovery stage of a stroke, when the individual generally receives full and comprehensive treatment; whereas the later sequelae of stroke, in particular the psychological disorders which develop, typically receive less attention.

Negative emotional reactions are common following a stroke. A stroke is associated with significant losses, as a fit and well person suddenly becomes disabled and dependent on others. According to Anderson,[4] the reaction of each patient is shaped by his or her premorbid personality, the individual's characteristic manner of coping with stress, support of family and friends, and the cognitive/perceptual deficits created by the stroke itself (Table 1). As will be clear from the review that follows, post-stroke mood disorders arise out of a complex interaction between psychological reactions to the disability and neurophysiological consequences of the brain damage itself. The challenge for the clinician is to identify the causal factors underlying the emotional disturbances and to tailor interventions accordingly.

In this chapter, whenever possible, a distinction will be made between the psychological

TABLE 1.   Factors Contributing to Post-Stroke Behavior*

Pre-stroke (premorbid) behavior
Psychological reaction to the stroke and subsequent disability
Neurobehavioral deficits: i.e., aphasia, apraxia, perceptual problems, etc.
Organic cerebral changes
Environmental situation and supports

* Data from Anderson.[4]

reactions observed and treatment strategies to be implemented during the **recovery phase** (i.e., in the 1- to 6-month interval post-stroke) and those psychological reactions and treatment strategies after 6 months post-stroke, referred to here as the **disability phase.** Given that many stroke patients spend a good part of the recovery phase at a rehabilitation facility, recommendations for treatment during this phase are directed to inpatient rehabilitation physicians and allied health care professionals. In contrast, management of problems during the disability phase is presumed to be implemented by health care providers who will be following patients and their families after discharge—physiatrists, primary care physicians, social workers, and psychologists.

As different teams of health care professionals are typically involved in patient care during the recovery and disability stages, continuity of care may be an issue. Problems with lack of continuity of care between the acute stage (during which time patients are typically treated by neurologists) and the recovery stage (when rehabilitation staff oversee patient care) have been noted by McCaffrey and Fisher.[47] Continuity of care between the recovery and disability phases poses an even larger challenge, given the transition from, respectively, hospital-based to community-based treatment. That patients may fall through the cracks after discharge was demonstrated in a study of 85 stroke patients within 6 months of discharge.[18] The researchers found a high incidence of psychosocial problems which included social isolation, decreased community involvement, new economic strain, disruption of family functioning, major depression, anger, and anxiety (Table 2). Despite the fact that a major depression was present in over one-third of the patients, it was rarely diagnosed. Moreover, none of these patients were utilizing existing stroke support groups or psychological or family services. This study demonstrates the need for careful follow-up of stroke patients after discharge and the need for ongoing psychosocial support upon entry into the community.

STAGES OF PSYCHOLOGICAL REACTIONS

Unlike most other physically disabling diseases, stroke has a sudden onset that leaves no time for advance preparation. Accordingly, the initial reaction to a stroke is often shock and denial. The stages of psychological reactions we observe in some of our stroke patients are not inconsistent with those seen in people going through a grieving process[85]; patients are, in essence, mourning the loss of their

TABLE 2.   Psychosocial Problems After Stroke Following Discharge[18]

Social isolation	56%
Decreased community involvement	43%
Economic strain causing a lifestyle alteration	46%
Disruption of family functioning	52%
Major depression	37%
Anxiety/anger	32%

functional and cognitive abilities. According to Worden,[85] the four tasks (stages) of bereavement include:

1. acceptance of the reality of the loss—i.e., working through the denial of the event;
2. letting oneself experience the pain of the loss;
3. adjusting to an environment in which the deceased (or, from our perspective, lost abilities) are missing;
4. reinvesting one's energy into another relationship (or into new activities and social roles that one is capable of engaging in).

The psychological reactions observed during the first two stages, denial and experiencing the pain of the loss, will be elaborated on in subsequent sections of this chapter.

It is important to note that not all patients experience these reactions. In fact, it has been cogently argued that depression is not an inevitable consequence of loss and that failure to experience distress is not pathological.[87] That is, many, but not all, patients will experience grief reactions following their strokes, and those who do not should not be forced to "confront" their denial or work through their grief. This is only necessary if the patients' failure to acknowledge the extent of their functional impairment compromises rehabilitation efforts or poses management problems. Moreover, those patients who do grieve may not necessarily progress through these stages in a linear fashion. That is, they might exhibit different reactions simultaneously or fluctuate back and forth between earlier and later stages. In addition, there is no set timeline for resolution of the grief. For instance, it has been found that even 4 to 7 years after losing a loved one, many bereaved have not yet achieved a state of resolution.[38] Similarly, it has been estimated that one-third of stroke patients have still not adjusted emotionally 2 to 3 years post-stroke.[36]

DENIAL

Denial is generally regarded as a protective emotional mechanism which allows the patient time to accept the reality of the loss and thereby avoid a sudden and profound depression. Denial should not be confused with anosognosia (neglect of the involved side), which is regarded as a separate phenomenon.[21] Denial often persists for the majority of the in-hospital rehabilitation phase. It is characterized by high expectations of recovery and denial by the patient that the disability is permanent. The denial is supported by the natural tendency for some spontaneous recovery, most rapid in the first few weeks or months after stroke. Attempts to confront denial are generally unsuccessful and nonproductive, serving only to make the patient more anxious and depressed.[21] The stroke survivor will frequently disbelieve confronting staff, and credibility will be undermined. In our experience, confrontation of denial is warranted only when the denial interferes with the rehabilitation process. The denial is best countered by discussing the disability and its possible permanence in a hopeful, optimistic, and gradual fashion.

It has been observed that this tendency to deny the presence of one's disability or to diminish its significance, also termed the **indifference reaction,** is more prevalent among right than left hemisphere-damaged patients.[14,27] It has been suggested[14] that the hypoarousal observed in right hemisphere-damaged patients[34] might underlie this indifference/denial reaction.

EMOTIONAL LABILITY

Some stroke patients easily and suddenly demonstrate extreme emotional responses to seemingly innocuous circumstances and can very quickly move from expressions of happiness to those of sadness. Laughing and crying are considered pathological when they are inappropriate to the situation and do not correspond with underlying emotional feelings. House et al.[37] noted that 1 in 5 stroke patients suffered from lability or "emotionalism" 6 months after stroke onset, whereas 1 in 10 patients continued to have these difficulties 1 year following the onset of the stroke.

Patients who have suffered bilateral subcortical infarcts (pseudobulbar palsy) are more susceptible to emotional lability and may suddenly weep or burst out laughing at the slightest provocation. However, emotional lability is also common after unilateral strokes, especially right hemispheric lesions, and appears related to depressed mood.[37] Since insight is often preserved, patients may become embarrassed by these emotional outbursts. Emotional lability may be partially relieved with antidepressant medications.[68]

ANXIETY

Anxiety is commonly seen shortly after the stroke, more frequently in patients with left hemispheric lesions.[40] There are many sources of anxiety—anxiety about recovery, management of present affairs, family members, and fear of dying or having another stroke. Anxiety is frequently associated with depression post-stroke and is more commonly seen with cortical lesions than with subcortical lesions.[81] It may be managed with continual reassurance and tangible feedback (through charting and graphing) of positive gains made during rehabilitation. In more severe cases, anxiolytics and psychotherapy may be necessary.[21]

CATASTROPHIC REACTIONS

Catastrophic reactions (extreme anxiety and anger reactions) are uncommonly seen, but when they occur they can be very disruptive and stressful to family members and caregivers. Catastrophic reactions, first described by Goldstein,[30] involve extremely disruptive emotional outbursts characterized by physically aggressive behavior toward family and staff, refusal to comply with directions, difficulty in settling down, swearing or other verbal abuse (within limitations of the aphasia), and an inability to be reasoned with. The cause of catastrophic reactions is not known,[78] though it has been suggested that they are observed more frequently in left hemisphere-damaged patients, who are quite sensitive to their limitations. Catastrophic reactions have been reported primarily in association with expressive or Broca's aphasia.[27] Fisher[21] reported that catastrophic reactions were more likely to occur when patients were presented with tasks they could not solve, i.e., those tasks that confront them with their limitations. It has similarly been suggested that the emotions may be triggered by a particular stressor, such as a demanding language test.[7] In our experience, however, discernible triggers are not always present.

Responding to the outbursts by restraining patients and/or threatening to punish them only aggravates the situation. Moreover, although medications, primarily sedatives, are often effective in subduing difficult patients, we have found that they often make patients so stuporous that they cannot participate in rehabilitation efforts. Assuming triggers are evident, catastrophic reactions usually diminish when the patient is removed from the frustrating situations.[47] Moreover, to decrease the likelihood of eliciting the reaction in the first place, it has been suggested that during assessments, easy tasks and more difficult tasks be alternated.[7]

AVOIDANT AND AGGRESSIVE BEHAVIOR

The concept of the rehabilitation process as punishment has been discussed by Fordyce[24] and is helpful in understanding patients' responses, particularly avoidant and aggressive behavior during the recovery phase. Punishment has two behavioral components: aversive (negative) events and the withdrawal of positive reinforcers. Both of these occur when a patient suffers a disabling stroke (Table 3). For all stroke patients, the entry into disability and consequent rehabilitation is forced and involuntary. Patients must learn to perform laborious therapies which they never performed before the stroke and which they do not value. Moreover, many of the patient's positive reinforcers (i.e., social contacts, material comforts, hobbies) are not as available during the recovery phase of the stroke. Escape or avoidance behavior and counteraggression or attack are two natural responses to perceived punishment.[24]

Some patients respond to aversive situations with aggressive behavior and anger which causes them to strike out (verbally and physically) at rehabilitation staff or family members. Alternatively, they might try to escape the aversive situation and accordingly may be unwilling or reluctant to participate in occupational and/or physiotherapy or to cooperate with nursing staff. Either reaction will compromise rehabilitation efforts or maintenance of gains once rehabilitation is completed. It is important for health care workers and family not to respond with negative sanctions (i.e., withholding privileges), as this will only increase the patient's perception of the disability as punishment. Instead, it has been our experience that an optimistic and positive approach, with praise given for participation in therapy and functional gains, are more likely to encourage the patient to "buy into" a rehabilitation program designed to maximize independence.

UNDUE CHEERFULNESS

Euphoric behavior has been reported in patients with right hemispheric lesions.[13,27,80] Patients with undue cheerfulness showed a greater frequency of lesions involving the frontal operculum.[80] It has been suggested that patients with frontal right hemispheric strokes are more susceptible to elevated mood disorders as a result of disruptions in frontal cortical interaction with the limbic system.[50,79]

TABLE 3.   Stroke Disability As Punishment*

Aversive stimuli
    Pain
    Negative cosmetic effect
    Forced practice of laborious therapies
    Prejudice toward disabled persons
    Excessive sympathy (pity) and overprotection by family and friends
Deprivation of positive reinforcers
    Removed from work, leisure activities, and people important to patient
    Prevented from achieving life goals

* Data from Fordyce.[24]

DEPRESSION

Depression is a common psychological sequela of stroke, occurring within 6 months of stroke in anywhere from 20 to 50% of stroke survivors, with 30% being the most commonly accepted figure.[16,18,19,42,54,57-61,63-65] Prevalence estimates are influenced, in part, by the diagnostic criteria used to identify depression. A major issue is whether the depression is a reaction to the significant losses (i.e., disability) faced by the stroke patient or whether it is intrinsically related to the brain damage itself. Robinson et al.[62] suggest that the etiology of post-stroke depression may differ depending on the time of onset of depression following brain injury. Specifically, they argue that patients who develop depression shortly after their stroke may have a neuroanatomic and neurophysiologic basis for their stroke, whereas patients who become depressed later on are responding to their intellectual and functional losses. In this section, we first consider the neurophysiological factors which may contribute to post-stroke depression and will predominantly focus on physiologically based treatment strategies. We then review the psychological causes and treatments of depression.

Diagnosis

Depression may present as an unexplained deterioration in the stroke survivor's level of functioning. Statements concerning dysphoria, guilt, hopelessness, and suicide or signs such as loss of appetite and insomnia are often indicative of depression. Depression has been underdiagnosed in stroke survivors. As alluded to earlier, Feibel et al.[18] identified moderate to severe depression in 37% of their sample, yet in very few cases had the depression been previously diagnosed or treated.

DSM III-R criteria for major depression are listed in Table 4.[3] The validity of applying DSM criteria in stroke patients has been criticized, since some of these criteria rely on verbal responses[53,69] and may be particularly difficult to establish in a stroke patient who is aphasic or cognitively impaired. This criticism applies even more so to the assessment of depression based on self-report inventories, such as the Beck Depression Inventory,[5] the Hamilton Rating Scale for Depression,[33] and the Zung Self-Rating Scale,[88] all of which have been used to assess depression in post-stroke patients. It should be noted that since six of the nine DSM III-R

TABLE 4.   DSM III-R Criteria for Major Depression*

At least *one* of the following, present for at least 2 weeks:

- Dysphoric mood, as indicated by subjective reports of being "depressed, blue, sad, or hopeless" or as indicated by observations by others
- Anhedonia: i.e., markedly diminished interest or pleasure in all or almost all activities. Can be indicated by subjective account or by others' observations of apathy most of the time

At least *four* of the following, present for at least 2 weeks:

- Appetite disturbance or significant weight loss or gain when not dieting
- Insomnia (particularly early morning awakening) or hyersomnia
- Psychomotor agitation or retardation
- Loss of energy, excessive fatigue
- Feelings of worthlessness, self-reproach, excessive or inappropriate guilt
- Diminished ability to think, concentrate, or make decisions
- Suicidal ideation/attempt or thoughts of death

---

* Data from the American Psychiatric Association.[3]

diagnostic criteria can be inferred from behavioral observations, the DSM III-R is less reliant on verbal responses than most other diagnostic tools. In this vein, Robinson et al.[62] have recently concluded that DSM criteria are appropriate for use in the post-stroke population.

Another strategy has been to diagnose depression in these patients solely on the basis of vegetative symptoms (i.e., sleep and appetite disturbance, fatigue, psychomotor retardation).[68] One problem with this approach to diagnosis, however, is that many of the vegetative symptoms may themselves be physical sequelae of the stroke[18] or, for that matter, many other medical conditions.[52]

It has been claimed that the **dexamethasone suppression test** is a good indicator of depression and a good predictor of response to tricyclic antidepressant medications.[20,43,54] However, the specificity of this test in diagnosis of post-stroke depression may be as low as 70% (indicating many false-positives)[54] and must be interpreted with caution.[53] Lipsey et al.[44] found that the dexamethasone suppression test lacked validity as a biological marker of depressed mood when compared with psychiatric interview.

Consequences of Post-Stroke Depression

The diagnosis and treatment of depression are important both to alleviate suffering and to promote recovery. Ebrahim et al.[16] found that among patients with a relatively good spontaneous recovery, depressed mood was associated with a longer hospital stay. In a study of patients with left hemispheric infarcts, cognitive or intellectual impairment was greater in depressed patients when compared to nondepressed patients, even when lesion volume and locations were taken into account.[63] Even more importantly, after 6 months nondepressed patients were significantly less cognitively impaired than depressed patients, who failed to show improvement.[63] In one reported case, a patient with a postoperative posterior right hemisphere lesion demonstrated visual-constructive deficits on neuropsychological testing typical of right hemisphere damage. Treatment of an associated depression with antidepressants not only helped to resolve the depression but also resulted in clinical resolution of the right hemispheric deficits.[22] Depression often reduces motivation with a consequent negative effect on functional abilities[51,74] and resumption of social activities[13] following discharge from rehabilitation. Accordingly, aggressive treatment of depression after stroke could be expected to have a significant impact on both cognitive recovery and rehabilitation of depressed stroke patients in general.

Neuropsychological Causes of Post-Stroke Depression

Depression may be a specific complication of stroke.[31] There is evidence that depression following a stroke may be related to the **anatomical site of brain damage,** although the nature of this anatomic relationship is not completely clear. The Johns Hopkins group[42,57-61,63-65] have carried out a series of studies on post-stroke depression, in particular exploring its relationship to the location of the lesion within the brain itself. They found that in a selected group of stroke patients, depression appeared to be more frequent in patients with left hemispheric lesions,[57-61,63-65] both cortical and subcortical.[76] Among these patients, the severity of depression correlated inversely with the distance of the lesion from the frontal poles.[57-61,63-65,76] Patients with subcortical, cerebellar, or brainstem lesions had much shorter-lasting depressions than patients with cortical lesions.[76,77]

This correlation of major depression to proximity of the lesion to the frontal pole has been confirmed by Sinyor et al.[75] and Eastwood et al.[15] Right hemispheric lesions failed to demonstrate a similar relationship with depression but were associated with a significantly higher incidence of undue cheerfulness.[76] Interestingly, patients who had both an anxiety disorder and a major depression showed a significantly higher frequency of cortical lesions, while patients with major depression only had a significantly higher frequency of subcortical (basal ganglia) strokes.[76]

The Johns Hopkins group found that diagnosable depressive disorders occurred in approximately 70% of stroke patients with left frontal lesions. They further hypothesized that depression in these cases may be due to stroke-induced damage to catecholamine pathways, which pass through the left frontal pole.[55-57,65] It has been suggested that catecholamine depletion may play a role in the etiology of depression.[7]

Although some support for hemispheric differences in depression has also been found by Finkelstein et al.,[20] Gianotti,[27] and Rosse and Ciolino,[70] others including Sinyor et al,[75] Eastwood et al.,[15] and Ebrahim et al.[16] were unable to replicate the interhemispheric differences found by the Johns Hopkins group. Moreover, Wade et al.[84] failed to find an association between right-sided weakness and depression. Robinson and his group[59] failed to confirm their previously established interhemispheric differences when looking at a larger number of patients. Finally, Folstein et al.[23] found that patients with right-sided lesions were more likely to suffer psychological symptoms of irritability, loss of interest, difficulty in concentrating, subjective memory loss, and depressed mood when compared to controls or patients with left hemispheric lesions.

As important as the contribution of Robinson and his group is to our understanding of post-stroke depression, there are weaknesses in their research, largely related to selection biases in their patient population which might be why their findings are not consistently replicated. These weaknesses are outlined by Malec et al.[46] and Ebrahim.[17] Thus, the association of post-stroke depression and left frontal hemispheric damage, although compelling, is not firmly established and should be accepted with caution.[53]

Pharmacologic Treatment of Depression

Pharmacologic treatment may be the most viable treatment option for depression. **Antidepressants** are indicated for persistent depressive mood with neurovegetative signs. In a randomized double-blind study, Lipsey et al.[43] found that **nortriptyline** significantly improved post-stroke depression when compared to an untreated matched control group. Treatment with 25 mg of nortriptyline per day, and the dosage was gradually increased until the serum levels were therapeutic (to a maximum of 100 mg daily). Unfortunately, the sample size was small and the dropout rate high (6 of 17) due to side effects. Accordingly, conclusions regarding the efficacy of nortriptyline in treating post-stroke depression are difficult to draw from this study. Borson[8] found that at the end of 6 weeks, depressed elderly patients receiving nortriptyline did better than a placebo group.

Reding et al.[54] looked at **trazodone HCl** (Desyrel, Mead-Johnson) in the treatment of both depressed and nondepressed stroke patients. A quarter of patients were withdrawn from the study because of side effects. Although the authors concluded that trazodone was useful in the treatment of depressed stroke patients, doubt has been raised as to whether such conclusions can actually be drawn from this study.[17]

Unfortunately, many depressed stroke patients are denied treatment with tricyclic antidepressants because of excessive concerns about **cardiac side effects.** Antidepressants can affect cardiac conduction and rhythm, heart rate, and blood pressure and should be used with caution, especially in elderly patients.[11] Orthostatic hypotension is a common cardiovascular side effect of tricyclic antidepressants. Patients with left ventricular dysfunction are more subject to orthostatic hypotension. One study showed that a substantial percentage of depressed patients with severe heart disease developed orthostatic hypotension when treated with imipramine.[28,29] Substantially less hypotension occurred when these patients were treated with nortriptyline.[67] Patients with bundle branch block are at much higher risk for developing second-degree heart block and orthostatic hypotension than are patients who have normal conduction or first-degree heart block.[8] Tricyclic antidepressants can be used even in patients with serious heart disease, some of whom have congestive heart failure.[8] Nortriptyline has been reported to not have the deleterious effects on left ventricular function. Unfortunately, antidepressant drugs have troublesome anticholinergic side effects and can be very sedating in the elderly stroke population.

There is some anecdotal evidence that **methylphenidate** (Ritalin, Ciba-Geigy) may be useful in patients with disabling depression with psychomotor retardation intractable to tricyclic antidepressants.[41] Methyphenidate, however, is highly addictive, may suppress appetite, and should be used very cautiously, especially in patients with ischemic heart disease or hypertension. Coll and Erickson[12] report, however, that in prescribed doses (5–10 mg/d) there are no significant side effects, even in elderly patients, and suggest that psychostimulants such as methylphenidate may be used while waiting for a trial of tricyclic antiidepressants to take effect. Nevertheless, methylphenidate should be used with caution and only as a last resort.

Electroconvulsive therapy (ECT) remains an alternative for those patients who fail to respond to antidepressants, are considered at high risk of suicide, or have marked neurovegetative or psychotic symptoms.[53] It has been shown to be relatively safe and generally efficacious in the treatment of depression in stroke victims,[49] though it should not be regarded within 3 months of the stroke. Thus, like methylphenidate, ECT should be used only as a last resort.

Psychological Causes of Post-Stroke Depression

Depression as a Response to Loss

Depression can be seen as a response to actual or perceived loss.[6] The loss can be that of a tangible resource, a loved one, social role, or valued aspects of oneself, i.e., personal characteristics and attributes.[35] Thus, depression in stroke patients can be regarded as an understandable reaction to the physical and intellectual losses which frequently accompany a stroke.[7,10,47] The reactive depression seen at this time so resembles a grief reaction that one can liken stroke to a "small death." The intensity of this reactive depression is likely dependent on a variety of factors (Table 5). However, to our knowledge, there has been very little quantitative research done in this area, with some exceptions.[26,32]

As McCaffrey and Fisher[47] suggest, the functional and cognitive impairment secondary to a stroke may result in a wide range of losses in the areas of finances, family status, personal appearance, and leisure and social activities. The losses would become more apparent to the patient in the disability phase, at which point

TABLE 5.   Variables Contributing to a Reactive Depression

Premorbid personality
Degree of physical loss
Amount of family/community support
Loss of self-esteem
Guilt feelings (stroke may be seen as punishment)
Intellectual deterioration due to sensory deprivation

functional gains will have reached a plateau and hopes for further recovery realistically diminished. At this point, the impact and permanence of the disability caused by the stroke can no longer be denied by the patient. One net effect of these losses would be a decrease in the level of positive (largely social) reinforcement, which has been implicated in the development and maintenance of depression.[39]

Most studies of post-stroke depression have shown the correlation between physical impairment and depression to be weak.[20,23,60,74] This is not particularly surprising, as the above-noted theories would lead one to predict that loss of functioning, as opposed to current functioning, should be related to depression. In this vein, Turner and Noh[83] found that change in functional health in an elderly disabled population was associated with depression, even after controlling for current functional health. Moreover, Ghesquiere[26] found that the perceived loss of valued aspects of oneself predicted depression in a group of stroke patients, even after controlling for perceived functional loss.

The practical implications of treating depression as a response to perceived loss (and, to a lesser degree, perceived threat) are elaborated more fully in the subsequent section. Put briefly, however, treatment might involve behavioral interventions to help patients increase the number of positive events in their lives and cognitive intervention to alter their interpretation of these events as well as to alter their views of themselves.

DEPRESSION AS A RESPONSE TO UNCONTROLLABLE EVENTS

Lack of perceived control has implications for emotional adjustment to stroke. There is a substantial body of research indicating that exposure to uncontrollable events, or more importantly, events that are experienced as uncontrollable, engender a state of passivity and hopelessness (termed **learned helplessness**), which leads to depression.[1,73,87] In this vein, it has been demonstrated that perceiving a chronic illness/disability and its consequences as beyond one's control predisposes one to depression.[2,9,71]

Stroke and its sequelae may easily be regarded by patients as unpredictable and uncontrollable events. The stroke itself, given its rapid, precipitous onset, may be seen by patients as unpredictable, and a future recurrence unpreventable. During the rehabilitation phase, the feelings of loss of control associated with the stroke may be further exacerbated by the hospitalization[47] if patients do not feel they have control over their recovery and are treated as passive rather than active recipients of care. Moreover, the uncertainty of prognosis at this time may further contribute to a sense of unpredictability and loss of control.[47] Patients may also be prone to perceiving events as beyond their control during the disability stage, at which point they have realized the limits to functional recovery imposed by their neurologic damage. Moreover, well-meant yet oversolicitous care by family members and friends that stifles the patients' autonomy will further compromise their sense of control. For example, stroke patients whose primary caregivers were overprotective of them felt that they had less control over their recovery and were more depressed at 9 months post-stroke than those whose caregivers were not overprotective.[82]

Interventions tailored to counter perceived lack of control are elaborated in the following section. In essence, the aim of such interventions is to enhance patients' sense of competence and mastery over their environment and to encourage active rather than passive participation in the rehabilitation process and in life in general. It is also important that positive reinforcement, when given, be dependent on the patient's behavior and not be indiscriminate; reinforcers that are not dependent on a patient's responses will compromise the patient's sense of control and can exacerbate the helplessness and depression.[73]

Psychological Treatment of Depression in Stroke Patients

Primeau[53] noted that individual psychotherapy and problem-focused family therapy might be helpful in managing depression, but also pointed out that the usefulness of these psychotherapeutic techniques in depressed stroke patients has not been well examined in controlled trials. However, the effectiveness of cognitive and behavioral therapies for treating depression in the elderly (reviewed and described by Gaylord and Zung[25]) has been well established. Assuming the stroke patient has a moderate degree of insight and has the cognitive and verbal abilities, there is no reason for these interventions not to be effective for this population during the rehabilitation and disability phases.

One promising model of a psychosocial intervention for depression during the rehabilitation process is provided by a pilot project, albeit uncontrolled.[45] In this study, 21 geriatric rehabilitation (mostly stroke) patients who were identified as being depressed were referred for individual psychotherapy with clinical psychology interns. Interns met with the patient, on average, three to four times a week for 30-minute sessions, for a total of 2 to 3 weeks. The interns were also responsible for coordinating a team approach to each subject's treatment, involving nurses and physical and occupational therapists. The interventions included making graphs of progress and goals and having team members appropriately reinforce the patients' progress; encouraging patients to seek information about their condition and to talk more openly and realistically about their disease and disability; helping patients make positive social comparisons (i.e., identifying others who were worse off than they were); increasing patients' pleasant activities (e.g., getting them involved in unit social activities and events); and relaxation training when appropriate. Thus, the intervention, which was active and very goal-focused, served to increase positive reinforcements that were dependent on the patients' behavior, promoted active participation in the rehabilitation process, and helped patients improve their self-image. At admission, these patients were predictably significantly more depressed than the normative control group. By the discharge date, depression scores dropped significantly in the treated group to levels comparable to those of the control group. Moreover, their rehabilitation success (quantified by aggregating objective independent ratings of goal attainment provided by the physical and occupational therapists) was equivalent to that of the normative control group. While these results are promising, the absence of an attention placebo group makes it virtually impossible to differentiate the specific from nonspecific treatment effects.

CONCLUSIONS

Although not all stroke patients experience emotional difficulties following stroke, psychological reactions to stroke, most notably depression, are nevertheless quite prevalent during the acute, disability, and recovery phases. Depression can be fairly readily identified using the DSM III-R criteria or, in the case of patients who are verbally intact, with self-report inventories (such as the Zung, Beck, and Hamilton rating scales). Unfortunately, in many cases, depression is underdiagnosed and consequently untreated, a situation which may compromise rehabilitation efforts (during the recovery stage) and the maintenance of functional gains during the disability stage.

In this chapter, we have reviewed evidence for the neurophysiological basis of psychological difficulties, the biological treatment approaches, as well as the psychological causes and treatments of these problems. In clinical practice (as well as in research), it is difficult to disentangle the neurophysiologic from psychological causes, though this need not impede treatment efforts. That is, more severe depression, regardless of its cause, is best addressed, in the first instance, psychopharmacologically, whereas less severe depression is best treated by cognitive-behavioral therapy.

How does one ensure that the psychological difficulties are adequately diagnosed and treated? During the hospitalization, consultation with psychiatric and/or psychological services for ambiguous and/or difficult cases can be quite helpful. The challenge after discharge is for the primary care physician to keep monitoring (through direct questioning) the patient's psychological health during follow-up visits; the stigma associated with psychological distress may prevent patients or their families from bringing up these concerns spontaneously. Psychotropic medications can be quite useful at this stage as well, though patients will have to be more closely monitored.

Obviously, improved access to outpatient services, day hospitals, maintenance therapy programs, long-term patient and family counseling, intermittent relief admissions, and a long-term multidisciplinary follow-up clinic would help to ameliorate many of the psychological problems that stroke patients and their families experience. These programs, however, would require an allocation of additional resources from a painfully dwindling supply. In their absence, the best approach is for continuity of care following discharge carried out by the original physicians and the rehabilitation team supported by a referral network of psychiatrists, psychologists, and/or social workers.

REFERENCES

1. Abramson LY, Seligman MEP, Teasdale JD: Learned helplessness in humans: Critique and reformulation. J Abn Psychol 87:49–74, 1978.
2. Affleck G, Tennen H, Pfeiffer C, Fifield J: Appraisals of control and predictability in adapting to a chronic disease. J Pers Soc Psychol 53:23–279, 1987.
3. American Psychiatric Association: Diagnostic and Statistical Manual III-R, 3rd ed, revised. Washington, DC, American Psychiatric Association, 1987.
4. Anderson TP: Rehabilitation of patients with completed stroke. In Kottke EJ, Stillwell GK, Lehmann JF (eds): Krusen's Handbook of Physical Medicine and Rehabilitation. Philadelphia, WB Saunders, 1982, pp 583–603.
5. Beck AT, Ward CH, Mendelson M, et al: An inventory for measuring depression. Arch Gen Psychiatry 4:561–571, 1961.
6. Beck AT, Clark DA: Anxiety and depression: An information processing perspective. Anxiety Res 1:23–36, 1988.
7. Benson DF: Psychiatric aspects of asphasia. Br J Psychiatry 123:555–556, 1973.

8. Borson S: Depression: Medical treatment works in the chronically ill. Geriatrics 43(2):19–23, 1988.
9. Bulman R, Wortman C: Attributions of blame and coping in the "real world": Severe accident victims react to their lot. Pers Soc Psychol 35:351–363, 1977.
10. Charaton FB, Fisk A: The mental and emotional results of strokes. NY State J Med 78:1403–1405, 1978.
11. Chutka DS: Cardiovascular effects of the antidepressants: Recognition and control. Geriatrics 45(1):55–67, 1990.
12. Coll P, Erickson RV: Mood disorders associated with stroke. Phys Med Rehabil: State Art Rev 3:619–628, 1989.
13. Cutting I: Memory in functional psychosis. J Neurol Neurosurg Psychiatry 42:1031–1037, 1979.
14. Denny-Brown D, Meyer JS, Horenstein S: The significance of perceptual rivalry resulting from parietal lesions. Brain 75:433–471, 1952.
15. Eastwood MR, Rifat SL, Nobbs H, et al: Mood disorder following cerebrovascular accident. Br J Psychiatry 154:195–200, 1989.
16. Ebrahim S, Barer KD, Nouri F: Affective illness after stroke. Br J Psychiatry 151:52–56, 1987.
17. Ebrahim S: Clinical Epidemiology of Stroke. Oxford, Oxford University Press, 1990.
18. Feibel JH, Berk SS, Joynt RJ: Unmet needs of stroke survivors. Neurology 29:592, 1979.
19. Feibel JH, Springer CJ: Depression and failure to resume social activities after stroke. Arch Phys Med Rehabil 63:276–278, 1982.
20. Finkelstein S, Benowitz LI, Baldessarian RJ, et al: Mood, vegetative disturbance and dexamethasone suppression test after stroke. Ann Neurol 12:463–468, 1982.
21. Fisher SH: Psychiatric considerations of cerebral vascular disease. Am J Cardiol 7:379–385, 1961.
22. Fogel BS, Sparadeo FR: Single case study: Focal cognitive deficits accentuated by depression. J Nerv Ment Dis 173:120–124, 1985.
23. Folstein MF, Mailberger R, McHugh PR: Mood disorder as a specific complication of stroke. J Neurol Neurosurg Psychiatry 40:1018–1022, 1977.
24. Fordyce WE: Behavioural methods in medical rehabilitation. Neurosci Biobehav Rev 5:391–396, 1981.
25. Gaylord SA, Zung WK: Affective disorders among the aging. In Carstensen LL, Edelstein BA (eds): Handbook of Clinical Gerontology. New York, Pergammon Press, 1987, pp 76–95.
26. Ghesquiere KJ: Affective response to stroke: The impact of perceived loss of and threat to self (masters thesis). London, ON, University of Western Ontario, 1991.
27. Gianotti G: Emotional behaviour and hemispheric side of the lesion. Cortex 8:41–55, 1972.
28. Glassman AH, Bigger JT Jr, Giardina EV, et al: Clinical characteristics of imipramine-induced orthostatic hypotension. Lancet i:468–472, 1979.
29 Glassman AH, Johnson LL, Giardia EV, et al: The use of imipramine in depressed patients with congestive heart failure. JAMA 250:1997–2001, 1983.
30. Goldstein K: Language and Language Disturbances. New York, Grune & Stratton, 1948.
31. Gresham GE, Fitzpatrick TE, Wolf PA, et al: Residual disability in survivors of stroke: The Framingham study. N Engl J Med 293:954–956, 1985.
32. Griffith VE: Observations on patients' dysphoria after stroke. BMJ 281:1608–1609, 1980.
33. Hamilton M: Development of a rating scale for primary depressive illness. Br J Soc Clin Psychol 6:278–296, 1967.
34. Heilman KM, Watson RT, Valenstein E: Neglect and related disorders. In Heilman LL, Valenstein E (eds): Clinical Neuropsychology, 2nd ed. New York, Oxford University Press, 1985, pp 243–293.
35. Hobfoll SE: Conservation of resources: A new attempt at conceptualizing stress. Am Psychol 44:513–524, 1989.
36. Holbrook M: Stroke and emotional outcome. J R Coll Phys Lond 16:100–104, 1982.
37. House A, Dennis M, Molyneux A, et al: Emotionalism after stroke. BMJ 298:991–994, 1989.
38. Lehman DR, Wortman CB, Williams AF: Long-term effects of losing a spouse or a child in a motor vehicle crash. J Pers Soc Psychol 52:218–231, 1987.
39. Lewinsohn PM, Biglan A, Zeiss AM: Behavioral treatment of depression. In Davidson PO (ed): The Behavioral Management of Anxiety, Depression, and Pain. New York, Brunner/Mazel, 1976, pp 91–146.
40. Lezak MD: Neuropsychological Assessment, 2nd ed. New York, Oxford University Press, 1983.
41. Lingam VR, Lazarus LW, Groves L, et al: Methylphenidate in treating post-stroke depression: A double-blind study. Lancet i:297–300, 1987.
42. Lipsey JR, Robinson RG, Pearlson GD, et al: Mood change following bilateral hemispheric brain injury. Br J Psychiatry 143:266–273, 1983.

43. Lipsey JR, Robinson RG, Pearlson GD, et al: Nortriptyline treatment in post-stroke depression: A double-blind study. Lancet i:297–300, 1984.
44. Lipsey JR, Robinson RG, Pearlson GD, et al: Dexamethasone suppression test and mood following strokes. Am J Psychiatry 142:318–323, 1985.
45. Lopez M, Mermelstein RJ: Enhancing geriatric rehab outcome through psychological intervention. Presented at the Annual Meeting of the Society of Behavioural Medicine, Boston, 1988.
46. Malec JF, Richardson JW, Sinaki M, O'Brien MW: Types of affective response to stroke. Arch Phys Med Rehabil 71:279–284, 1990.
47. McCaffrey RJ, Fisher JM: Cognitive, behavioural and psychosocial sequelae of cerebrovascular accidents and closed head injuries in older adults. In Carstensen LL, Edelsten BA (eds): Handbook of Clinical Gerontology. New York, Pergammon Press, 1987, pp 277–288.
48. Moskowitz E, Lightbody FEH, Freitag NS: Long-term follow-up of the post-stroke patient. Arch Phys Med Rehabil 53:167–172, 1972.
49. Murray GB, Shea V, Conn DK: Electroconvulsive therapy for post-stroke depression. J Clin Psychiatry 47:258–260, 1986.
50. Nauta WJH: The problem of the frontal lobe: A reinterpretation. J Psychiatr Res 8:167–187, 1971.
51. Parikh RM, Robinson RG, Lipsey JR, et al: The impact of post stroke depression on recovery in activities of daily living over a 2-year follow-up. Arch Neurol 47:785–789, 1990.
52. Popkin MK, Callies AL, Colon EA: A framework for the study of medical depression. Psychosomatics 28:27–33, 1987.
53. Primeau F: Post-stroke depression: A critical review of the literature. Can J Psychiatry 33:757–765, 1988.
54. Reding MJ, Orto LA, Winter SW, et al: Antidepressant therapy after stroke. Arch Neurol 43:763–765, 1986.
55. Robinson RG, Shoemaker WJ, Schlumpf M, et al: Effect of experimental cerebral infarction on catecholamines and behavior. Nature 255:332–333, 1975.
56. Robinson RG, Coyle JT: The differential effect of right vs. left hemispheric cerebral infarction on catecholamines and behaviour in the rat. Brain Res 188:63, 1980.
57. Robinson RG, Szetela B: Mood change following left hemispheric brain injury. Ann Neurol 9:447–453, 1981.
58. Robinson RG, Price TR: Post-stroke depressive disorders: A follow-up study of 103 patients. Stroke 13:635–641, 1982.
59. Robinson RG, Starr LB, Kubos KL, Price T: A two-year longitudinal study of post-stroke mood disorders: Finding during the initial evaluation. Stroke 14:736–741, 1983.
60. Robinson RG, Kubos KL, Starrr LB, et al: Mood disorders in stroke patients: Importance of location of lesion. Brain 107:81–93, 1982.
61. Robinson RG, Starr LB, Price TR: A two year longitudinal study of mood disorders following stroke: Prevalence and duration at six months follow-up. Br J Psychiatry 144:256–262, 1984.
62. Robinson RG, et al: A two-year longitudinal study of post-stroke mood disorders: In-hospital prognostic factors associated with six-month outcome. J Nerv Ment Dis 173:221–226, 1985.
63. Robinson RG, Bolla-Wilson K, Kaplan E, et al: Depression influences intellectual impairment in stroke patients. Br J Psychiatry 148:541–547, 1986.
64. Robinson RG: Post-stroke mood disorders. Hosp Pract (15 Apr):83–88, 1986.
65. Robinson RG, Bolduc PL, Price TR: Two-year longitudinal study of post-stroke mood disorders: Diagnosis and outcome at one and two years. Stroke 18:837–843, 1987.
66. Rodin J: Aging and health: Effects of the sense of control. Science 233:1271–1276, 1986.
67. Roose SP, Glassman AH, Giardina EG, et al: Cardiovascular effects of imipramine and bupropion in depressed patients with congestive heart failure. J Clin Psychopharmacol 7:247–251, 1987.
68. Ross ED, Rush A: Diagnosis and neuroanatomical correlates of depression in brain damaged patients. Arch Gen Psychiatry 38:1344–1354, 1981.
69. Ross ED, Gordon WA, Hibbard M, et al: The dexamethasone suppression test, post-stroke depression and the validity of DSM-III-based diagnostic criteria. Am J Psychiatry 143:1200–1201, 1986.
70. Rosse RB, Ciolino CP: Effects of cortical lesion location on psychiatric consultation referral for depressed stroke inpatients. Int J Psychiatr Med 15:311–319, 1986.
71. Schulz R, Decker S: Long-term adjustment to physical disability: The role of social support, perceived control and self-blame. Pers Soc Psychol 48:1162–1172, 1985.
72. Schulz R, Tompkins CA, Rau MT: A longitudinal study of the psychosocial impact of stroke on primary support persons. Psychol Aging 3:131–141, 1988.
73. Seligman ME: Fall into helplessness. Psychol Today 7:43–48, 1973.

74. Sinyor D, Amato P, Kaloupek DG, et al: Post-stroke depression: Relationships to functional impairment, coping strategies and rehabilitation outcome. Stroke 17:1102–1107, 1986.
75. Sinyor O, Jacques P, Kaloupek D, et al: Post-stroke depression and lesion location. Brain 105:537–546, 1986.
76. Starkstein S, Robinson R, Price TR: Comparison of cortical and subcortical lesions in the production of poststroke mood disorders. Brain 110:1045–1059, 1987.
77. Starkstein S, Robinson R, Price TR: Comparison of spontaneously recovered versus nonrecovered patients with poststroke depression. Stroke 199:1491–1496, 1988.
78. Starkstein SE, Boston JD, Robinson RG: Mechanisms of mania after brain injury. J Nerv Mental Dis 176:87–100, 1988.
79. Starkstein SE, Robinson RG: Aphasia and depression. Aphasiology 2:1–20, 1988.
80. Starkstein SE, Robinson RG, Honig MA, et al: Mood changes after right-hemisphere lesions. Br J Psychiatry 155:79–85, 1989.
81. Starkstein SE, Cohen BS, Federoff P, et al: Relationship between anxiety disorders and depressive disorders in patients with cerebrovascular injury. Arch Gen Psychiatry 47:246–251, 1990.
82. Thompson SC, Sobolew-Shubin A, Graham MA, Janagian AS: Psychosocial adjustment following a stroke. Soc Sci Med 28:234–247, 1989.
83. Turner RJ, Noh S: Physical disability and depression: A longitudinal analysis. Health Soc Behav 29:23–37, 1988.
84. Wade DT, Legh-Smith J, Hewer RA: Depressed mood after stroke: A community study of its frequency. Br J Psychiatry 151:200–205, 1987.
85. Worden JW: Grief Counselling and Grief Therapy. New York, Springer, 1982.
86. Wortman CB, Brehm JW: Responses to uncontrollable outcomes: An integration of reactance theory and the learned helplessness model. In Berkowitz L (ed): Advances in Experimental Social Psychology. New York, Academic Press, 1975, pp 277–336.
87. Wortman CB, Silver RC: The myths of coping with loss. J Consult Clin Psychol 57:349–357, 1989.
88. Zung W: A self-rating depression scale. Arch Gen Psychiatry 12:63–70, 1965.

TIMO ERKINJUNTTI, MD, PhD
VLADIMIR C. HACHINSKI, MD,
FRCPC, MSc(DME), DSc(Med)

13. DEMENTIA POST STROKE

From the Department of Clinical
    Neurological Sciences
University of Western Ontario
    and
The John P. Robarts Research
    Institute
London, Ontario
Canada (TE, VCH)
    and
The Department of Neurology
University of Helsinki
Helsinki, Finland (TE)

Reprint requests to:
Dr. Timo Erkinjuntti
Department of Neurology
University of Helsinki
00290 Helsinki
Finland

Stroke may relate to dementia in different ways: it may cause, contribute, or only coexist with the cognitive impairment. Stroke may be the main cause of vascular dementia. However, it often unmasks or modifies an underlying impairment, such as Alzheimer's disease. Patients with a history of cerebrovascular disease seem to be at considerable risk for dementia. As some of these vascular factors can be modified by treatment, more attention should be paid to those persons at risk both for stroke and dementia, and the interactions of different causes should be analyzed in more detail.

Vascular dementia has commonly been considered a dementia syndrome evolving in connection with multiple ischemic lesions of the brain. It is not a disease entity; it is a syndrome. Vascular dementia may be related to different vascular factors and pathophysiologic changes in the brain. Currently, no precise knowledge exists regarding the extent to which these factors cause, compound, or only coincide with the cognitive loss. Most likely, they act in combination, not only adding to but multiplying the impairments. The current concept, causes, and diagnosis of vascular dementia are reviewed in detail in this chapter.

Evaluation of cognitive abilities, emotion, and social skills is part of the clinical evaluation of stroke patients and those with suspected cognitive impairment. We should abandon the use of dementia as an identifier. Instead, the focus should be on early changes in a person's cognitive abilities, personality, and mood, which may signal the prelude of early dementia. Thus, we should examine the brains of persons at risk of vascular damage and at risk of dementia. A practical clinical approach to vascular risk factors, stroke, and dementia is outlined here.

RELATIONSHIPS BETWEEN STROKE AND DEMENTIA

Stroke may relate to dementia in different ways: it may cause, contribute, or only coexist with the cognitive impairment (Table 1). Stroke may be the main cause of dementia syndrome, as in vascular dementia. However, stroke may be only contributing to the cognitive impairment, although it often is clinically an important factor. A recent stroke may finally overcome the brain's compensatory capacity and, for the first time, clinically manifest symptoms related to preexisting conditions affecting the brain. These conditions include chronic cardiovascular and metabolic disorders (arterial hypertension, diabetes), head trauma, other CNS diseases (epilepsy), and use of alcohol or drugs. In addition, preexisting Alzheimer's disease or other degenerative dementing disorders are common, especially in the older age groups. Also, loss of the brain's compensatory capacity with normal aging renders aged normal subjects at higher risk.

Focal ischemic infarcts and ischemic white matter changes may also modify and/or aggravate the cognitive impairment. Those patients with Alzheimer's disease who have diffuse white matter changes, leuko-araiosis, have been reported to show a faster progression and more severe degree of dementia syndrome.[23,37] However, tiny infarcts may be seen in aged brains without any clear cognitive consequences.[104]

Stroke and Risk of Dementia

A recent stroke cohort study has shown that stroke increases the risk of dementia by a factor of nine.[101] The risk is highest in the age group 70–79 years of age, with an odds ratio of 31.2. The frequency of dementia 3 months after stroke was, in the series of patients aged 60 years and over, 26.3%. It was 14.8% for those aged 60 to 69 years, 28.3% for those aged 70 to 79, and 52.3% for those aged 80 years and older.[101] Besides age, lower education was also associated with an increased risk of dementia. Of the 66 stroke patients with dementia, the primary cause was Alzheimer's disease in 36.4%. Thus, cooccurrence of dementia and stroke as such does not establish a causal relation. In this series, vascular dementia was the diagnosis in 56% and other disorders in 7.6%.[101]

The incidence of dementia after stroke is not well known. In a small series of young stroke patients (mean age 47 years), 3 of 37 became demented during the 4-year follow-up.[65] In a stroke databank cohort, the 1-year dementia rate was 5.4%

TABLE 1.   Relationships Between Stroke and Dementia

Stroke as a cause of cognitive impairment and dementia
Multiple infarcts
Large infarcts
Single infarct in strategic location
Stroke contributing to cognitive impairment and dementia
Unmasking underlying impairment(s)
Modifying or aggravating the impairment(s)
Stroke only coexisting with cognitive impairment and dementia

in persons aged 60 years and over and 10.4% in those aged 90 years and older.[24] In this study the diagnosis and differential diagnosis of dementia were not based on a more detailed clinical workup.

Patients with a history of cerebrovascular disease seem to be at considerable risk for dementia (odds ratio 5.7 to 31.2),[101] which is higher than that for those with head trauma (odds ratio 2.0–5.3).[85] Some of these vascular factors can be modified by treatment, and thus more attention should be paid to persons at risk both for stroke and dementia (see later discussion).

Predictors of Dementia after Stroke

The clinical characteristics that predict dementia after stroke are still poorly known. Besides age and lower education,[101] one preliminary series related the risk of dementia after stroke to a history of previous stroke, myocardial infarction, and stroke due to large-artery atherosclerosis.[103]

Brain imaging findings and the risk of dementia after stroke have been studied in few series. In a series of stroke patients, CT findings related to dementia included the total volume of infarcts, number of infarcts, thalamic and cortical medial cerebral artery location, and cerebral atrophy, but not white matter changes or deep infarcts.[70] In a similar study, Tatemichi et al.[103] found that the presence of cortical atrophy, cortical temporo-occipito-parietal infarcts, total number of infarcts, and white matter changes were associated with dementia in stroke patients, whereas the volume or deep location of the infarcts was not. In patients with multiple lacunae, those with dementia more often had extensive white matter changes, especially in the frontal areas.[44] In an MR study on stroke patients, dementia was associated with central atrophy only, and not with location of the infarcts or white matter changes.[52] On the other hand, in the series of Liu et al.,[69] dementia was associated with total volume of white matter changes, central atrophy, left parietal infarcts, and the total volume of infarcts, but not with deep location of infarcts seen on MR. A small MR series of patients with lacunar strokes related dementia to the extent of white matter changes, as well as to central and cortical atrophy.[98] Thus, many studies indicate that a patient with a history of stroke and more extensive white matter changes could be at a higher risk for dementia.

Cognitive Aspects of Stroke

The cognitive aspects of stroke have been often neglected, as the concept of stroke is related to acute focal symptoms and signs. Thus, the relation to motor and sensory changes is emphasized, and more subtle early cognitive symptoms may be overlooked. In addition, ischemic events may show only diffuse symptoms and signs, such as cardiac arrhythmias and systemic hypotension causing general cerebral dysfunction, or episodes with impaired consciousness, confusion, or amnesia combined with apraxic-ataxic gait or dysequilibrium clinically judged to be related to compromised cerebral circulation.[79] In addition, ischemic events may even be silent.[58] Thus, the focusing on the more obvious motor and sensory aspects of stroke may divert attention from the analysis of the neurobehavioral aspects of stroke.

Some important clinical stroke syndromes with cognitive impairment(s) are listed in Table 2.[72,111] In particular, mild slowing of mental processes and executive functioning, impairment in learning and short-term memory, as well as personality changes should be taken into account.

TABLE 2.   Important Clinical Syndromes Related to Stroke and Cognitive Impairment

Large vessel territories	
Carotid artery	Contralateral motor weakness, sensory loss. Aphasia (if dominant hemisphere). Visuospatial disturbances
Anterior cerebral artery	Contralateral leg weakness. Slowing of mental processes and abnormal executive functioning. Decreased verbal output. Apraxia. Depression.
Middle cerebral artery	Contralateral motor weakness, sensory loss. Aphasia (global, Broca, Wernicke, or conduction type), alexia, agraphia, acalculia (if left hemisphere). Constructional difficulty, hemi-neglect (if right hemisphere).
Posterior cerebral artery	Visual field defect (contralateral), visual agnosias, alexia without agraphia (left hemisphere), amnesia (severe bilateral lesion, more verbal left-sided).
Inferior parietal branch (left)	Gyrus angularis syndrome: agraphia, acalculia, alexia, finger agnosia, right-left disorientation, anomia, memory impairment (verbal).
Border zones	Aphasia (transcortical), apraxia, visuospatial disturbances, memory impairment.
Small vessel territories	
Lenticulostriate arteries and deep white matter arteries	Pure motor hemiparesis, pure sensory stroke, homolateral ataxia and leg weakness, dysarthria, dysphagia, emotional lability (pseudobulbar syndrome), extrapyramidal syndrome, gait disorder (apractic-ataxic), incontinence. Slowing of mental processing and abnormal executive functioning. Changes in mood. Memory impairment.
Thalamic branches	Decreased attention and consciousness (early in the course). Variable motor and sensory symptoms. Aphasia (left). Memory impairment (more verbal left-side).

VASCULAR DEMENTIA

Vascular dementia has commonly been considered a dementia syndrome, evolving in connection with multiple ischemic lesions of the brain without other changes known to cause dementia.[26,29,50] It is not a disease entity; it is a syndrome. Vascular dementia may be related to different vascular factors and pathophysiologic changes in the brain. Currently, no precise knowledge exists regarding the extent to which these factors cause, compound, or only coincide with the cognitive loss. Most likely, they act in combination, not only adding to but multiplying the impairments.

The resulting imprecision in definition and diagnosis has bred confusion regarding incidence, prevention, and treatment of the syndrome. In addition, a tendency for categorization has spread,[109,114] which may prevent analyzing the types of vascular factor and changes involved. Further, dementia should not be used as an identifier; instead, the focus should be on the early changes related to vascular risk factors (brain at risk for stroke) and to cerebrovascular disorders (brain at risk for vascular dementia).

TABLE 3. Pathophysiologic Changes Related to Vascular Dementia

Focal ischemic lesions	Other factors related to ischemia
Location	Focal gliosis (incomplete ischemic necrosis)
Side	Border zones around focal infarcts
Number	Selective vulnerability
Volume	Functional factors
White matter changes	Focal changes
Location	State dependent and remote effects
Extent	Unknown factor(s)
Type	

Factors Related to Vascular Dementia

Several changes in the brain have been related to vascular dementia (Table 3).[19,27,35,78,86,87,100] Previously the total volume of infarcted brain was regarded as the most important factor.[105] This may still be the mechanism in those few cases where the infarct size reaches the critical threshold and overcomes the brain's compensatory capacity.[100] However, because the volume of infarcts is often small, other factors have been explored, including site, side, and number of the infarcts.[19,30]

Few neuroradiologic[2,32,63] and neuropathologic studies[19,22,30,56,90,105] have analyzed the location and types of vascular lesions in vascular dementia. These studies indicate that bilateral ischemic lesions are of importance.[30,56,69] Location of the infarcts may well be a factor[2,32,63]; some studies emphasize deep infarcts,[44,56,98] other studies lesions affecting the limbic- and paralimbic areas and frontal connections,[29,95] and some studies cortical infarcts especially in the temporal and parietal cortices.[32,69,70,103] Controversy exists regarding the number and volume of the infarcts.[19,30,69,70,103,105] In addition, the diffuse white matter changes may be an important factor, as it may cause disconnection of cortical structures.[56,69,98]

Besides focal ischemic infarcts, other changes related to ischemia could have an effect. These include focal gliotic areas or incomplete ischemic necrosis,[66] areas of selective vulnerability (e.g., area CA1 in the hippocampus[18]), cortical areas with laminar necrosis,[1] and also lesions in the myelinated fibers, which may be related to dysfunction of oligodendrocytes.[110] Functional factors should be considered, such as remote cortical changes related to focal infarcts and white matter changes.[38,64] Change in state-dependent functions could be a factor, including cholinergic and noradrenergic cortical afferents or in the activating effects of the thalamo-cortical afferent pathways.[8,60] The role of these noninfarct and functional factors in the genesis of vascular dementia is not yet well established. In addition, other contributing factors may yet be uncovered.

Vascular Mechanisms Related to Vascular Dementia

Various vascular mechanisms are related to ischemic lesions of the brain (Table 4). The atherothrombotic stroke, lacunar strokes, ischemic white matter changes, cardiac embolic events, and hemodynamic mechanisms are those most often related to vascular dementia.[26] In most cases, several vascular factors are involved.

Large-Vessel Arteriopathies. Atherothrombotic stroke—i.e., artery-to-artery embolism and thrombosis of an extracranial or intracranial artery in association with large-artery atherosclerosis—is the most common cause of vascular lesions in

TABLE 4. Vascular Mechanisms Involved in the Evolution of Vascular Dementia

Large-vessel arteriopathies	Cardiac embolic events
Artery-to-artery embolism	Hemodynamic changes
Thrombosis/occlusion of an extra-	Hemorrhages
or intracranial artery	Intracerebral hemorrhage
	Subarachnoidal hemorrhage
Small-vessel arteriopathies	Hematologic factors
Lacunar strokes/infarcts, "lacunar state"	Hereditary diseases
Diffuse ischemic white matter lesions,	Isolated infarcts
"Binswanger's disease"	Unknown mechanism(s)
Granular cortical atrophy	

the cerebral cortex.[24,57] Rarely, other large-vessel arteriopathies are involved, such as fibromuscular dysplasia or Takayasu's arteritis.

Small-Vessel Arteriopathies. Arteriolosclerosis, also termed lipohyalinosis of the deep penetrating arteries of the brain, leads to lacunar infarcts and destruction of the white matter.[7,41] It also leads to two entities associated with dementia: the lacunar state (*état lacunaire*) and subcortical arteriosclerotic encephalopathy (Binswanger's disease). Because the clinical pictures and neuropathologic findings are similar,[7,86] they likely represent the same entity and their separation into two types is not encouraged.[33,86] In addition to lacunar infarcts, extensive white matter changes are seen. The white matter changes include patchy loss of myelin, astrocytic gliosis, rarefaction and cavitation of the white matter with scattered microcystic areas (spongiosis), *état criblé* (widening of the perivascular spaces), and arteriolosclerosis.[7,82] The white matter changes are located primarily in the watershed or arterial border zone areas.[76] The cortical U-fibers connecting cortical areas are often spared, as they are irrigated by cortical rather than medullary arteries.

The pathogenesis of these white matter changes has been related to changes in the walls of the perforating arteries,[81] hypoperfusion and ischemia,[20] focal cerebral edema and hypoxia related to hypertension or acidosis,[39] and slowing of venous drainage of the deep white matter.[12]

Inflammatory or noninflammatory arteriopathies affecting primarily the small vessels can cause multiple cerebral infarcts and lead to a vascular dementia.[29] Granular cortical atrophy is a state with multiple microinfarcts of the cortex and involvement of the small leptomeningeal vessels.[83,117] It may also be associated with dementia. Cerebral amyloid angiopathy is related to multiple intracerebral hematomas[15,48] and in some cases to extensive white matter changes.[46,71]

Cardiac Embolic Events. Cardiac embolic events are the second most common factor responsible for vascular lesions of the cerebral cortex,[24,57] and various heart disorders give rise to embolic strokes,[13] the most prevalent being atrial fibrillation, acute myocardial infarction with mural thrombosis, and rheumatic heart diseases.

Hemodynamic Changes. Hypoperfusion of the brain caused by various cardiopulmonary disorders, with or without carotid occlusion, causes multiple vascular lesions of the brain, especially in the watershed areas.[21,106] Vascular dementia due to cardiac arrhythmias has been documented.[4,96] In addition, hemodynamic factors may secondarily aggravate an already compromised mental status.

The concept of chronic ischemia as a cause of vascular dementia is attractive.[14] However, so far it has not been supported by clear scientific evidence.[43]

Isolated Infarcts.   Isolated infarcts may occasionally be the cause of vascular dementia, including bilateral hippocampal infarcts,[18] bilateral thalamic lesions,[47] an infarct in the left thalamus,[45] bifrontal infarcts, bilateral infarcts of the fornix or of the gyrus ginguli,[11] or an infarct in the left angular gyrus.[9]

Hemorrhages.   Intracerebral hematoma and subarachnoid hemorrhage can cause widespread brain destruction. However, probably because of their high fatality rates, these conditions are seen less often in cases of vascular dementia. Multiple intracerebral hematomas leading to dementia have been described in association with cerebral amyloid angiopathy.[15,48]

Other Factors.   Hematologic factors include hyperviscosity-induced dementia[77] and hyperlipidemic dementia,[73] which are linked to increased red blood cell aggregation and blood viscosity. Hereditary diseases also have been described as a cause of vascular dementia.[29]

Subtypes of Vascular Dementia

It has been suggested that vascular dementia be divided into subtypes.[26,95] The two most commonly referred to clinical types or syndromes are the **cortical** and **subcortical** vascular dementias.[26,72,86] Cortical vascular dementia is related to atherothrombotic strokes, cardiac embolic strokes, and cortical watershed infarcts. Subcortical vascular dementia relates to lacunar infarcts and deep white matter changes, including the so-called lacunar state and Binswanger's disease.[26,72,86]

Typical clinical features for cortical vascular dementia are lateralized sensorimotor changes and abrupt onset of cognitive impairment and aphasia.[26] In addition, some combination of different cortical neuropsychological syndromes has been suggested to be present in cortical vascular dementia.[72] Subcortical vascular dementia is characterized by pure motor hemiparesis, bulbar signs and dysarthria, depression, and emotional lability.[26] Other features include slowing of mental processing, deficits in executive functioning, and aspontaneity.[7,56,72,94,95] Although selected cases with more accentuated subcortical or cortical features may well be found, especially among early cases, most cases have both cortical and subcortical symptoms.[26] Also, neuropathologically verified cases mostly demonstrate both cortical and subcortical pathology.[19,30,105] However, vascular dementia may arise from deep lesions only,[56,86] and cases with lesions only in the association cortex are rare, the gyrus angularis syndrome being one example.[9]

The question as to whether the clinical pictures in subcortical and cortical vascular dementia reflect different disease entities or merely an expression of the same causes with differences related to the site of the lesions is still open.[26] On the other hand, the cases related to more specific diseases, such as arteriopathies of the brain vessels, could be diagnosed and classified as their own entities.

Criteria of Vascular Dementia

Current uncertainties in the definition of vascular dementia have been highlighted, which includes both the definition of dementia and that of vascular dementia.[29,36]

Definition of Dementia.   Dementia is a syndrome, not a disease. It is usually regarded as an acquired syndrome of cognitive decline due to some organic disease affecting the brain.[5,6,89,113,114] Dementia is characterized by global cognitive impairment, including decline of memory and other cognitive functions such as abstract thinking, in comparison with the patient's previous level of function. In addition, this decline has to be of sufficient severity to interfere with the person's usual social activities; thus, dementia always includes a social dimension.

Some definitions require progressive cognitive decline,[89] while others do not carry a connotation as to prognosis, and dementia may be progressive, static, or remitting.[5,6,113,114] Which combination of cognitive impairment should be required is another question. Some of the definitions require only short-term memory impairment,[5,113,114] while others also require long-term memory loss.[6,89] The DSM-III-R definition requires some combination of short- and long-term memory impairment with one of the domains including abstract thinking, judgment, aphasia, apraxia, agnosia, constructional difficulty, or personality change.[6] Others include slightly different combinations. Also, there are differences in defining the social functioning. Finally, these criteria do not include more detailed guidelines for measuring impairment in a given cognitive or social domain, nor do they state what degree of impairment in each domain qualifies for the diagnosis. Thus, unfortunately there is no clear international agreement on the concept and criteria of dementia to be used.

Definition of Vascular Dementia.   Uncertainty in the concept and causes of vascular dementia has generated questions regarding the definition. In addition, as the effects of focal brain lesions on the evolution of cognitive impairment cannot always be assessed accurately, it limits the judgment of the relationships between ischemic lesions and cognitive changes.

The most widely used clinical criteria for vascular dementia have been those of the DSM-III[5] and DSM-III-R[6] for multi-infarct dementia. These criteria are based on clinical descriptions only and include, besides dementia, features suggestive of focal ischemic brain lesions such as stepwise deterioration, "patchy" distribution of deficits, focal neurologic symptoms and signs, and evidence of significant cerebrovascular disease that is judged to be etiologically related to the disturbance. However, these clinical features are not defined in detail, and brain imaging data are not used. Consequently, these criteria also overlap with a number of cases with Alzheimer's disease and vascular changes, giving a low specificity of the antemortem diagnosis as verified postmortem.[3,108]

In order to achieve a higher rate of accuracy of the antemortem diagnosis, more strict criteria for vascular dementia based on the infarct concept have been proposed.[27,28] These criteria include, besides dementia,

> "evidence of clinical history and/or findings in clinical examination indicating stroke/strokes (i.e., event of focal cerebral dysfunction of vascular origin) and/or findings on brain imaging (e.g., CT, MR) compatible with vascular lesions of the brain (infarct/infarcts and/or moderate to severe degree of ischaemic white matter change) indicating multiple cortical and/or deep vascular lesions of the brain which are judged to be causally related to the disturbance."[27,28]

By using these criteria, the antemortem accuracy of the diagnosis of vascular dementia as verified postmortem was over 80%.[30] However, these results reflect a selected sample, and a number of cases related to vascular changes may have been excluded. Thus, the sensitivity may drop with an increase in specificity.

Recently, Chui et al.[14] and Roman et al.[87] have suggested similar criteria based on clinical history of stroke, presence of ischemic lesions on brain imaging, and the clinical assumption that these two have a relation. Knowing the limitations, the criteria of Roman et al.[87] may well serve as a starting point for further discussion and studies. However, only a large prospective clinical neurologic, neuropsychological, neuroradiologic, and neuropathologic study can overcome the obstacles.

DIAGNOSTIC APPROACH

Symptomatic Diagnosis

The main levels in the clinical assessments of related stroke and dementia include the symptomatic diagnosis and the etiologic diagnosis. The most important symptomatic categories, besides dementia, include delirium, circumscribed neuropsychological syndrome, and functional psychiatric disorders, especially depression.

Delirium. The essential feature of delirium is reduced attention and disorganized thinking.[6,68] In addition, reduced level of consciousness, disturbances in perception and sleep-wakefulness cycle, increase or decrease of psychomotor activity, disorientation, or memory impairment is present. The onset is relatively rapid, and the course typically fluctuates. In addition to cerebrovascular diseases, the causes of delirium include a variety of disorders including heart and lung diseases, infections, nutritional deficiencies, endocrine diseases, electrolyte disorders, head trauma, drugs, and intoxications.[67,68] Predisposing factors include old age, chronic cardiovascular disease and other systemic disorders, and other preexisting brain damage. Most of the disorders leading to delirium are treatable, but without proper treatment they may lead to permanent brain damage and even death. Although demented patients, especially those with vascular dementia, are at a greater risk for delirium, one cannot diagnose dementia in the presence of delirium, because its symptoms interfere with the proper assessment of dementia.

Circumscribed Neuropsychological Disorders. The differential diagnosis should include circumscribed memory disorder, amnestic syndrome, and aphasia.[62,74,111]

Amnestic syndrome is characterized by impairment in both short- and long-term memory. It may result from any pathologic process that causes damage, mostly bilaterally, to the limbic- and paralimbic structures and to the diencephalon, including the hippocampal formation and the medial dorsal nucleus of thalamus and their connections.[91] In addition to cerebrovascular diseases, causes include head trauma, surgical intervention, herpes simplex encephalitis, and thiamine deficiency.[91]

Aphasia is related to lesion(s) in the dominant hemisphere (Table 2). It is of diagnostic importance, as it often prevents testing of patient's other higher cortical functions. Cases with severe aphasia are excluded using the recent criteria for vascular dementia.[87]

Functional Psychiatric Disorders. Both subjective and objective changes in cognitive functions, especially in memory, are seen in a variety of functional psychiatric disorders: affective disorders including depressive and manic syndromes, schizophrenic disorders, other psychotic disorders, anxiety disorders, somatoform disorders including conversion disorder, and dissociative disorders including psychogenic amnesia.[6,112] The most prevalent are depression and anxiety, where the objective cognitive impairment is often mild, showing changes in attention, concentration, short-term memory, and speed of processing. Lists of clinical characteristics for distinguishing dementia from depression have been published.[99] One proposed scheme for coordinating work on affective illness and dementia divides the relationships between depression and dementia into four categories[40]:

1. depression presenting as dementia,
2. depression with secondary dementia,
3. dementia presenting as depression, and
4. dementia with secondary depression.

Affective disorders after stroke include depression, mania, apathy, and hyperemotionalism. The most common is depression, which is reported in up to 60% of patients with stroke.[93] Depression after stroke also affects patients' cognitive abilities,[59] especially in those with left hemisphere stroke.[10,84] In some series, post-stroke depression has been related to more anterior lesions in the left hemisphere.[92] On the other hand, mania and apathy are related more to right hemisphere lesions.[93] Affective disorders affect patients' rehabilitation and mentation and may represent differential diagnostic difficulties. These problems are discussed more in detail in chapter 12.

CLINICAL ASSESSMENT OF COGNITIVE IMPAIRMENT

In all patients with stroke, and especially in those with suspected cognitive impairment, a short mental status test should be part of the clinical examination. The Mini Mental State Examination (MMSE)[42] can be used as a simple screening test and also as a simple measure of overall abnormality. However, it is limited in that it emphasizes language and does not include the timed elements or recognition portion of the memory tests. It is also relatively insensitive to mild deficits and is influenced by education and age.[102,118] Using a cut-off point of 24 in a stroke cohort, it gave 84% sensitivity and 76% specificity in diagnosing dementia according to the modified DSM-III-R criteria.[102] Besides MMSE, other proposed screening instruments for vascular dementia include the four-word memory test with 10-minute delayed recall, cube drawing test for copy, verbal fluency test (number of animals named in 1 minute), Luria's alternating hang sequence or finger rings and letter cancelation test (neglect).[87]

Often more detailed neuropsychological tests and test batteries are needed. These should cover the main areas of cognitive abilities including orientation, attention, memory, language and verbal output, visuospatial abilities, executive functions, motor control and praxis, and speed of information processing.[16] In the future, we may even have stress tests for cognitive impairment. A history of decreased alcohol tolerance, and unusual susceptibility to side effects of medications, especially of those with anticholinergic effects, may signal the brain's decreased compensatory capacity.

Assessment of persons' social functioning is also part of basic evaluation, including activities of daily living (ADL) such as dressing, feeding, and toileting, instrumental activities of daily living (IADL) such as use of telephone, shopping, handling finances, and more complex social functions (such as work) and activities.[116] In addition, emotion should be assessed including depression, anxiety, changes in personality, delusions, and hallucinations.

In conclusion, evaluation of cognitive abilities, emotion, and social skills is part of the clinical evaluation of stroke patients and those with suspected cognitive impairment. Especially important domains include speed of processing, executive functions, learning, personality, and mood.

Diagnosing the Causes of Cognitive Impairment

Strategy. The main strategy in the evaluation of underlying causes in patients with cognitive impairment include diagnosis of the specific causes, especially the potentially treatable conditions; evaluation of secondary factors able to affect the cognitive functioning; and diagnosis of other causes, including Alzheimer's disease and vascular dementia.

Causes. Most of the diseases that afflict the brain directly or indirectly may present as cognitive impairment and dementia. In addition to the two most common causes, Alzheimer's disease and vascular dementia, dementia may be caused by various degenerative brain diseases, deficiency states, drugs and toxins, endocrine disturbances, infections, intracranial conditions, and systemic illnesses. A number of these specific causes of cognitive impairment are potentially treatable and have all been the subject of reviews.[17,61]

Clinical Workup. The diagnosis and differential diagnosis of these conditions is based on the clinical interview and examination, chest radiograph, electrocardiogram, screening laboratory tests, and brain imaging including CT or MR. In addition, electroencephalography or quantitive electroencephalography, as well as single photon emission tomography (SPECT), may also be used. The clinical chemical parameters most commonly measured include erythrocyte sedimentation rate, hemoglobin, leukocyte count, vitamin B_{12}, glucose, potassium, sodium, calcium, kidney, liver, and thyroid function tests. Plasma lipids may also be tested, along with tests for syphilis and AIDS. In some cases, an analysis of the cerebrospinal fluid is needed.

Secondary Factors. A person's cognitive capacity may be worsened by secondary factors. These include emotional changes (depression, anxiety, paranoid symptoms), sleep disorders (insomnia, excessive daytime sleepiness, hypopneas, and apneas), medication (anticholinergic and sedative drugs, alcohol), a number of medical conditions (cardiopulmonary and metabolic abnormalities, deficiency states, infections), and environmental factors (sensory deprivation, excess of sensory input, social isolation).[36]

Differentiation Between Alzheimer's Disease and Vascular Dementia. Alzheimer's disease is a degenerative dementing disorder of unknown cause. Its clinical picture is characterized by insidious onset and slowly progressive intellectual deterioration, absence of symptoms and signs indicating focal brain damage, and absence of any other specific disease affecting the brain.[75] Its diagnosis is based mainly on exclusion. In selected series, the antemortem accuracy of the diagnosis is as high as 80 to 90%.[97,108] However, no reliable biological marker for Alzheimer's disease is yet known.[53,55] Diagnosis of Alzheimer's disease combined with other factors, such as stroke, remains a problem.

In contrast, vascular dementia is assumed to be related to strokes and other ischemic changes in the brain. Thus, these patients often show in their clinical history, neurological examination, or brain imaging scans, findings compatible with ischemic changes of the brain (Table 5). Ischemic Scores have been also useful in the differential diagnosis.[49,88] In typical cases the differentiation between vascular dementia and Alzheimer's disease, using common clinical tools, is straightforward.[35] Clinical problems include vascular dementia patients who demonstrate insidious onset and nonstepwise progression of the cognitive symptoms, often without a clear clinical history of stroke. A problem is Alzheimer's disease patients who have focal symptoms (e.g., aphasia) early in the course, as well as patients with combined vascular and degenerative changes. In particular,

TABLE 5.   Clinical Features Related to Vascular Dementia

Course
   Relatively abrupt onset (days to weeks) of cognitive impairment.
   Often stepwise deterioration (some recovery after worsenings) and fluctuating course (e.g.,
      difference between days) of cognitive symptoms.
   In some cases (20–40%) an insidious onset and progressive deterioration.

Neurologic/psychiatric signs
   Clinical neurologic findings indicating focal brain lesions in early cases: mild motor or sensory
      deficits, decreased coordination, brisk deep tendon relfexes, Babinski's sign.
         Bulbar signs including dysarthria and dysphagia
         Gait disorder: hemiplegic, apractic-ataxic, small-stepped
         Unsteadiness, unprovoked falls
         Urinary frequency and urgency
         Psychomotor slowing, abnormal executive functioning
         Emotional lability
   Preserved personality and insight in mild and moderate cases.
   Affective disorders: depression, anxiety, affect lability.

Comorbid findings
   History of cardiovascular diseases (not always): arterial hypertension, coronary heart disease,
      cardiac arrhythmias.

Radiologic findings
   CT or MR: Focal infarcts (70–90%). Especially bilateral infarcts in limbic- and paralimbic areas,
      cortical association areas, and watershed territories. Diffuse or patchy white matter changes,
      leuko-araiosis (70–100%), especially more extensive involving more than 25% of the total white
      matter area.

   SPECT or PET: Patchy reduction of regional cerebral blood flow.

   EEG: Compared to Alzheimer's disease, more often normal; if abnormal, more focal findings.
      Overall, abnormality increases with more severe intellectual decline.

Laboratory investigations
   No known specific tests.
   Often findings related to concomitant diseases: hyperlipidemia, diabetes, abnormalities on ECG.

the last two groups of patients remain problematic, until a sensitive and specific antemortem marker for Alzheimer's disease is available or until more detailed knowledge exists as to which types and locations of ischemic brain changes are most critical.

White Matter Changes Are Not Always Ischemic in Origin.   Patchy or diffuse areas of white matter changes are referred to as leuko-araiosis.[51] Tiny areas of leuko-araiosis are seen among aged, neurologically normal subjects.[54] Small areas have been seen on CT scans in up to 40% of Alzheimer's disease patients and on MR images in up to 70% of cases.[29,34] However, these changes are usually small and limited to periventricular areas. In contrast, patients with vascular dementia typically demonstrate large areas of leuko-araiosis extending to deep white matter.[25,31]

Unfortunately, the analysis of leuko-araiosis has been usually restricted to its presence or absence, and the location, extent, and type of leuko-araiosis have not been studied in detail. The tiny periventricular changes (e.g., caps and periventricular linings) differ in regard to causes, risk factors, and clinical consequences from the spots in the deep subcortical white matter (the undefined bright objects) and from the diffuse, dense leuko-araiosis extending from periventricular areas to the deep white matter.[29] In addition, hyperintensities located in the vascular centrencephalon, in the centrum semiovale, in the watershed areas, and close to the ventricles may have different profiles of causation. Besides the arteriolar changes and their consequences, changes in venous drainage and changes in cerebrospinal fluid hydrodynamics may play a role.[29]

White matter has limited ways to react to different pathogenetic factors. These include loss of myelin and oligodendrocytes, loss of axons, astrocytic gliosis, widening of cell spaces, widening of perivascular spaces, extra- and intracellular edema, and focal changes including infarcts, lacunae, vascular ectasia, and cysts.[29,34,35] Leuko-araiosis seen on CT or MR is often an endstage due to a variety of pathogenetic mechanisms. Thus, leuko-araiosis should not be used as a synonym for ischemic change, as it may be caused by a number of other conditions (Table 6).[29,34,107]

ACTION NEEDED: RECOGNIZE THE BRAIN AT RISK!

Despite the uncertainties related to the concept and causes of vascular dementia, much can be done. One important prerequisite is that we abandon the use of dementia as an identifier. Instead, the focus should be early changes in person's cognitive abilities, personality, and mood which may signal the prelude of early dementia. Thus, we should examine the brains at risk for vascular damage and at risk for dementia. A practical clinical approach to vascular risk factors, stroke, and dementia is outlined in Table 7. The effects of stroke prevention have been established to some extent.[80,115] However, we do not yet know precisely if these interventions will prevent and slow the progression of cognitive impairment or the dementia state. Prospective clinical studies are needed to solve these questions. Meanwhile, the proposed approach could well be adopted.

TABLE 6. Causes of Patchy or Diffuse White Matter Changes (Leuko-Araiosis) on Brain Imaging Other Than Those Related to Vascular Dementia

Leukodystrophies with defective myelination	Brain irradiation and/or methotrexate medication
Adrenoleukodystrophy	
Globoid cell leukodystrophy	Encephalitides
Metachromatic leukodystrophy	Subacute sclerosing panencephalitis
	Progressive multifocal leukoencephalopathy
Hemodynamic disorders	HIV encephalopathy
Neonatal anoxia	Other infections
Hypoxia-ischemia	
Cardiopulmonary arrest	Arteriopathies
	Systemic lupus erythematosus
Hypertensive encephalopathy	Temporal arteritis
	Other inflammatory and noninflammatory
Subarachnoid hemorrhage	arteriopathies
Arteriovenous malformations	Neurosarcoidosis
Cerebral amyloid angiopathy	Multiple sclerosis
Cerebral venous thrombosis	Alzheimer's disease
Polycythemia	Creutzfeldt-Jakob disease
Cerebral edema	Other conditions
Recent stroke	Hepatic coma
Trauma	Uremia
Metastases	Hypoglycemia
	Gangliosidoses
Hydrocephalus	Mucopolysaccharidoses
Obstructive	Muscular dystrophy
Normal-pressure hydrocephalus	

TABLE 7.   Vascular Risk Factors for Stroke and Dementia: A Practical Approach

Factor	Possible Action Needed
Brain at risk of vascular damage	
Age	—
Race	—
Smoking	Stop smoking.
Arterial hypertension	Diagnose, treat.
Arterial hypotension	Diagnose: orthostatic test, 24-hour monitoring. Often iatrogenic side effect!
Hyperlipidemia	In early, younger cases, treat.
Cardiac diseases, atrial fibrillation	Diagnose. Anticoagulation.
Cardiac surgery	Calcium blockers (?)
Brain at risk of dementia	
Transient ischemic attack	Diagnose cause/mechanism.
Stroke	Aspirin, ticlopidine, anticoagulation, carotid endarterectomy.
"Silent cerebral infarcts"	Action as in stroke patients
Mild cognitive deficits	Screen, diagnose.
Brain at Dementia State and Risk of Progression	
Etiologic diagnosis	Diagnose, treat. Especially the potentially treatable conditions

Types of vascular lesions:
    Large-artery disease
    Cardiac embolic
    Small vessels disease
	Diagnose and treat according to cause: aspirin, ticlopidine, anticoagulation, carotid endarterectomy

Secondary factors affecting the cognitive abilities
    Depression
    Metabolic disorders
    Alcohol
    Medication
    Sleep disorders
	Diagnose, treat, avoid.

ACKNOWLEDGMENTS

Dr. T. Erkinjuntti is supported by the Paavo Nurmi Foundation, Helsinki, Finland. Dr. Vladimir C. Hachinski is a career investigator with the Heart and Stroke Foundation of Ontario, Canada.

REFERENCES

1. Adams JH, Brierley JB, Connor RCJ: The effects of systemic hypotension upon the human brain: Clinical and neuropathological observations in 11 cases. Brain 89:235–268, 1966.
2. Aharon-Peretz J, Cummings JL, Hill A: Vascular dementia and dementia of the Alzheimer type: Cognition, ventricular size, and leuko-araiosis. Arch Neurol 45:719–721, 1988.
3. Alafuzoff I: Histopathological and immunocytochemical studies in age-associated dementias [Dissertation] Umeå, Sweden, Umeå University, 1985.
4. Anonymous. Cardiogenic dementia. Lancet i:27–28, 1977.
5. American Psychiatric Association: Diagnostic and Statistical Manual of Mental Disorders (DSM-III), 3rd ed. Washington, DC, American Psychiatric Association, 1980.
6. American Psychiatric Association: Diagnostic and Statistcal Manual of Mental Disorders (DSM-III-R), 3rd ed, revised. Washington, DC, American Psychiatric Association, 1987.
7. Babikian V, Ropper AH: Binswanger's disease: A review. Stroke 18:2–12, 1987.
8. Baron JC, D'Antona R, Pantano P, et al: Effects of thalamic stroke on energy metabolism of the cerebral cortex. Brain 109:1243–1259, 1986.

9. Benson DF, Cummings JL, Tsai SY: Angular gyrus syndrome simulating Alzheimer's disease. Arch Neurol 39:616–620, 1982.

10. Bolla-Wilson K, Robinson RG, Starkstein SE, et al: Lateralization of dementia of depression in stroke patients. Am J Psychiatry 146:627–637, 1989.

11. Bousser MG: Les conceptions actuelles des démences artériopathiques. Encephale 3:357–372, 1977.

12. Burger PC, Burch JG, Kunze U: Subcortical arteriosclerotic encephalopathy (Binswanger's disease): A vascular etiology of dementia. Stroke 7:626–631, 1976.

13. CETF: Cardiogenic Brain Embolism: The Second Report of the Cerebral Embolism Task Force. Arch Neurol 46:727–743, 1989.

14. Chui HC, Victoroff JI, Margolin D, et al: Criteria for the diagnosis of ischemic vascular dementia proposed by the State of California Alzheimer's Disease and Treatment Centers. Neurology 42:473–480, 1992.

15. Cosgrove CR, Leblanc R, Meagher-Villemure K, Ethier R: Cerebral amyloid angiopathy. Neurology 35:625–631, 1985.

16. Cummings JL: Subcortical dementia as a manifestation of cerebrovascular disease. New Iss Neurosci 1992 (in press).

17. Cummings JL, Benson DF (eds): Dementia: A Clinical Approach, 2nd ed. Stoneham, MA, Butterworth-Heinemann, 1992.

18. Cummings JL, Tomiyasu U, Read S, Benson DF: Amnesia with hippocampal lesions after cardiopulmonary arrest. Neurology 34:679–681, 1984.

19. DelSer T, Bermejo F, Portera A, et al: Vascular dementia: A clinicopathological study. J Neurol Neurosurg Psychiatry 96:1–17, 1990.

20. DeReuck J, Crevits L, DeCoster W, et al: Pathogenesis of Binswanger chronic progressive subcortical encephalopathy. Neurology 30:920–928, 1980.

21. DeReuck J, Schaumburg HH: Periventricular atherosclerotic leukoencephalopathy. Neurology 22:1094–1097, 1972.

22. DeReuck J, Sieben G, DeCoster W, VanderEecken H: Dementia and confusional state in patients with cerebral infarcts: A clinicopathological study. Eur Neurol 21:94–97, 1982.

23. Diaz F, Merskey H, Hachinski VC, et al: Improved recognition of leuko-araiosis and cognitive impairment in Alzheimer's disease. Arch Neurol 48:1022–1025, 1991.

24. Easton JD, Hart RG, Sherman DG, Kaste M (eds): Diagnosis and management of ischemic stroke: Part 1. Threatened stroke and its management. Curr Probl Cardiol 1–76, 1983.

25. Erkinjuntti T: Differential diagnosis between Alzheimer's disease and vascular dementia: Evaluation of common clinical methods. Acta Neurol Scand 76:433–442, 1987.

26. Erkinjuntti T: Types of multi-infarct dementia. Acta Neurol Scand 75:391–399, 1987.

27. Erkinjuntti T: Dementia: Clinical diagnosis and differential diagnosis, with special reference to multi-infarct dementia [Dissertation]. Helsinki, University of Helsinki, 1988.

28. Erkinjuntti T: Clinical diagnosis and differential diagnosis of multi-infarct dementia. Rec Adv Cardiovasc Dis 11(suppl 1):35–47, 1990.

29. Erkinjuntti T, Hachinski VC: Rethinking vascular dementia. Cerebrovasc Dis 1992 (in press).

30. Erkinjuntti T, Haltia M, Palo J, et al: Accuracy of the clinical diagnosis of vascular dementia: A prospective clinical and post-mortem neuropathological study. J Neurol Neurosurg Psychiatry 51:1037–1044, 1988.

31. Erkinjuntti T, Ketonen L, Sulkava R, et al: Do white matter changes on MRI and CT differentiate vascular dementia from Alzheimer's disease? J Neurol Neurosurg Psychiatry 50:37–42, 1987.

32. Erkinjuntti T, Ketonen L, Sulkava R, et al: CT in the differential diagnosis between Alzheimer's disease and vascular dementia. Acta Neurol Scand 75:262–270, 1987.

33. Erkinjuntti T, Sipponen JT, Iivanainen M, et al: Cerebral NMR and CT imaging in dementia. J Comput Assist Tomogr 8:614–618, 1984.

34. Erkinjuntti T, Sulkava R: Brain imaging and diagnosis of dementia. In Gottfries CG, Levy R, Clinke G, Tritsmans L (eds): Diagnostic and Therapeutic Assessments in Alzheimer's Disease. Guildford, Wrighton Biomedical Publishing Ltd, 1991, pp 17–31.

35. Erkinjuntti T, Sulkava R: Diagnosis of multi-infarct dementia. Alzheimer Dis Assoc Dis 5:112–121, 1991.

36. Erkinjuntti T, Sulkava R, Hachinski VC: Diagnostic assessments and criteria for memory disorders in clinical drug trials. In Canal N, Hachinski VC, McKhann G (eds): Guidelines for Drug Trials in Memory Disorders. New York, Raven Press, 1992.

37. Erkinjuntti T, Sulkava R, Palo J, Ketonen L: White matter low attenuation on CT in Alzheimer's disease. Arch Gerontol Geriatr 8:95–104, 1989.

38. Feeney DM, Baron J-C: Diaschisis. Stroke 17:817–830, 1986.

39. Feigin I, Popoff N: Neuropathological changes late in cerebral edema: The relationship to trauma, hypertensive disease and Binswanger's encephalopathy. J Neuropathol Exp Neurol 22:500–511, 1963.

40. Feinberg T, Goodman B: Affective illness, dementia, and pseudodementia. J Clin Psychiatry 45:99–103, 1984.

41. Fisher CM: Lacunar strokes and infarcts: A review. Neurology 32:871–876, 1982.

42. Folstein MF, Folstein SE, McHugh PR: "Mini-mental State": A practical method for grading the cognitive state of patients for the clinician. J Psychiatr Res 12:189–198, 1975.

43. Frackowiak RSJ, Pozzilli IC, Legg NJ, et al: Regional cerebral oxygen supply and utilization in dementia: A clinical and physiological study with oxygen-15 and positron tomography. Brain 104:753–778, 1981.

44. Fukuda H, Kobayashi S, Okada K, Tsunematsu T: Frontal white matter lesions and dementia in lacunar infarction. Stroke 21:1143–1149, 1990.

45. Graff-Radford NR, Eslinger PJ, Damasio AR, Yamada T: Nonhemorrhagic infarction of the thalamus: Behavioral, anatomic, and physiologic correlates. Neurology 34:14–23, 1984.

46. Gray F, Dubas F, Roullet E, Escourelle R: Leukoencephalopathy in diffuse hemorrhagic cerebral amyloid angiopathy. Ann Neurol 18:54–59, 1985.

47. Guberman A, Stuss D: The syndrome of bilateral paramedian thalamic infarction. Neurology 33:540–546, 1983.

48. Gudmundsson S, Hallgrimsson J, Jonasson TA, Bjarnason O: Hereditary cerebral haemorrhage with amyloidosis. Brain 95:387–404, 1972.

49. Hachinski VC, Iliff LD, Zilhka E, et al: Cerebral blood flow in dementia. Arch Neurol 32:632–637, 1975.

50. Hachinski VC, Lassen NA, Marshall J: Multi-infarct dementia: A cause of mental deterioration in the elderly. Lancet ii:207–210, 1974.

51. Hachinski VC, Potter P, Merskey H: Leuko-araiosis. Arch Neurol 44:21–23, 1987.

52. Hershey LA, Modic MT, Greenough PG, Jaffe DF: Magnetic resonance imaging in vascular dementia. Neurology 37:29–36, 1987.

53. Hollander E, Mohs RC, Davis KL: Antemortem markers of Alzheimer's disease. Neurobiol Aging 7:367–387, 1986.

54. Inzitari D, Diaz F, Fox A, et al: Vascular risk factors and leuko-araiosis. Arch Neurol 44:42–47, 1987.

55. Iqbal K: Prevalence and neurobiology of Alzheimer's disease: Some highlights. In Iqbal K, McLachlan DRC, Winblad B, Wisniewski HM (eds): Alzheimer's Disease: Basic Mechanisms, Diagnosis and Therapeutic Strategies. Chichester, John Wiley & Sons, 1991.

56. Ishii N, Nishihara Y, Imamura T: Why do frontal lobe symptoms predominate in vascular dementia with lacunes? Neurology 36:340–345, 1986.

57. Jorgensen L, Torvik A: Ischaemic cerebrovascular diseases in an autopsy series: Part 1. Prevalence, location and predisposing factors in verified thrombo-embolic occlusions, and their significance in the pathogenesis of cerebral infarction. J Neurol Sci 3:490–509, 1966.

58. Kase CS, Wolf PA, Chodosh EH, et al: Prevalence of silent stroke in patients presenting with initial stroke: The Framingham Study. Stroke 20:850–852, 1989.

59. Kase CS, Wolf PA, Kelly-Hayes M, et al: Intellectual decline following stroke: The Framingham study. Neurology 37:11, 1987.

60. Kataoka K, Hayakawa T, Kuroda R, et al: Cholinergic deafferentation after focal cerebral infarct in rats. Stroke 22:1291–1296, 1991.

61. Katzman R: Differential diagnosis of dementing illnesses. Neurol Clin 4:329–339, 1986.

62. Kirshner HS (ed): Behavioral Neurology. A Practical Approach. New York, Churchill Livingstone, 1986.

63. Kitagawa Y, Meyer JS, Tachibana H, et al: CT-CBF correlations of cognitive deficits in multi-infarct dementia. Stroke 15:1000–1009, 1984.

64. Kobari M, Meyer JS, Ichijo M, Oravez WT: Leukoaraiosis: Correlation of MR and CT findings with blood flow, atrophy, and cognition. AJNR 11:273–281, 1990.

65. Kotila M, Waltimo O, Niemi M-L, Laaksonen R: Dementia after stroke. Eur Neurol 25:134–140, 1986.

66. Lassen NA: Incomplete cerebral infarction—Focal incomplete ischemic tissue necrosis not leading to emollision. Stroke 13:522–523, 1982.

67. Lipowski ZJ (ed): Delirium. Springfield, IL, Charles C Thomas, 1980.

68. Lipowski ZJ: Delirium in the elderly patient. N Engl J Med 320:578–582, 1989.

69. Liu CK, Miller BL, Cummings JL, et al: A quantitative MRI study of vascular dementia. Neurology 42:138–143, 1992.

70. Loeb C, Gandolfo C, Bino G: Intellectual impairment and cerebral lesions in multiple cerebral infarcts: A clinical-computed tomography study. Stroke 19:560–565, 1988.
71. Loes DJ, Biller J, Yuh WTC, et al: Leukoencephalopathy in cerebral amyloid angiopathy: MR imaging in four cases. AJNR 11:485–488, 1990.
72. Mahler ME, Cummings JL: The behavioural neurology of multi-infarct dementia. Alzheimer Dis Assoc Dis 5:122–130, 1991.
73. Mas J-L, Bousser M-G, Lacombe C, Agar N: Hyperlipidemic dementia. Neurology 35:1385–1387, 1985.
74. McEvoy JP: Organic brain syndromes. Ann Intern Med 95:212–220, 1981.
75. McKhann G, Drachman D, Folstein M, et al: Clinical diagnosis of Alzheimer's disease: Report of the NINCDS-ADRDA Work Group under the auspices of Department of Health and Human Services Task Force on Alzheimer's Disease. Neurology 34:939–944, 1984.
76. Moody DM, Bell MA, Challa VR: Features of the cerebral vascular pattern that predict vulnerability to perfusion or oxygenation deficiency: An anatomical study. AJNR 11:431–439, 1990.
77. Mueller J, Hotson JR, Langston JW: Hyperviscosity-induced dementia. Neurology 33:101–103, 1983.
78. Munoz DG: The pathological basis of multi-infarct dementia. Alzheimer Dis Assoc Dis 5:77–90, 1991.
79. NINCDS. National Institute of Neurological Communications Disorders and Stroke: A classification and outline of cerebrovascular diseases: II. Stroke 6:564–616, 1975.
80. Norris JW, Hachinski VC: Stroke prevention: Past, present, and future. In Norris JW, Hachinski VC (eds): Prevention of Stroke. New York, Springer-Verlag, 1991, pp 1–15.
81. Okeda R: Morphometrische Vergleichsuntersuchungen an Hirnarterien bei Binswangerscher Encephalopathie und Hochdruckencephalopathie. Acta Neuropathol (Berl) 26:23–43, 1973.
82. Olszewski J: Subcortical arteriosclerotic encephalopathy. World Neurol 3:359–375, 1962.
83. Pentschew A: Die granuläre Atrophie der Grosshirnrinde. Arch Psychiat Nervenkr 101:80–136, 1933.
84. Robinson RG, Bolla-Wilson K, Kaplan E, et al: Depression influences intellectual impairment in stroke patients. Br J Psychiatry 148:541–547, 1986.
85. Rocca WA, Amaducci LA, Schoenberg BS: Epidemiology of clinically diagnosed Alzheimer's disease. Ann Neurol 19:415–424, 1986.
86. Roman GC: Senile dementia of the Binswanger type: A vascular form of dementia in the elderly. JAMA 258:1782–1788, 1987.
87. Roman GC, Tatemichi TK, Erkinjuntti T, et al: Vascular dementia: Diagnostic criteria for research studies: Report of the NINDS-AIREN International Work Group. Neurology 1992 (in press).
88. Rosen WG, Terry RD, Fuld PA, et al: Pathological verification of ischemic score in differentiation of dementias. Ann Neurol 7:486–488, 1980.
89. Roth M, Huppert FA, Tym E, Mountjoy CO (eds): CAMDEX: The Cambridge Examination for Mental Disorders of the Elderly. Cambridge, UK, Cambridge University Press, 1988.
90. Rothschild D: Neuropathologic changes in arteriosclerotic psychoses and their psychiatric significance. Arch Neurol Psychiatry 48:417–436, 1942.
91. Signoret J-L: Memory and amnesias. In Mesulam M-m (ed): Contemporary Neurology: Principles of Behavioral Neurology, 3rd ed. Philadelphia, FA Davis, 1987, pp 169–192.
92. Sinyor D, Jacques P, Kaloupek DG, et al: Post-stroke depression and lesion location: An attempted replication. Brain 109:537–546, 1986.
93. Starkstein SE, Robinson RG: Affective disorders and cerebral vascular disease. Br J Psychiatry 154:170–182, 1989.
94. Stuss DT, Benson DF: The Frontal Lobes. New York, Raven Press, 1986.
95. Stuss DT, Cummings JL: Subcortical vascular dementias. In Cummings JL (ed): Subcortical Dementia. New York, Oxford University Press, 1990, pp 145–163.
96. Sulkava R, Erkinjuntti T: Vascular dementia due to cardiac arrhythmias and systemic hypotension. Acta Neurol Scand 76:123–128, 1987.
97. Sulkava R, Haltia M, Paetau A, et al: Accuracy of clinical diagnosis in primary degenerative dementia: Correlation with neuropathological findings. J Neurol Neurosurg Psychiatry 46:9–13, 1983.
98. Tanaka Y, Tanaka O, Mizuno Y, Yoshida M: A radiologic study of dynamic processes in lacunar dementia. Stroke 20:1488–1493, 1989.
99. Tanzi RE, Gusella JF, Watkins PC, et al: Amyloid beta protein gene: cDNA, mRNA distribution, and gene linkage near the Alzheimer locus. Science 235:880–884, 1987.

100. Tatemichi TK: How acute brain failure becomes chronic: A view of the mechanisms and syndromes of dementia related to stroke. Neurology 40:1652–1659, 1990.
101. Tatemichi TK, Desmond DW, Mayeux R, et al: Dementia after stroke: Baseline frequency, risks, and clinical features in a hospitalized cohort. Neurology 42:1185–1193, 1992.
102. Tatemichi TK, Desmond DW, Paik M, et al: The mini-mental state examination as a screen for dementia following stroke (abstract). J Clin Exp Neuropsychol 13:419, 1991.
103. Tatemichi TK, Foulkes MA, Mohr JP, et al: Dementia in stroke survivors in the stroke data bank cohort: Prevalence, incidence, risk factors, and computed tomographic findings. Stroke 21:858–866, 1990.
104. Tomlinson BE, Blessed G, Roth M: Observations on the brains of non-demented old people. J Neurol Sci 7:331–356, 1968.
105. Tomlinson BE, Blessed G, Roth M: Observations on the brains of demented old people. J Neurol Sci 11:205–242, 1970.
106. Torvik A: The pathogenesis of watershed infarcts in the brain. Stroke 15:221–223, 1984.
107. Valentine AR, Moseley IF, Kendall BE: White matter abnormality in cerebral atrophy: Clinicoradiological correlations. J Neurol Neurosurg Psychiatry 43:139–142, 1980.
108. Wade JPH, Mirsen TR, Hachinski VC, et al: The clinical diagnosis of Alzheimer's disease. Arch Neurol 44:24–29, 1987.
109. Wallin A: (A consensus on dementia diseases: 1. Classification and investigation.) Lakartidningen 87:3856–3865, 1990.
110. Wallin A, Blennow K: The pathogenetic basis of multi-infarct dementia. Alzheimer Dis Assoc Dis 5:91–102, 1991.
111. Walsh K (ed): Neuropsychology: A Clinical Approach, 2nd ed. London, Churchill Livingstone, 1987.
112. Wells CE: Pseudodementia. Am J Psychiatry 136:895–900, 1979.
113. World Health Organization: Manual of the International Statistical Classification of Diseases, Injuries and Causes of Death, 9th Revision, vol 1. Geneva, WHO, 1977.
114. World Health Organization: Mental, behavioural and developmental disorders. In: The International Classification of Diseases, 10th Revision (ICD-10). Geneva, WHO, 1989, pp 25–31. (MNH/MEP/87.1).
115. Wolf PA, Belanger AJ, D'Agostino RB: Management of risk factors. Neurol Clin 10:177–191, 1992.
116. Woods RT: Activities of daily living in dementia. In Gottfies CG, Levy R, Clincke G, Tritsmans L (eds): Diagnostic and Therapeutic Assessments in Alzheimer's Disease. Petersfield, Wrighton Biomedical Publ, 1991, pp 71–80.
117. Yates PO: Vascular diseases of the central nervous system. In Blackwood V, Corcellis JAN (eds): Greenfield's Neuropathology, 3rd ed. London, Edward Arnold Ltd, 1976, pp 86–147.
118. Ylikoski R, Erkinjuntti T, Sulkava R, et al: Correlation for age, education and other demographic variables in the use of Mini-mental state examination in Finland. Acta Neurol Scand 85:391–396, 1992.

COLLEEN CHURCHILL, BSW, MSW

14. SOCIAL PROBLEMS POST STROKE

From the Rehabilitation Unit
University Hospital
London, Ontario
Canada

Reprint requests to:
Colleen Churchill, BSW, MSW
Rehabilitation Unit
University Hospital
339 Windermere Road
London, Ontario N6A 5A5
Canada

A stroke is characterized by rapidly developing signs of focal cerebral dysfunction of vascular origin lasting more than 24 hours. The term *stroke* includes infarcts due to athero-thrombosis or emboli as well as intracerebral and subarachnoid hemorrhages. The annual incidence of stroke is approximately 1 to 2 per 1000 persons, with up to half a million new cases in the United States annually.[36,58] Stroke survivors live an average of 7 years after stroke.[3,34] There are an estimated 1.7 million stroke survivors in the United States[58]; of these, 15% require long-term institutional care,[27] while 70% are left with a significant functional disability in the realms of mobility, activities of daily living, social integration, and gainful employment.[28]

What is often not appreciated about a stroke is that in addition to the effect it has on the stroke victim, it also has a significant effect on the immediate family. The management of stroke patients too often focuses on the acute care phase, when patients receive full and comprehensive treatment. Later sequelae, in particular psychosocial problems, are frequently downplayed by health care professionals. As a result, the psychological and social consequences of stroke often do not receive appropriate attention.

Feibel et al.[22] reviewed 85 patients with an acute stroke within 6 months after discharge. Among these 85 patients, there was a significant incidence of psychosocial problems including social isolation, decreased community involvement, new economic strain, disruption of family functioning, major depression, anxiety, and anger (Table 1). Major depression was present in over one-third of patients but was rarely treated. None of the patients utilized the existing

TABLE 1. Psychosocial Problems Following Discharge After Stroke*

Social isolation	56%
Decreased community involvement	43%
Economic strain causing a lifestyle alteration	46%
Disruption of family functioning	52%
Major depression	37%
Anxiety/anger	32%

* Data from Feibel et al.[22]

stroke support groups or psychological or family services. This study demonstrated the need for careful follow-up of stroke patients after discharge and the need for ongoing psychosocial support on entering the community. The psychological problems encountered by stroke patients is discussed in some detail in the previous chapter. This chapter will focus on family and social issues which further complicate stroke patients over the long term.

FAMILY PROBLEMS

The effects of a stroke on the patient's family are not often fully appreciated. A stroke in one family member inevitably affects the entire well-being of the family unit. Fortunately, contrary to popular belief, in our experience most families are supportive. Reasons for refusal to take the patient home after a stroke include the fact that the family relationship was poor prior to the stroke, there are major barriers to home care (e.g., spouse with poor health), and the family was disenchanted with previous home support or lack of community resources.

CAREGIVER'S STRESS

The brunt of the long-term care of the stroke survivor falls onto family caregivers and, in particular, one primary caregiver. Silverstone and Horowitz,[44] in their review on caregiving provided to frail elderly individuals, pointed out that there is no family caregiving system; rather, one family member occupies the role of primary caregiver and is the primary provider of direct care. The primary caregiver will usually be the spouse. Otherwise, the care of the stroke survivor will fall onto a daughter or son. Only in the absence of a spouse or child do other relatives become primary caregivers. Friends and neighbors only occasionally serve as the primary caregiver. Apart from the primary caregiver, other family members generally play only minor roles.[30,51] Brocklehurst et al.[10] noted that although friends and relatives provide the primary caregiver with significant support shortly after discharge home (in the form of assistance with transferring and supervising the stroke patient), there was little help forthcoming from these individuals 1 year after the stroke. If new care demands develop, it is the family (generally the primary caregiver) who must meet those demands.[44]

When the care demands of the stroke survivor become overwhelming, institutionalization may follow. Placement of elderly individuals in a chronic care facility occurs more often because of deterioration of the caregiver's health or decompensation in the face of continuous stress than it does because of increased care requirements.[8,14,30]

ADJUSTMENT PROBLEMS FOR CAREGIVERS

Family members providing care for stroke victims face their own adjustment problems, as their own personal needs are often sacrificed to meet the needs of the stroke survivor. In the case of stroke, Silverstone and Horowitz[44] noted that families often find themselves in a position of having to provide skilled nursing assistance for which they are not experienced and for which they have received no training. They often have no choice but to learn by trial and error.[44] Family roles often become reversed, as other family members struggle to fill the void left by the stroke survivor. For instance, the wife of a stroke victim may have to perform tasks previously performed by her husband. A child may need to become a parent to his or her parents. Mobility may be limited and traveling becomes a difficult chore. Sanford[41] and Brocklehurst et al.[10] both noted that lifting problems were not tolerated well by caregivers. There are generally limited opportunities for rest, putting the primary caregiver under great stress.

Spouses provide the most extensive and comprehensive care, tolerating greater levels of disability than other caregivers; however, these individuals also report the highest level of stress when compared to other caregivers.[44,52] Unfortunately, the needs of other family members may be compromised over a preoccupation with the stroke victim's needs. One study conducted 2 to 3 years after the stroke found that 36% of stroke victims and 32% of primary caregivers had not adjusted to the stroke[29]; it did not always follow that if the stroke survivor had adjusted, the primary caregiver had also done so.

Coughlan and Humphreys,[15] in their study of stroke survivors and spouses 3 to 8 years after the stroke, noted that 41% of patients and 32% of spouses reported much less enjoyment of life. Patients' loss of enjoyment was attributed primarily to residual disabilities, loss of independence, and lack of occupation. For spouses, the chief causes of loss of enjoyment were loss of companionship, increased domestic responsibility, and interference with leisure and social activities. Webster and Newhoff[56] noted that stroke patients experienced a variety of common problems, including having to assume duties formerly assigned to the spouse, lack of people to confide in or talk to, and lack of personal time alone.

Caregivers of stroke survivors suffer higher rates of depression and greater rates of deterioration in their own health.[35] Caregivers at greatest risk of ongoing depression are the spouses of younger, more severely impaired patients with lower household incomes, smaller social networks with whom they visit frequently, and lower levels of future optimism and expectation.[52] Adjustment by the caregiver, generally the spouse, is not related to the severity of the patient's disability in terms of paralysis, level of activities of daily living functioning, or severity of aphasia, although caregivers of aphasics in general have more difficulty adjusting.[35] Kinsella and Duffy[35] suggest that adjustment by the caregiver is most often influenced by the presence or absence of behavioral problems in the stroke survivor. In contrast, Evans and Northwood[19] reported that the burden of caregivers is associated more with changes in stability and family support than with patient behavior problems. Mykyta[40] identified communication difficulties, altered role relations, overprotection, and guilt as common problems for the primary caregivers of stroke patients.

Stroker[50] studied the impact of a disabled family member on the significant other. Although this study was of a descriptive nature and consisted of a very small sample size, their study revealed that subjects were coping relatively well. In this study, subjects had some difficulty with feeling overprotective and overcommitted to the disabled family member.

Wade et al.[55] studied the effects of living with and looking after survivors of a stroke in a 2-year longitudinal study on a community sample of patients. The purpose of the study was to determine the effects of stress on the mood of the primary caregiver. Their study revealed that increased anxiety was the most commonly reported change 6 months after the stroke. Significant depression was also seen in 11 to 13% of caregivers over the first 2 years after the stroke.

Recent research has been optimistic regarding the impact of stroke and disability on family support or caregivers. Bishop et al.[6] indicated that couples in a stroke sample did not differ from couples in a matched community sample on level of morale, family functioning, or subjective health rating. Unks[53] found that elderly wives of stroke patients had morale scores that were comparable with those of the general public. Silliman et al.[43] reported that relatives felt better about themselves because they had learned to manage the illness. MacKay and Niac[39] reported that a majority of families reported a closer relationship with the patient. In their study, they described the majority of their stroke sample as moderately happy and confident.

It is important to note that these recent studies indicate that good family functioning is possible following a stroke in one of its members. However, stroke survivors and families will continue to have real problems with practical concerns, such as transportation and socialization. There is some evidence that as time progresses following the stroke, caregivers may become less well adjusted.[35]

FAMILY ADJUSTMENT STAGES

Stages of family adjustment after a severe disability affecting a family member have been identified (Table 2).[7,9,29] Silverstone and Horowitz[44] noted that when a healthy, elderly individual suddenly becomes disabled, a severe family crisis ensues. Denial among family members that the neurologic deficits may be permanent is common in the first few months following a stroke. Initial relief over survival and hope for a complete recovery eventual turn to feelings of despair when the hoped for recovery fails to take place. At this point, a spouse or other caregiver may be able to express anger or resentment toward the stroke victim. However, as

TABLE 2. Stages of Family Adjustment to Severe Disability

Acute
   Shock and confusion
   Relief that the patient did not die
   High anxiety

Rehabilitation/treatment
   Denial of permanence of disability
   High expectations of recovery
   Often family members express helplessness and anxiety by questioning the competence of
     care; however, they are reluctant to openly criticize.
   Fears about future
   Grieving

Acceptance of disability
   Full acceptance of permanence of the disability
   Family attitude changes to actively seeking means to better accommodate to changes in the
     patient-family system.
   Information previously denied or rejected is now readily accepted.
   Feelings of frustration, despair, and depression
   Hidden and guilt-ridden feelings of anger and hostility can now be expressed toward the
     patient.

time progresses, family members come to accept or learn to cope with the permanence of the disability.

BEHAVIORAL ISSUES

Brocklehurst et al.[10] noted that the major problems for primary caregivers were related to the stroke survivor's behavior—the need for constant supervision and loss of sleep due to nocturnal restlessness. Coughlin and Humphreys[15] found that personality changes were noted by the caregiver in two out of three stroke survivors 3 to 8 years after the stroke. The change was for the better in 5%, for the worst in 82%, and not clear in 13%. The main changes reported in their study were irritability and loss of self-control, lower frustration tolerance, emotional lability, self-centeredness, and reduced initiative. Marked personality changes were reported in one-quarter of the patients.[15]

EDUCATION AND COUNSELING FOR CAREGIVERS

Limited family education and counseling given in the early stages following a stroke result in significantly better stroke knowledge, problem-solving, communication, and global family functioning when compared to controls.[21] With time, a new equilibrium is reached as the family adjusts roles to accommodate the changed capabilities of the disabled family member. Unfortunately, this new equilibrium may take years to establish, and in some cases the family decompensates under the burden of care required by stroke survivors. Family coping and reintegration are often dependent upon how well family members communicate and problem-solve.[21]

Families of stroke patients may need considerable support for many years after the stroke.[29] Holbrook[29] points out that stroke survivors and their families need continuity of care so that when new problems develop, they will know who to turn to for help.

QUALITY OF LIFE AFTER STROKE

Having a stroke is an unexpected event, and the amount of recovery is unpredictable. Stroke survivors returning home are frequently faced with one difficult task after another, the majority of which were simple or automatic for them to perform prior to the stroke. The end result is that the stroke patient often experiences fear and anxiety regarding the future.

Goodstein[26] reported that the psychological and social impact of stroke on the individual is devastating. Ahlsio et al.,[1] in their study of disablement and quality of life following stroke, found that stroke survivors who still suffered from tiredness, memory difficulties, impairment of motor function, and vertigo had limited opportunities for leisure and social functions. They also found that subjective measurement of quality of life failed to improve with time, even if independence and the ability to perform activities of daily living improved dramatically. Sjogren[46] suggested that life quality is closely related to leisure activities. He found that the stroke survivors' frequency of active leisure participation decreased following their stroke, and these individuals became passively discontented.

Lawrence and Christie[38] studied 45 people who had suffered a stroke 3 years previously. The patients were interviewed along with their families and close friends. They found that the stroke had devastated many people's lives: patients and caregivers ceased work prematurely, their interpersonal relationships deteriorated, and over 70% viewed their future with uncertainty or gloom. Physical disability in itself was less important than individuals' responses to their disability; inappropriate and dysfunctional responses were present in over half the sample. Astrom et al.[2] concluded that major depression early after stroke, functional disability, and an impaired social network interacted to reduce life satisfaction for long-term survivors of stroke.

From these studies it becomes apparent that quality of life and leisure activities diminish to a considerable degree following a stroke. These studies indicate the need for a greater awareness about how a stroke affects a person's perceived quality of life.

SOCIALIZATION

Lack of socialization is a common complaint of many stroke victims and their caregivers. Feibel and Springer[23] measured socialization by compiling five categories of social activities—work, hobbies/sports, pastimes, community activities, and socializing. Twenty-seven percent of stroke patients reported a reduction in socialization of at least two-thirds, whereas another 36% of patients reported a reduction of between one-third to two-thirds. Isaacs et al.[33] found that socialization is a key factor in adjustment. They reported that no patient went out by public transportation during the first 6 months. Also, of the 21 patients who they surveyed for 1 year, 1 was out of the house on more than 100 occasions, 11 went out between 10 and 100 times, and 9 went out less than 10 times or not at all. Holbrook[29] found that 72% of primary caregivers reported that the stroke had an adverse effect on their social life.

Physical disability itself appears to be the major factor leading to loss of socialization.[13,54] Although physical disabilities such as hemiplegia and urinary incontinence frequently limit social contacts, our experience is that self-consciousness about impaired mobility, communication problems, depression, or other sequelae of stroke frequently prevent stroke patients from resuming their previous social activities.

Hyman[32] reported that social reintegration was more problematic for women and for those with more education. It was speculated that this contrast between women and men may be due to differences in body image. Research has indicated a relationship between body image and feelings of stigma and outcome of physical rehabilitation.[32]

Labi et al.[37] found that many stroke survivors do not return to a normal social life, even after physical disability has ceased to be a serious obstacle. Their findings also indicated that stroke survivors who live alone are less likely than those who live in a family context to suffer decreased outside socialization. It is felt that family support is important initially but later may become overprotective to the detriment of the stroke survivor's long-term adjustment. The study by Astrom et al.[2] provides prospective data regarding the global situation in a population base sample of long-term survivors of stroke as well as information on the development of changes over time. Compared with the general elderly population, patients 3 years after a stroke had more psychiatric symptoms, lower functional ability, and a pronounced reduction of life satisfaction. Contacts with close family members were maintained over the 3 year follow-up period. However, contact with other relatives, friends, and neighbors declined early after the stroke and remained lower than in the general elderly population.

These studies reveal the importance of psychosocial intervention prior to a stroke survivor's discharge from hospital and the need for ongoing psychosocial intervention while in the community. Patient and family counseling in these areas may lessen some of these later difficulties. Fortunately, there has been greater emphasis placed on community resources for stroke victims (and their spouses) with senior centers, public transportation for the disabled, easier access to public places, and stroke clubs and groups, all of which aid in socialization.

FUNCTIONAL CONSEQUENCES

While stroke rehabilitation programs do not appear to influence neurologic or intrinsic recovery, they do increase the stroke survivors level of independence. Some 90% of patients undergoing intensive rehabilitation eventually return home.[45,47,48] Following a stroke, an individual may be unable to perform activities of daily living (dressing, grooming, bathing, and feeding), lack mobility skills (transfers, bed and wheelchair mobility, and ambulation), and be unable to communicate. These activities of daily living skills are often reacquired through exposure to an intensive rehabilitation environment designed to maximize the stroke patient's independence. Being able to transfer independently or pull up one's pants after toileting may seem like a mundane issue, but it is often the ability to perform these types of tasks which determines whether stroke survivors will be able to remain in their own homes or require institutionalization. The difference in quality of life to the individual stroke victim and eventual savings to society are obvious.

Rehabilitation nurses and therapists encourage the patient to dress, groom, and transfer themselves, even though it may take longer than if the attendant assisted them. Unfortunately, patients are frequently capable of performing activities in the hospital that they seem unable to carryover with at home[4]; this may occur because of depression and lack of motivation on the part of the patient and/or because the relatives find it easier to perform these tasks themselves.[29] Family members, in their attempts to be supportive, may make the patient dependent again by not allowing him or her to perform these activities themselves.[25] Families must be warned that their often good intentions may lead to deterioration in the stroke survivor's level of independence. Too often because of lack of resources and inadequate follow-up, these issues remain unresolved and many of the gains acquired through intensive rehabilitation efforts may be lost.

DRIVING

Resumption of driving often represents the final step toward independence and reintegration into the community. However, driving a car is one of the most complicated of learned skills, requiring good vision and intact reflex responses, rapid decision-making, and careful attentiveness. If one or more of these factors is impaired, then the individual's driving skills need to be retested or a decision made that the patient not drive. In the case of significant hemi-neglect or homonymous hemianopsia, patients should not be allowed to drive. A recent seizure is also a contraindication to driving. Ensuring the car has an automatic transmission and power steering and brakes makes driving easier and safer.

Zomeren et al.[60] in their review of acquired brain damage in driving reached the following conclusions:

1. About half of all subjects studied still held a valid driver's license;
2. Brain-damaged drivers could not, in general, be seen as risky drivers, although some individuals showed decreased driving skill and risky behavior in traffic; and

3. Statistics showed no increase in traffic violations or accidents in groups of neurologic patients with acquired brain lesions or disease.

Problems noted of brain-damaged drivers include visual-spatial impairment, impassivity, and poor judgment of traffic situations. If health professionals find it difficult to judge the patient's ability to return to driving or have concerns about their competence to drive, the patient must undergo a formal driving assessment. In the case of stroke patients, the driving assessment should take place with a specialized program that focuses on cognitive ability to operate a motor vehicle along with operational skills.

VOCATIONAL ISSUES

Vocational counseling should be considered for all patients employed at the time of their stroke. For those with significant deficits, the decisions to return to employment may need to be delayed for several months to allow maximum neurologic and functional recovery to occur. The remaining skills of the stroke survivor must be carefully measured against the demands of the particular job. Unfortunately, many stroke survivors are not successful in returning to work.

Coughlin and Humphreys[15] studied 170 surviving stroke patients 3 to 8 years after a stroke. All were under the age of 65 at the time of their stroke. Of those still under 65 years of age at follow-up, only 30% of the men were in paid employment, and the majority of those had reduced the number of hours worked or had changed the nature of their work. Of those women under 60 years of age at the time of follow-up, only 17% were in paid employment. Patients without hemiplegia were employed significantly more often (11 of 18, 61%) than those with left hemiplegia (9 of 32, 28%) or right hemiplegia (2 of 37, 5%).[1,5]

Howard et al.[31] studied 379 patients who were employed before cerebral infarction and living 1 year afterward. This study attempted to determine what factors influenced their return to work. They found age, occupation, degree of disability, race, and the hemisphere infarcted to be significant. Younger patients with less disability were more likely to return to work. Patients employed in professional managerial positions were more likely to return to work than patients in blue collar or farming positions.

Brooks et al.[11] found that only 29% of stroke survivors returned to work after a 7-year period. Isaacs et al.[33] studied 29 stroke survivors who were followed for 3 years or until they died. They reported that before admission, 11 stroke patients had been in fulltime employment and 8 had full household duties. After discharge, none returned to any form of employment, 1 returned to full household duties, and 2 to partial duties.

These studies all demonstrate that stroke survivors tend to not return to their previous employment. The inability to return to work frequently leads to financial and emotional concerns for stroke survivors and their family members.

It would appear obvious that the neurologic impairments following a stroke restrict the person's ability to return to work. Unfortunately, there is very little research as to which programs and techniques increase the likelihood of a stroke survivor's returning to the workforce. In the past, efforts have been made through neuropsychological evaluation, cognitive rehabilitation, physiotherapy, and psychological counseling to enhance the patient's ability to return to work. A relatively new approach to job retraining has been explored by Wehman et al.[57] This study of supportive employment found that this program allowed more individuals with strokes to return to work. Wehman et al.'s[57] concept of supported employment consists of intensive time-limited training and compensatory strategies provided at the job site, followed by extended assessment and support services to assist with job retention. Supportive employment requires further research to demonstrate its overall effectiveness in assisting stroke survivors' return to employment.

SOLUTIONS

There are no easy solutions to the social problems which develop following a stroke. Greater attention to these problems on the part of health professionals would benefit both patients and families in adjusting to these difficulties. It is always tempting to recommend increasing resources allocated to long-term stroke survivors in an attempt to deal with these problems. However, it is apparent that an improvement in outpatient services, day hospitals, maintenance therapy programs, long-term patient and family counseling, intermittent relief admissions or respite care, and a long-term multidisciplinary follow-up clinic would help to ease or alleviate many of the social problems that these individuals experience.

Continuity of care following discharge is essential. Patients need to have professionals available to serve as a resource if only for information, to help them deal with crises which develop. This is best done by the regional physicians and the original rehabilitation team. As well, community support groups are of great benefit in providing socialization. More research into the long-term impact of stroke on social functioning is needed.

ACKNOWLEDGMENT

Special acknowledgment is extended to Miss Sue Merritt and Mrs. Cheryl Hill for their secretarial support during the preparation of this manuscript.

REFERENCES

1. Ahlsio B, Britton M, Murray V, Theorell T: Disablement and quality of life after stroke. Stroke 15:886–890, 1984.
2. Astrom M, Asplund K, Astrom T: Psychosocial function and life satisfaction after stroke. Stroke 23:527–531, 1992.
3. Anderson TP, McClure WJ, Athelson G, et al: Stroke rehabilitation: Evaluation of its quality by assessing patient outcomes. Arch Phys Mcd Rehabil 59:170–175, 1978.
4. Andrews K, Stewart J: Stroke recovery: He can but does he. Rheum Rehabil 18:43–48, 1979.
5. Binder LM: Emotional problems after stroke. Stroke 15:174–177, 1984.
6. Bishop D, Epstein NB, Keitner G, et al: Stroke: Morale, family functioning, health status and functional capacity. Arch Phys Med Rehabil 67:84–87, 1986..
7. Bleiberg J: Psychological and neuropsychological factors in stroke management. In Kaplan PE, Cerullo LJ (eds): Stroke Rehabilitation. Stoneman, MA, Butterworth, 1986, pp 210–212.
8. Boxell J, McKercher G: Needs of caregivers of elderly attending day hospital. Can Fam Phys 36:45–49, 1990.
9. Bray GD: Reactive patterns in families of the severely disabled. Rehabil Counsel Bull (Mar):236–239, 1977.
10. Brocklehurst JC, Morris P, Andrews K, et al: Social effects of stroke. Soc Sci Med 15:35–39, 1981.
11. Brooks N, McKinlay W, Symington C, et al: Return to work within the first seven years after head injury. Brain Injury 1:5–19, 1987.
12. Callahan D: Families as caregivers: The limits of mortality. Arch Phys Med Rehabil 69:323–328, 1988.
13. Christie D: Aftermath of stroke: An epidemiological study in Melbourne, Australia. J Epidemiol Community Health 36:123–126, 1982.
14. Colerick EJ, George LK: Predictors of institutionalization among caregivers of patients with Alzheimers disease. J Am Geriatr Soc 34:493–498, 1986.

15. Coughlan AK, Humphreys M: Presenile stroke: Long-term outcome for patients and their families. Rheum Rehabil 21:115–122, 1982.
16. Doolittle N: Stroke recovery: Review of literature and suggestions for future research. J Neurosci Nurs (3):169–173, 1988.
17. Espmarch S: Stroke before 50: A follow-up study of vocational and psychological adjustment. Scand J Rehabil Med (Suppl 2):1–107, 1973.
18. Evans R, Bishop D, Matlock A: Family interaction and treatment adherence after stroke. Arch Phys Med Rehabil 68:513–517, 1987.
19. Evans RL, Northwood L: Social support needs in adjustment in stroke. Arch Phys Med Rehabil 64:61–64, 1987.
20. Evans RL, Miller RM: Psychosocial implications and treatment of stroke. Soc Casework: J Contemp Soc Work (Apr):242–247, 1984.
21. Evans RL, Matlock AL, Bishop DS, et al: Family interaction after stroke: Does counselling or education help? Stroke 19:1243–1249, 1988.
22. Feibel JH, Berks S, Joynt RJ: Unmet needs of stroke survivors. Neurology 29:592, 1979.
23. Feibel JH, Springer CJ: Depression and failure to resume social activities after stroke. Arch Phys Med Rehabil 63:276–278, 1982.
24. Fordyce WE: Behavioural methods in medical rehabilitation. Neurosci Biobehav Rev 5:391–396, 1981.
25. Garraway WM, Akhtar AJ, Hockey L, Prescott RJ: Management of acute stroke in the elderly: Follow-up of a controlled trial. BMJ 281:827–829, 1980.
26. Goodstein RK: Overview: Cerebrovascular accident and the hospitalized elderly—a multidimensional clinical problem. Am J Psychiatry 140:141–147, 1983.
27. Gresham GE, Phillips TF, Wolf PA, et al: Epidemiologic profile of long-term stroke disability: The Framingham study. Arch Phys Med Rehabil 60:487–491, 1979.
28. Gresham GE, Fitzpatrick TE, Wolf PA, McNamara PM, Kannel WB, Dawber TR: Residual disability in survivors of stroke: The Framingham study. N Engl J Med 293:954–956, 1985.
29. Holbrook M: Stroke and emotional outcome. J R Coll Phys Lond 16:100–104, 1982.
30. Horowitz A: Family caregiving to the frail elderly. Annu Rev Gerontol Geriat 5:194–246 and 249–282, 1985.
31. Howard G, Till JS, Toole JF, et al: Factors influencing return to work following cerebral infarction. JAMA (2):226–232, 1985.
32. Hyman MD: Stigma of stroke: Its effects on performance during and after rehabilitation. Geriatrics 26:132–141, 1971.
33. Isaacs B, Neville Y, Rushford I: The stricken: The social consequences of stroke. Age Aging 5:188–192, 1976.
34. Kannel WE, Wolf PA, Verter J: Risk factors for stroke. In Smith RR (ed): Stroke and the Extracranial Vessel. New York, Raven Press, 1984, pp 47–57.
35. Kinsella GJ, Duffy FP: Psychosocial readjustment in the spouses of aphasic patients. Scand J Rehabil Med 11:129–132, 1979.
36. Kistler JP, Ropper AH, Heros RC: Therapy of ischemic cerebral vascular disease due to atherothrombosis (second of two parts). N Engl J Med 311:100–105, 1984.
37. Labi M, Phillips P, Gresham G: Psychosocial disability in physically restored long-term stroke survivors. Arch Phys Med Rehabil 61:561–565, 1980.
38. Lawrence L, Christie D: Quality of life after stroke: A three year follow-up. Age Aging 8:167–172, 1979.
39. MacKay A, Niac BC: Strokes in the young and middle-aged: Consequences to the family and to society. J R Coll Phys Lond 13:106–112, 1979.
40. Mykyta LJ: Caring for relatives of stroke patients. Age Aging 5:87–90, 1976.
41. Sanford J: Tolerance of debility in elder dependents by supports at home: Its significance for hospital practice. BMJ 3:471–473, 1975.
42. Schulz R, Rompkins CA, Rau MT: A longitudinal study of the psychosocial impact of stroke on primary support persons. Psychol Aging 3:131–141, 1988.
43. Silliman RA, Fletcher RH, Earp JL, Wagner EH: Families of elderly stroke patients: Effects of home care. J Am Geriatr Soc 34:643–648, 1986.
44. Silverstone B, Horowitz A: Issues of social support: The family and home care. In Dunkel RE, Schmidley JW (eds): Stroke in the Elderly. New York, Springer, 1987, pp 169–185.
45. Sivenins J, Pyorala K, Heinonen OP, et al: The significance of intensity of rehabilitation of stroke—A controlled trial. Stroke 16:928–931, 1985.
46. Sjogren K: Leisure after stroke. Int Rehabil Med 4:80–87, 1982.

47. Smith ME, Garraway WM, Smith DL, Akhtar AJ: Therapy impact on functional outcome in a controlled trial of stroke rehabilitation. Arch Phys Med Rehabil 63:21–24, 1982.
48. Strand T, Asplund K, Eriksson S, et al: A non-intensive stroke unit reduces functional disability and the need for long-term hospitalization. Stroke 15:29–34, 1985.
49. Strickland R, Alston J, Davidson J: Negative influence of families on compliance. Hosp Community Psychiatry 32:349–350, 1981.
50. Stroker R: Impact of disability on families of stroke clients. Neurosurg Nurs 15:360–365, 1983.
51. Tobin SS, Kalys R: The family in the institutionalization of the elderly. J Soc Iss 37:145–157, 1981.
52. Tompkins CA, Schulz R, Ran MT: Post-stroke depression in primary support persons: Predicting those at risk. Consult Clin Psychol 56:502–508, 1988.
53. Unks RP: The relative influence of social, physical, and psychological factors on the morale and life satisfaction of elderly wives of stroke patients. Dissert Abstr Int 44:2585, 1985.
54. Wade D, Langton-Hewer R, Skilbeck C, David R (eds): Stroke: A Critical Approach to Diagnosis, Treatment and Management. Chicago, Year Book, 1985, pp 261–284.
55. Wade D, Legh-Smith J, Hewer R: Effects of living with and looking after survivors of a stroke. BMJ 293:418–420, 1986.
56. Webster EJ, Newhoff M: Intervention with families of communicatively impaired adults. In Beasley DS, Davis GA (eds): Aging: Communication Processes and Disorders. New York, Grune & Stratton, 1981, pp 229–240.
57. Wehman P, Inlow D, Altman A, et al: Return to work for individuals recovering from stroke or traumatic brain injury: Three case studies. Can J Rehabil 5:45–50, 1991.
58. Weinfield FE (ed): The National Survey of Stroke. Stroke 12(suppl 1):1–71, 1981.
59. Williams SE, Freer CA: Aphasia: Its effect on marital relationships. Arch Phys Med Rehabil 67:250–252, 1986.
60. Zomeren AH, Brouwer WH, Minderhound JM: Acquired brain damage and driving: A review. Arch Phys Med Rehabil 68:697–705, 1987.

TRILOK N. MONGA, MD, FRCPC, MRCP(I)

15. SEXUALITY POST STROKE

From the Rehabilitation Medicine
  Service
Houston VA Medical Center
  and
Department of Clinical Physical
  Medicine and Rehabilitation
Baylor College of Medicine
Houston, Texas

Reprint requests to:
Trilok N. Monga, MD, FRCPC,
  MRCP(I)
Rehabilitation Medicine Service
Houston VA Medical Center
2002 Holcombe Boulevard
Houston, TX 77030

Stroke is the third most common cause of death and one of the major causes of long-term disability. Despite its prevalence, there are very few studies that have comprehensively examined the long-term effects of stroke on sexuality.[34] Most of the research in this area has either a small sample size or includes subjects under 60 years of age[3,12,19,41]; however, our experience is that stroke is most common in elderly subjects. In other studies, the only specific sexual behavior assessed was frequency of coitus, with very little reference to attitudes or physiologic function.[19,41]

When considering sexuality issues in stroke patients, it is very important to remember that age is not a major factor in the decline of sexual functioning. Understanding of physiologic changes of aging and sexuality in the elderly is a prerequisite to any discussion regarding sexuality in stroke patients. Sexuality in aging has recently been reviewed by Kleitsch and O'Donnell.[20]

PHYSIOLOGIC CHANGES OF AGING

There is some decrease in serum testosterone levels after the age of 50 to 55 years. However, this change is accompanied by a decrease neither in libido nor in general sexual activities.[4,44]

Ability to attain an erection without direct stimulation diminishes, and there is a need for more time and caressing to achieve erection. Erection may not be as firm as in younger men. There is greater tendency to lose the erection during intercourse. Detumescence occurs more rapidly, and the refractory period increases with age.[28,29] A decrease in the frequency and firmness of nocturnal erections occurs with aging, and some of the medications that suppress or alter REM sleep will further reduce the frequency and firmness of erection at night. Depression has similar effects. Reduced penile sensitivity has been reported in the elderly which may lead to diminished sexual activity.[8]

In women, there is distinct change in sex hormones production, starting at middle age and becoming most dramatic at menopause. Rate and amount of vaginal lubrication are decreased during sexual arousal; vaginal walls become thinner and undergo a reduction in length.[28] There is usually a loss of elastic tissue. Changes in the labia minora and majora that occur during sexual arousal diminish with aging. Although women retain their ability to achieve orgasm throughout their lives, the duration of stimulation needed to achieve orgasm increases. Sexual desire does not normally diminish following menopause.

Master and Johnson[28] found that older women who continued to have sexual intercourse once or twice a week maintained adequate lubrication and had normal-sized vaginas. It appears there is adequate support for the old saying "use it or lose it."

Although sexual activity is a vital part of normal life, society tends to deny the sexuality of persons who are elderly or physically disabled. They are, in fact, often considered asexual.[34]

SEXUALITY IN THE ELDERLY

Kinsey et al.[21,22] were the first to focus attention on the sexual behavior of the elderly. It is now well established that regular coitus may continue into the seventh, eighth, and even ninth decades.[28] Other studies[10,37,38,48] have also found that sex continues to play an important role in the lives of many elderly. Moreover, studies on sexual function indicate that basic physiologic responses remain essentially intact with advancing age.[28] In a recent study by Starr and Weiner,[47] 75% of the respondents reported that sex feels as good as, or better than, when they were young. In the same study, 76% of the subjects felt that sex was a positive effect on their health, and 91% of the women indicated that they were orgasmic sometimes, most of the time, or always. They[47] concluded that in elderly people who were sexually active and have a partner, the rate of sexual decline in performance may not be as great as heretofore believed.

Renshaw[39] reported that the most common sexual problems among the elderly were secondary impotence in men and orgasmic dysfunction in women. The decline in male erection response was, no doubt, the most limiting factor in the sexual relationship of the elderly.

SEXUALITY IN STROKE PATIENTS

Magnitude of the Problem

Various authors have reported a marked decline in many of the aspects of sexuality[3,34,43,44] (Table 1). Muckleroy,[36] however, stated that the stroke patient regularly experiences a change in sexual activity, but this is not necessarily a problem. According to him, it is rare for either partner to view this loss as a significant one.

Libido

The profound effect of strokes on patients' performance-oriented sexuality is well documented. The earliest study by Kalliomaki et al.[19] described sexual behavior in stroke patients younger than 60 years, an age that we find does not

TABLE 1. Sexuality Problems Identified in Stroke Patients

Decline in libido	Orgasmic difficulties
Decline or cessation of coital activity	Poor satisfaction with sexual activity
Lack of or poor erection	Lack of enjoyment with sexual activity
Poor vaginal lubrication	Hypersexuality
Absence of ejaculation	

represent most stroke patients. According to these authors, cerebrovascular accident tends to diminish libido and the frequency of coitus. In this study, the decline was more common in patients with right-sided paralysis as compared to those with left-sided weakness. The study was based on personal interviews with patients; however, there was no mention whether or not spouses were involved in the study. In a study of elderly stroke patients (mean age at onset, 68 years), 75% of men and 60% of women reported normal libido pre-stroke, while only 21% of men and 12% of women reported normal libido post-stroke.[34] However, no decline in libido or desire was noted by Bray et al.[3]

Coital Frequency

Various studies have reported decline in the frequency of intercourse. Many of these patients stopped having intercourse completely. In one of these studies, 9 men (11%) and 10 women (29%) reported no coital activity before their cerebrovascular accident, while 50 men (64%) and 19 women (54%) reported no coital activity after stroke.[34] Sjogren, Damber, and Liliequist[44] reported that the decrease in frequency of intercourse appeared to be more common in males than in females. In their study, 41% of males had ceased and 31% had decreased frequency, whereas 17% of the females had ceased and 42% had decreased frequency. The authors also noted marked changes in the coital situation following stroke; thus, 31% of males and 27% of females had ceased commonly termed foreplay. In another study by Sjogren and Fugl-Meyer,[45] the changes in frequency of intercourse was related to the degree of cutaneous sensibility impairment and levels of dependence in primary and activities of daily living, but not with degree of motor impairment. On the other hand, the degree of motor impairment was a main factor causing sexual dysfunction in a study by Fugl-Meyer and Joasko.[11]

Erection and Vaginal Lubrication

Problems with erection in men and vaginal lubrication in women have been reported. In a study by Sjogren and Fugl-Meyer,[46] 64% of the males had difficulty in achieving erections post-stroke as compared to 21% reporting such problems before stroke. Monga et al.[34] reported that 73 men (94%) had normal erection before stroke as compared to only 30 men (38%) who had normal response after cerebrovascular accident. In the same study, the female patients experienced problems with lubrication after the stroke; 63% of women had normal vaginal lubrication before stroke and only 29% had normal lubrication post-stroke.

Ejaculation and Orgasm

Problems with ejaculation and orgasm are also very common in stroke patients. Bray et al.[3] reported that only 1 of 11 women experienced orgasm post-stroke as compared to 5 women who regularly had orgasms before the stroke. In the study by Monga and colleagues,[34] most women became anorgasmic after the stroke, and premature ejaculation was prevalent in the male population in the post-stroke period. Fifteen women (43%) and 4 women (11%) had normal orgasm before and after stroke, respectively. Similarly 17 men (22%) and 57 men (73%) reported premature ejaculation before and after stroke, respectively. Other studies have reported similar problems to a greater or lesser extent.

Enjoyment and Satisfaction with Sexual Activity

Other findings that have been described include declined leisure activities,[26,45,49] enjoyment, and satisfaction with the level of sexual activity in the post-stroke period.[34] Sjogren[42] found a decline in mutual verbal and nonverbal responsiveness, a decrease in frequency of caressing and touching with intention of having sex, and a decrease in intimate caressing or foreplay following stroke. He noted that 31% of men and 27% of the women had ceased foreplay altogether. Spectatoring occurs when these patients remove themselves from an active sexual role and are instead preoccupied by attempts to observe and evaluate their own and their partners' performance.

SEXUALITY IN APHASIC PATIENTS

Available information regarding sexual problems in aphasic patients is limited. Kinsella and Duffy[23] stressed that a sudden loss of ability to communicate effectively influenced several aspects of life, including the marital relationship. Wiig[52] looked at the sexual readjustment in 100 persons with aphasia and reported that the physically intact aphasic with relatively good auditory comprehension and nonverbal communication ability exhibited the least problems in sexual adjustment, irrespective of expressive language ability. Wiig's findings implied that sexual readjustment was easier for aphasic patients if they could interpret other people correctly. Her results indicated that males, especially right hemiplegics, questioned their adequacies and capabilities, whereas female aphasics were concerned regarding their attractiveness.

LONG-TERM EFFECTS OF STROKE ON SEXUALITY

Life Adjustment

The only studies published on the long-term effects of cerebrovascular accident on sexuality are from Viitanen et al.[51] and Sjogren et al.[45] Sjogren and colleagues, in their study on adjustment to life after stroke, reported that while changes in frequency were temporally independent, changes in leisure activities were less pronounced for subjects examined later than 12 months after stroke. They commented that subjects with previously known arterial hypertension, myocardial infarction, or diabetes mellitus had changed relatively little in their sexual function or lifestyle than those without these ailments. This probably represents pre-stroke decline in sexual functioning.

In a population of 62 stroke patients with a follow-up of 4 to 6 years, Viitanen et al,[51] in a prospective long-term study of life after stroke, reported that 61% of the population experienced a decreased general and/or domain-specific satisfaction with life. Twelve of these subjects (15% of respondents) had decreased in four or more aspects, while 14 (18%) had decreased in only one aspect. Except for contact with friends, where 85% were as satisfied before as after the stroke, changes in all the items of domain-specific life satisfaction were significantly associated with changes in global life satisfaction. Reduced satisfaction with sex life was noted in

42 married subjects in their study. This study comes from Sweden, and whether or not the results can be generalized to all patient populations is difficult to state.

In another study on sexual adjustment of men who had strokes, Hawton[16] reported that the interest in sex returned for the great majority of 35 patients. These subjects had been living with a partner and had been sexually active before the stroke. The interval between the strokes and the interviews averaged 6.2 months (SD 5.4), the shortest interval was 3 months, and in all but 3 patients the interviews took place within 1 year of the stroke. This kind of experience has not been reported by other investigators. The authors do comment that the men who reported full return to their previous interest in sex tended to be younger than those whose interest in sex had failed to return or had returned partially. In this study, there were only 2 patients over the age of 70 years.

Nature of the Problem

Sexual dysfunction in stroke patients is complex and multifactorial in nature (Table 2). It can be said that the sexual problems in these patients are never a consequence of "stroke" alone; rather, it may be due to a variety of associated medical conditions, such as the high prevalence of diabetes, hypertension, and coronary artery disease. The situation is compounded by a multitude of psychosocial factors including role changes, loss of self-esteem, and fear of rejection by the spouse, just to mention a few. Other factors which may influence sexual functioning are cognitive, sensory, and motor deficits, incontinence, and poor coping skills.

None of the above factors have been systematically investigated, and subjective loss of potency in male patients has not been objectively verified by penile plethysmography. In one study,[45] cessation of sexual intercourse was most common among those patients who did not regain independence after their strokes.

Sidedness of Lesions. Kalliomaki et al.[19] reported that impairment of sexual interest was more common with dominant hemispheric lesions as compared to nondominant hemispheric involvement; however, Sjogren et al.[44] reported no significant correlation between side of lesion and any of the sexual parameters which were investigated. Monga et al.[34] reported a lesser decline in sexuality, as measured on an index of sexual function, among women with right-sided lesions. In this study, the sexual function of the four groups (left and right hemispheric lesions in male and female patients) was compared. A single index of sexual function before and after was established: the sexual function data thus produced had a minimum value of 8 points and a maximum value of 30 points. Twenty-six diabetic patients were excluded from the analysis. Sexual function of the four groups was comparable before stroke. Although there was a decline in sexual function for all groups after stroke, the sexual function of the four groups after stroke was not comparable. The women with right-sided lesions had a less marked decline in index of sexual function than any of the other three groups. No

TABLE 2. Nature of the Sexuality Problems in Stroke Patients

Fear of having another stroke	Side effects of medications
Fear of rejection by the partner	Severity of disability
Fear of poor performance	Contractures and spasticity
Concomitant medical conditions	Cognitive deficits

significant difference between men with right and left lesions in the degree of decline of sexual function was noted. However, there was a marked difference between women having left- and right-sided lesions in the severity of decline of sexual function, with the latter showing a much smaller decline. The authors concluded that the severity of cognitive deficits may contribute to this sexual decline.[34] This conclusion was based upon a finding, which previously was reported by Inglis et al.,[18] that right-sided lesions in women did not reveal as severe cognitive deficits as the left-sided lesions in women or both right- and left-sided lesions in men.

Those patients who had a higher frequency of sexual activity before their stroke were more likely to resume sexual intercourse after their strokes.[16]

Alcohol and Medications.   Alcohol can contribute to the decline in sexual performance, particularly in men. As a central nervous system depressant, alcohol can cause erectile problems. Hawton[16] reported that up to 80% of chronic alcoholics experienced decreased sex drive and ejaculation dysfunction.

Antihypertensives, antidepressants and hypnotics can contribute to erectile difficulties and ejaculatory dysfunction. Hagan, Wallin, and Baer[15] reported a positive correlation between antihypertensive usage and erectile dysfunction; however, in the study by Sjogren et al,[44] there was no such association. Other medications which may influence sexual performance include anxiolytics, antihistamines, muscle relaxants, and cimetidine.

Autonomic Dysfunction.   Autonomic nervous system dysfunction as a factor leading to sexual decline in stroke patients was suggested by Monga et al.[32] in their study of cardiovascular effects of exercise in stroke patients. They reported a significantly less increase in both systolic and diastolic blood pressure with upper limb exercises as compared to age- and sex-matched control subjects. No such difference was noted with lower limb exercises. They concluded that a lack of response may suggest an underlying autonomic dysfunction.[32]

In another study[33] involving stroke patients, autonomic nervous system functioning was examined and compared with that in an age-matched control group of normal elderly. Abnormalities of skin temperature on the hemiparetic side as compared to the normal side were noted; no such findings were present in the control subjects. Similarly, abnormalities in Valsalva maneuver and heart rate variation with change of posture were detected in stroke patients. The abnormalities were more marked in patients who had symptoms of autonomic nervous system dysfunction. It was concluded that these findings suggest autonomic system dysfunction in stroke patients.

Fear of Another Stroke.   One of the main factors identified in the decline of sexual function was the fear that sexual intercourse might precipitate another stroke.[34] Other investigators have also found that fear is one of the factors responsible for the decline of sexual functioning.[23,44]

The reasons for this fear appear to be similar to those reported in patients with myocardial infarction. Block, Maeder, and Hinsley[2] studied patients with acute myocardial infarction and reported that average frequency of sexual intercourse declined from preinfarction rates. In their study, the decline did not correlate with measures of patients' health or activity levels or the results of exercise tests. The authors found the main reason for reduction in sexual activity to be psychosocial, the principal factors being depression, fear of relapse, or fear of sudden death. Sudden death during intercourse in patients with myocardial infarction does occur; however, it is very rare. Ueno[50] reported that the occurrence of death during intercourse or shortly thereafter was 0.6% of all deaths. Sudden death during or after intercourse has not been reported in stroke patients.

Fear of Rejection or Failure Besides the fear of having another stroke or myocardial infarction, these patients also have the fear of rejection by their spouse and fear of failure. Master and Johnson,[29] Rykken,[40] and Starr and Weiner[47] suggested that a major cause of sexual dysfunction in the elderly couple was the "fear of failure" in the aging male. According to these authors, the fear of failure and its accompanying anxiety become a self-fulfilling prophesy. In time, the man will withdraw from sexual activity with his spouse altogether.

Diminished Self-Image. Stroke often leads to a loss of status and a diminished self-image. Reduced self-esteem resulting from inability to perform intercourse according to expectations has been reported.[3,45] Not surprisingly, the incidence of depression is quite high. The reported incidence varies from 20 to 60% (*see* Chapter 12). Decrease in the frequency and firmness of erections may be a clinical manifestation of depression, with resultant decline in sex drive and desire. Beaumont[1] reported that depressed men suffer erectile dysfunction and some women report difficulty reaching an orgasm.

Coping Skills and Role Changes. Sjogren et al.[44] contend that sexual dysfunctions in the hemiplegic may be explained in terms of poor coping skills rather than by endocrine deficits. According to these authors, there was no organic background for common sexual dysfunction; therefore, they concluded that the dysfunction was a result of a change in sex role, the custodial attitude of the partner, and dependency in self-care. A stroke patient may become distressed and less willing to initiate a sexual encounter while his spouse has to assist him with toileting and other self-care activities. Other investigators have also identified the role change and role conflict as contributing factors that influence sexual function in stroke patients (Crossman et al.,[7] Goldstein et al.,[13] Fugl-Meyer and Jaasko[11]). The patient's spouse may abruptly become the wage earner, family decision-maker, and household manager, in addition to the responsibility of providing care. Social isolation, such as reduced contact with friends, less social interactions, and lack of time for leisure activities may add to further frustrations and influence sexual relationships with the partners. Marron[27] cautioned that rejection of the stroke patient by the partner may reflect previous marital discord within the couple.

Hypersexuality. Although hyposexuality is quite common in stroke patients, some patients may present with hypersexuality. Monga et al.[35] have described three patients with hypersexuality and deviant sexual behavior as a post-stroke complication. Symptoms in these patients were similar to the findings described in the Kluver-Bucy syndrome.[24]

ASSESSMENT

It is strongly recommended that assessment should include an in-depth interview of both partners to determine sexual history, sexual behavior, and functioning before the stroke (Table 3). Any psychosocial disorders (depression,

TABLE 3. Assessment of Sexuality in Stroke Patients

Complete history and physical examination	History of alcohol consumption
Pre- and post-stroke sexuality	Interview both partners
Cognitive and functional status	Need for and side effects of current medications
Psychosocial functioning and coping skills	Personal preferences of sexuality expression

anxiety, etc.) and factors that may interfere with sexual functioning should be noted. Patients and spouses should be interviewed together and separately, so that it can be determined how the couple has been coping with stresses resulting from stroke, with special reference to the sexuality-related concerns. Interviewing separately also provides insight of the partners preferences about methods of sexual expressions. This also may help to unmask some of the concerns in respect to perceived extramarital relationships on the part of the healthy partner. Sometimes it is possible that both partners do not desire sexual activity as part of the relationship.

Medical history should include details of past and present medical diagnosis, history of any surgical procedures, drug usage, endocrine function, and other neurologic deficits or diseases. Special note should be made of diseases that may influence sexuality (e.g., diabetes mellitus, renal failure). History of excessive alcohol consumption, use of antidepressants, tranquilizers, sedatives, and hypotensives should be explored.

Because of the relatively high incidence of depression in these patients, as well as the significant decrease in the frequency and firmness of nighttime erections that occurs in even potent elderly men, past or present history of depression should be considered in the assessment of sexuality in stroke patients.

In male patients who have problems achieving satisfactory erections and those who have a strong desire to remain sexually active, further investigations should be considered (Table 4). These include urodynamics, penile biothesiometry, dorsal nerve somatosensory evoked potentials (SSEP), and nocturnal penile tumescence (NPT). However, the absence of nighttime erections should not lead to the conclusion that the dysfunction is wholly or even partially organic in nature, since this could be due to an underlying depression. There is no information available regarding the use of nocturnal penile tumescence in the evaluation of sexuality in male stroke patients. Measurement of serum testosterone level may not be of much help either in diagnosis or management of the patient, as relationship between testosterone levels and sexuality in older men has been found to be only modest. Sjogren et al.[44] measured serum testosterone levels and found the values within the predicted range. Responses to HCG stimulation were also adequate.

The traditional organic versus psychogenic approach to sexual dysfunction in stroke patients is a gross oversimplification. Most of the sexual problems encountered by stroke patients result from a complex interaction of psychological and physical factors including the side effects of medication.

TREATMENT

As the problem is multifactorial in nature, the management of these patients requires a multifaceted approach (Table 5). The first and foremost task for those caring for these patients is to be aware of sexual dysfunctioning in stroke patients. Sexual counseling and discussion should not be left to the orderlies or staff

TABLE 4. Sexuality Assessment in Selected Patients

Urology consultation
Penile biothesiometry
Dorsal nerve somatosensory evoked potentials (SSEP)
Nocturnal penile tumescence

TABLE 5. Management Approaches to Sexuality in Stroke Patients

Remove communication barriers	Retrain cognitive and perceptual deficits
Reassure regarding:	Adjust medications
Acceptance	Manage depression
Performance	Improve coping skills
Safety	Suggest alternative positions
Improve functional status	

members who feel uncomfortable in discussing sexual issues with the disabled. Conine and Evans[5] remind us that stroke patients will discuss sexual concerns with people they feel comfortable around.

Before sexual counseling can begin, assessment of the cause or causes of sexual dysfunction should be carried out. An erection occurring during the morning or sleep may indicate that impotence is not organic in nature.

In preparing for the discussion of sexuality in this elderly population, one must carefully consider their own feelings and attitudes towards sexuality so that the information and counseling provided is free from judgment and bias. Mims and Swenson[31] have developed the sexual model "to provide a frame-work for self assessment, for client assessment, and for intervention." According to these authors, the development of behaviors regarding sexuality is based upon personal experience and societal influence and that there are various levels of development. They explained that the "life experience level" involved the development of personal destructive and intuitively helpful behaviors that may result in conflicting messages regarding sexuality. The authors believe that attaining the "basic level" awareness is necessary in order to assist other individuals with sexual concerns. This awareness is created by the interaction of perceptions, attitudes, and cognition and that awareness is fluid and constantly changing due to the changes in sexual mores.[31]

It is this author's opinion that the topic of sexuality should be discussed at an early time during the recovery from stroke and that it should not be delayed. The most appropriate time might be when the patient is going home for a weekend pass or at a time when the patient mentions concerns regarding sexual function. It is my experience that most patients welcome an open and honest discussion of this topic and welcome any suggestions that one may be able to provide.

Several concerns need to be addressed in this discussion. These include problems with self-image, self-esteem, communication blocks between the partners, problems related to sensory/perceptual deficits, weakness, contractures, and bowel and bladder incontinence. The fear of having another stroke or a heart attack, fear of rejection, and fear of performance need to be discussed as well.

Permission-giving is a fundamental intervention,[17] and reassurance should be provided that concerns and questions following stroke are normal. Furthermore, patients should be reassured regarding the safety of exercises and intercourse. There are no data available to indicate that sexual intercourse will or may precipitate another stroke; moreover, exercises within limits of fatigue have been found to be safe.[32] The patient should be asked to notify the physician of any shortness of breath, chest pain, or dizziness experienced during the exercise, and the clinician needs to be cautioned in prescribing unsupervised exercises with the upper limbs.

Medications may need to be adjusted or changed to drugs with fewer side effects on sexual function. Empirical use of antidepressants and tranquilizers should be discouraged. If spasticity is considered to be interfering in sexual performance, dantrolene sodium could be tried to relieve some of the increased tone.

Attempts should be made to improve the functional status of the patient and make him or her as independent as possible. Female patients with symptoms of vaginal dryness and dyspareunia may be relieved of symptoms with a local estrogen preparation.

If depression has been diagnosed, this should be treated effectively by medication or, if required, psychotherapy. Partners of stroke patients with sensory deficits should be encouraged to explore erogenous zones in which sensation remains intact. Various means of sexual expressions, such as hugs, kisses, caresses, and verbal affection need to be explained to the couple.

The need for marital counseling should be assessed and provided. Sjogren[42] has emphasized the importance of role changes and increased dependency in self-care as major factors that contribute to the decline in frequency of intercourse and interfere with positive attitudes toward sexuality. Once the problem of custodial care has been identified, then it is possible to facilitate alternative ways of providing care to maintain the previous relationship and sex roles.

Unlike spinal cord-injured patients, the role and need for penile implantation have not been looked into, and similarly no reports of papaverine injections in stroke patients have been identified. However, urology consultation is in order if there is any question of prostatic problem or among those who are keen to explore the possibility of having any of these procedures carried out.

Information regarding alternate sexual positions for couples in which one partner has residual physical impairments resulting from stroke should be provided. Conine and Evans[5] and Fugl-Meyer and Jaasko[11] offer suggestions on methods of enhancing sexual performance in male hemiplegics. Both suggest that the patient should lie on the affected side so that the unaffected arm is free to caress the partner. In this position, with a pillow wedged behind the male's back, a rear entry is easiest. The female partner may need encouragement to increase her active participation. If this position is not possible, the male can remain supine during intercourse and the female partner can adopt a top superior position. The authors have provided more details as how to manage with the problem of incomplete erection and perform hand stimulation.[5] Costello Smith[6] also recommended that stroke patients assume a mutual side-lying or supine position with their partners to facilitate intercourse. Patients with shoulder pain should avoid the side-lying position, and a supine position should be adopted. McCormick, Riffer, and Thompson[30] have given several alternate positions for these patients. The partner may need to be reminded that the patient may neglect stimuli from the affected side because of perceptual and sensory deficits.

There have been many options, suggestions, and recommendations put forward concerning treatment and management of these patients. However, there is no information available to support the above approaches as effective in management of sexual dysfunction. There is a need for further research regarding the outcome with various treatment approaches, including sexual counseling with the team framework.

SUMMARY

Marked decline in many aspects of sexuality has been reported. The common problems which have been identified include a decline in libido, coital frequency, vaginal lubrication and orgasm in women, and poor or lack of erection and ejaculation in male patients. Patients experience lack of enjoyment and poor satisfaction with sexual activity during the post-stroke period. The decline appears to be multifactorial in nature, with the major factors influencing sexuality comprising poor coping skills, psychosocial adjustment to the impairment and disability resulting from stroke, fear of having another stroke, and, to a certain extent, the severity of sensory, perceptual, and cognitive deficits.

The first step in management is a complete assessment of the medical, functional, and psychosocial status of the patient. An in-depth interview with both partners to determine sexual history and behavior before and after stroke should be carried out, followed by appropriate interventions. Interventions should focus upon reassurance, adjustment of medications, and counseling regarding coping skills, alternate positions, and means of sexual expressions and satisfaction. No information is available regarding the value of urodynamics, penile biothesiometry, dorsal nerve SSEP, and nocturnal penile tumescence in the diagnosis of impotence in stroke patients.

REFERENCES

1. Beaumont G: Sexual side of cloipramine (Anafranil). J Int Med Res 5(suppl 1):37–44, 1977.
2. Block A, Maeder J, Hinsley J: Sexual problems after myocardial infarction. Am Heart J 90:536–537, 1975.
3. Bray GP, De Frank RS, Wolfe TL: Sexual functioning in stroke patients. Arch Phys Med Rehabil 62:286–288, 1981.
4. Brown WA, Monti PM, Corriveau DP: Serum testosterone and sexual activity and interest in men. Arch Sex Behav 7:97–103, 1978.
5. Conine TA, Evans JH: Sexual reactivation of chronically ill and disabled adults. J Allied Health 11:261–270, 1982.
6. Costello Smith P: The sexual recovery of stroke patients. Sex Med Today 5:6–11, 1981.
7. Crossman L, London C, Barry C: Older women caring for disabled spouses: A model for supportive services. Gerontologist 21:464–470, 1981.
8. Edwards AE, Husted JR: Penile sensitivity, age and sexual behavior. J Clin Psychol 32:697–700, 1976.
9. Ford AB, Orfirer AP: Sexual behavior and chronically ill patient. Med Aspects Hum Sex 1:51–61, 1967.
10. Freeman JT: Sexual capacities in aging male. Geriatrics 16:37–43, 1961.
11. Fugl-Meyer AR, Jaasko L: Post-stroke hemiplegia and sexual intercourse. Scand J Rehabil Med 7:158–166, 1980.
12. Goddess ED, Wagner NN, Silverman DR: Post-stroke sexual activity of CVA patients. Med Aspects Hum Sex 13(3):16–29, 1979.
13. Goldstein V, Regnery G, Wellin E: Caretaker role fatigue. Nurs Outlook 29(1):24–30, 1981.
14. Griggs W: Sex and the elderly. Am J Nurs 78:1352–1354, 1978.
15. Hagan MJ, Wallin JD, Baer RM: Anti-hypertension therapy and male sexual dysfunction. Psychosomatics 21:234–237, 1980.
16. Hawton K: Sexual adjustment of men who had strokes. J Psychosom Res 28:243–249, 1984.
17. Herring BE: Sexual changes in patients and partners following stroke. Rehabil Nurs (Mar-Apr):28–30, 1985.
18. Inglis J, Ruckman M, Lawson JS, et al: Sex differences in cognitive effects of unilateral brain damage. Cortex 18:257–275, 1982.
19. Kalliomaki JL, Markkanen TK, Mustonen VA: Sexual behavior after cerebral vascular accident: Study on patients below age 60 years. Fertil Steril 12:156–158, 1961.
20. Kleitsch EC, O'Donnell PD: Sex and Aging. Phys Med Rehabil: State Art Rev 4:121–135, 1990.
21. Kinsey AL, Gebhard PH: Sexual Behavior in the Human Female. Philadelphia, WB Saunders, 1953.
22. Kinsey AC, Pomeroy WB, Martin CE, Gebhard PH: Sexual Behavior in Human Male. Philadelphia, WB Saunders, 1948.
23. Kinsella GH, Duffy FD: Psychosocial readjustment in the spouses of aphasic patients: A comparative survey of 79 subjects. Scand J Rehabil Med 11(3):129–132, 1979.

24. Kluver H, Bucy PC: Preliminary analysis of functions of temporal lobes in monkeys. Arch Neurol Psychiatry 42:979–1000, 1939.
25. Leshner M, Fine HL, Goldman A: Sexual activity in older stroke patients. Arch Phys Med Rehabil 55:578–579, 1974.
26. Lobi MLC, Phillips TF, Gresham GE: Psychosocial disability in physically restored long term stroke survivors. Arch Phys Med Rehabil 61:56–71, 1980.
27. Marron KR: Sexuality with aging. Geriatrics 37(9):135–138, 1982.
28. Master WH, Johnson VE: Human Sexual Response. Boston, Little Brown and Company, 1966.
29. Master WH, Johnson VE: Human Sexual Inadequacy. Boston, Little Brown and Company, 1970.
30. McCormick GP, Riffer DJ, Thompson MM: Coital positioning for stroke afflicted couples. Rehabil Nurs 11(2):17–19, 1986.
31. Mims FH, Swenson M: Sexuality: A Nursing Perspective. New York, McGraw-Hill Book Co., 1980.
32. Monga TN, DeForge DA, Williams J, Wolfe LA: Cardiovascular responses to acute exercise in patients with cerebrovascular accident. Arch Phys Med Rehabil 69:937–940, 1988.
33. Monga TN, Miller T, Biederman HJ: Autonomic nervous system dysfunction in stroke patients. Arch Phys Med Rehabil 68:630, 1987.
34. Monga TN, Lawson JS, Inglis J: Sexual dysfunction in stroke patients. Arch Phys Med Rehabil 67(1):19–22, 1986.
35. Monga TN, Monga M, Raina MS, Hardjasudarma M: Hypersexuality in stroke. Arch Phys Med Rehabil 67:415–417, 1986.
36. Muckleroy RN: Sex counselling after stroke. Med Aspects Hum Sex 11(12):115–116, 1977.
37. Newman G, Nichols CR: Sexual activities and attitudes in older persons. JAMA 173:33–35, 1960.
38. Pfeiffer E, Verwoerdt A, Wang HS: Sexual behavior in aged men and women: 1. Observation on 254 community volunteers. Arch Gen Psychiatry 19:753–758, 1968.
39. Renshaw DC: Geriatric sex problems. J Geriatr Psychiatry 17:123–148, 1984.
40. Rykken DE: Sex in the later years. In Silverman P (ed): The Elderly as Modern Pioneers. Bloomington, IN, Indiana University Press, 1988, pp 158–182.
41. Sadoughi W, Leshner M, Fine HL: Sexual adjustment in chronically ill and physically disabled population: Pilot study. Arch Phys Med Rehabil 52:311–317, 1971.
42. Sjogren K: Sexuality after stroke with hemiplegia: II. With special regard to partnership adjustment and to fulfillment. Scand J Rehabil Med 15(2):63–69, 1983.
43. Sjogren K: Leisure after stroke. Int Rehabil Med (suppl 7):140, 1980.
44. Sjogren K, Damber JE, Liliequist B: Sexuality after stroke with hemiplegia: 1. Aspects of sexual function. Scand J Rehabil Med 15(2):55–61, 1983.
45. Sjogren K, Fugl-Meyer AR: Sexual problems in hemiplegia. Int Rehabil Med 3(11):28–31, 1981.
46. Sjogren K, Fugl-Meyer AR: Adjustment to life after stroke with special reference to sexual intercourse and leisure. J Psychosom Res 26:409–417, 1982.
47. Starr BD, Weiner MB: The Starr-Weiner Report on Sex and Sexuality in the Mature Years. New York, McGraw-Hill, 1981.
48. Thienhaus OJ: Practical overview of sexual function and advancing age. Geriatrics 43(8):63–67, 1988.
49. Trudel L, Fabia J, Bouchard JP: Quality of life of 50 carotid endarterectomy survivors: A long term follow-up study. Arch Phys Med Rehabil 65:310, 1984.
50. Ueno M: The so-called coital death. Jpn J Legal Med 17:535, 1963.
51. Viitanen M, Fugl-Meyer KS, Bernspan B, Fugl-Meyer AR: Life satisfaction in long term survivors after stroke. Scand J Rehabil Med 20:17–24, 1988.
52. Wiig EH: Counseling the adult aphasic for sexual readjustment. Rehabil Counseling Bull 17(2):110–119, 1973.

INDEX

Entries in **boldface type** signify complete articles.

Hemorrhage *(cont.)*
  intracerebral *(cont.)*
    neurogenic pulmonary edema and, 65
    seizures and, 78–79
  subarachnoid, 29, 55, 201
    ECG changes in, 62–63
    myocardial infarction and, 64
    neurogenic pulmonary edema and, 65
    prevention of, 49–50
    seizures and, 79–80
Heparin, 48
Heterotopic ossification, 155
Hip
  contracture of, 153
  heterotopic ossification of, 155
Homocysteinemia, as stroke risk factor, 44
Honolulu Heart Program, 57
Hospital bed-days, for stroke care, 5
Hospitalization rate, for stroke, 5
Hyperlipidemia
  as post-stroke dementia risk factor, 201
  as stroke risk factor, 10, 11, 29, 44
  treatment of, 67–68
Hypersexuality, 231
Hypertension
  intracerebral hemorrhage and, 29
  as seizure risk factor, 76
  during stroke, 65
  as stroke risk factor, 5, 10, 11, 56, 65
    post-stroke disability and, 29
    survival time effects of, 67
    treatment of, 44
Hyperuricemia, as stroke risk factor, 44
Hypnotics, as sexual dysfunction cause, 230
Hypoarousal, in right hemisphere-damaged
    patients, 181
Hypotension
  during stroke, 65
  as stroke risk factor, 60–61

Illicit drug use, as stroke risk factor, 10, 11, 44
Imipramine, for urinary incontinence control,
    109–110
Impotence, 226
Incidence, of stroke, 213
  antihypertensive drugs and, 56
  decline of, 5
  international rates of, 6–7
Incontinence. *See* Urinary incontinence
Independence, of stroke survivors, 219
Indifference reaction, 181
Infarction
  lacunar, 28–29
  post-stroke dementia and, 197, 199, 200, 201
Infection, as stroke risk factor, 44
Institutionalization, of stroke survivors, 36, 214
Instrumental activities of daily living,
    assessment of, 204
Ischemia, cerebral, mitral valve prolapse and,
    59–60

Ischemic heart disease
  post-stroke, 44, 66–67
  prevention of, 43

Jackson's syndrome, 34
Joint contractures. *See* Contractures

Kegel pelvic floor exercises, 107–108
Ketazolam, as spasticity therapy, 125
Kinetron II gait training device, 174–175
Knee
  flexion contractures of, 154
  force-of-gravity line of, 122, 123
Kwashiorkor, 95

Lacunar state, 200
Lacunar syndrome, 28–29
Language deficits. *See also* Aphasia
  left-hemisphere stroke-related, 31
Laryngeal paresis, 90
Lateral foot pain, 155
Laughing, pathological, 182
Learned helplessness, 188
Leuko-araiosis, 206–207
Libido, of stroke survivors, 226–227
Lipids
  as post-stroke dementia risk factor, 201
  as stroke risk factor, 10, 11, 29, 44
Loss, depression response to, 187–188
Lower extremity disorders, **147–159.** *See also*
    Contractures
  assessment of, 150–151
  energy expenditure during, 148–149
  features of, 147–148
  follow-up approach to, 156–157
  fractures, 155
  gait analysis of, 163
  lesion specificity and, 149–150
  long-term complications of, 153–156
  orthotics for, 148, 152, 167–171
    ankle-foot, 167–169
    ankle-foot, toe-inhibiting, 169–170
    ankle-foot, tubular-style, 170
    knee-ankle-foot, 170–171
  outcome of, 156
  spasticity, 124
  treatment of, 152–153
Lupus anticoagulant, as stroke risk factor, 44

Magnetic resonance angiography, 50, 51
Malnutrition, of stroke survivors, 94–95, 98
Marital counseling, 234
Marital problems, of stroke survivors, 38, 231
Medical Research Council motor testing scale,
    150–151, 163
Menopause, sexual desire following, 226
Methylphenidate, as depression therapy, 187
Migraine, as stroke risk factor, 11